Also by Roger Warner

Haing Ngor: A Cambodian Odyssey
(with Haing Ngor)

# Back Fire

The CIA's Secret War
in Laos and Its Link to
the War in Vietnam

# Roger Warner

Simon & Schuster

New York   London   Toronto   Sydney   Tokyo   Singapore

SIMON & SCHUSTER
Rockfeller Center
1230 Avenue of the Americas
New York, NY 10020

Copyright © 1995 by Roger Warner
All rights reserved,
including the right of reproduction
in whole or in part in any form.

SIMON & SCHUSTER and colophon are registered trademarks
of Simon & Schuster Inc.

Designed by Levavi & Levavi

Manufactured in the United States of America

1   3   5   7   9   10   8   6   4   2

Library of Congress Cataloging-in-Publication Data

Warner, Roger.
Back fire : the CIA's secret war in Laos and its links to the
Vietnam War / Roger Warner.
p.      cm.
Includes bibliographical references and index.
1. Vietnamese Conflict, 1961–1975—Laos.   2. Vietnamese Conflict,
1961–1975—Secret service—United States.   3. Laos—Politics and
government.   I. Title.
DS559.73.L28W37 1995
959.704´34—dc20                     95-5758
CIP
ISBN 0-684-80292-9

PHOTO CREDITS
1, 4, 6, 7. Buell family; 2, 8, 9. Paru; 3. Vint Lawrence; 5. Dave
Kouba; 10. Tom Ward; 11, 12. Roger Warner Collection

back • fire (-fīr) *n.*   1 a fire started to stop an advancing prairie fire or forest fire by creating a burned area in its path   2 a premature ignition of fuel or an explosion of unburned exhaust gases in an internal-combustion engine, sometimes preventing the completion of the compression stroke and reversing the direction of the piston 3 an explosive force toward the breech, rather than through the muzzle, of a firearm—*vi.* -fired', -firing   1 to use or set a backfire   2 to explode as a backfire   3 to have an unexpected and unwelcome result; go awry; boomerang [his plan *backfired*]

—*Webster's New World Dictionary of American English*

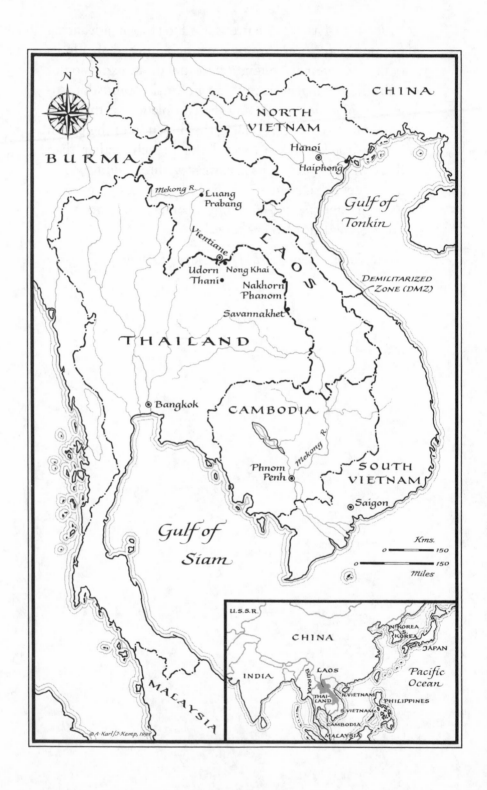

# Contents

1

Vang Pao, commander of the CIA-supported tribal forces in Laos, at a hilltop position near Nakhang, 1965.

Bill Lair, the shy, quiet CIA operative who started Operation Momentum, in his Thai police uniform with parachute wings.

2

Anthony ("Tony Poe") Poshepny—half of the early U.S. team at Long Tieng. A brave, outspoken CIA paramilitary officer famous for his alcohol consumption.

3

Vint Lawrence, the other half of the American team at Long Tieng.

4

The airstrip at
Long Tieng, the
center of the
CIA's tribal
operation.

5

Edgar "Pop" Buell
giving a stump
speech in a tribal
village in Laos.

6

USAID's
Dr. Charles Weldon
and Buell with Bill
Young of the CIA at
a *baci* ceremony,
having good-luck
strings tied around
their wrists.

7

Vang Pao on payday for the troops, with bundles of Laotian money on the table.

8

9

1968: Pat Landry (*far left*), Bill Lair (*face partly hidden*), and Ted Shackley (*with glasses*) receive the Order of the Million Elephants from the King of Laos. Prime Minister Prince Souvanna Phouma stands at the far right.

10

The King of Laos distributes
gifts to Hmong girls.
General Ouane Rattikone
*(in sunglasses)*, the drug-
dealing commander-in-chief,
looks on.

The two royal half brothers,
Prince Souphanovong of the
Pathet Lao, and Prime
Minister Prince Souvanna
Phouma, in 1973.

11

Two Hmong resistance soldiers in the tattered remnants of their U.S.–supplied uniforms, after the Americans left Laos and the communists took over.

# Preface

In the hinterlands of Southeast Asia lies an obscure country called Laos. Along one side runs the largely unnavigable Mekong River, upstream from Cambodia and Vietnam. The rest is a jumble of mountains, with few roads, and widely scattered settlements of primitive tribal people.

Isolated, lost in tropical lethargy, and poor, Laos is an unlikely place for American intervention. Except for opium, a drug of dreamlike reveries, it produces little of value to outsiders. Its inhabitants are among the least war-like in the world. Nonetheless, during the depths of the Cold War era, when Laos was quaintly and officially known as the Kingdom of Laos, Land of the Million Elephants and the White Parasol, it became the site of a large, strange conflict in which America played a major role.

Here the sparks were struck that led to the larger Vietnam War. A coup in Laos in 1960 led the Americans and the Soviets to a proxy fight and nearly to war with each other, until they both backed down, and much of the fighting moved to a flatter, more populous country next door, South Vietnam. From 1963 to 1973, behind a bizarre front of "neutrality," Laos was a secret annex to the main Vietnam theater, overseen by the U.S. ambassador, run by the Central Intelligence Agency, and bombed by the U.S. military, without the consent of Congress.

Because Laos was off-limits to the press in the years that mattered most, its story has been known only in general terms until now. It is a story of unlikely allies, of Americans "going native," and Iron Age hillbillies calling in jet strikes. And it is a story of deceptions—of outside nations denying that they were fighting in the kingdom, ambassadors and politicians lying to each other, and earnest, committed Americans discovering only when it was too late that they had been deceiving themselves.

*Back Fire* is the inside story of the Laos war, based on lengthy research and interviews. In a larger historical sense, it provides the long-missing jigsaw piece of the Vietnam War, the piece that finally makes the big picture whole. But it is also a saga in itself, a nonfictional account of a fifteen-year, multi-billion dollar covert effort. The people in this book are the Americans who were key to the U.S. undertaking in this strange Asian kingdom. They gave the program there its direction, from its brilliant early success through its troubled middle years to its ultimate tragedy. They made a difference; and the war in turn forever changed their lives.

# The Coup

Unlike the later and larger war in Vietnam next door, there were never more than a couple thousand Americans in Laos. Of those Americans, only about a dozen were key players. They came to the kingdom by what seemed like random chance, arriving over the course of several years, and once there it took them awhile to invent or discover their roles.

The first on the scene was a short, grizzled, balding forty-seven-year-old farmer from Indiana. In late May 1960, a local newspaper announced his departure as follows:

> Edgar Buell, a lifelong resident of the Edon area, embarked Saturday on a job which offers as an inducement long hours of back-breaking work with archaic tools in a disease-infested land.
>
> International Voluntary Services, an organization dedicated to the better understanding among people throughout the world, is sending Mr. Buell to Laos in southeastern Asia to further its diplomatic work.
>
> Mr. Buell, who farms west of Edon, will be in Laos for two years. He describes his assignment as "people-to-people" work.
>
> "I'm supposed to show them modern farming methods and at the same time a better way of life. This isn't a white collar job. I'll get my hands plenty dirty," he said.
>
> Mr. Buell explained that farming in Laos is 150 to 300 years behind American methods. Such primitive tools as the hoe and wooden plow are used by most of the country's land tillers. Oxen and elephants do the pulling. Opium and rice are the chief exports.
>
> Communism and a high disease rate are other problems he will face.

For that backbreaking work in a disease-infested land where the communists lurked in the shadows, International Voluntary Services, a private forerunner to the Peace Corps, was prepared to pay Edgar Buell sixty-five dollars a month. That was a pay cut even for a dirt farmer, but money was not Buell's motivation. His wife had died the year before, and he was grief-stricken and lonely. For his own mental health, he wanted to get away from home and, being halfway around the world, Laos was as far away as possible.

He flew first to Washington, D.C., for an IVS orientation session, where he learned that Laos's former colonial power, France, had withdrawn several years before, and that America had rushed in to fill the political vacuum. The king of Laos was only a figurehead, and right-wing strongmen, weak neutralists, and communist-backed nationalists were struggling for control of the government. The United States was determined to see a friendly regime in place, and IVS, with its low-cost self-help projects, was a part of the effort to keep Laos free of communist domination.

From Washington, Buell flew to Chicago and westward in short hops powered by propellor and turboprop planes. In letters to his grown children he wrote of seeing the Rocky Mountains for the first time from the air. He was amazed, flying over the Pacific, at the sight of clouds underneath. "Just looked like one big white, soft plush rug under you," he wrote. "Gave you a good feeling, like something would catch you if you fell, and hold you and you would just be there forever. You had a feeling of being in space."

There was a touch of the poet in this Indiana farmer, even if he wasn't much at spelling or grammar. "Now this old boy has saw quite a lot," he declared from Hawaii, "but I have never saw anything as beuitful as these islands were from the air. The sun was right. Oh so beuitful I can't explain. If it were only so I could have said to someone, just anybody I love, Oh Look, Look. Flowers, big flowers everywhere, in the little towns, on the farms, in the fields. The mountains are pretty. My eyes are tired. Only wish I could show it to you."

There was no detail too trivial to be conveyed to the folks at home, for this was Buell's first trip outside the United States and he was amazed by everything he saw. He wrote a postcard inbound to Wake Island and another outbound. From Japan, he wrote, "Hi. Made it to Tokyo. Our first real look at Orental buildings and Customs. Nice hotel chairs beds and all close to floor." He sent one more postcard from Hong Kong. "Good morning. Beuitful sunrise on the water. Have ate and shaved." Exhausted, he slept for most of the flight to Vientiane, the administrative capital of Laos, where he arrived in June 1960.

With a population of thirty-five thousand, Vientiane was the largest settlement in the kingdom. Buddhist monks in saffron robes walked about carrying parasols for shade. Portraits of the king adorned the walls of the buildings. Two open-air markets and a handful of Western-style shops handled most of the commerce. The people were the friendliest, and laziest, Buell had ever seen. Most of them belonged to the country's dominant ethnic group, the Lao, who cultivated rice and lived in houses built on stilts in lowland areas along the Mekong River. The muddy, mile-wide river, filled to its banks with the run-off from the monsoon rains, was also a national boundary, and on the other side was Thailand, with a language and Buddhist culture almost exactly the same.

As Buell learned, most lowland Lao identified with the Thais, their richer, more Westernized cousins to the south across the river. To his surprise, there were more ethnic Lao in Thailand than in Laos itself, which made him wonder why Laos was a country at all. Meanwhile, Laotians from other ethnic groups identified with their own tribes, or with the Vietnamese and Chinese to the east and north. Between the Americans, who were trying to expand their influence from Thailand, and the communists, who were trying to expand their influence from China and North Vietnam, Laos was in chaos.

Near the end of June 1960, Buell moved a hundred miles north of Vientiane to a little market town called Lat Houang. He lived in a crude little house with no glass on the windows and an outhouse out back. When it rained he drank runoff water from the roof; otherwise he filtered it from a muddy stream. He cooked on an oil stove until that blew up and then changed to a campfire outside in the yard. The living conditions reminded Buell of his childhood on the family farm in Indiana, and didn't faze him in the slightest.

His job was to teach rural vocational skills on an elementary school level. "How to saw boards straight, how to use soap and water, what it means to boil water," he explained to his family. "How to better raise live stock. Here they don't belive in castration. What God gave you, you are to keep." He was surprised at the backwardness of his students. "You will be unable to belive this," Buell wrote, in a letter typical for its misspellings, grammatical errors, and solid common sense, "but these people are not yet to the wheel age. They never fix nothing. They just cant figure out why it broke. Now dont get me wrong, these people are not dummies, in some ways very smart and Oh so friendly. They are so Dam willing, but you can't belive grown men that far back. They know nothing about Modern life."

Though his own daily work was no more glamorous than farming in Indiana, he was proud to be part of the American mission. Nearby, on an area of rolling grasslands known as the Plain of Jars, a handful of U.S. Army Special Forces soldiers wearing civilian clothes helped train the Royal Lao Army. A few other Americans who traveled about upcountry Laos in small planes worked for a branch of the government whose name he would speak only in a whisper. Elsewhere in the forested mountains of Laos were communists and "pro-communists"—advisers from the North Vietnamese Army, and units of the Laotian leftist insurgency, the Neo Lao Hak Sat, generally known as the Pathet Lao. As a people, the Vietnamese had been trying to take over Laos for centuries, long before communism existed; their own country was crowded and they wanted more land. But Buell, a fervently patriotic American, saw the struggle for Laos in terms of Cold War morality, as a struggle between free world good and communist evil.

If being part of a cause made Buell feel important, so did the respect he got from the local people. What confirmed his elevation in status to himself was an incident with a middle-aged Lao woman from a nearby village. He had been observing the local agricultural scene closely, and he had given the woman an envelope of red kidney bean seeds. Dropping to her knees, she placed her palms together and then raised her hands up in front of her forehead in a Buddhist gesture of respect called the *wai.* Nobody had ever thanked Buell on her knees before, and he was touched.

A little over two weeks after arriving at Lat Houang, Buell was invited to a dinner hosted by the Lao military commander for the nearby Plain of Jars. That evening he met the commander's number two, a Maj. Vang Pao, who was also the highest-ranking officer from an ethnic group called the Meo.

The Meo, like other Laotian hilltribes, lived at higher elevations than the lowlanders, planted rice on hillsides rather than in diked paddies, and worshipped animist spirits instead of Buddha. When one of IVS's teenage Meo boys got a Meo nurse pregnant, Buell went to their wedding in a tribal village a two hours' hike uphill from the nearest road. The Meo men wore baggy black trousers that stopped at their shins. The women wore turbaned headdresses, heavy silver necklaces, embroidered blouses, trousers, and waist sashes with embroidered panels hanging down fore and aft. Everybody drank *lao-lao,* or rice whiskey, at the wedding. Hiking out of the village Buell got lost with some inebriated companions. Long after dark when they had been on the trail for hours, they stumbled into a native hut and got directions to the road, which was nearby, and where some other Americans were waiting for them. Buell had enjoyed himself at the wedding and was no worse for wear.

Thus, when there was a coup in Vientiane a few days later Buell had already had his first taste of upland and lowland Laos, and he took it all in stride.

◆

Though Buell was a novice in Asia, with an entry-level job, spoke his own language ungrammatically, and could speak only a few phrases of Lao, he got along perfectly with ordinary Laotians. He treated them with rough-hewn courtesy and common sense, and never patronized them. He had gray hair, which helped—Asians respect age—and being the same size as the locals (five feet five) made him seem unthreatening. On a local level he was already making a difference and representing his country well. Thus it is no exaggeration to say that if the U.S. government had had many more Buells in Laos, the coup might never have happened, for he was an exception and American arrogance and clumsiness was the rule.

Few Americans knew how to operate effectively in Laos. It was one of the poorest countries in the world. It had no paved roads outside Vientiane, few schools, and an illiteracy rate of more than 90 percent. Its grand-sounding name not withstanding, Laos didn't have a million elephants—probably a couple thousand, though nobody had ever bothered to count. Its greatest handicap was a mentality of passive resistance to change. To call the lowland Lao easygoing was an understatement. Every American knew the story of the Lao farmer who had been given fertilizers to double his crop yield; after that the farmer only worked half as hard as before.

Yet there was much that was deceptive and even admirable in the Laotians' ability to resist outsiders' plans for their improvement. The Laotians liked things as they were. Nobody starved. They admired Westerners but knew they were incapable of doing what the Westerners did. There was a kind of magical perversity about the place that turned straightforward attempts to Westernize Laos into the purest folly.

The U.S. caused the coup unintentionally. Starting in 1957 the U.S. had spent more on foreign aid to Laos per capita than it had on any other nation. It worked out to about $150 per Laotian, twice the average person's annual income, though the average Laotian didn't get a penny of the aid. Some of the money went to support pro-American candidates in an election. They won by lopsided, not to mention embarrassing, victories in balloting that was obviously rigged. Other money went to a program to support the local currency, the kip. The Americans bought truckfuls of kip above the black-market rate, burned the banknotes, and gave the Laotian government dollars in exchange. Realizing that bags of nearly worthless kip could be traded for dollars, Laotian merchants imported Mercedes and other luxury goods with their cheaply obtained American money, and then exported them to Thailand at a profit. The tiny class of rich elite got richer, and the poor were no better off than before.

The Royal Lao Army's entire budget was paid by the U.S. government, with much of the payroll going to nonexistent units. Graft was everywhere. Most Laotians were too apathetic to care, but a few lower-ranking officers were both angry at the generals for their corruption and angry at the Americans for appearing to encourage it. One of these disgruntled nationalists was a five-feet-two-inch captain named Kong Le, commander of the army's elite Second Lao Paratroop Battalion.

In early August 1960, the captain's American advisers, including a CIA paramilitary specialist, put him through a theoretical training exercise on occupying a city. The advisers chose Vientiane as their concrete example. They suggested he take over the radio station and the airport and then major street intersections, the post office, and so on. They offered him innovative ideas, such as giving his soldiers little transistor radios, so he could give them instructions once the radio station was captured.

The American advisers didn't speak Lao, a tonal language difficult for outsiders to master. (The Laotians always giggled when foreigners tried to say the word for "I" and said "penis" by mistake.) Thus they had no idea what the outwardly docile Laotians were really thinking. After his CIA case officer went to bed, the captain and his men took over Vientiane according to the script the Americans had prepared. From the captured radio station he gave his orders over the airwaves. His soldiers were wearing little transistor radios, which were presents from the U.S. government. Within a few days he was broadcasting speeches whose message was, Foreigners, go home.

For safety, about seven hundred Americans were evacuated across the Mekong and several hundred miles to the south to Bangkok, the capital of Thailand. Less than fifty were left in Laos, one of whom was Edgar Buell.

In the United States, the Laotian crisis, as it was called by the media, was portrayed as an ungrateful rejection of American aid and as a dangerous flirtation with communism. In Laos itself, there was a kind of unreality to the "crisis," which simultaneously managed to seem both serious and make-believe, though that was how the kingdom often seemed to outsiders. In Vientiane, ordinary people took their midday snoozes in the shade. The soldiers draped their laundry to dry on the barrels of their field guns and grinned politely at every *farang,* or foreigner, who walked by.

From August through October 1960, Vientiane was in a state of confusion. Honest but hopelessly naive, the captain who had mounted the coup proclaimed himself a "neutralist," a man of the nonaligned political center. He asked a fellow neutralist, a former prime minister and distant relative of the king named Prince Souvanna Phouma, to form a government. Quietly and quickly, this fledgling government was penetrated by agents of North Vietnam, who were far better suited to this kind of work than their clumsy counterparts in the CIA.

Taking advantage of the confusion, left-wing Pathet Lao units seized control wherever they could. At the same time, down the Mekong River from Vientiane in the town of Savannakhet, army units vaguely loyal to the right-wing elite gathered under the command of a general overthrown in the coup. The country was splitting apart.

Buell and the other Americans in the Plain of Jars were cut off from the outside world, but were not threatened by the peaceable Laotians. Buell played pinochle with a small group of plainclothes U.S. Army trainers. He went out visiting his Lao and hilltribe acquaintances, who had begun calling him "Mr. Pop," since it was easier for them to pronounce than "Buell" (which they twisted into "Bure"). He wondered how the corn and soybeans were doing on the farm in Indiana, and how the Detroit Tigers were doing in the American League standings. And he wrote letters home.

"Now quit your Dam worrying," Buell admonished his family. "You know I can take care of myself. They are not going to shoot me or stab me either. I love this work, people and all. As for the folks at home understanding, to Hell with it. *Cao ji.* Understand. Then *De ji* which means stay or be happy."

Buell wrote that he didn't know whether, or when, the U.S. government would intervene. But he agreed with his Special Forces friends that any effort would have to be staged from across the Mekong River in Thailand. He added, a bit cryptically, "You know our Buddys across the border are not dumb."

# The Quiet Texan

In Washington, the Eisenhower administration was divided over the Laotian crisis. How should the U.S. government react? In the Pentagon, some generals proposed invading the little kingdom while others counseled restraint. The CIA was split between support for the rightists and the neutralists. At the State Department, senior bureaucrats proposed making an example out of Laos, while a junior foreign service officer named William Sullivan helped draft an accommodationist plan to partition Laos into communist, neutralist, and royalist areas.

President Eisenhower's position was not to take a position. He was nearing the end of his second term in office, and there was an election coming up between his own vice president, Richard Nixon, and Senator John F. Kennedy of Massachusetts. Whatever the outcome of the election, Eisenhower didn't want to start anything for his successor to inherit.

This lack of clear direction from the top, together with the anarchy in Laos, created an unusual opportunity for men on the scene to guide events from the bottom up.

◆

On the morning of October 19, 1960, at the military end of an airport outside Bangkok, Thailand, two Americans removed the rear seats from a small single-engine plane. On the plane's fuselage appeared the markings Helio Courier—its make and model—and Air America, the name of a charter airline operating in eastern Asia. To the untrained eye, the Helio was a perfectly normal-looking aircraft, with a tiny rear wheel, two larger front wheels, and wide, boxy wings affixed to the top of the cabin.

With the back seats removed to maximize the cargo space, the two men stacked identical parcels wrapped in brown paper inside. The young sandy-haired pilot, Ron Sutphin, didn't ask the "Customer" what the packages contained. As long as the plane wasn't overweight, the cargo was none of an Air America pilot's business.

When the unmarked parcels filled the cabin from the floor to the ceiling, the Customer, an unobtrusive, stoop-shouldered man wearing glasses, asked Sutphin if he might go along. His accent, more a twang than a drawl, hinted at origins somewhere south of the Mason-Dixon line. Sutphin told him to jump in. They taxied to the runway, revved the engine, and took off in less than a hundred feet, rising almost vertically into the muggy air. The pilot banked and leveled out on a northeast heading, over the central plains of Thailand.

Below them lay a checkerboard of irregularly shaped rice fields with low earthen dikes. Houses on wooden stilts stood alongside muddy canals in which naked children swam and played. Here and there, in groves of bananas and coconut palms, rose Buddhist temples, or *wats,* with multicolored tile roofs and golden ornaments on the eaves. Beyond the plains lay dark green jungled mountains, with hardly a road or a settlement to break the tufted green surface of the treetops.

It was near the end of the rainy season, and the cloud cover increased the farther they flew toward their destination, the town of Savannakhet, on the other side of the Mekong River, in the Land of the Million Elephants and the White Parasol. There, a right-wing Lao general overthrown in the coup had gathered some ragtag army units. But the general's men were poorly trained and, since they had not been paid in months, were close to mutiny.

By no great coincidence, the Customer, whose name was Bill Lair, was flying to Savannakhet to see the general. It was a three-hour flight and he began to chat with Sutphin. Lair had never flown in a Helio, a relatively new plane, and he asked what it could do.

Sutphin said it was a STOL plane, meaning Short Takeoffs and Landings. It could fly very slowly—less than forty miles an hour when necessary—and land and take off from rough, improvised strips on mountainsides. Because the Helio didn't need airports, Sutphin declared, it was perfect for north Laos, where most of the action was, in the mountainous territory bordering North Vietnam and China.

Lair mulled that over for a while. He was silent for what seemed the longest time. Finally he asked Sutphin what he would do if the Helio's engine quit in midair.

Sutphin switched off the engine. All noise and vibration ceased. He put on full flaps, extending the rear surface area of the wings. He steered through a hole in the clouds. When the airspeed slowed to fifty-five miles an hour the front or leading edge of the wings popped forward and down— "slats," Sutphin called them. Now the Helio was drifting down as softly as a feather. Fifty miles an hour, then forty-five.

"I could put her there," said Sutphin, pointing at a rough clearing in the jungle. "Or else over there or there."

"Or you could restart your engine," said Lair, as the treetops loomed in front of them. Sutphin got the motor started, and the little plane climbed up through the clouds.

Lair remarked that he could see how a plane like that could be useful.

There was another long silence, and to fill it Sutphin started talking about north Laos, which he compared to a chess game, always changing. It was fascinating, he said, to watch the U.S. and the other side making their moves and countermoves. A few of the players were unusual, too— especially Vang Pao, the only officer in the Royal Lao Army who was from the Meo hilltribe.

Lair said he had heard of Vang Pao.

Sutphin was off and talking about the Laotian royalists and the pro-communist Pathet Lao, and how both of them had been trying to take over the country before the coup threw off their calculations. He went on and on, glad for an audience. Then he took another look at the Customer, whose occasional laconic remarks had prompted him into saying more than he had intended. It didn't add up. Lair seemed humble and self-effacing. He talked so slowly that even his thought process seemed slow. But it dawned on Sutphin that Lair's meekness just might be camouflage.

"Are you an adviser?" Sutphin asked, meaning a plainclothes U.S. Army Special Forces trainer.

"Nope," Lair replied.

"Then you're a new spook, aren't you?" asked Sutphin. "You work for the CIA, right?"

Lair just shrugged his shoulders.

The Helio crossed above the flat brown ribbon of the Mekong River and landed in a Savannakhet soccer field with plenty of room to spare. They were in Laos. It looked like Thailand, the same skinny, curving coconut palms and vase-shaped acacia trees and rusting tin roofs. The language was nearly the same and so were the Buddhist *wat*s and the women in sarongs and people lounging in the shade. Only the tropical languor had intensified. The loudest sounds were the chirping of birds and the buzzing of flies. It was as though they had entered a country in a permanent daydream. A jeep drove out to meet them. Lair got into the jeep with the plain brown-wrapped parcels piled high in the back seat. Inside the parcels was Lao currency, kip—the first installment on a million-dollar payment to the Laotian right.

But Lair had more on his mind than a countercoup when he went to see the general.

◆

A few days later five teams of five Asian men each crossed the Mekong from the Thai to the Laotian side by ferry. The teams, who wore green fatigues without identifying insignias, reported to the battalion commanders of the rightist Lao army. Each team member was cross-trained in several specialties—weapons handling and instruction, first aid, radio communications, and so on. They looked and spoke like the Lao, and within minutes they blended in as though they had always been there. In the following weeks more Air America cargo plains flew into Savannakhet with money, weapons, ammunition, and American advisers.

In late November 1960, after the rainy season had ended, and after John F. Kennedy had won the U.S. presidential election, the re-equipped right-wing Lao force began trudging along the roads upriver toward Vientiane, 250 miles away. The five-men teams kept the battalions in touch with one another and advised the genially corrupt general in charge, whose name was Phoumi Nosavan. When the dusty army neared an enemy stronghold, the advisers arranged to ferry part of the force to Thailand, upriver by land a ways, and then back across to Laos again, neatly avoiding a battle. The advisers thought it best to save Phoumi's limited fighting capacity for Vientiane.

In Moscow and Washington, the imminent clash of fourth-rate Laotian armies attracted interest at the highest levels of government. In the war rooms in the Kremlin and the Pentagon, the planners pointed at their wall maps and drew the same conclusion: With communist China and North Vietnam on one side and fragile U.S. allies like Thailand and South Vietnam on the other, the Kingdom of Laos was a perfect place from which to control the rest of Southeast Asia. Or if not perfect, at least worth denying to the enemy.

The Soviets knew that the Americans had already supplied the rightists with arms and equipment. On December 4, 1960, the Soviet Union began airlifting supplies to the so-called neutralist army in Vientiane. Capt. Kong Le's idealistic coup was giving way to a potentially dangerous showdown between the superpowers.

As the rightist army slowly trudged toward Vientiane, Bill Lair stayed behind in Savannakhet in a rented house. He studied troop movements on topographical maps. He sent off coded reports from an upstairs radio room. In his free time he sat in the back of local restaurants eating *quiteo,* the local soup, and watching the clean little gecko lizards climbing up the walls and blinking in the light. He smoked cigars and thought about hill-tribes and waited for events to unfold with a patience acquired in a long immersion in Asia.

He was an unlikely man to find at the center, the very turning point, of an international crisis. He did not exude power or glamour or heroism; he was the last man to be noticed in a crowd. But his obscurity was deliberate, and his presence there was the result of a long-thought-out plan.

◆

James William Lair was a fifth-generation Texan, and the only son of a man killed in an oilfield accident. As a quiet, shy boy in a threadbare household, he read adventure novels and dreamed of becoming a pilot in his nation's service. He was a freshman at Texas A&M when the Japanese attacked Pearl Harbor. He tried to join a navy training program for pilots, and when he was rejected for bad eyesight, joined the army as a private. He was only seventeen, and he had to persuade his mother to cosign his enlistment papers.

In World War II, his armored unit provided covering fire for tanks from highly maneuverable half-tracked vehicles. His fellow privates included city kids who had never walked on grass, Puerto Ricans who could barely speak English, farmers' sons who could barely read. They didn't have much training. During the Normandy invasion, Lair and everyone else around him panicked the first time they came under enemy artillery fire. Gradually, however, they taught themselves the necessary combat skills and learned to rely on one another. Eventually, they became the kind of tight-knit, gung-ho bunch whose wounded go AWOL from the hospitals and re-join their buddies, to avoid being transferred anywhere else.

Attached to a tank battalion, they stayed in combat for about a year, pushing eastward through France into Germany, and finally stopping at the banks of the Elbe River, when they met their erstwhile allies, the Soviets, coming the other way. An instinctive mistrust hung between Lair's company and the Soviet forces on opposite sides of the river. Lair and the other enlisted men thought that they might as well cross the river, fight the communists, and get the next war over with. The Cold War began then and there, on the banks of the Elbe and in other places like it, in the spring of 1945, even before World War II was over.

Expecting to work in the Texas oilfields like his father before him, Lair returned to Texas A&M to get a degree in geology. But he was always looking for an Elbe to cross. In his senior year the CIA recruited on campus, looking for veterans to hire as paramilitary instructors. Feeling that the U.S.

had unfinished business to take care of, Lair joined the intelligence agency. Like millions of American men of his generation, he was a Cold War idealist, practical in some ways and naive in others. He was a true believer in the fight against communism, and he assumed that his own government would always be on the side of the good.

When Lair arrived in Thailand for his first CIA assignment, in 1951, the Korean War was under way some two thousand miles to the northeast. In Thailand and other countries of Southeast Asia, the U.S. government was trying to contain China's southern flank in case the fighting spread. The Strategic Air Command was building long runways in Thailand to base its nuclear bombers. The CIA put politicians and generals on its payroll, and supported anticommunist exile groups. To prepare for the remote chance of Chinese troops pouring through the buffer zone of Laos into Thailand, the CIA also decided to train members of the Thai national police in the skills of guerilla warfare. Lair and another novice were put in charge of that effort, which was given a low priority.

Lair had hardly seen Asians before, much less worked with them. To his surprise, he discovered that he could relate to the Thais as fellow human beings. He learned to speak their language from them, haltingly and with a Texas twang. They parachuted from planes together and learned to live on wild foods from the indigenous people of the forests.

He began to re-create among the trainees the camaraderie, that special unit feeling, he had known in his platoon in World War II. Nobody told him how to do it, and it was only later that he realized that his talent for getting on the Thais' wavelength was unusual. Most Thais outwardly deferred to Caucasians, just as the Lao did. Most Americans played into the role of the great white leader, posture erect, shoulders back, bellowing commands. Lair hunched his shoulders, lowered his gaze, and spoke quietly and sincerely. He never lost his temper. He waited humbly for days at a time, when necessary, in the anteroom of Thai officials if he needed their help. He solved problems before they arose. His calm demeanor matched the Thai cultural ideal of gentlemanly behavior, and his policemen welcomed him as one of their own.

When the Chinese invasion failed to materialize and his program was canceled, Lair convinced first the Bangkok CIA station chief and then the strongman running Thailand to let him organize his best training graduates into an elite police unit. The Thai strongman, Gen. Phao Sriyanonda, who knew Lair worked for the CIA, accepted on the condition that Lair also become an aboveground, legitimate officer in the Thai police. The CIA was delighted to have one of its own men serve in the Thai government without even a cover story—or better yet, with a cover story that happened to be true. Lair's marriage to a Thai woman from a prominent Bangkok family sealed his career path. From then on, Thailand would be his second country. He would work faithfully in its interests, as long as they didn't conflict with the interests of the U.S. government and the CIA.

Lair's new force was called the Police Aerial Resupply Unit, or Paru. The commander was a Thai, and Lair was the commander's best friend and the unit's guru. Mostly they worked in the jungles, training villagers to defend themselves against outlaw gangs in Thailand's wild border areas. On a shoestring budget, and unknown to the outside world, they also cap-tured opium smugglers, survived the coup when the army took over from the national police, and befriended Thailand's king, a constitutional monarch who became their discreet, behind-the-scenes patron. When the U.S. ambassador to Thailand, William J. Donovan, visited their training camp, Lair felt honored, for "Wild Bill" Donovan had run the Office of Strategic Services (OSS), the CIA's predecessor, and his presence there was like the passing of the torch. The CIA's Far East chief, Desmond FitzGerald, visited the camp after that, followed by the CIA's director, Allen W. Dulles.

In the mid-1950s, the Paru set out to acquaint themselves with the tribes in the mountains of Thailand's north. Most lowland Thais despised the mountain people, or hilltribes, for being unclean and for lacking a written form of their own languages; but the Paru admired the hilltribes for their toughness and their hunting skills with homemade muskets. The biggest tribe was the Meo, a particularly hardy bunch who covered terrain like mountain goats, hiking scores of miles at a rapid gait and never getting tired. Asked about their leaders, many Meo mentioned a young fellow tribesman in Laos by the name of Vang Pao.

By the end of the 1950s, the Paru had cleaned up Thailand's border re-gions and were ready for another assignment. There were hilltribes, Lair knew, throughout the mountains on China's southern flank. None of the hilltribes liked the lowland Chinese, who had never treated them well; and there was a potential for recruiting and arming the hilltribes to serve as nui-sance or tripwire forces in case the Chinese pushed south. But in practical terms Lair always knew that his next assignment would have to be Laos, the buffer state that separated Thailand from China and North Vietnam. The languages and cultures of upcountry Thailand and Laos were practi-cally the same. His Paru could operate as easily in Laos as at home. He wanted the Paru to find a new role for their sake, for Thailand's, and for the CIA's, but he also had his own reasons. He was a Cold Warrior, and the Mekong was his Elbe.

◆

On December 14, 1960, after the Laotian neutralists had formally allied with the Pathet Lao and Hanoi, the rightist army finally attacked Vientiane.

It was a sloppy battle. The rightists had American-supplied artillery and heavy machine guns. The neutralists had artillery from the Soviets. Both sides let loose from a safe distance in the Buddhist belief that since they were not aiming at individual enemies they could not be blamed for any deaths. Entire neighborhoods of thatched-roof shacks were set ablaze by incendiary shells. Even the American embassy was hit, and an old blackened stupa, or Buddhist monument, nearby toppled over on the street. Once inside Vientiane, the rightists celebrated. They were too busy partying to listen to their Paru advisers, who urged them not to let the neutralists escape. With no one following, the neutralists retreated northward in good order, away from the Mekong River.

Lair arrived in Vientiane by plane while smoke was still billowing in the air. On another flight came Desmond FitzGerald, chief of the Far East division of the Directorate for Plans, the covert action branch of the CIA. FitzGerald was an Ivy League adventurer, a charming aristocrat whose allergy to tropical sunlight forced him to wear skin powder and gloves. He called a general meeting in the office of the CIA's station chief for Laos and asked Lair to attend. FitzGerald started the meeting by thanking Lair and his organization and heaping on the praise.

FitzGerald knew that the rightists wouldn't have won any kind of victory, sloppy or otherwise, if it hadn't been for their Paru advisers. He also knew the Paru existed because of Lair, and that they followed him personally. Men who raised and led their own armed forces were rare in the outfit—much more rare than FitzGerald liked.

The real victory the Far East chief savored, however, was one of *technique,* as that term is used in the intelligence trade. The information the Paru teams had radioed on every skirmish and bivouac had been accurate every time. The U.S. government had never had good inside information from Laos before—and if it had, FitzGerald didn't need to remind anyone in the room, Kong Le would never have mounted his original coup. The U.S. had acted only as a catalyst, helping the Laotians while staying on the sidelines. There had been no news leaks about the CIA's role. The outfit hadn't spent much, either—a million dollars was small change for a successful coup d'etat.

FitzGerald asked Lair and the Paru to stick around and find other useful work to do. Lair rented a house on the western edge of Vientiane, near the airport. He left his shoes outside the door and moved in with his teams. He ate rice with them, and he spoke to them in Texas-accented Thai. They set up their radios and spread out their maps. And they waited.

◆

Allowed to escape from Vientiane, the neutralists marched north and joined their Pathet Lao allies. Together they forced right-wing troops from a crucial three-way road junction. From it, they controlled all traffic between Vientiane, the old royal capital of Luang Prabang, and the area of grasslands in north-central Laos, the Plain of Jars.

Soviet airplanes dropped the neutralists and Pathet Lao weapons and supplies. Soviet and North Vietnamese advisers helped them plan for their next big confrontation with the forces of the West.

The Laos war had just begun.

# The Meeting

The Plain of Jars gets its name from dozens of containers carved from solid rock and left on its grassy landscape like a giant's tea set. The jars are as high as a man's chest, many times broader, and too heavy to move without a crane. Nobody knows what ancient civilization made them or what it used them for. They just sit there, covered in lichen, an unsolved mystery and minor tourist attraction.

The importance of the plain is geographical. Though less than ten miles across, it is the biggest area in northern Laos that is flat, or close to flat. Around it in all directions rise wild mountains, with spectacular limestone escarpments poking up here and there through the heavy forest canopy. The few roads of northern Laos converge in or near the Plain of Jars, and that makes it a favorite gathering point and logistical center for any army.

In the last week of December 1960, Edgar Buell was still living in Lat Houang, in a valley that feeds into the Plain of Jars. He supposed that the Pathet Lao and the neutralists were coming but he didn't know when. The Meo army officer, Vang Pao, previously the deputy commander of the plain, had taken over the top army job and was trying to keep the lowland soldiers in the garrison loyal to the royalists. For insurance, Vang Pao was quietly handing out weapons from the government armory to fellow tribesmen. Buell learned that the Meo had created resistance networks before. The tribe didn't fear the neutralists or the Pathet Lao much, but it considered the Pathet Lao's main backers, the North Vietnamese, a dangerous enemy. The North Vietnamese border was only about fifty miles away.

On the night of December 30, 1960, Buell stayed up late using his farm midwifery skills on a pregnant Laotian woman. By the time he delivered the healthy baby it was nearly dawn on the thirty-first. He returned to the IVS compound, where Meo friends warned him that the Pathet Lao were about to arrive in Lat Houang.

Buell, another American, and two Meo boys who worked with them drove to an airstrip, where a hastily arranged evacuation plane was landing. Enemy soldiers approached within sight as their plane took off. The escape, Buell wrote to his family, was the most exciting thing that had happened to him in his lifetime.

The plane flew them south to Bangkok, Thailand, to join the rest of the Americans evacuated from Laos. Though it was midnight on New Year's Eve, Buell was whisked off to see the U.S. ambassador to Thailand. He talked with the ambassador for an hour, and then went off to brief military and civilian intelligence staffers until four A.M. He was their authority on the Plain of Jars area, though he hadn't lived there long. They asked him to keep his mouth shut, stay out of sight, and make sure the two Meo boys with him didn't talk to strangers. Buell was happy to oblige.

Six months after leaving home, this Indiana farmer found himself in the midst of an international crisis. He had escaped from the communists by the thinnest of margins, and ambassadors and spooks were asking his opinions and hanging on his every word. He was bursting with patriotic pride, and his letters home were full of hints and sideways winks of matters too secret to divulge. He loved the excitement, and vowed to go back and help the Meo if he had the chance.

◆

Ron Sutphin, the Air America pilot, was also in north Laos on December 31, 1960. In the early morning the airstrip where he had parked his Helio overnight came under mortar attack. Fragments of the exploding shells punched tiny holes in the wing. Hastily airborne, he headed for the Plain of Jars with his Customers, two CIA case officers. As they flew over the southern edge of the plain, ground soldiers fired at them with rifles and they saw a pillar of dust up ahead. Trucks carrying troops were heading for the big Xieng Khouang airfield. The neutralists and Pathet Lao were on the verge of capturing the Plain of Jars.

Sutphin got to the airfield ahead of them. Landing and taxiing onto the mat of pierced-steel planking, the CIA men jumped out and drove off to join Vang Pao, who was in the town of Xieng Khouang some distance away. There were cargo planes at the airstrip, and Sutphin was getting the other pilots moving when a message came back from one of the case officers telling him to pick up Vang Pao's family, who had fled southeast in a French truck.

Airborne again, over hilly country between the plain and the Mekong valley, Sutphin spotted the truck in a village of scraggly thatched huts called Tha Vieng. Outside the village, low earthen dikes in a dry rice field had been flattened to make a crude airstrip. A crowd had collected, mostly women with the heavy silver necklaces and embroidered black costumes of the Meo. Among them were Vang Pao's wives and members of his extended family. A dozen women and children climbed in the Helio, filling the cabin until they were sitting on one another's laps and lying on the floor. Overloaded, the Helio rose sluggishly off the makeshift airfield and landed heavily less than an hour later at Wattay Airport outside Vientiane. A crowd had gathered to meet the plane and at the back of it stood a meek-looking *farang* wearing glasses, Bill Lair.

By this time Sutphin knew that Lair was both an undercover CIA paramilitary officer and an aboveground major in the Thai police. He went back with Lair to the Paru house near the airport. Spreading out his navigational charts, Sutphin began to explain what had happened that day, retracing all the stops.

When he finished, Lair asked him to go over parts of his story again. What about the size and placement of units of the attacking army? Did Vang Pao have Meo civilians with him or lowland Lao soldiers? Where was Vang Pao now? The two men pored over the maps again as Lair meticulously checked and rechecked the facts.

Around them, looking over their shoulders, stood the Thai Paru, wearing fatigues with no insignias. They didn't speak, but they appeared to understand what was being said. At the table, Bill Lair kept patiently directing the questions back to Vang Pao, always boring in and never losing track. And gradually, it dawned on the pilot what a long and subtle hand Lair was playing.

◆

The next day, New Year's Day 1961, President Eisenhower held an unusual holiday cabinet meeting at the White House. The subject was Laos. The discussions covered the takeover of the Plain of Jars, the known presence of Soviet advisers, and published (though erroneous) news reports that North Vietnamese and mainland Chinese forces had taken part in the fighting.

"In view of the present situation in Laos," Press Secretary James C. Hagerty announced later, "we are taking normal precautionary actions to increase the readiness of our forces in the Pacific, including measures to increase the airlift capability of the Pacific command."

An aircraft carrier group, with two carriers, several destroyers, and 1,400 marines got under way in the South China Sea. Army and marine paratroopers on Okinawa went on standby alert, and the air force shifted troop transport planes from bases in the continental U.S. to the Philippines.

Members of the Southeast Asian Treaty Organization (SEATO) met in Bangkok. In New York, the Laotian representative to the United Nations said that his government would appeal to the Security Council if the situation got worse.

◆

Lair drove from the Paru house down the airport road toward the U.S. embassy downtown.

Of all the streets in Vientiane, the airport road was the ugliest, being the only one without trees and shade. Until the year before it had been a handsome boulevard, with two central lanes lined by a double row of fine old trees, and then two more lanes outside the shade trees. But that was before an American contractor had tried to improve the traffic flow. Without consulting anyone, he cut down the trees and paved over the stumps, creating a bleak four-lane highway. Now the cars, oxcarts, bicycles, and pedicabs wove and drifted from side to side at the same slow speed as before, but under the harsh, punishing glare of the tropical sun.

The rest of Vientiane had a more traditional small-town Oriental appearance. Down the shaded side streets, lined with acacia and jacaranda trees, Lair glimpsed single-file lines of barefoot monks walking in measured silence in their orange and yellow robes. The monks were making their early morning rounds, stopping for housewives who knelt and placed gifts of food in their begging bowls, and then *wai*'d to show respect. Women scurried off to market, wearing *pasin*s, fancy versions of sarongs, with silver-link belts around their waists. The tang of woodsmoke from cooking fires drifted through the streets, and thin stray dogs rummaged through garbage heaps.

At the CIA station, next to the U.S. embassy, a few blocks from the Mekong, Lair went to see the station chief, Gordon Jorgensen, to ask permission to go upcountry to see Vang Pao. Jorgensen said he thought it was a pretty good idea. In the CIA station, Vang Pao was considered a wild card because of his tribal background. Some of the political action officers had gotten to know him, had given him a radio, an anvil, and some surplus sweaters, things like that, but in the chaos of the countercoup and the takeover of the Plain of Jars, it was unclear what Vang Pao was going to do. The political action officers wanted to work with Vang Pao themselves, but Lair had better credentials as the de facto leader of the Paru.

Jorgensen asked Lair how he would get there. Lair said that a flight of H-34 helicopters had just landed at the airport. If the station chief could arrange it, he would be on his way.

Jorgensen said he would arrange for a chopper, but wanted Lair back the same day. His unspoken message was that he didn't want any Americans taken captive upcountry, that he had enough headaches already.

Lair went back to his house to get the Paru's Thai commander, Col. Pranet Ritchenchai. They took a five-man Paru team with full field gear and weapons. It took until midafternoon to get the flight clearances—in Laos everything takes longer than it is supposed to. Finally they met their pilot, who was wearing civilian clothes and had a quarter-inch haircut.

The pilot had previously served aboard a U.S. aircraft carrier in the Gulf of Siam. He and other marine pilots had flown H-34 helicopters, a relatively new and powerful model with a bulbous, protuberant nose, over the length of Thailand and across the Mekong to Vientiane. In a deal quietly arranged by higher authorities the H-34s had been turned over to Air America, and the chopper pilots retired from the Marine Corps and joined Air America the same day. The pilot admitted to Lair that he didn't know where he was, let alone where he was going.

Lair produced a topographical map and offered to navigate from the copilot's seat. He told the pilot not to worry, he'd been around these parts a long time.

With Lair and the Thais inside, the chopper rose from the tarmac and clattered over the Mekong, heading downstream. The river surface had dropped lower as the dry season progressed, exposing massive sandbars. To the south stretched Thailand's rice paddies, already turning a tawny gold as the harvest season approached. To the north, the first mountains of Laos were in sight, a curving escarpment rising three thousand feet above the Vientiane plain. Farther downstream from Vientiane, the hills crowded the river's edge, then fell away again, leaving a wide span of flat bottomland, through which passed a little tributary, the Nam Ngiap. Lair told the pilot to follow it north.

Upstream, the tributary narrowed to a canyon, then broadened out again, with a strip of farmland and rice paddies on either bank. The mountainside to their right was partially in sunlight, the shadow of their chopper fluttering and rippling with the contours of the land. Already the afternoon was coming to a close. Over the engine noise and the whop-whop-whop of the rotor blades, the pilot shouted that it was time to go back soon. Lair shouted back that he knew their location and they wouldn't get lost. In fact, he had never been to upcountry Laos before.

Fifty miles later on a hillside below, Lair saw a small man wearing baggy black trousers that ended at his shins. He told the pilot to put the chopper down. Lair ran to the startled Meo farmer and asked him if Vang Pao was around. The Meo nodded and said sure, somewhere. Lair gestured for Pranet to talk to the farmer. The pilot yelled over the engine noise that it was time to get off the ground, he didn't want to wait till it was dark.

Lair turned to Pranet and asked if he was willing to stay overnight with the team. Of course, the Paru commander said. He believed that it was in Thailand's interest for him to meet Vang Pao. He knew that the station chief wanted Lair back, that otherwise Bill would have stayed, too. At Pranet's signal, his five-man team jumped out of the chopper, eager and alert, into unfamiliar territory.

The next day a coded radio message from Pranet reached Lair in the Paru house in Vientiane. "We found Vang Pao," the message read. "He's the one we've been looking for. Come back, so you can meet him too."

Lair arranged for another chopper. On his way back to the mountains he thought about that message: *He's the one we've been looking for.* He scarcely noticed the flight itself, or the collection of thatched and tin-roof huts known as Tha Vieng. Vang Pao's men, some uniformed soldiers in the lowland army, others Meo partisans in baggy black, had been on the run for days, sleeping in the fields or in the huts of relatives. On the run, but running well, kept in order by their short, vivacious leader with the slanting eyes. For that was what Lair noticed. Just Vang Pao himself, and Pranet off to the side, nodding, affirming Lair's perceptions.

◆

Vang Pao was about five feet five, with a ready smile and white even teeth. A small wart on his left eyebrow seemed like a punctuation mark in a rounded, lively face.

He was a mountain man who had learned the ways of the Lao lowlanders, and some of the ways of the *farang*s. Though he had never heard of Lair, he had been preparing for the meeting for years, just as Lair had been getting ready for him—two men with long paths ready to converge.

He was born in 1931 in Nong Het, east of the Plain of Jars near the Vietnamese border, the middle son of a peasant with a thatched hut, a rice field, and an opium patch. The Vang clan was small and unimportant. Whether to make up for his lowly origins, or because he had been granted an extra-large spark of life, Vang Pao always outdid other boys his age. With his restless energy, hot temper, and natural ability to lead, he caught the eyes of Touby LyFoung, the tribe's political spokesman in what was then the French colonial government, and Touby's friend Chao (meaning "Prince") Saykham, the hereditary ruler of the province. The two older men were looking for protégés, and Vang Pao was looking for mentors. In March 1945, when he was fourteen and World War II was drawing to a close, Vang Pao became a courier for French soldiers hiding from Japanese occupation troops in the villages and limestone caves of the area. To support the French, Saykham and Touby organized a partisan tribal force, and from it Vang Pao got a taste of the hit-and-run tactics of guerilla warfare.

When the war was over, he joined the national police. His training brought him out of the mountains and down to the Mekong valley, to the old royal capital of Luang Prabang. He was the only tribesman in the police academy, and others treated him poorly, for the lowland Lao believe the people of the hills to be racially inferior. "Meo," the word outsiders called Vang Pao's people, means "barbarian" in Chinese. But the Meo call themselves Hmong, which in their own language means "free people."

Vang Pao finished first in his class of eighty. He also won a 3,500-meter foot race against his police classmates, soldiers, students, and royal guards; the crown prince, who later became king, awarded him a silver cup. It was heady stuff for the boy from the mountains, and it convinced him that his people could benefit from an alliance with the lowlanders without having to leave the mountains or take on lowland ways.

Vang Pao's home province of Xieng Khouang bordered on the part of French Indochina that was to become North Vietnam. In 1950, when Ho Chi Minh's communists carried their independence fight into Laos, to spread out the French forces, Vang Pao was a police sergeant, with other Meo policemen serving under him. His French commander asked him to go after a wily Vietnamese captain who had been plaguing the region.

Vang Pao found the captain in the house of a village chief. Before dawn one morning, Vang Pao and his men opened fire on the chief's house. There was nothing chivalrous about it, no telling the enemy to wake up and fight, but hilltribes have never operated that way. Stoic and cruel, they expect no quarter and they give none.

The Vietnamese captain and most of his men died on the chief's wooden floor. One escaped, and as daylight arrived Vang Pao followed bloody tracks to a cave. The Vietnamese soldier inside refused to surrender. Vang Pao lobbed grenades inside. On the corpse he found safe-conduct passes and detailed communist battle plans. ("The Vietnamese adore paperwork," Vang Pao said later, adding, "not me.")

Vang Pao and his men returned to base, where the French officers staged a feast in their honor. They drank and ate and sang. At the height of the celebration the French commander came up to Vang Pao and told him to sleep well that night because he was going out again in the morning. According to the captured documents, the dead captain had scheduled a meeting with another Vietnamese force in the district, and Vang Pao was going to show up for it.

Another ambush, another firefight. More grenades. More Vietnamese dead, and more documents.

The French commander decided that Sergeant Vang Pao should become an officer. He radioed for the written entrance exam for the officer candidate course in the Laotian military training school.

The exam arrived by parachute, drifting down from a circling messenger plane. The test was entirely in French. Vang Pao had picked up a few hundred words of gutter French in the barracks and bordellos, but his five years of formal schooling had been in the Lao language. He sat down to take his exam and tried to figure out what the letters of the *farang* alphabet meant.

The French commander paced behind him, back and forth. Grammar and verb tenses, he remarked, had nothing to do with the ability to lead soldiers through elephant grass. Then the Frenchman started dictating the answers to the young Meo. But only dictating, Vang Pao emphasized when he told this story years later. ("It is not true, as it is sometimes said, that he guided my hand," Vang Pao insisted. "Whorehouse of shit! I know how to write!")

Soon after his graduation from officer candidate school the gendarmerie was dissolved and its men transferred into the regular military. Lt. Vang Pao joined a program headed by a Col. Roger Trinquier, who reported to the French high military command in Hanoi, but who was also connected to the Service de Documentation Extérieure et du Contre-Espionage, or SDECE—the French equivalent of the CIA.

Trinquier wanted to train and arm the hilltribes to help fight against the communists. But he never had much support from his superiors and he was always short of funds. His solution was to buy the Meo's opium crop from Touby LyFoung and from other tribal leaders across the border in northern Vietnam. He flew the raw opium to Cap St. Jacques on the coast of southern Vietnam, and had it trucked to the Binh Xuyen bandits, who managed Saigon's opium dens. The bandits split their profits with Trinquier, and Trinquier split his take with Touby LyFoung, who became rich enough to set up another household in Vientiane.

With his opium money, Trinquier flew five hundred Meo to Cap St. Jacques for paramilitary training and back to Laos again. Whatever its morality, this French drugs-for-guns deal had little effect. The five hundred lightly armed tribesmen could not stop the seven thousand Vietnamese communists who invaded in 1953. The Vietnamese drove toward Luang Prabang in another attempt to make the French spread their defenses over a wider area.

At the time Vang Pao was living in an unhappy little base where the ethnic Lao and hilltribe soldiers quarreled and nobody got along with the local population. When the Vietnamese neared the base, the men of his garrison went on the run, fleeing one ambush after another. Because of the ethnic frictions, Vang Pao's French commander ordered the unit to break up, the Lao to go off by themselves and the French to go with the Meo under Vang Pao. The Lao failed to cover their tracks and the Vietnamese followed in hot pursuit. Vang Pao's men brushed their tracks carefully. They hid in caves. Hungry and exhausted, but safe, they ate wild bamboo shoots and the fibrous hearts of banana trees.

Weeks later Vang Pao led them onto the grassy, gently rolling countryside of the Plain of Jars. Tribal scouts loyal to Touby LyFoung had already warned the French high command of Vietnamese positions nearby. When elements of the Vietnamese force emerged on the plain soon afterwards they were strafed, bombed, and blown to bits on the open ground by the French air force.

When Vang Pao saw airpower destroy the Vietnamese who had been chasing him all over the mountains, he had a revelation. It was like eating the apple of knowledge. He wanted airpower himself, and tanks and artillery. The bigger the weapon, the better. Though his background had prepared him only for small-scale, hit-and-run guerilla warfare, he didn't want to be typecast. Guerillas couldn't stop a big enemy force by themselves. But airpower and conventional forces, working with information from tribal scouts, had done exactly that.

From that time on Vang Pao longed to come down from the mountains, to become a conventional warrior with planes and big guns. But he had no chance to nourish those ambitions under the French, whose days in Indochina were rapidly coming to a close. In 1954 the French Expeditionary Corps established a big, heavily fortified base in the valley of Dienbienphu, just over the border from Laos in northern Vietnam. From there the French expected to block any further invasions of Laos. They were unprepared when the Vietnamese communists, or Viet Minh, laid siege from the surrounding hills. As the communists tightened the noose, shelling the French in their trenches, and firing antiaircraft guns at the resupply planes, Vang Pao was sent at the head of a four-hundred-man Meo column to achieve whatever was possible in the way of reconnaissance or harassment. Dienbienphu fell before he got there, and the next morning a conference began in Geneva to negotiate France's exit from its Indochinese colonies.

In the years that followed, with France gradually pulling out and the United States coming in, Vang Pao became a captain and then a major in the sleepy, inefficient Royal Lao Army. In 1959 he met his first U.S. military training teams and CIA officers, but the Meo partisans of Trinquier's time had gone back to their villages, and the concept of irregular warfare did not attract much American interest. Then Capt. Kong Le's coup of August 1960 threw Laos into civil war.

Vang Pao believed, as Kong Le did, that the lowland generals had gotten too rich and fat on stolen American aid. But he also knew that the Pathet Lao and North Vietnamese would penetrate Kong Le's new neutralist regime. The North Vietnamese were his enemy. Because of that, Vang Pao felt he had to support the anticommunist Laotian right, or royalist, side. Most men of his tribe felt the same way and so did his old mentor, Chao Saykham, the lowland governor of Xieng Khouang Province. But Touby LyFoung, Vang Pao's other mentor and his tribe's political spokesman, was known to favor neutralism. Touby was in Vientiane and impossible to reach.

By his own account, Vang Pao called in an important shaman, or spirit doctor, who got out his bells, pulled a black hood over his eyes, and began to chant and dance, or "shake." Once in his trance, the shaman crossed from the mortal everyday world into the parallel world of the spirits. He invoked the souls of their ancestors, and promised a sacrifice of one white cow and one black cow if the ancestors got through to Touby. Three days later Touby appeared by plane. The cows were slaughtered, and Touby bowed to the wishes of the majority and switched to the royalist side.

Now that he had a tribal consensus, Vang Pao was ready to move. Some of his old Meo partisans from French days had gathered, knowing they would be needed. He marched them into the nearby military base and issued them government weapons. From Savannakhet, the rightists sent 200,000 kip, which had come from Lair, to pay the regular troops. For a brief, shining moment, Vang Pao was both the royalist commander of the Plain of Jars and a leader of his hilltribe. But when the neutralists fled north from Vientiane and joined forces with the Pathet Lao, and the Soviets brought in heavy weapons, he decided to retreat, and to mobilize his people for guerilla resistance in the mountains.

Vang Pao left with Chao Saykham and a collection of civilians, soldiers, and Meo irregulars on foot by the back road southeast from the plain, a rutted jeep track known as Route 4. Part of the way to the Mekong, at the village of Tha Vieng, Vang Pao decided to send the civilians on ahead. He regrouped his remaining men and waited for U.S. aircraft to arrive. He was expecting Americans, but the tough, courteous Thais were a pleasant surprise.

To Lair, the general outlines of Vang Pao's story were plain to see by the way he carried himself and by the way he ran his camp. Vang Pao was in charge. His men obeyed his every word. Even in retreat they were well organized and their discipline was good.

Pranet had been right. Vang Pao was the man they had been looking for. Together Pranet and Lair had worked the wild borders of Thailand for a decade, looking for local leaders to develop. They had never seen a people as ripe for partisan war as the Meo of Laos, or a leader as accomplished as Vang Pao. He was perfectly at home in his environment. With his upward-tilting eyes in that keen, intelligent face, he reminded Lair of a miniature Genghis Khan.

◆

As Vang Pao, Lair, and Pranet sat and talked, they heard yelling from the river. One of Vang Pao's Meo had fallen into the river and drowned. The camp was in the foothills and the Meo home was the mountain peaks, where the streams were small. The tribesmen didn't know how to swim.

When the body was recovered and the commotion quieted down, the three men returned to their conversation.

Bill Lair asked Vang Pao what he planned to do.

Vang Pao answered as a tribesman rather than as an officer in the low-landers' army.

"This is our home," Vang Pao replied, sweeping his hand toward the hills and behind him toward the Plain of Jars. "We own all of these mountains. I've been in touch with the communists. They've been around here for years. But my people cannot live with them. Their life is too different from ours. We have only two choices: We fight them, or we leave. There is nothing else we can do. If you give us the guns, we will fight them."

Lair said, "How many men can you arm, do you think?"

"At least ten thousand."

In nine years in Thailand, Bill Lair had built the Paru up to four hundred men.

In those years Lair had learned to judge Asian characters. He had come up against almost every form of scam and fakery imaginable. He looked at Vang Pao, and his instinct told him that Vang Pao was telling the truth.

"If the Meo were armed," Bill Lair asked, "would they try to become autonomous, or would they be loyal to the Laotian government?"

"I am loyal to the king of Laos," Vang Pao replied.

"Neither the Laotian government nor the U.S. government could support a Meo independence movement. What do your people want to do?"

Vang Pao said, "They want to keep their way of life and follow their own leaders. They want to fight the communists. They will follow me, and I am loyal to the king."

It was a hedge, not a commitment, but it sounded true.

Lair did not commit either.

"I'll see what I can do," was all he said.

It was dark by the time he got back to the U.S. embassy in Vientiane. Jorgensen was gone, but he had left a note for Lair to come over to his house for dinner. Lair went over and found Desmond FitzGerald with the station chief.

His two bosses knew that the options the government was weighing for Laos boiled down to invading with a conventional military force and then getting bogged down Korea-style, or else sitting back and letting the Soviets win by default. There had to be a better way. They asked him what he believed the outfit ought to do, and Lair paused to collect his thoughts.

He always thought before he spoke, and he had a Thai mannerism of lowering his gaze when addressing people he didn't know well, so as not to appear aggressive. The combination worked well on *farang*s, who saw that he was shy and listened sympathetically and dropped their guards; and then they were always surprised when he lifted his gaze to theirs and they saw his smouldering intensity, his eyes clear and almost fierce. FitzGerald had gotten the Lair treatment before, and he was always impressed with Lair's sincerity. But the Far East chief was always full of enthusiasm for field proposals, and he had to guard against his normal reactions. For it was one thing to like what somebody was doing in the field and what he was proposing to do, and quite another to change the outfit's policy, not to mention trying to change the policy of the U.S. government.

Lair started talking, hesitantly and in his Texas twang.

Vang Pao could probably do what he said, Lair said. Raise a paramilitary force, not a real army but a large guerilla force of ten thousand men. If a conventional army drove into the mountains of Laos, Vang Pao wouldn't try to defend any particular piece of terrain. He'd just make it expensive, attacking the enemy here and there and in the rear. Typical guerilla operation. The Meo would probably give a good account of themselves with small-scale harassment raids. The communists would have a hard time wiping them out.

Nobody but the Meo stood between the Plain of Jars and the Mekong, Lair said. Whether the U.S. objective was to save the lowland towns on the Mekong, or to deny territory to the communists so as to be in a stronger position for negotiations, or even just to collect intelligence, arming the Meo was a good bet. It wouldn't cost much. The Meo wanted to be armed, and they were ready to fight.

FitzGerald didn't react, even when Lair raised his eyes.

But the Meo would only follow their own kind, said Lair, and they would only fight to defend their territory and their way of life. There was more to be gained from doing it their way, and keeping Vang Pao in charge, than from trying to change them. The fewer outsiders the better. No Americans were needed in the field. The Paru were perfectly qualified to advise Vang Pao, to train the Meo and the other tribes, and to serve as a link between the tribes and the outfit. From Vientiane, the outfit would advise on the overall direction of the program and provide the equipment and the money.

It wouldn't take much money, either, Lair pointed out—the leaner the better. Cheap, reliable, surplus World War II weapons from existing stocks would be just right. Weapons of that vintage were hard to trace back to the U.S. government since they were so common. Similarly, the Paru would be hard to trace to the U.S. government since they looked exactly like the lowland Lao. That way the operation could be reversible. Low cost, easy-in, easy-out. A classic approach.

Another long pause from Lair, and more silence from FitzGerald.

The weak part of the proposition, Lair said, was that in the end the Meo were probably going to lose if the North Vietnamese kept on pushing. The North Vietnamese were disciplined and organized, probably the best soldiers in Asia. If the communists wanted Laos badly enough, the Meo were going to lose whether the U.S. helped them or not.

What could be done, if the operation was run right, said Lair, was prepare an exit for the Meo. There was a Laotian province called Sayaboury on the "Thai," or south, side of the Mekong. The river was one edge of Sayaboury Province and the other was a mountainous land border with Thailand. There were already some Meo in Sayaboury and others on the Thai side of the border, and they passed back and forth as though the border didn't exist. Vang Pao's Meo should go there, said Lair, if they had to leave. If Vang Pao couldn't stay in Sayaboury, the Thais might take him in Thailand, and make him a border security force.

Lair finished by saying that he knew the Thais pretty well and he thought they'd be willing to make a deal.

FitzGerald didn't say anything, and neither did the Vientiane station chief.

Lair figured they hadn't bought it. He went back to the Paru house by the airport for the night. As he went to sleep he thought about the miniature Genghis Khan and wondered what would happen to him.

Early the next morning at the station, FitzGerald told Lair that he liked the plan after all. Lair should write up a proposal immediately and send it to D.C., with a copy to Saigon, where FitzGerald was going.

Lair typed an eighteen-page proposal in one sitting. He cabled it through regular CIA channels, and three or four days later the answer came back from headquarters. The return cable said that the proposal had merit. As a first step, Lair was authorized to arm and train one thousand men, taking whatever steps were necessary. The project would be called Operation Momentum.

Copies of the return cable were addressed to the station chiefs in Bangkok and Vientiane. Except for coordinating overall policy with them, Lair would run Momentum on his own. He would have no day-to-day obligations to either station. The Meo operation would be funded directly from headquarters through a special account that Lair would control.

Once in a great while, the CIA sets up a money pipeline directly to a field operation, bypassing the bureaucracy of the station chiefs. But only in extraordinary situations and only for projects cleared at the highest levels. To anybody who knew how to read the tea leaves, the message was clear: Desmond FitzGerald wanted Bill Lair to handle the Meo operation personally, without interference, and with the help of the Paru. And the director of Central Intelligence had agreed.

# Momentum Begins

At the start of Operation Momentum, in early January 1961, Bill Lair was a GS-13 employee of the U.S. government, the civilian equivalent of a major. He had never worked in Washington and he had only made brief visits to the CIA headquarters, on the Mall near the Reflecting Pool.

He knew that Laos was taking up the time of senior government officials, but not that it was the most time-consuming foreign policy crisis in the waning days of the Eisenhower administration. He had no inkling that the day before John F. Kennedy's inauguration, Eisenhower would tell the president-elect, "If Laos is lost to the Free World, in the long run we will lose all of Southeast Asia."

Lair had lived in the boondocks of Asia for almost a decade. A practical-minded field man, he was not particularly interested in the domino theory, or counterinsurgency theories, or in theories about anything, though he understood them perfectly well. He had organized and trained the Paru, while staying out of the spotlight and carefully finessing the question of who was in charge. Now he and the Paru wanted to organize the Meo in the same way.

Pleased with the support he was getting from headquarters, but not giving it much thought, Lair decided to go up and talk to Vang Pao again, and set up the trainings as quickly as possible. Vang Pao's force had been attacked the night after their first meeting and they were on the run again, farther up in the mountains. Pranet, the Thai Paru leader, had radioed that he would stay behind at a meeting point to show Lair the way.

Lair flew upcountry with another helicopter pilot fresh out of the marines. They picked up Pranet at the meeting place and took off again toward Vang Pao's position higher in the mountains. They clattered along, rising up to a transverse ridge with trees growing on top. Sitting in the copilot's seat, Lair saw that they were awfully near the ridgeline. He wondered how close the pilot was going to get to the trees before flying over them.

It was like watching a movie in slow motion. The ridge and the trees got closer and closer, filling up the movie screen. Then the chopper hit the trees head-on and reality broke through. Branches yielded to the Plexiglas. The H-34 fell and hit the ground with a thump but with enough speed to keep moving forward. Overhead, the rotor broke with a loud snap. The motor roared uselessly, and the wounded helicopter went into a body slide down the steep slope of the far side of the ridge.

The chassis slid frontwards and then sideways. As Lair held his arms in front of his face, the H-34 skied over bumps and jumps, faster and faster. It slammed into a grove of trees, caromed off, hit still more trees, flopped over on its side, and finally lurched to a halt.

Lair was out of his seat belt and twenty-five yards away before he knew how he had gotten there. He turned around to look.

The helicopter lay on its side, a great metal carcass.

Not a soul was stirring.

Then Lair heard a voice call out, "Bill, you okay?"

Lair went cautiously back to the overturned helicopter. He climbed up on its side and peered in. There was a strong smell of high-octane gas. The pilot and Pranet were still in their seat belts, dazed.

"You okay, Bill?" Pranet asked again.

"You guys better get the hell out of here before this thing blows up," Lair warned.

Pranet climbed out. The pilot shook himself, climbed out, walked off, and sat under a tree a safe distance away with his head in his hands.

The thin mountain air had fooled the pilot, who wasn't used to flying at such high altitudes. Lacking lift, he had tried to pull up directly over the ridge even while he was losing control, instead of banking around to the rear and spiraling up to a higher elevation.

As they sat on the hillside, the shock gradually wearing off, they saw they were near a collection of thatched huts. An old man was running toward them from the village, barefoot, with baggy black pants flapping around his shins.

He was the Meo village chief, the *naiban*. The little toes on his feet stuck out to the sides almost at right angles, for better traction. He had probably never worn shoes. He looked at the helicopter, then at the skid tracks it made down the mountainside, then at Lair. He shook his head and declared that he didn't want to ride in one of those machines. Evidently he thought helicopters landed that way normally.

They walked down the hill to the old man's village. The houses were built of handsawn slabs of wood placed vertically with gaps between them, and thatched roofs above. The women and girls sat in the doorway doing their embroidery; they wore sashed, embroidered skirts and silver necklaces and turbaned hats. In front of some of the houses were strips of bamboo woven into a hexagon and placed on a stick, a sign that the woman within had recently given birth and nobody except the family should enter and disturb the spirits. Above other doorways were curved, sharpened pieces of bamboo or wood hanging from twisted ropes to keep the evil spirits away.

The headman invited them into his dirt-floor house. The inside was smoky from the cooking fire, and the smoke caught in the beams of light shining through the gaps in the walls. He removed the cloth cover from a heavy old radio desk set equipped with a hand crank, a microphone, and a continuous-wavelength, or Morse code–type, key. He cranked the generator handle a few times. " *'Allo, 'allo?*" he said into the microphone, and then tapped the keys a few times. " *'Allo, 'allo?*" The headman was also the chief of an older system of militia, the Auto Défense de Choc ("Self-Defense Shock Force"), organized and equipped by the French many years before. " *'Allo, 'allo?*"

Lair looked out the door at the helicopter scattered in pieces on the hillside and told Pranet to get ready to spend the night.

The messages from the radio reached Vientiane, and the next day a replacement chopper arrived. It ferried them without incident to Vang Pao and his band, a couple of mountain ridges away.

Lair told Vang Pao the U.S. government was ready to arm the first thousand men. They would start by training three companies of a hundred men each, with the Paru as instructors. For the training they needed to find a remote place where they could air-drop supplies. It would have to be remote, Lair said, because the other side was going to see the parachutes and would come in as fast as they could.

Vang Pao said that a base called Pha Khao would do. It was on the west side of a nine-thousand-foot mountain massif called Phu Bia, south of the Plain of Jars. He thought it would take the enemy about three days to get there.

Lair and the Paru devised a three-day training course and Air America dropped the weapons by parachute. The training was a variant of a course the Paru had given many times in Thailand to help villagers protect themselves against armed outlaw gangs. It was very simple. On the first day the recruits learned how to use their personal weapons, the rifles. The next day they learned team weapons—machine guns, mortars, and bazookas. The last day they learned tactics, such as setting up ambushes with tripwires attached to hand grenades.

Early on the fourth day Vang Pao went out on the periphery of the base, setting up tripwires and stationing his men behind rocks and trees. Just as he predicted, the Pathet Lao came charging up the hill. The Pathet Lao, who were no better soldiers than their lowland royalist brethren, walked right into his ambush. Then they ran away, leaving their dead sprawled on the hillside.

It was the Meo's first victory.

Lair was hugely pleased. Neither he nor the Paru had done any of the fighting. They'd just pushed the training button and the Meo had done everything else by themselves. The tribesmen were natural guerilla fighters and Vang Pao was a hands-on leader, the only kind that counted in the mountains. And the best thing of all, thought Lair, was that everybody at Pha Khao had black hair and almond eyes except himself. He was the only non-Asian, and he was getting out of there because he wasn't needed anymore.

It was a classic operation, deniable and reversible. The profile was so low there was no profile at all.

◆

Within days after Lair returned to Vientiane, Americans from the outfit started reporting for duty. Lair was aghast. He hadn't asked for any *farang*s in his original proposal, except for one financial man in the office. But Desmond FitzGerald had sent them, and Lair didn't have the clout to keep them out.

The first to arrive was Lloyd "Pat" Landry, a gruff Cajun from the gulf coast of Texas. Landry's fellow officers used words like "nasty," "rough," and "sarcastic" to describe him. But Lair had known Landry ever since their college days at Texas A&M and they had always gotten along fine. After a few short trips to work with the Meo, during which he realized that the Paru were better field instructors than he, Landry came back to the office to be Lair's deputy. It was the right niche for him. He played tough cop to Lair's nice cop. Blunt and hard-driving, Landry worked fiendishly long hours, piecing intelligence reports together, arranging logistics, doing whatever needed to be done.

The second American was "Tony Poe," a balding paramilitary specialist who charged into their office, snarled greetings at the two of them, and hurried out as fast as he could. Poe's real name was Anthony Alexander Poshepny. He had never bothered changing it legally. Poe hated offices and paperwork of any kind. He carried all his belongings in one duffel bag, and he didn't wear rings or watches—anything, he boasted, that might get caught in a parachute in a night drop.

Poe had run paramilitary missions in the Korean War. Later he worked with Tibetan Khamba tribesmen, training them for a rebellion against the mainland Chinese. In 1958, Poe went to Indonesia, where he and Landry tried to jump-start a revolution on the island of Sumatra. The revolt there fizzled out, and Poe and Landry ended up on the run and quarreling with each other, until they were rescued by a submarine, the USS *Tang*. The two men didn't like each other much, but Laos was where the action was, and Poe wanted to get in on it no matter what.

While Poe presided over the opening of dirt airstrips north and northeast of the Plain of Jars, and the Paru were doing all the real work, another American paramilitary officer named Jack Shirley showed up in Vientiane. To Bill Lair, it was yet another case of not wanting Americans in general but welcoming individual Americans because he had no choice.

Shirley, who had assisted Lair in the very early years of the Paru, had also been the best man at Lair's wedding. He was a solid little guy, and highly competent when he applied himself, which wasn't often. If you wanted to make an in-depth tour of the bars and bordellos of Thailand, Jack Shirley was the perfect guide—relaxed and genial and very good company. Lair made sure Shirley applied himself, and sent him with a Paru team east of the Plain of Jars, only twenty-five miles from the North Vietnamese border, a dangerous assignment.

And then Bill Young came in, a jungle boy with extraordinary family credentials. Young's grandfather, a Baptist missionary, had converted thousands of Lahu tribespeople in the mountains of Burma to Christianity. Young's father, Harold, moved the family mission to northern Thailand and ran an intelligence net into southern China for the CIA, with the help of Lahu tribesmen and Bill's older brother. Growing up with hilltribe boys as friends, Bill Young spoke fluent Lahu, Thai, and Lao; and he could walk and hunt just as well as hilltribesmen and live for months off wild game. No other American had those skills, but people in the CIA always talked about Bill Young wistfully, in terms of his remarkable potential. He had a history of leaving work on the spur of the moment to chase women, and he resented taking orders from anybody except Bill Lair, whom he had known through his family for years.

For all his flaws, Bill Young was the only American capable of operating in the boondocks of Laos by himself without Paru to help him, so Lair sent him west of the Plain of Jars, on foot, with an escort of tribesmen, to open up sites along the escape route to Sayaboury.

And still the Americans kept arriving, unasked-for by Lair. More Agency paramilitary officers appeared, followed by U.S. Army officers. In Vientiane, Lair jousted for turf with a Special Forces lieutenant colonel named Arthur "Bull" Simons, who ran training sites in southern Laos and wanted to take over the Meo operation in the northeast, too. As a compromise, a Special Forces training team went up to Vang Pao's headquarters to work alongside the CIA. The Green Berets, who had bristle haircuts and military postures, wore Viet Cong–style black pajamas, on the dubious theory that it would help them blend in.

Bill Lair liked the Green Berets as individuals. He felt the same about the CIA men under him. It was not their fault that they had the wrong skin color for covert work in Asia. But there it was. With the possible exception of a few long-timers like Bill Young and himself, Americans didn't belong in upcountry Laos. They were visible for miles, and they couldn't speak any languages that the tribesmen understood.

Lair also believed that there was a danger of the Meo developing an unwarranted dependence on *farang*s. Few of the Meo had seen white men and airplanes up close before. They didn't know much about Western people or technology. Having Americans around might give them an artificial level of confidence—might encourage them to take risks that they would reject if they were advised by people from their own part of the world.

The Paru made better advisers for the Meo. They had years of experience training other Asians. They blended in. They didn't need interpreters, and they knew how to live in the jungles. If American credentials were what mattered, the Paru had those, too. During the late 1950s, Lair and the Paru officers had gone through U.S. Army Ranger training in Fort Benning, Georgia, and through advanced courses in company and battalion tactics. They all had their jump wings, too. What more could anybody want?

But Lair's misgivings about the use of Americans were not obvious to others in early 1961. Even with the *farang*s, Operation Momentum was succeeding and expanding fast. As soon as the first thousand Meo were trained, approval was given to train the rest, and the numbers climbed up toward the ten-thousand-man mark. At the Paru headquarters in the Thai seaport town of Hua Hin, the most promising young tribesmen took leadership courses and learned secure radio communications. In upcountry Laos, about a hundred Paru in five-man teams ran trainings for Meo, under the nominal direction of about a dozen Americans. The Paru and the Americans were all over the place, opening sites, arranging for trainings, sending out reconnaissance teams, advising Vang Pao, seeking and choosing lower-level leaders.

The CIA warehouse on Okinawa prepackaged the weapons and ammo for the trainings. The civilian contract airlines, Air America and Bird & Sons, parachuted the materials to the new dirt landing sites, or Lima Sites, as they became known. The airlines shuttled case officers and Paru from one rough mountain strip to the next with their H-34 helicopters and their remarkable Helio Couriers.

Everything was happening very rapidly. Success followed success. Old Meo resistance networks were springing to life, tribal village leaders signing up one after the next. The village patrols, armed with surplus weapons, ambushed enemy forces in their neighborhoods, killing a few here, a few there, before vanishing into the hills. The high ground belonged to the Meo, and the leftists and neutralists hadn't figured out how to react. This worried Lair, who knew it was only a matter of time. The North Vietnamese hadn't started fighting yet.

# Shooting at the Moon

Operation Momentum was only a small, hidden part of America's ever-broadening response to the Laotian crisis. Four hundred more U.S. Army trainers and advisers arrived in the little kingdom, along with new weapons and half a dozen propellor planes for the royalist forces. Five hundred U.S. Marines landed in helicopters across the Mekong River from Vientiane, in Thailand. Two thousand more marines vanished from a movie set in Japan, where they had been appearing as extras in a film entitled *Marines, Let's Go!,* and stood by in reserve.

Not to be outdone by the army and marines, the U.S. Air Force proposed mass bombing raids on the Plain of Jars. Looking at the bigger picture and foreseeing that any major U.S. intervention in Laos would lead to a Soviet or Chinese response, the Joint Chiefs of Staff proposed a 140,000-man expeditionary force equipped with tactical nuclear weapons. With nuclear weapons, said the chiefs, victory could be assured.

The CIA, unwilling to place all its bets on Lair and Operation Momentum, set up another operation called Millpond under the command of another covert operator, Harry C. "Heinie" Aderholt. An air force major on long-term loan to the CIA, Aderholt was already running Momentum's logistics. He was an old friend of Lair's, and he knew Laos fairly well.

With help from Air America and the U.S. Air Force, Aderholt assembled a temporary, unofficial air fleet of World War II–era B-26 bombers with the markings removed. He proposed night bombing raids on targets near the Plain of Jars: the towns of Xieng Khouang and Ban Ban; and Route

7, which connects the plain and the two towns with North Vietnam. His idea was not total annihilation of the Soviet airlift and the Soviet advisers. It was more like a quick, efficient mugging in an alleyway, a warning to the other side to stay away. In CIA headquarters, high-level officials considered timing Aderholt's raids to coincide with the upcoming invasion of the Bay of Pigs in Cuba, for which a comparable covert air fleet had been assembled.

Aderholt's favorite civilian pilot, Ron Sutphin, flew to the island of Taiwan and led a formation of B-26s back to Takli air base in central Thailand. The pilots were a mixed bunch, some from Air America, the rest from the air force but "sheep-dipped"—wearing civilian clothes and carrying phony civilian papers.

The pilots waited at Takli. And waited. Eventually, a few of them flew at night over the Mekong and across the narrow Laotian panhandle to North Vietnam. They dropped supplies to resistance groups, who marked their locations with fires in the shapes of prearranged letters of the alphabet.

The sole American bombing raid over Laos was, apparently, a night flight of Sutphin's. Staying low to avoid radar, he flew through mountain passes, banking steeply when the black shapes of hillsides blocked the stars ahead. He dropped two 500-pound bombs on Route 7 near Ban Ban. However, several days later reconnaissance photos showed that the craters were filled and the dirt surface repaired like new.

The pilots waited for Washington to order them on their joint bombing raid. Nothing happened. The higher-ups were weighing their options, procrastinating. Months later Millpond's temporary air fleet was disbanded, and without explanation the pilots were sent back to their normal jobs.

◆

In Bangkok, Edgar Buell thought he was going to play a starring role in a major military attack on the Plain of Jars. His intense excitement gradually turned to disappointment and then disgust as he realized that nothing of the sort was going to happen at all.

Agitated and depressed, and knowing nothing of Millpond or Momentum, he went sightseeing with the Meo boys from Lat Houang. They visited Buddhist temples, went on boat rides in Bangkok's canals, went to movies and racetracks and Thai nightclubs. He got more and more restless as the days passed. Finally, toward the end of January 1961, the boys were sent off to the Paru communications school at Hua Hin, Thailand, and Buell was told that there was some kind of new program going on with the Meo.

He returned to Vientiane. Since his last visit there, the Mekong River had dropped far below its banks, shrunken to a narrow dry-season chan-

nel between sandbars. The U.S. embassy put him to work arranging supplies for Meo refugees. The new job put him in daily contact with the civilian pilots, a cheerful, profane bunch who welcomed Buell to their nightly
poker games and visits to raunchy nightclubs. He met them at the airport
when they flew in with blankets, medicine, pots and pans, and rice. He
stockpiled the supplies, loaded them into smaller planes, and often rode
along on the relief flights as a cargo handler.

By plane and helicopter, he landed in squatter camps in the hills around
the Plain of Jars. Crude huts made from branches and leaves and white
domed tents made from cargo parachutes dotted the slopes. Turbaned
women with breasts hanging out their blouses nursed hungry, dirty infants.
Old crones with neck goiters and stoic, bronze-skinned men carrying
homemade muskets straggled in from the forests, hungry and tired. At
home in Indiana, Buell had always helped society's underdogs, the pregnant teens and the children of the poor. In Laos, his heart went out to the
tribal people, whom he felt were getting a raw deal, run over by the communists and not given much support by the U.S. government.

When he got back to Vientiane, he vented his anger against bureaucrats
who fouled up his logistics pipeline or who insisted on following unnecessary rules—"educated fools," Buell called them. Sometimes he walked into
meetings at the embassy straight from the refugee camps, dirty and smelly
and needing a shave. He was often the lowest-ranking person there, but he
had moral authority to make up for it, and more to the point, he also had
the quiet backing of Bill Lair. Always on the lookout for help in the field,
Lair had spotted Buell and asked the embassy to treat him with special con-
sideration.

As a result of CIA support, Buell's career took off. IVS more than doubled his salary, to $150 a month. The U.S. ambassador to Laos gave Buell
an award for his work in Lat Houang, and his colleagues applauded as Buell
walked forward shakily to receive the certificate. The ambassador called
him "Pop" Buell, the nickname by which he was beginning to be known.

"Do you see now why I came back to Laos?" Buell wrote home. "Really
I belive I am wanted.

"Tonight I am going to try and find a poker game. Not many Americans
here."

◆

One of the few Americans in Vientiane was Lair himself, who was del-
uged by administrative chores for the Meo operation. On an evening in
March 1961, he was working late in his office when he heard heavy gunfire breaking out in all directions. It sounded as though another coup attempt was under way. He decided to stay inside to see if he could find out

what was going on from CIA channels, and wondered glumly which case officer had been neglecting his duties this time.

The firing went on from all directions, the thump of mortars and the rat-tat-tat of machine guns. He listened carefully for answering volleys and for concentrated firing near the city's strategic points, but he couldn't pick up a pattern that made sense.

Then the electricity went off. Lair looked out the window. In the semi-darkness, the merchants of the town were hurriedly closing the accordion-like grills in front of their shops. He saw an ordinary Lao woman wearing a *pasin*, the long national dress with a belt of silver links around her waist, firing a pistol in the sky.

"What's happening?" Lair shouted at her. "Who are you shooting at?"

"The frog's eating the moon! The frog's eating the moon!" the woman answered, closing her eyes and squeezing off another round.

Lair went down to the street. Up in the cloudless sky, a disk-shaped shadow was moving across the coppery face of the moon—an eclipse in progress, he deduced. But among the locals on the street the consensus was that a cosmic frog had gotten hungry. Soldiers at their posts, policemen in the streets, ordinary citizens—everybody had joined to scare the celestial frog away, firing whatever weapons they had.

From the Laotian point of view it was a close call. The moon nearly disappeared from sight. But by shooting at the moon, the Lao got the frog to disgorge its food, a little at a time. Gradually, the disk grew larger and the light returned. An hour later the shadow-frog had vanished from the sky.

The spattering of gunfire continued desultorily until the celebrants cooled down or ran out of ammunition. The thin stray dogs of Vientiane barked and yelped. Bodies of innocent civilians shot by trigger-happy soldiers were carried away on stretchers. Oil lamps and candles appeared, and the moonlight, restored to its wan silvery power, cast its rippling reflections on the Mekong River.

Afterwards the joke among Americans was that shooting at the moon had worked, and that the science of the outside world had proved to be an illusion.

◆

A few weeks after the eclipse, on March 23, 1961, President John F. Kennedy held a news conference in Washington, D.C. The setting was the brand-new auditorium at the State Department's headquarters, in the low-lying region near the Potomac known as Foggy Bottom. On the stage, a white cloth covered a large vertical stand mounted on rubber wheels. The print journalists were all assembled and the TV cameras aimed; and moments before Kennedy walked in, the white cloth was dramatically jerked away to reveal three gigantic maps of Laos.

The maps purported to show the territory held by the various warring groups in Laos on three separate dates. Communist territory was shown in red, neutralist in white, royalist in blue. On the first map, from before the August 1960 neutralist coup, the red area was a few pockets of territory along the North Vietnamese border. On the second map, after the rightist recapture of Vientiane in December 1960, the red had become an irregularly sized strip. On the third map, dated just before the news conference, the red area had become a very large menacing blob that included the entire region in and around the Plain of Jars like a metastasizing cancer.

Though the reporters had no way of knowing it, the third map was bogus. A true map would have shown rough concentric circles, with the Plain of Jars red, then a blue-colored doughnut shape around it, and then more red outside the blue. The blue doughnut was high ground controlled by Vang Pao. But the rapid mobilization of the Laotian hillbillies was a success the White House didn't want to advertise.

The president stepped to the podium and said he wanted to make a brief statement about Laos. He called it "Lay-oss." Most of his advisers had been pronouncing the name "Louse," with one syllable, instead of the more usual "Lah-ose," with two. Kennedy didn't think the American people would take a country called "Louse" seriously. So "Lay-oss" it was throughout his speech, though most Americans didn't notice, having barely heard of the place anyway.

"It is, I think, important for all Americans to understand this difficult and potentially dangerous problem," Kennedy announced to his audience. "In my last conversation with General Eisenhower, the day before the inauguration on January 19, we spent more time on this hard matter than on any other thing. And since then it has been steadily before the Administration as the most immediate of the problems that we found upon taking office."

Kennedy didn't mention the pressure he had gotten from the Pentagon to send in regular American troops, nor his growing dismay at Phoumi's royalist forces, who ran away from the Pathet Lao and the neutralists at every opportunity, and continued to invent stories of Chinese and even Russian combat troops facing them upcountry. He didn't mention the sense of unreality about Laos that had begun to make itself felt in the Oval Office—that it might as well have been Louse, a tiny, mythical country that was hard to get out of your hair once you had gotten infected.

Presidents only say what they have to say in public; and this was a vintage Kennedy public performance. He came across as tough and balanced, preparing the American public for war if necessary, but at the same time sending signals to Moscow that peace talks would be welcomed. "First, we strongly and unreservedly support the goal of a neutral and independent Laos. . . . Secondly, if there is to be a peaceful solution there must be a cessation of the present armed attacks by externally supported Communists. . . . No one should doubt our resolution on that point. . . . Thirdly, we are earnestly in favor of constructive negotiation among the nations concerned and among the leaders of Laos. . . .

"My fellow Americans," Kennedy concluded, "Laos is far away from America, but the world is small. Its two million people live in a country three times the size of Austria. The security of all Southeast Asia will be endangered if Laos loses its neutral independence. Its own safety runs with the safety of us all—in neutrality observed by us all. I want to make it clear to the American people and to all the world that all we want in Laos is peace, not war; a truly neutral government, not a cold war pawn; a settlement concluded at the conference table and not on the battlefield."

Kennedy was genuinely alarmed at the Soviet airlift into the Plain of Jars, which was running to about fifty tons of equipment and supplies a day, the largest Soviet aerial supply operation since the Second World War. But he couldn't afford to do much about it. Laos had no seaports or railroads, or paved roads upcountry. The Pentagon didn't have much airlift capability, and had told him that if he committed just ten thousand troops—a fraction of what the generals claimed was necessary—it would leave him without a strategic reserve to use in other global hot spots.

And there were many hot spots at that time. There was the Belgian Congo, which had much of the world's copper supply. The Belgian colonialists were moving out of the Congo and the United Nations and everyone else were moving in. There was Cuba, which the CIA was about to invade, using a 1,200-man force of anti-Castro exiles. Above all, there was Berlin, which the Soviets were threatening to seal off; if they did, much of America's airlift capacity would be needed there. With so much at stake in the rest of the world, it was hard to see how a distant little country like Laos deserved a major commitment.

Kennedy didn't want to "lose" Laos, but he decided he could settle for a draw. That meant siding with some of the "neutralist" Laotians the U.S. government had been struggling against, like Kong Le and his favorite politician, the on-again, off-again prime minister, Prince Souvanna Phouma. Souvanna Phouma had flirted with the enemy, visiting Moscow and Beijing, but Kennedy was willing to overlook that. To get the other Laotian factions and the interested nations to agree to "neutralization," the president exercised those familiar instruments of policy, the carrot and the stick.

His big stick was the further buildup of U.S. military force, in Thailand, in the Gulf of Siam and the South China Sea, and elsewhere in the region. Kennedy was artfully vague about it in his news conference, leaving his assistants to brief the reporters off the record. The next days' newspapers reported movements of the 7th Fleet, the readiness of combat troops in Okinawa, marines, paratroopers, helicopters, heavy artillery, and so on. It was secret-with-a-wink and hush-hush-but-here-are-the-details, which only added to the excitement and helped send signals to the Soviets of American determination.

The carrot was a series of exploratory moves to see whether the Americans and the Soviets couldn't make some kind of deal. The British wanted to prevent a ground war in Asia; and the French showed a proprietary interest as the former colonial power in the region. Even India got in the picture. As members of the international nonaligned movement, the Indians sympathized with the Laotian neutralists, though they were on good terms with the Soviets, too. An idea came into focus of reviving a multinational peace conference in Geneva, Switzerland, a forum that had been used to extricate the French from Indochina in 1954.

Kennedy's carrot-dangler was Averell Harriman, heir to a wealthy railroad family, a former governor of New York, and a perennial figure in Democratic party politics. Harriman flew off to Asia and arranged a meeting with Prince Souvanna Phouma, who agreed to everything Harriman proposed. The neutralist prince, Harriman decided on the spot, would do just fine. Souvanna Phouma spoke perfect French, smoked a pipe, and was calm and rational. Forget about his playing footsie with the communists, Harriman told Washington. It didn't matter. The prince was the best man to deal with.

That accomplished, the tall, craggy Harriman flew to the old royal capital of Laos, Luang Prabang, for the cremation of the previous Lao king. The late king—a distant cousin of Prince Souvanna Phouma's—had died a year and a half before, but the court soothsayers and astrologers waited until the stars and planets were properly aligned and until they could find a sandalwood tree trunk large enough to hollow out and make into a funeral urn. In the meantime they kept the body pickled in a vat.

The cremation was another one of those infrequent events that brought the normally unfathomable spiritual life of Laos right to the surface, like shooting at the frog on the moon. The finished urn was ten feet high, gracefully proportioned, and entirely covered in real gold. It stood on a sort of gold palanquin with curtains and tassels, which was mounted on a carriage ornamented with heads and elongated bodies of mythical serpents. The carriage rode on rubber whitewall tires, and was pulled by a double line of men in scarlet trousers and white coats holding ropes. It was the kind of overdone and faintly incongruous pageantry found in Asian kingdoms safely out of the way of Western progress.

Harriman and the other foreign dignitaries stood around looking appropriately somber, though the locals laughed and smiled as the urn with the king's body inside was placed on the crematorium and the flames took hold. Being devout Buddhists, the lowland Lao saw happiness in death. The soul of the old king was released to be born again, if that was his karma, and that seemed certain, what with the astrologers waiting so long to get the timing right. And meanwhile, if the rightist forces had just been roundly defeated once again, and the leftists and their Soviet and North Vietnamese comrades were only thirty miles away, and blocking the road between Luang Prabang and the administrative capital of Vientiane, maybe that was karma, too. Acceptance, passivity, and a kind of charming incompetence were ingrained traits of the lowland Lao. They practiced government by default.

The Land of the Million Elephants and the White Parasol was falling apart, and so was the American will to do much about it. Halfway around the world, the Bay of Pigs invasion, sponsored by the CIA and backed by the Pentagon, had upstaged Laos as the foreign policy crisis of the moment. Harriman hurried back to Washington.

Laos was far away from America, as Kennedy had said, but Laos, Cuba, and America were all connected in his thinking. After the Bay of Pigs the president decided he couldn't trust the judgment of either the CIA or the Pentagon. If he had still entertained any lingering ideas of a ground war in Laos, he dropped them now. There would be no massive American invasion. The way out was through diplomacy. He told Harriman to figure out a way to salvage the Laotian mess.

# Vang Pao's Mistake

After his victorious skirmish at Pha Khao, Vang Pao set up headquarters a few mountains away at Padong, an old opium-trading base. Padong had a long grassy airstrip and a few wooden buildings dating back to French colonial days. It sat on a plateau surrounded by wild tea bushes, with a high peak above it to the south. Across the valley to the north rose a lower ridgeline populated by Meo villages. Beyond the ridge lay the Plain of Jars, still occupied by the enemy alliance—the neutralists, the Pathet Lao leftists, Soviet advisers, and various North Vietnamese.

At Padong, Vang Pao played host to his own alliance, an assortment of tribal leaders, Thais, American pilots, spooks, and soldiers. It was a lively scene. He walked around with a theatrical strut, followed three paces behind by his newest wife, a seventeen-year-old beauty from the Moua clan. Nicknamed "the Field Wife" by the Americans, she cooked daily meals for the guests, who sat at long tables in a tent and ate with varying enthusiasm her sticky rice and dishes of what seemed like gristle and uncleaned pigs' intestines. During meals Vang Pao's men dragged captured enemy soldiers and spies into the tent for his rulings. With a summary wave of his hand, he let them go, or had them thrown into jails made from holes in the ground or taken away to a rat-tat-tat of bullets.

Padong drew tribesmen like a magnet. *Naiban*s hiked in with their wives and the men of their village in tow, ready to join the cause. Ready to discard their baggy black pants for the olive green fatigues that had suddenly become a status item in the mountains. Old men, skinny and palsied, came up to Vang Pao, begging to be allowed to join, and craving the M-1 carbines that shot farther and straighter than their homemade flintlock muskets. "Just once in my life I want to kill a Vietnamese. Then I can die happy," they declared.

The Meo were a people with a deep ancestral yearning. Their elders spoke of a long-ago golden age when they had lived in cities and had known how to read and write. Padong was their center for resisting the Vietnamese, an enemy of several generations' standing; but it was connected to those far older myths as well. It was the place where they were going to begin their tribal renaissance, with the help of the all-powerful Americans.

It was a place of great symbolic value, and that, apparently, was why Vang Pao decided to defend Padong when the enemy forces massed in the southern Plain of Jars. Normally, guerilla commanders won't give up their mobility to face heavily armed conventional forces head-on because that means fighting on the enemy's terms. Bill Lair gently discouraged Vang Pao from defending Padong, but didn't order him not to. Lair believed in letting Vang Pao make his own decisions, even if he made mistakes.

In any event, Vang Pao was deaf to advice. He had a naive and touching faith that American help made him infallible. In a few short months he'd brought the tribal leaders into his alliance, and now they were flying in planes and seeing the ground from the air and doing things they'd never dreamed of before. He thought they were ready to grow out of their guerilla ways.

His disillusionment began with the news of the Bay of Pigs, which he heard on his shortwave radio on about April 18, 1961. How, Vang Pao demanded angrily of the Americans around him, could the great country that had won two world wars fail with the invasion of a little island off its coast? He couldn't believe it; he was shaken; he had used America's prestige and its reputation to help recruit his fellow tribesmen.

The CIA case officers stationed at Padong, Bill Young and an older explosives specialist, were just as dumbfounded as Vang Pao by the Bay of Pigs fiasco. Another American, his Special Forces adviser, diplomatically replied that he didn't have the information but would try to find out. He never found the answer, but a few days later a plane arrived with U.S. Army uniforms, which the Green Berets donned in place of their black pajamas. No more disguises for them.

Vang Pao was not mollified by having a few uniformed American soldiers on his side. By then, the Pathet Lao and the North Vietnamese had begun an offensive against his new bases all across northeast Laos. A race had begun, with the Meo trying to protect their gains, and the other side trying to take as much territory as possible before cease-fire negotiations began.

To everybody but Vang Pao and his followers, the matchup looked un-equal. The North Vietnamese were well-trained conventional troops who were willing to take casualties, if necessary. They excelled at technical skills, like the aiming and coordination of artillery, which the tribal forces knew nothing about. The Meo were good at small, sting-and-fade guerilla at-tacks, but the concept of discipline was alien to them. They tended to run away if the other side made more noise with their weapons. Nothing could stop them from wandering off to hunt or to visit their wives. Highly su-perstitious, they often asked shamans to cast split buffalo horns on the ground for clues to the spirits' intentions. Their morale depended on their perception of luck, and the Bay of Pigs was unlucky.

From the southern Plain of Jars, an enemy force began to move toward Padong. The force consisted of North Vietnamese artillery units, plus ground units that varied in composition from pure North Vietnamese to pure Pathet Lao and in between. (Bill Young swore he heard Chinese as well as Vietnamese voices on the radio, which added to everybody's jitters.) The enemy began by attacking the low ridge that separated Padong from the plain.

Initially the Meo on the ridge stood their ground. They believed that with the United States behind them they could not lose. When the enemy shelling grew heavier, the Special Forces team leader, Captain Bill Chance, put a 4.2-inch mortar, a heavy but portable tube-like weapon with shells four-and-a-fifth inches in diameter, on a helicopter and went over to help out. The Green Berets set up the mortar and lobbed off some shells, ad-justed their range, and silenced the enemy positions. Then a day or two later the enemy opened up from somewhere else.

Captain Chance, an astute, well-liked West Point graduate, thought they should abandon Padong, filter away, and then regroup somewhere else. He couldn't convince the Meo commander to follow his advice, and the CIA men were following Lair's instructions to let Vang Pao make his own de-cisions. But as the enemy shelling got heavier Vang Pao agreed to let non-combatants leave. The women and children began walking out to the south, to the rear base of Pha Khao, a day-and-a-half to two days' hike away. Only the lovely young Field Wife stayed, in the thatched hut she shared with Vang Pao.

On May 3, 1961, as a result of Averell Harriman's diplomatic efforts with the Laotian neutralists, the Soviets, and other outside nations, an official cease-fire was proclaimed in Laos. But the cease-fire had no effect in Padong. The incoming artillery fire, much of it from U.S.-made 75mm and 105mm howitzers the enemy had captured from the royalists, was inter-mittent. Six rounds one day, 110 the next, no real pattern, everyone scam-pering into the trenches for cover. The Americans counted the incoming shells and radioed the numbers to Vientiane for relay to Harriman, who had gone to Geneva to set up peace negotiations.

The strain began to tell on the CIA men. The explosives expert, who was frustrated at the inability of the tribal forces to learn technical skills, had a nervous breakdown after a planned demonstration of booby traps nearly blew up in his face. Lair had him evacuated and replaced him with Jack Shirley, who had narrowly escaped with his life from a North Vietnamese attack east of the Plain of Jars.

The CIA contingent now consisted of Shirley, who was in charge, and Bill Young, who didn't like Shirley much. Young, too, questioned the wisdom of trying to hold a fixed position with what was supposed to be a guerilla force. Then an accidental sighting of the Field Wife bathing naked in a stream reminded Young (by his own later account) that he was sorely missing female company. He started wandering off to outlying encampments, returning when he felt like it, in hilltribe style. This angered Jack Shirley, who didn't like Young much, either.

On May 13, a pure North Vietnamese force assaulted a cone-shaped base called Muong Ngat, eighty miles to the east. Using heavy machine guns with overlapping fields of fire, the Meo and Paru defenders on the summit mowed down hundreds of attackers. But the North Vietnamese kept on charging up the hill in human waves until they swarmed over the top and killed all the defenders. At this news, morale at Padong plummeted.

On May 15, the day before the opening of Harriman's peace conference in Geneva, the enemy began its full-scale attack on Padong. With heavy losses, the North Vietnamese took the ridge between the camp and the Plain of Jars. They built new roads for their artillery and set up their big guns in the lee of the ridge, where it was hard for the 4.2-inch mortar to hit them. The enemy patrols became larger and bolder, probing for weaknesses.

As the shelling grew heavier, a Special Forces man went AWOL under one bombardment, but he returned eventually. Chafing under Shirley and not liking the situation, Bill Young hiked over the mountain to the south without asking permission. He never came back.

The last piece of safe high ground was the big mountain above Padong itself. At the Americans' urging, Vang Pao garrisoned the peak, but the tribesmen he sent there came down a few days later complaining that they had no water. Soon a Meo patrol discovered a telephone line on the mountain. They cut the line and set up ambushes. Nothing happened. Chance and Shirley believed that the enemy was waiting for the rainy season to begin, when the United States couldn't send in its planes or helicopters. It was already smoke season, that period at the end of the dry season when the tribes set fire to the mountainsides, to clear fields. Between the smoke and low-lying clouds and fog, visibility was poor.

On May 31, an Air America H-34 helicopter came in from the rear base, Pha Khao. It clattered over Padong and flew past. There was no enemy artillery fire just then and everybody on the ground idly watched the pilot turn into the wind to land. When a cloud drifted off the mountain, the pilot flew into the cloud and then, losing his bearings, crashed into the mountainside.

Vang Pao's men recovered the bodies promptly. They wrapped the dead carefully in parachute cloth, made sturdy coffins from packing crates, and put the dead inside. An honor guard stood by the coffins all night, until another chopper arrived to carry the bodies. Vang Pao was really very good about it, very respectful of the Americans. But the accident showed that the spirits were angry, and his tribesmen began slipping away by ones and twos.

The crash also shook Vang Pao and reduced his willingness to take risks. About twenty miles away, the Pathet Lao were holding three American prisoners—an American newsman named Grant Wolfkill and two Green Berets, Sgt. Orville Ballenger and Capt. Walter Moon. At Padong, Captain Chance and his men planned several rescue attempts and scheduled helicopters for the transportation, but each time Vang Pao managed to delay them. First he said the antiaircraft fire would be heavy. Then he said the prisoners had been moved. Later Chance came to believe that what Vang Pao said was not necessarily true, and that the Meo leader just didn't want to be responsible for any more Americans being killed. (Eventually, Wolfkill and Ballenger were released, but the Pathet Lao shot and killed Moon in the house at Lat Houang where Edgar Buell had lived until a few months before.)

While Captain Chance stayed at the base, Jack Shirley flew around in helicopters, attending to the nuts and bolts of resupply and gathering information to send to Lair and Landry in Vientiane. When he landed at a big scraggly civilian encampment at a place called Yad Mo, a short, balding white man with glasses walked up to the helicopter. He claimed that he was a good friend of Vang Pao and that his name was Pop Buell. The Indiana farmer started climbing in the helicopter, but Shirley, who had never even heard of him before, blocked his way. Buell looked as though he was going to lose his temper, then reluctantly backed off.

Shirley returned to Padong alone. No sooner had he landed in the helicopter than Vang Pao got in. Something big had happened in his absence; according to Shirley's later recollections, the whites showed almost entirely around the Meo commander's irises. Shirley asked Vang Pao where he was going. Vang Pao, staring off in space, mentioned some airstrip and said he was going to get some rice.

Shirley told the chopper pilot to take Vang Pao wherever he wanted and not to come back, that Padong was closed for the day. The chopper took off with Vang Pao.

From the radio shack, a Paru brought Shirley a decoded message from Pat Landry. It said that the Vientiane station had received reliable information that the North Vietnamese were about to attack at such-and-such coordinates at 1600 hours. Shirley looked at his watch: 1550. Ten minutes to four. He checked his map. The coordinates matched the ground at his feet.

Shirley, Chance, the rest of the Special Forces team, and the Paru got everybody moving. They took what they could carry and smashed the rest of their equipment. They set fire to their thatched huts and headed for the ridge to the south. There were about a half-dozen Americans, a dozen Thais, and four to five hundred Meo, including the Field Wife. They were carrying their wounded. Nobody panicked. Heavy small-arms fire snapped through the trees overhead, coming from the mountain above them.

The Americans and the Paru helped cover the rear until darkness fell. Then many of the tribespeople fanned out in small groups, as was their practice. It began to rain. About midnight some of the Meo still in the column turned on their flashlights, after being told not to, and the enemy shells came in again.

Shirley, Chance, and the Field Wife were in a muddy field when the mortar shells came in. The shells just kind of plopped into the wet ground and sprayed mud. Children cried and mothers clapped hands over their mouths, and the smoke from the mortars lay close to the ground like a surreal fog, making it hard to see anything.

When daybreak came at last, they heard a distant clatter to the south. A few minutes later H-34 helicopters landed in a clearing nearby. Chance, Shirley, the Field Wife, and the Paru scrambled inside.

They had made it out of Padong without too many casualties, but the tribesmen were badly demoralized. Even with American help, they had been no match for the Vietnamese fighting machine.

The Americans couldn't figure out why they had defended Padong in the first place.

Vang Pao met them at Pha Khao and so did Edgar Buell. Everyone was tired and discouraged except for the Indiana farmer, who was eager to help in any way possible in the changing, evolving Laos war.

◆

In Geneva, where the Laos peace conference was taking place, a new player studied the cables from Vientiane. His name was William Sullivan. The year before, in Washington, he had proposed a Laos partitioning plan to his superiors at the State Department. The plan hadn't been accepted, but it got him noticed, and Averell Harriman had chosen him to be deputy head of the U.S. delegation over men far his senior.

Thirty-eight years old, with prematurely gray hair and clear blue eyes, Sullivan carefully scrutinized the reports of Padong's fall and the enemy mop-up operations that followed. Facts were his weapons, and the other side's cease-fire violations were ammunition at the negotiating table.

Sullivan and Harriman had decided to occupy the moral high ground at Geneva. They needed to avoid being accused of cease-fire violations in return. With that in mind, the State Department and the CIA worked out a negotiating strategy that amounted to a ruse. On June 27, 1961, the CIA discontinued arms drops to the Meo. Rice and nonmilitary supply flights went on as before. While Geneva was under way, the United States wished to pretend that its aid to the Meo was merely humanitarian assistance to refugees.

So Sullivan had reason to keep track of the Meo operation. It was part of the complex, shifting Laos mosaic, though not a terribly important part. The three-way struggle for power among the lowland leftist, rightist, and neutral factions absorbed far more of his attention. For that matter, he was well aware that Laos as a whole was only a minor part of America's regional and global concerns.

Smart and ambitious, Sullivan was drawn to geopolitics, that high-level game where a nation's moves on one continent affected its positions on others, like planetary chess. In Washington, he had watched in fascination as the Kennedy administration's inner circle first weighed military intervention in Laos, and then considered the consequences in the rest of Asia and ultimately the effect on American forces in Europe. Ultimately the president himself had decided that Laotian neutrality made more sense for the United States than intervention. If the North Vietnamese violated a neutrality agreement in Laos later on, and the U.S. had to make a stand, it made more sense to do so next door in South Vietnam, where there were seaports, roads and railroads, and a military organization that at least by local standards was relatively professional.

With Kennedy's decision, Laos had become subordinate to South Vietnam as a focus of U.S. efforts in the region. There were fourteen nations at the Geneva conference, and a few, like Thailand and North Vietnam, cared very much what happened to Laos, their next-door neighbor; but the Americans and the Soviets were playing a game of geopolitical maneuver in which Laos was only a pawn.

The conference bogged down, and Harriman went back to Washington, leaving Sullivan in charge on a day-to-day basis. Sullivan sat through hostile harangues, negotiated minute changes in draft agreements, cabled back to Foggy Bottom, read piles of incoming cables, consulted with other delegations—and drank. Drinking was part of his job. The Soviet delegation, equally bored, was amenable to bending elbows after hours. It was the best way to get to know one another informally, and to explore new initiatives. The USSR, it turned out, didn't want to fight a war in Laos either.

Sullivan and two other Americans from the delegation invited the top three Soviets to dinner at the bachelor apartment the Americans shared. The meal went well, and later they went together to a bar, where they played the piano, drank, and talked in fractured French that seemed to improve as time wore on. They stayed long past the usual closing hour, as they realized when the Soviets checked their watches and abruptly hurried home.

Back at their own apartment, the Americans were vaguely aware of room and closet doors being ajar and of an unusual number of cars parked outside on the normally deserted street. But it was not until the next morning, when the local CIA representative and a liaison with the Swiss police stopped in to see them, that they learned what had happened. When the Soviet delegation hadn't returned to their own quarters on time, the KGB had sent a team to Sullivan's apartment to search it and then hide in the bushes. Other KGB teams drove to the railroad station and the airport to block the Soviet diplomats' supposed defection and escape from the country.

With the Soviet delegation mistrusted by its own government, informal diplomacy wasn't going to accomplish much.

It became clear that the Geneva negotiations were going to take a very long time. Though the problems of the little kingdom were unsolved, the atmosphere of crisis faded.

Six months after the conference opened, in November 1961, President Kennedy decided to send U.S. advisers and support troops to South Vietnam.

# The Withdrawal

After the Padong defeat, Bill Lair went upcountry to console Vang Pao, who had lost face among his people and was angry that the Americans were negotiating with his enemies. Lair told him that the U.S. State Department was talking to the neutralists, and even to the Pathet Lao, but that his own outfit, the CIA, was still only aiding the right. He encouraged Vang Pao to try to raise the morale of the tribal forces, to go back to guerilla tactics and prepare for the day when the Americans would leave. Lair didn't know *when* the U.S. was going to leave, but it was only a matter of time. He wanted the Meo to be self-sufficient, to have the best chance of surviving on their own.

Vang Pao continued sulking and there was not much to be done about it. He had a mercurial temperament, but he was still the leader of the tribal irregular forces, and he still had Lair's support.

Back in Vientiane, Lair worked behind the scenes with the embassy program to aid Meo civilian refugees. The North Vietnamese, ignoring the cease-fire, had continued to attack the Meo, driving forty to fifty thousand tribespeople into the forests. With the trainings and arms drops on hold, helping these hungry and bedraggled Meo was the best way to keep Vang Pao's fragile coalition from collapsing.

The rainy season monsoon and the lack of roads in the mountains made it hard to deliver relief supplies. The only way was by air. The American pilots broke through the cloud cover in areas they knew to be safe and flew through narrow, winding valleys to reach their targets, constantly calcu-

lating whether they had room to turn and bank to avoid hitting the mountainsides. (About twenty Americans died in plane crashes in this period.)
On the ground in the muddy, squalid refugee settlements, about a dozen
overworked Americans spent weeks on end distributing rice, pots and
pans, soap, cloth, sewing needles, blankets, and tarps to tribespeople in
need.

Of these Americans on the ground, Lair's favorite was Edgar Buell. He
had watched Buell at work and marveled at the grizzled farmer's skills. Entering new settlements, Buell took candy from his pockets and threw it to
the ragged Meo children, who scrambled to pick it up, laughing in delight.
Then he sat down with the *naiban*s to draw up the *ban si*, the village list—
who came from where, the number of families. From it he tallied the
amount of rice and clothing needed. Then he found a stump or box to
stand on and started talking in broken Lao, surrounded by tribespeople.
An Old Gold cigarette dangled from Buell's lips, and if the sun was out he
had his shirt off to fight a persistent fungal infection on his chest.

Buell always told the refugees to stick together and help one another.
That everybody was at the same level. That he had lost his own wife. That
he used to be a farmer himself in America. That the rice from the planes
was temporary help, until they could grow their own rice again. They
should all work together and support Vang Pao and fight the communists
who were trying to take their country away. Laos is your country, Buell told
them. Don't depend on us Americans. We won't stay here forever. You
must rely on yourselves.

Lair never paid Buell a dime. He never bothered running a security
check on him, and never asked him to become a source, or agent. He
arranged for Buell to be assigned responsibilities for refugees in Vang Pao's
stronghold south of the Plain of Jars, and gave him help with plane flights
and supplies when needed. In turn, Buell fed a steady stream of information to the CIA. The relationship between the two men was informal, but
close. In December 1961, when Desmond FitzGerald came to Vientiane,
Buell and the U.S. ambassador were the only non-CIA men invited to a
party in FitzGerald's honor.

During this post-Padong period Lair's greatest frustration was finding
CIA officers as effective in the field as Buell. A lot of them talked a good
game or enjoyed being the towering white man to whom Laotians deferred.
But there weren't many who liked staying in the boondocks for months at
a time.

The Padong defeat was too much for Jack Shirley, who went back to
Thailand and out of the Laos picture. Lair brought Tony Poe down to be
the titular American at the Meo trainings. Poe was a paramilitary man, a
"P.M.er," or "knuckledragger." Wearing a Marine Corps drill instructor's

hat, with a flat brim and the four dents in the crown, Poe got the trainings going again, bellowing at the Meo recruits as though they were in boot camp.

What Lair wanted most was an extension of himself—a subtle, low-key man to work alongside Poe on the political and intelligence-gathering aspects of the Meo program. Such a person would be Vang Pao's personal adviser, and he would have to work well with hilltribes and the Paru, too.

The most obvious candidate was Bill Young, because he spoke the languages and understood the cultures. In the CIA station, the standard joke about Young was that he was American on the outside and a Lahu tribesman inside. Believing that this humorous assessment was largely true, Lair didn't hold Young's going AWOL at Padong against him, any more than he held it against Vang Pao. It was proven practice for people raised in mountain ways to run when attacked, so they could regroup and fight again. But that didn't excuse the overall pattern of Young's behavior. Others complained that Young wasn't showing up for meetings, that he wasn't doing work he'd promised. Young and Pat Landry didn't get along either, and Lair didn't want to undercut his hardworking deputy.

So Lair kept on looking for an adviser for Vang Pao, and he began sending Young farther and farther into the periphery. He told Young to scout some sites that had been suggested as new bases for the Meo. One of them was a bowl-like valley called Long Tieng, southwest of the Plain of Jars.

Young flew to Long Tieng in a Helio Courier with Ron Sutphin, the most talented pilot on Air America's staff. Sutphin loved stunt flying. He had gained local fame for flying in one end of Air America's hangar in Vientiane and out the other at the dead-low speed of thirty-five miles per hour with a foot clearance on the top and sides. Sutphin approached Long Tieng from the next valley over, rode the thermals up a ridge, and flipped the plane over at the top, flying *upside down* into the Long Tieng valley until he had gained airspeed. Then he righted the Helio and came in low toward a cornfield in the valley bottom, landing just beyond the corn stalks on a path. Young nearly lost his breakfast on the control panel.

"Just wanted to see if you were awake," Sutphin told him. (Shortly afterwards Sutphin transferred out of Laos to a higher-paying position with Air America's management.)

Young reported to Lair that Long Tieng would make a good base. It was an attractive, isolated valley with some chunks of limestone karst poking up vertically from the valley floor, including two conical formations that looked like a pair of breasts. There was a little hamlet near the corn patch, a few miserable thatched huts belonging to some people of the midslopes known as Lao Theung, but those were the only inhabitants.

Fine, said Lair, who sent Young farther west, opening more bases, bringing the alliance to more village chiefs. Young's route led from the Plain of

Jars toward the Mekong River and across to the Laotian province of Sayaboury on the far side. He set up airstrips there; and Lair flew Vang Pao to Sayaboury a few times, getting him focused on using it as a fallback.

And finally Lair sent Young north of Sayaboury to far northwestern Laos, in the Golden Triangle opium-trading region, as near as possible to the Burmese area where Young's father and grandfather had worked as missionaries. Young set up a tiny, one-American operation in the far northwest among the locals there, mostly the Shan.

Lair saw a couple of possibilities for Young. He could rebuild his family's old intelligence network up into southern China, which had been rolled up by the Chinese communists some years before. Or he could organize the dominant local tribe, the Yao or Mien, as the Meo had been organized. But as a practical matter he did not expect much of Bill Young, the "jungle boy" who had not lived up to his extraordinary potential.

◆

On the other side of the world, in Princeton, New Jersey, a college senior named James Vinton Lawrence marched around the athletic fields with his classmates in the spring of 1961. An art history major, Lawrence had no firm plans for a career. He had joined ROTC, the Reserve Officers Training Corps, to make the best of his military service obligation. Then one day the dean of his college called him in and suggested that Lawrence might be interested in talking to "a gentleman from the CIA," as the dean put it.

Lawrence's father, also a Princeton man, had served in the CIA's predecessor, the OSS, during World War II. His father had left government service soon after the war, but the Ivy Leaguers dominating the agency had long memories for family names and social connections. The old boy network was recruiting on campus. The younger Lawrence, known as Vint, accepted the offer. Joining the CIA seemed like an exciting and glamorous way for him to serve his country.

After college graduation he reported to CIA headquarters, in dirty gray wooden buildings near the Reflecting Pool on the Mall in Washington, D.C. (Not long after, headquarters would move to a new building in Langley, Virginia.) Lawrence did his intelligence training at Camp Peary, Virginia—"The Farm"—the usual courses in techniques of collecting information and running agents. He and his classmates were to become "F.I.s," or foreign intelligence men, but before they could start they had to take an additional paramilitary course, on the off-chance that they might have to attack an enemy outpost or capture a radio station someday.

They went through jump school together, and then they flew down to Fort Sherman in the Panama Canal Zone. There they took the same courses

that Special Forces took, but whereas the Green Berets vied with one another to run the fastest routes and complete the courses in the quickest
possible times, the young F.I.s devised shortcuts and made life miserable
for their instructors. They were itchy to start their intelligence careers, and
they didn't want to get sidelined into knuckledragger business, which they
perceived as a lower-order occupation.

Learning that he would be going to Laos to work with the Meo, a people who lacked their own alphabet, Lawrence packed in his duffel bag
thirty or forty books by J. D. Salinger, Barbara Tuchman, Oliver Wendell
Holmes, Nietzsche, Toynbee, and others. He left from Idlewild Airport in
New York on February 20, 1962, as John Glenn was orbiting the earth.

He island-hopped across the Pacific to Hawaii, Wake Island, Tokyo, and
Hong Kong. En route to Bangkok, one of his fellow passengers was a U.S.
Army major heading for Laos, too. At the Bangkok airport, a CIA colleague
pulled Lawrence aside and whisked him through customs. Lawrence had
misgivings about that—he thought the special treatment might have compromised their identities. Then he ran into the army major again outside
the terminal and found it awkward that they had to avoid offering him a
lift into town, but that was the problem with being in the outfit and living
the double life. You never told people what you did and you always worried that they'd find out.

Bangkok was a large and flourishing gateway to the region and a city
that all the Laos hands knew. On his first night there, Lawrence was taken
for a tour of the red-light nightclubs, a standard initiation ritual for Americans. He was suitably impressed. Golden-skinned, black-haired women
laughed beguilingly at his first attempts to learn their language and came
over to sit in his lap. He found it difficult to think of them as prostitutes.
They were a traditional part of Thai society, friendly and free of guilt. Like
other Americans before him, Lawrence had entered a part of the world
where there were few women of his own background. His only realistic
choice was between exploring the local scene or doing without the company of women at all.

For the next few days Lawrence toured the flat, formless city, riding in
low-ceilinged buses like a giant in a dollhouse. He visited a temple with a
reclining Buddha statue more than two hundred feet long. He threaded
his way through a market reeking with odors, and took a boat across the
Chao Phraya River to see Wat Arun, the Temple of Dawn, across from the
royal palace.

Then he flew to Vientiane. After Bangkok, it was a letdown—few paved
streets, few telephones, little electricity or hot water, and dust everywhere.
The Mekong River was a mile wide and empty, except for a few human beings the size of specks far out on the sandbars.

According to his cover story, Lawrence was an army artillery officer assigned to the joint liaison support group working out of the U.S. embassy. He was actually paid by the military and received military benefits. He wore civilian clothes, though; and he was supposed to work for Bill Lair, which was news to Lair.

Nobody was expecting Lawrence at Meo Alley, the compound the Agency kept for Operation Momentum. The Americans there were so casual and unmilitary-like that it was hard for Lawrence even to figure out the chain of command. That evening one of them took him to a Vientiane nightclub, the Vieng Ratray, nicknamed the Green Latrine, where the nightlife was like Bangkok on a smaller scale, cheerful and raunchy and inexpensive.

The next day Lawrence went back to Meo Alley. He met Lair briefly and learned that nothing definite had been decided about his working in Laos. This was Lair's indirect way of saying that he hadn't asked for Lawrence, and hadn't decided whether to palm him off on somebody else.

That night Lawrence joined a group that went out to a French restaurant with Lair. With them were other J.O.s, junior officers on their first assignment. Lawrence ordered steak tartare. Lair started talking, partly to brief the newcomers and partly to gauge what they had already learned about Laos, Thailand, and other nearby countries. In his low-key, mild-mannered way, Lair was trying to teach them what had succeeded and what had failed in the past, to help them understand what the outfit was trying to accomplish.

The next day, violently ill from eating raw meat in a country without refrigeration, Lawrence learned that he had a job on a sixty-day trial basis. He would be working for Pat Landry on logistics and training for the Meo Special Operations Teams, which were being trained at the Paru headquarters at Hua Hin, southwest of Bangkok.

From then on, he was immersed in a world of drop zones and signals, of battalion strengths and deployments, of second-guessing Desmond FitzGerald and Averell Harriman, of Vang Pao and the Paru and of opportunities for stay-behind warfare in Laos that were just too good to miss, or so people said. He was faced with questions he didn't feel qualified to answer. Should the training groups be set up by area of origin or should they be mixed? Should Meo who had been given leadership training at Hua Hin go back to the villages they had come from or move to new areas? He plunged in and made his recommendations to Landry, who listened skeptically and didn't comment.

Still trying to get his bearings, Lawrence went out drinking with older American case officers at night and asked them for advice: Trying to change the Meo or the Thais in any fundamental sense was useless, they told him.

Nothing gets done by ordering these people around. Success grows out of building common ground. Personal relationships make things work. Don't take anything for granted. See everything for yourself, make up your own mind. Get off your butt. There's a lot to be done before we have to abandon these poor people.

This advice was directly traceable to Lair, who had put his stamp on the operation. And yet though these older officers respected Lair, they did not socialize with him much. He was a man apart, serene and calm, detached and almost disengaged.

Lair had never asked for *any* of the Americans sent to him but of those who arrived he preferred J.O.s on their first assignments as these younger men were more open to instruction. Lair invited them to his house for drinks in the evenings, and as they sat around he advised them on working in Asian cultures. Never show anger to Asians, said Lair. Never lose control of your emotions or you will lose Asians' respect forever. Never threaten anyone unless you are prepared to fulfill that threat.

When the J.O.s asked questions Lair paused, rotated his cigar in his fingertips, and out came quiet, sincere answers that always hit the mark. His way of talking was so slow that Lawrence often reached the conclusion ahead of him. And yet, Lawrence realized, he was already adopting Lair's conclusions as his own. It took awhile to realize how subtle Lair was, how many steps he thought ahead of everybody else, how wise he was behind the meek facade. This Texan, thought Lawrence, was more Oriental than the Orientals themselves.

At the end of his probationary period Lawrence was accepted by Lair and began making trips upcountry. After hot, dusty, grubby Vientiane, he was glad to be in the fresh, cool mountain air. The sheer limestone rock formations and the traditional costumes of the Meo women appealed to him. He found himself wondering why anybody ever left the mountains, though the silvery wreckage of a C-46 cargo plane near Pha Khao suggested the danger in trying to go almost anywhere.

He came to Pha Khao as Pat Landry's envoy to a farewell party for a Green Beret training team, or "L-Taggers," the Laos Tactical Advisory Group. The team leaving Pha Khao had replaced the team that had defended Padong, and now they were being replaced by somebody else. Lawrence was obliged to avoid mentioning that he worked for the outfit, but the Green Berets figured it out for themselves and looked at him with a respect he didn't think he deserved. He gained more points by speaking to Vang Pao in French, which none of the others could do. Everybody sat at a long table with two glasses apiece, one for Japanese beer and one for scotch. Little Meo girls kept coming around and filling the glasses. Lawrence managed to sit through the toasts and the Meo singing and Vang

Pao's giving of gifts. Afterwards, flying from one airstrip to the next, he fell asleep.

As he made more flights in the following weeks, landing at short, rough strips that twisted left and right and up and down, he began connecting the names of bases with the names and faces of their leaders. It was another universe, with its crude orange airstrips and its little brown tribal soldiers in green fatigues, and lowland Lao who kept turning out to be Thai Paru in disguise. The mountains, which looked more like the Appalachians than the Rockies, were beautiful and silent, except for birdcalls and crickets and the occasional far-off sputtering of gunfire. From hilltop positions with trenches in the orange laterite, he looked over landscapes mantled in green, the fog filling the valleys below and stray wisps clinging to the hillsides and the jagged peaks and ridges getting bluer and paler in the distance. The magic of radio and aircraft were all that linked him to other friendly mountaintop positions and to the towns along the Mekong.

He ran into Vang Pao occasionally, and then on a long day of flying around by chopper they rode together. They landed at a civilian refugee encampment that Vang Pao had ordered to move a week before, but had not budged. Vang Pao yelled and ranted and screamed at the *naiban*, who yelled back just as loudly, not giving an inch.

Vang Pao explained to Lawrence that the village would move the next day.

"If we stayed the night would they still move?" Lawrence asked, in French.

"The day after," Vang Pao replied, with a little smile.

While waiting for ground fog to clear, Vang Pao sat by a little fire with his arms clasped around his knees, humming and looking pleased. He asked Lawrence to fly with him again, to help control and direct the choppers.

◆

With the Geneva conference deadlocked, Bill Sullivan traveled to Laos in March 1962 to meet with the neutralist leader, Prince Souvanna Phouma, who was up on the Plain of Jars in a little town called Khang Khay. Souvanna Phouma's half brother, Prince Souphanouvong, the leader of the Pathet Lao, happened to be there, too. Sullivan had seen them both across the table in the Palais des Nations in Geneva, but he wanted to talk with them on their own turf.

It was a strange meeting except by Laotian standards, which often remind Westerners of *Alice in Wonderland*. The two rival princes were friends, even though they led separate factions, neither one of which was royalist. Neither prince saw anything unusual in that.

Souvanna Phouma, the neutralist, welcomed Sullivan cordially. He was a habitual pipe smoker with a thoughtful expression on his face; and by training a civil engineer, with a university degree from France. To prove his neutrality, he told the American diplomat where tanks given to his forces by the Soviets were hidden under trees. Then he brought his guest to a nearby smoky shack to see his younger half brother, a handsome, vain, resentful man with a pencil moustache.

The two men shared the same father, but Souphanouvong, the Pathet Lao spokesman, had been born to a concubine rather than to a princess of royal blood. The difference in birth was believed to be the first of many insults to his pride. Like Souvanna Phouma, he had also earned an engineering degree from a university in France, but when he had returned to Laos, then still a French protectorate, he was offered a job at a lower salary than French engineers. Justifiably angered, Souphanouvong moved to Vietnam, where jobs were more plentiful. He married a vain, beautiful Vietnamese woman who disliked colonialism even more than he did.

In September 1945, during a brief period when Americans were supporting anticolonialist Asians, a U.S. general flew Souphanouvong up to Hanoi to introduce him to another promising Asian nationalist named Ho Chi Minh. The two men quickly formed their own alliance behind the Americans' backs. Ho sent Souphanouvong off to Laos on foot with an escort of armed Viet Minh soldiers to organize a resistance against the French. When they got to the Laotian border, Souphanouvong ordered the Vietnamese to take off their Liberation Army insignias and replace them with the Lao royal insignia, the white three-headed elephant. When they arrived in Savannakhet along the Mekong River, no one knew what to make of them, a Vietnamese force in Lao insignia—wolves in sheep's clothing.

In 1947, Bill Sullivan first met Souvanna Phouma and Souphanouvong. Sullivan was in Thailand on his first posting as a foreign service officer. The two princes, then active in a genteel anticolonial movement called the Lao Issara, were living in Thailand in exile from the French colonial authorities. (A third Lao prince lived across the street from Sullivan in Bangkok. His bodyguard was Phoumi Nosavan, later the military leader of the right wing.) Souvanna Phouma had taken a job with the Bangkok electric light company, which made him a popular dinner guest among wealthy hosts who wanted to avoid electrical blackouts in the middle of their parties. Souphanouvong, the younger and more radical brother, was in Bangkok recuperating from injuries sustained when a French plane strafed him as he tried to cross the Mekong River by boat. Sympathetic Americans in the Bangkok legation had donated blood for his emergency treatment and for his subsequent surgery. Sullivan wasn't sure, but he had a hazy recollection that he might have given Souphanouvong a pint of blood himself.

Fifteen years later, in the smoky shack on the Plain of Jars, Sullivan and the "Red Prince" traded pleasantries. But when the American tried to pin down the Pathet Lao leader on the subject of the North Vietnamese, Souphanouvong replied angrily that there were no North Vietnamese troops in Laos. Sullivan countered with specific North Vietnamese unit numbers and locations. The neutralist Souvanna Phouma slipped out the door to avoid the confrontation. A Pathet Lao bodyguard positioned himself a few feet away from the American with a compact automatic rifle, then noisily switched the safety off and pointed the barrel at Sullivan's head.

Sullivan did not budge. They argued about the North Vietnamese for several more minutes before Souphanouvong waved his hand dismissively and the bodyguard lowered the rifle.

Both men knew that neither of them was telling the truth. The Pathet Lao leader pretended that there were no North Vietnamese in Laos, which was pure Wonderland. The American pretended that U.S. aid to the Meo was strictly humanitarian. The fact that they were both dissembling gave them something in common. The angry tone subsided. The two men went outside, where the conciliatory Souvanna Phouma rejoined them.

They had lunch together. Souphanouvong, the Red Prince, personally cooked the venison and served it to Sullivan, while making small talk in perfect French. He couldn't have been more charming.

◆

In Vientiane, the American press corps was starting to become aware of a middle-aged Hoosier playing Rice God to the hilltribes. In the spring of 1962, a journalist from *The Saturday Evening Post* asked to go upcountry with Pop Buell. The embassy gave permission and so did Bill Lair, who knew that Buell could be trusted to keep his mouth shut about the CIA's role in Operation Momentum.

Buell and *The Saturday Evening Post* reporter, Don Schanche, took a Helio upcountry in bad weather with low visibility. Their view from the plane was limited to massive looming shadows in the mist ahead. The pilot snaked through passes not much wider than his wingspan, and across plateaus where tall trees nearly brushed the fuselage. Finally, they landed at "Lang Tien," as Schanche called it, also known as Long Cheng and Long Tieng—the valley Bill Young had scouted a little over six months before.

From a cluster of huts next to a cornfield, it had grown to about a dozen hamlets with about 1,250 Meo and 350 Lao Theung in the valley proper and more scattered in the surrounding hills. A new school with a thatch roof and split-bamboo sides taught 150 children; and there were buildings for military trainings, too.

Dearest to Buell's heart was a little irrigated garden where he had been teaching the Meo to grow vegetables in lowland style. From time to time he came up to Long Tieng and gave the gardens a good squirt of DDT, his favorite pesticide. But the vegetables weren't ready for harvest yet and the people were hungry. That afternoon a big C-46 made an airdrop of rice sacks and tools.

Buell, Schanche, and the local Meo chief hiked to a Lao Theung settlement that night for a party in Buell's honor. They climbed a ladder to a hut up on stilts, lit by lanterns made from cloth dipped in pig fat. They sat on low bamboo stools and drank with long thin straws from an earthen jar in the middle on the floor filled with a kind of sweet rice moonshine topped with a floating mash.

The men jabbered and sucked at their straws, and the level of the jar dropped as the brain alcohol levels rose. After a while the journalist noted that the Laotians' tones of voice and facial expressions had changed. Now the Meo chief was asking something of Buell, who was listening hard with a worried expression. What were they saying? the journalist wanted to know.

"I'll try to give you this exactly the way he said it to me," Buell told Schanche. "Here it is: 'Before the trouble came, the Meo people did not need help. When the trouble came, we heard about the Thing.' "

The Thing was the Meo chief's concept of the great forces of the outside world, something like the United States and the United Nations combined. In the chief's vocabulary, the North Vietnamese communists were "the Others."

" 'Until the Others came we could have beaten the Pathet Lao with our muskets and crossbows,' " Buell continued, still quoting the chief. " 'But we kept on fighting them and we thought we were fighting for the Thing. We were told that the Thing would come to help us. But so far the Thing has not been much help. Now we wonder if the Thing will move us to another country where we can live in peace. Will it?' "

That was a good question. The Thing—a bunch of poker-playing pilots and the Rice King and the CIA and the Thais—was sending in planes and dropping supplies and helping the natives. But the natives were smart enough to know that however many bags of rice they got, and whether or not they learned to irrigate vegetable patches and spray them with DDT, they were on the losing end. They were getting beat up by the Others, and they were on the run, one mountain to the next, with no guarantees.

Pop Buell had gone silent.

"You answer him," he finally told Schanche. "That's what I thought the Thing was for, too."

In June 1962, after another flare-up in the Laos civil war, Schanche's article came out in *The Saturday Evening Post*, a magazine known for its Norman Rockwell sentimental cover art of rural Americana. The piece was entitled "An American Hero: The exclusive story of how an American farmer has devoted his life to a one-man crusade for freedom and democracy in war-torn, Communist-infiltrated Laos."

The American public was yearning for good news from Asia, and the Buell story made people feel good about themselves. Newspapers quickly put out their own versions, portraying Buell as a kind of folk hero and ignoring the failure of the Thing. "Pop Buell Conducts 1-Man Crusade In Laos," proclaimed a midwestern newspaper as soon as *The Saturday Evening Post* story came out. "A retired Indiana farmer, conducting a one-man crusade for freedom against Communist aggression in Laos, has made the difference between life and starvation for 50,000 to 60,000 primitive Meo tribesmen." And variations on that theme kept appearing, one after another.

Buell took shrewd advantage of his newfound fame. On the one hand, he enjoyed telling reporters that most of what they wrote was baloney, which put them on the defensive, because they knew he was right. On the other hand, he used the publicity for leverage with the "educated fools" of the U.S. embassy bureaucracy. He was the famous "Pop" Buell, and they had to think twice before crossing him.

Beyond that, Buell decided that he was willing to be the public face of the Meo program, the guy the journalists could go up and see every once in a while. He was even willing to take credit for the whole operation—to pretend that it was his operation, rather than Bill Lair's. This was fine with Lair, who wanted to deflect attention away from the CIA.

And this had practical repercussions. In July 1962, Averell Harriman and Bill Sullivan finally wrapped up an agreement in Geneva—"a good bad deal," as Harriman described it to President Kennedy. The neutralist Souvanna Phouma would become prime minister and all three factions, neutralist, Pathet Lao, and royalist, would get seats in a coalition cabinet. All foreign military personnel were to leave the unified and officially neutral Laos—the Americans, the Soviets, the North Vietnamese, and anybody with a weapon who wasn't Laotian. Unarmed civilians like Buell would be allowed to stay for development projects and assistance to refugees.

The American program to help refugees—rice drops, schools, rudimentary medical clinics—was run by a branch of the State Department, the U.S. Agency for International Development, or USAID. Edgar Buell transferred from IVS to USAID and became its top field man in Xieng Khouang Province, in the center of the Meo operation. He moved to a base called Sam Thong, about seven air miles from Long Tieng, southwest of the Plain of Jars. He scrounged a folding field desk from the departing Green Berets and set up shop at one end of a warehouse along the runway.

Over the summer months of 1962, until October 6, the day before the deadline agreed to in Geneva, all 666 American military personnel withdrew, including the Special Forces trainers. The Soviet military advisers withdrew from Laos, too. The North Vietnamese withdrew forty soldiers past the checkpoints, leaving an estimated five to seven thousand behind.

The Americans protested the North Vietnamese noncompliance, but not loudly. The U.S. government was putting most of its money, manpower, and energy into the larger fight next door in South Vietnam. If the effort succeeded in South Vietnam, the Americans believed, Laos would take care of itself.

By then, the United States had about ten thousand military advisers and support troops in South Vietnam, including tactical advisers in the field. It had a small detachment of American air force pilots covertly flying missions in propellor-driven fighter-bombers with South Vietnamese markings. In the Central Highlands, along the mountainous border with southern Laos, the CIA had organized the local hilltribes, known as montagnards, in a program loosely modeled on Momentum, though staffed in part by Green Berets. And in the capital, Saigon, CIA operatives and others from the U.S. embassy had access to, and some influence over, South Vietnam's president, Ngo Dinh Diem.

Admittedly, Diem was no George Washington. His inept and corrupt regime had alienated vast sectors of the South Vietnamese people. It faced both southern communist insurgents, whom it called the Viet Cong, and infiltrators from North Vietnam.

South Vietnam was a troubled country, but it was where the action was, as far as Americans were concerned. In the Cold War crusades, it was the new Holy Land, the place where battles would be fought. Remote, obscure Laos was fading from sight.

# Udorn and Long Tieng

When the American military withdrew from Laos in October 1962, the CIA kept some aces up its sleeve. A hundred Thai Paru stayed behind, unknown to the outside world. Speaking Lao and looking like the Lao, these Thai police teams ran the radios, advised Vang Pao's field commanders, and kept Operation Momentum functioning. The Paru reported to their commander, Colonel Pranet, in Thailand, who reported to an overseer from the Thai military. But Bill Lair was a Paru lieutenant colonel, and he was held in such esteem by the Thais that he might as well have been in charge, such was the harmony and cooperation among them.

Lair was also allowed to keep two Americans in upcountry Laos, in Vang Pao's new headquarters, Long Tieng. One was Tony Poe, the hard-charging veteran paramilitary trainer, and the other was Vint Lawrence, the twenty-two-year-old Princeton graduate.

A third American, not under Lair, worked out of Pakse in the southern Laos panhandle, watching over the tribals and a large force of North Vietnamese near the South Vietnamese border. A skeleton staff of Americans also remained at the Vientiane CIA station, but with the general "drawdown" from Laos, the rest of the CIA officers, including Lair and his deputy, Pat Landry, crossed to the Thai side of the Mekong.

At first, Lair and Landry moved to the Thai town of Nong Khai, just downstream from Vientiane, where the Mekong River ferry met the railroad line from Bangkok. Nong Khai was a small, pleasant town with the usual open-air markets and Buddhist *wat*s and some restaurants built on stilts over the sloping banks of the river. But it was too obvious a place from which to run a secret operation, and their house lacked secure "commo," or communications. To send and receive coded radio messages they had to travel to Udorn Thani, a larger and less scenic town some thirty-five miles to the south.

Udorn had a huge concrete runway built by the U.S. Strategic Air Command in the early l 950s in case of nuclear war with China. A few times a week commercial flights landed in Udorn and took off again, but the rest of the time the place was nearly deserted. The CIA already owned a building just off the runway, a nondescript wooden structure known as AB-1, with air conditioners sticking out of the windows, aerials protruding from the roof, and a radio room inside. Apparently it had been built for visiting friendlies, like Taiwanese intelligence teams, who occasionally stayed there to eavesdrop on radio signals from the Chinese mainland. Lair and Landry moved their office there and rented houses in town to live in.

With this second move, Lair was promoted to a new level, "chief of base" at Udorn, reporting to the CIA chief of station in Laos. Lair was responsible for CIA paramilitary operations in Laos (except for those in the far south, which were under the man in Pakse, Roy Moffitt). At the same time Lair continued to serve in the Thai police, turning his Thai payroll check over to the CIA as the rules required. He went often to the office Pranet and the Paru's army minders set up outside the Udorn air base. He made monthly trips to the Paru headquarters at Hua Hin in Thailand. But his original program of training rural Thai villagers in self-defense began to die on the vine. Operation Momentum in Laos was taking all of his time.

He was at work in Udorn at seven in the morning. The radio room brought him the cable traffic from CIA headquarters, the Vientiane station, Long Tieng, and the roughly twenty Paru teams scattered through rural Laos. He and Landry, who sat at facing desks, read the cables and talked them over to see how the mosaic changed. It was *always* changing, with operations being planned or starting or ending and intelligence reports coming in along with requests for supplies. For some of the messages Lair could think of no suitable reply. He put them in a stack on his desk—his "worry file"—and went through them the next morning to see whether changing events put the matter in a new light.

Unless he visited Pranet or flew to Laos for the day, Lair stayed in the office until dinnertime. Then he and Landry went out to eat at Thai restaurants and came back to the office for a few more hours. They liked it there, with just the two of them and a financial officer and the commo guys in the other rooms. They didn't have any other staff or secretaries, and didn't want them, either. Everything went by "cable," meaning encrypted radio messages. They hand-printed their outgoing messages in block letters and brought them to the commo rooms, and by the time the messages were encoded, or incoming messages decoded, out came a machine printout, in English. It was a good, simple system, and it enabled them to stay in close touch with the men in the field.

Though his tribal operations in Laos had been scaled back—most of the effort was restricted to the Meo around the Plain of Jars—Lair felt the Geneva accords were a blessing in disguise. He had a couple of hand-picked Americans in Long Tieng and his Paru teams upcountry, close to what he had wanted in the first place. He didn't have to joust for turf with the U.S. military anymore. Momentum was small and low-profile again, just the way he liked it. He was a little worried for Vang Pao and the local commanders, who were running short of weapons and ammunition, but he figured it was better for them to run a lean, self-reliant guerilla operation than to depend on overabundant American supplies.

So Lair was pleased with the way things were going. Udorn was a benign, safe place. He and Landry used their real names around town. They didn't have fences around their houses or guards at the gate. For Lair, all that was lacking was a personal life. Except for monthly visits to Bangkok to see his wife and two children, he was living by himself and working longer hours than were healthy.

Knowing of Lair's situation, Vang Pao sent two young women of his tribe to help Lair around his house. They kept Lair's house clean and did some cooking. They dressed in the style of the Thais and the lowland Lao, with simple blouses and sarongs, and left their sandals outside the house. One of them, the sister of Vang Pao's chief of staff, was quite good-looking.

She walked in on him barefoot late one evening when he was sitting down mulling over his day. Lair was tired. Fourteen hours at the office again. He noticed that her expression was a little out of the ordinary. She had something on her mind.

She asked him how many wives he had. He said he had just one.

After a long pause she remarked that Vang Pao was a big man.

Lair couldn't quite see the connection, but he replied that, yes, Vang Pao was a very important man.

"He has many wives," she said.

"Yes, he does," agreed Lair.

"If you're going to be a big man, you ought to have more wives," she said.

It dawned on him what she was getting at.

Bill Lair reflected that his wife in Bangkok wouldn't like being part of a harem very much.

"If you don't have more wives, you'll never be a big man," the young woman added.

She looked steadily at him across the room. She was there. She was available.

Did he want to be a big man or not? The question had occurred to Lair many times in his CIA career, but never quite like that before.

◆

With the exodus of U.S. soldiers and advisers from Laos, the CIA's assistance to the Meo, previously an open secret among Westerners in Vientiane, went to the deepest shade of black. Outside the Agency, knowledge of the two Americans in Long Tieng was restricted to a very few people at the highest levels in Washington. To have Poe and Lawrence found out would risk the Geneva accords and America's posture in the region.

As a result, after October 1962, Vint Lawrence and Tony Poe seldom left the Long Tieng valley and never went to Vientiane. They lived in a thatched hut with split-bamboo sides and a dirt floor, just like the Meo. They had no electricity or running water. It was a primitive, isolated existence, and their primary mission, at first, was simply hiding their white skins from the enemy and from the white aircraft of the International Control Commission (ICC), which occasionally flew overhead in an ineffectual attempt to verify compliance with the Geneva agreements.

Yet the two men were not entirely cut off from the outside world. For better or worse, they were connected to their employer's worldwide enterprise of collecting information and applying pressure to communist regimes. On New Year's Day 1963, a cable from headquarters informed them that they were going to get a special airdrop. They laid out prearranged signals on the valley floor and a plane that had flown directly from the depot at Okinawa appeared overhead. Parachutes blossomed and wooden crates swung gently to the ground. They pried the crates open eagerly. Inside, to their disappointment, they found half a ton of Spam, half a ton of beans, and half a ton of rice, leftovers from the Bay of Pigs.

During that period Vang Pao felt a little like the Cuban exiles in the abortive invasion himself—betrayed by the Americans, hurt, caged, and angry. He told Poe and Lawrence that he was thinking of pulling out of the operation. It struck him as absurd that U.S. planes still dropped rice to his people but not weapons or ammunition. The Meo had been forced into defensive positions, and the other side was making all the gains.

The two Americans could only try to soothe relations with Vang Pao, bide their time, and concentrate on collecting intelligence information. Since Poe avoided office work of any kind, the intelligence task was left to Lawrence. Every day the Paru teams sent coded reports on enemy and neutralist activities in their regions, using field radios powered by hand-cranked generators. Lawrence took the information, added whatever he had learned from Vang Pao and his staff, and wrote a condensed daily situation report, or sit rep. He gave it to the Paru in the radio room, and the Thais used one-time pads to encode the report before sending it over the airwaves to Udorn for Lair and Pranet.

Another of Lawrence's tasks was helping Pop Buell, two valleys away in Sam Thong, with the logistics of supplies for refugees. Because the CIA's radio net was better than USAID's, Lawrence and the Paru kept track of refugee numbers, rice requests, drop signals, and so on. Buell, in exchange, was constantly picking up information from refugee groups and passing it on to Lawrence and the Paru.

Lawrence got along well with Buell. He also liked the Paru, particularly their leader at Long Tieng, Captain Makorn, who reported to Pranet in Udorn. Makorn advised Vang Pao, just as the two Americans did; and Makorn's subordinates acted as Vang Pao's staff officers until Meo could be trained to fill those functions. The Paru worked with Lawrence on intelligence reports and with Poe on weaponry. They ran the commo room, and they interpreted between the Americans and the tribesmen until Lawrence learned enough phrases of Lao and Meo to be able to communicate himself.

Determined to understand the Meo, and to improve his relationship with Vang Pao, Lawrence began studying the tribe's culture while learning their language. He sat down with one tribesman after another, tracing family lineage, where they came from, what they were doing. He had long talks with shamans about their beliefs. He asked them why they "rode" so hard, jumping up and down for hours in their trances, chanting and clanging cymbals, with black cloth hoods over their eyes. They explained that the hoods helped them see into the spirit world. He sought out an old and wrinkled woman herbal healer who began bringing him specimen plants. Lawrence dried and pressed the plants, sketched them on paper, and asked her questions about them and their medical uses.

Gradually, Vang Pao saw that Lawrence was genuinely interested in his people, and he began to open up, revealing a personality with many sides. He had a violent, brutal side—he kept prisoners in sleeved fifty-five-gallon barrels in holes in the ground, and he was not averse to summarily executing prisoners or even offenders and miscreants from his own tribe. But he came from a culture that had survived in a harsh environment by being brutal and stoic. He was stubborn, another trait common to his people. He was strong-willed, energetic, and intuitive. He could tell at a glance when Lawrence entered the room whether the young American had good or bad news on the intelligence front. Highly emotional, he wept when his people suffered defeats, or when yet another village had to go on the run.

As a kind of insurance policy, Vang Pao was storing about a ton of opium under his house in Long Tieng. He made no secret of it. Opium possession was legal in Laos. Opium cultivation was traditional to his people. He didn't smoke the stuff himself, and he didn't allow his soldiers to—it made them too lethargic—but he wanted to be able to sell it to outsiders. It was like an emergency bank account, in case the Americans left entirely.

Lawrence understood Vang Pao's position, but he was obliged to state his employer's line, making sure Vang Pao understood that if he got caught doing anything with drugs the CIA would pull out of the operation. It was an ambiguous situation and difficult to resolve. Lawrence wasn't in a position to tell Vang Pao to destroy the opium under his house, only not to get in trouble for selling it. And so the opium stayed.

The tall young American and the tribal commander began to talk about the outside world. On politics, Vang Pao's views were black and white—capitalism was good, communism bad, period. He rejected Lawrence's attempts at introducing shades of gray. The world was divided into good guys and bad guys, said Vang Pao, and if you were smart you went along with what the good guys said.

It was fascinating to Lawrence. As he recalled years later, Vang Pao was "strategically simple-minded and tactically brilliant. He had enough tricks up his sleeve tactically that he would play like a cat with a mouse, in terms of how to do this and that in a given campaign. But his strategic concepts were unreal.

"He thought I was a prince in my own country. He said, 'You're a prince, aren't you?' He thought I was a prince because I didn't fuck the local girls, and because I wasn't a drunk like Tony. Vang Pao had five wives, then. And he would say, 'If you ever want a wife, Monsieur Vin', just let me know.' " Lawrence was following the rule that Lair insisted upon upcountry, and that Pop Buell and his people had begun to follow, too. By staying celibate among the tribals, they avoided entanglements and jealousies that interfered with their work.

"We had a wonderful joking relationship, and one in which there was very rarely rank pulled," Lawrence remembered. "In some ways there was no rank to be pulled. The choice of operations was his. He could pull rank on me, but I could cut off his money. The trade-off was that I never tried to influence except in large issues his choice of military targets, and he never bothered me when I was poking my nose around trying to find out what was going on within the Meo community.

"He served twenty, thirty, forty people every night for dinner, wherever he was. He could be squatting in a hut, or in a cabin up at six thousand feet and freezing cold, or at his house at Long Tieng. He would always have people come, and he'd always listen. He'd always argue, and he'd always help.

"It was like trying to run a bunch of Allegheny Mountain Men. I mean, they had *no* compunction about coming up and giving him bloody hell if they didn't like something. Some old fart would come in and start scream-ing at Vang Pao for this, for that, and the other thing. There was absolutely no barrier of deference given to Vang Pao by the people. They'd laugh with him, they'd joke with him. And this would go on from nightfall for three or four hours almost every night.

"It was like a walking, talking civics session on how people become po-litically aware. How they learn to identify with the guy across the ridgeline whom they've hated, like the Hatfields and the McCoys. Trying to make po-litical connections with people. And Vang Pao's enormously powerful mes-sage was that you had to learn to fight for something larger than yourself."

There was only one American at these nightly tribal meetings, which *al-lowed* the chemistry, put it more on tribal terms, than if there had been two Americans or more. There was only Lawrence, and he sat quietly at Vang Pao's side and listened, without needing an interpreter.

Tony Poe was never there at night. He was not interested in learning lo-cal languages and being culturally sensitive. Poe wasn't a listener. He liked to talk.

◆

At Long Tieng, Poe's self-assigned job was eliminating the slack from the Meo operation. He hated laziness and inefficiency. He loved weapons and soldiering, and always wore a floppy U.S. Marine Corps campaign hat as a symbol of the standards he was trying to uphold.

All day long he paced around while Paru and Meo tried to keep up at his side. Intense and short-tempered, he exuded urgency. He gesticulated with his hands, and his voice jumped an octave when he emphasized his points. Generally, he got his messages across, though he never learned to speak Lao or Meo well. Now, with the Geneva stand-down, he did not have enough to do, and he was restless.

At the end of the afternoon, when the planes stopped flying, and the smells of woodsmoke and cooking drifted from the thatched huts, Poe changed gears. With a bottle of White Horse scotch, supplied to him by the pilots at negligible cost, or with locally made rice whiskey, which was free and tasted like sake flavored with kerosene, Poe held forth to a circle of admirers, most of them English-speaking Paru. Sometimes they were joined by American pilots staying overnight, and sometimes by Pop Buell.

Poe liked being the center of attention. He was a ham actor and a nat-ural storyteller. His own accounts of his life changed on successive tellings, but he was basically a navy brat who joined the marines during World War II and was wounded on Iwo Jima. (He sometimes claimed that he was a Hungarian refugee.) After the war he got his degree from San Jose State and joined the outfit, where he was the leader in his class at The Farm—

loud, opinionated, a raconteur of stories about his sexual exploits. His first assignment was Korea, where he displayed the excess zeal and humorous insubordination that became his trademark. He liked to tell his listeners at Long Tieng that after the Korean War began winding down he was sent back to headquarters for a psychiatric examination.

It was a classic Poe story. The doctor, he said, was a woman who was academically overeducated but physically attractive. She wore glasses and had big breasts. "Listen," Poe said he told her. "You shouldn't even be in this business. People like me are *animals*. That's why we're alive." She demurely took out a piece of paper with an ink blot on it, a Rorschach test. "What does this remind you of?" she said.

"A guy who's just had an orgasm," said Poe.

"Why are you telling me this?" she demanded. He reached over the desk and grabbed her, as she pressed a button on her desk and alarm bells went off in the hall. She wiggled loose and he was chasing her around the desk and grabbing at her blouse as the security guards burst in.

Poe said he had been saved by Desmond FitzGerald, the patron saint of knuckledraggers, who sent him away from headquarters to keep him from getting fired. "FitzGerald saved my ass many times. Lotta guys wanted to nail me. They thought I was some kind of nut. But he got me a lot of these good jobs." For about the next six years, until he went to Laos, Poe served at FitzGerald's bidding. "Five- or six-month deals," he said. "We don't have to talk about 'em. If it's Asia, I've been there. You didn't lack for anything to do."

Poe joined Pat Landry for the failed officers' uprising in Indonesia in 1958, but most of his operations centered on encouraging rebellions against mainland China's communist regime. One of them involved a Moslem ethnic group in southwestern China whose leader had left the mainland when the communists took over. These Moslem Chinese, Poe said, were better trainees than the Meo—it was the plan for using them that he objected to: "I said I wasn't going to sign off on it. The project was *zero*. There was *no* possibility of these Moslem guys succeeding. No reception for 'em. The area is so sparsely populated and the Chinese communists had everybody under their fucking thumbs. What the hell are you going to do? It means that you're going to have to resupply 'em. You can't resupply 'em—that gives the whole project away. Five-man teams are all right, but a hundred men—you're talking about a *tremendous* operation." The marines had taught Poe that a commander should put his men's welfare ahead of his own, and Poe felt proud to cancel this project for the sake of the Moslem men.

Poe's longest assignment, off and on for four years, was with the Khamba tribesmen of Tibet, in training camps in northern India and in the Colorado Rockies. The Chinese communists had invaded Tibet in 1950 and a widespread Tibetan resistance arose, eventually aided by the CIA. "We don't talk about that," said Tony Poe. "No comment. No comment," as he winked and dropped broad hints of standing with the Khamba tribesmen on the clifftops of the rooftop of the world, looking down at the roiling white rivers far below. "No fucking comment, but those Khambas are the best people I ever worked with.

"I never saw people that loved their weapons like those fuckers. They slept with 'em, which is not so good, you know, because it let off a lot of moisture. We told 'em, get your body fluids on 'em and it's going to rust. Re-clean it, re-dry it, re-oil it. But you talk about *shooting*. We put diesel drums down in a valley. We dig a hole down there, next to the barrels, way down, so we're indefilated. We had instructors up on a hill with the Khambas, a thousand fucking meters away, and the guys working telescopic sights. Incendiary bullets, *pch-oo ka-chung*, and the damn barrels burning. With such short time in training, these guys were *great*.

"They weren't what you'd call clean," Poe added, mock-serious. "I have to say that. They'd just turn around, stick their asses out the window, and shit. Shit right out of the window. All of 'em. 'Ey. You look at their god-damn women, you wouldn't even want to screw 'em. You couldn't even get a hard-on, they smelled so bad. You got a wife, you got ten brothers, they all screw your wife. Not for the sex. It was just part of the deal."

Poe told his audience at Long Tieng that he rated the Khambas first, the Moslem Chinese second, and the Meo third.

"Hey, training is different with every native group," said Poe. "Wherever you go, according to their education, the area, and the culture. You can only go so far in training. The Meo can't absorb technical stuff, like the elevation of a weapon, the difference in aiming at targets a hundred and six hundred meters away, for example. You can't get them to understand because with their old muzzle loaders, they're shooting at targets thirty meters away or so. Why can't you just fire straight at the target? they want to know. We draw it on paper, the arc of the bullet, and they say they don't know what the hell we're talking about. Mortars are a waste of time with them. It's very difficult, because they have no basic foundation in education. We aren't dealing with educated people, French, English, Europeans. We're dealing with people that don't know shit."

Poe always said what he thought, and if he offended anybody's sensibilities, so much the better. "I'm an obnoxious bastard," Poe declared, with relish. "That's one of my biggest faults. I've talked to a lot of big people and made 'em lose face." That he was the first to admit his flaws made him easier to take.

He was trying to tell his audience at Long Tieng that he already had misgivings about the Meo operation, but he always cloaked this information in humorous and exaggerated stories about himself. His listeners under-stood, but they weren't going to make a big deal out of it, and they also didn't object to the way he talked about women and indigenous Asian peo-ple. They were men in a man's world, and what mattered most was staying entertained in the isolated valley where there was little to do in the evenings, except to watch the Tony Show. And to drink.

Poe had been a teetotaler until coming to Laos. He started drinking, he explained later, to show solidarity with his troops. "I drank *lao cao*, white lightning," Poe said. "Touch a match to it and it'd burn. I could drink that shit by the quart. By the *quart*. You get a big headache, but you just take a bunch of Bayer aspirin.

"Drink didn't affect my performance. I drank only in the evenings. From five o'clock in the morning, I'm moving. Five o'clock in the morning I was up and ready to go. There was never a morning that I couldn't get up at five. I am, physically, a bad sonofabitch. I cover a lot of territory. I can walk a hundred fucking kilometers. And I had a lot of things to do.

"I've never been drunk on the job. Well, a little whiskey here and there, but never failing on the job. Just telling big people to go fuck themselves. But that should have been done anyway. At night I get loaded, and then at five o'clock in the morning I'm as sober as Judge Roy Bean."

# Hard Rice

In Washington, the man with his hand on the aid spigot for Laos was Averell Harriman, the assistant secretary of state for Far Eastern affairs.

Harriman was an autocrat with formidable style. Kennedy nicknamed him "the Crocodile" for his negotiating wiles and the disapproving, half-lidded expression Harriman assumed when he wanted to intimidate his opponents. The Geneva accords had been Harriman's achievement, and he had a proprietary interest in seeing them preserved. That meant preserving the fragile truce among the rightist army along the Mekong, Kong Le's little neutralist army on the Plain of Jars, and the Pathet Lao forces upcountry. Whether the Meo ever got another bullet or another surplus M-1 carbine was completely up to him.

When the CIA came calling on him at the State Department, armed with reports from Lawrence and Lair about North Vietnamese attacks on Meo villages, the elderly Harriman ostentatiously turned his hearing aid off. He didn't want the Meo wiped out, but it was far more important to him to avoid a clash between the U.S. and the USSR over anything having to do with Laos, for the sake of the larger geopolitical game.

The CIA petitioner to Harriman was Desmond FitzGerald's deputy, William Colby. A small owlish man with round glasses, Colby had previously served as Saigon station chief, and he was adamantly opposed to North Vietnamese expansion wherever it occurred. He made impassioned arguments for supporting the Meo. When Harriman cupped a hand over his ear, Colby repeated his arguments in a louder and louder tone. Without more ammunition, Colby pointed out, Vang Pao couldn't even slow the North Vietnamese down. What good would the Geneva accords be if the North Vietnamese took over Laos?

When Harriman still pretended he couldn't hear, Colby started shouting, losing his temper.

Harriman looked at Colby with his cold, implacable, half-lidded expression. Finally he approved one resupply flight here, another there. Just enough to keep the operation alive, and to show the Agency who was boss.

◆

Harriman's former deputy, Bill Sullivan, was also in Washington, helping plan the State Department's position on Vietnam. Since the United States had abstained from major fighting in Laos to be able to fight on better terms in South Vietnam, it made sense to study how a war in South Vietnam might play out.

The Pentagon commissioned the Rand Corporation, a think tank based in Santa Monica, California, to come up with a war game. This simulation of a ten-year Vietnam conflict, code-named Omega, was played out in Washington over a week's time, with government leaders taking the roles of both friendly and enemy commanders. There were two opposing teams. The Blue Team represented the Americans, the South Vietnamese, and their allies. The Red Team represented the North Vietnamese and their Soviet and Red Chinese backers.

Bill Sullivan was appointed leader of the Red Team's "action" group, which played the war game eight hours a day. His senior group leader, who set policy and played on occasional breaks from his regular job, was Gen. Maxwell Taylor, the White House military adviser. Taylor told Sullivan to "accept heavy casualties, exploit propaganda opportunities, and be brazen about disregard for the truth." Taylor cast himself as Ho Chi Minh and Sullivan as General Giap, the tough military commander of North Vietnam's troops.

By the week's end, a decade of simulated war reached its conclusion in a make-believe 1972. The red forces were everywhere on the map of Indochina. They had overrun most of Laos, South Vietnam, and Cambodia. They had taken heavy casualties, but their command structure was intact. Most strikingly, Sullivan recalled later, "We had bogged down 500,000 American troops in the quagmire of Indochina and had involved a large portion of the U.S. Navy and Air Force. We had caused great expenditure of the United States budget on this feckless enterprise and had provoked great agitation and unrest in the American population, especially on university campuses. Moreover, we had all but isolated the United States in the United Nations and in world opinion. We had driven the U.S. Congress to the brink of revolt over the seemingly endless war."

Some of the Omega players, including John McCone, a conservative Californian who was then CIA director, reluctantly accepted the game's results. McCone had been policy leader of the Blue Team. His crushing defeat at the hands of the Red Team turned him into something of a closet dove on Vietnam.

Others, however, especially the air force chief of staff, Gen. Curtis LeMay, were convinced that the assumptions upon which Omega was based were flawed. In the spring of 1963 a review of the game results was held in the giant underground bunker of the National Military Command Center, the room that inspired memorable scenes in the satirical film *Dr. Strangelove*. Secretary of State Dean Rusk, Secretary of Defense Robert McNamara, the Joint Chiefs of Staff, various presidential advisers, and junior staffers like Sullivan were there. General LeMay declared that the Rand Corporation had underestimated the air force's ability to bomb the North Vietnamese into submission. The air force demanded a replay with amended rules.

Another war game, Omega II, was held with the air force included. This time Sullivan was a member of the red policy team, playing the role of a Chinese representative. The results were about the same: The U.S. lost decisively.

In the years ahead, people who knew about the war games wondered how very bright men like Rusk, McNamara, Taylor, and Sullivan could ignore the evidence of the Omega games. The answer was hard to piece together, but Sullivan himself believed that larger geopolitical considerations were the key.

The reasons Kennedy and Rusk decided that the U.S. government should make a stand in South Vietnam, said Sullivan, did not solely pertain to South Vietnam itself. "There was an appearance to us of a sort of coordinated effort going on," he recalled, between the Soviet Union and mainland China, the two great communist powers. The Chinese were supporting a communist movement in the island nation of Indonesia. The Soviets were providing logistics support to the North Vietnamese. "And had there been a success with both these endeavors," continued Sullivan, "you would have had a pincer movement that would have cut off all the Japanese sea-lanes to the Middle East and everywhere else. Japan would inevitably have had to accommodate itself to the communists. So the strategic importance of sea-lanes to Japan, and the prospects of a success by the Chinese in Indonesia, and as we looked at it the Soviets in Indochina, together were the compelling things that drove Rusk and Kennedy to think of taking a stand in Vietnam.

"Now, an awful lot of people later got into the act on Vietnam," added Sullivan wistfully, "who had no comprehension of what the original strategy was all about."

◆

In the minds of Washington officials, Laos had become an annex to Vietnam. "The wart on the hog of Vietnam," Secretary of State Dean Rusk called it.

At the White House, the State Department, and the Pentagon, nobody spent much time thinking about Laos anymore. The Geneva accords were supposed to have fixed the Laotian problem, and unless there was a compelling reason to renounce them, the accords would stay in place. The new focus was on Vietnam, and the old notions about a big fight with the communists in the remote kingdom had become obsolete.

Gradually, however, it became apparent that there were advantages to *pretending* to abide by the Geneva accords while supporting a small war in Laos on the quiet. After all, this was what the North Vietnamese were doing, and on a much larger scale—publicly supporting the neutrality of Laos while secretly undermining it with thousands of their troops up-country.

A succession of events helped bring CIA paramilitary officers back across the Mekong and encouraged the return of regular supply flights of "hard rice," a euphemism for weapons and ammunition.

The first event was a rebellion on the Plain of Jars in March 1963. Kong Le, the tiny former paratroop captain, was over his head as the commander of the neutralist army. He did not know what to do with all the emissaries from communist and capitalist countries who came flying in to see him and offering help with strings attached. So he did nothing, in classic Lao fashion, hoping that the conflict would resolve itself. Tired of his procrastination, the Pathet Lao and North Vietnamese recruited his number-two man, who mounted a coup attempt against him. Fighting broke out between Kong Le's "old" neutralists and the "new" neutralists further to the left.

Vang Pao's spies and roadwatch teams reported that Pathet Lao troops were moving out of the town of Xieng Khouang, near the southeast corner of the Plain of Jars, to put pressure on Kong Le, who was in the northwest corner, blocking the roads that led toward Vientiane and Luang Prabang. Vang Pao decided on a diversionary attack to harass the Pathet Lao and make them pull back.

He reviewed his plans with Vint Lawrence, who made sure the impetuous Meo commander had thought through all the steps. Vang Pao had some artillery pieces, and the CIA sent up some new weapons—rockets. The rockets were navy surplus—small, portable, and cheap—and Tony Poe and the Paru experimented with steel racks to fire them from.

The idea was to find someplace above the Plain of Jars where the Meo could set up their weapons and fire into the Pathet Lao military barracks, causing havoc and confusion. Another Meo base north of the Plain of Jars would send tribesmen down on additional harassing raids.

The artillery pieces were disassembled, put on H-34 helicopters, and reassembled on the site. Vang Pao helped set up, load, and fire the weapons. Small rockets whooshed through the air, and howitzers boomed.

"Vang Pao was beside himself with excitement," Vint Lawrence wryly recalled. "He just assumed he was a superb artilleryman and that without any training whatsoever he would be able to fire one of these things. And one was always sort of hiding one's head, because he really didn't know what the fuck he was doing." The barrage stopped only when the tribesmen ran out of ammunition.

Though the Meo missed most of their targets, they succeeded in getting the enemy troops to pull back. To Lawrence's mind, this was an expensive but worthwhile undertaking. The goal was not to capture territory but to make life so uncomfortable for the enemy that they would hesitate to go on the offensive.

The Meo had struck a very small blow, but it was a blow nonetheless, and the politico-military spectrum was changing. The neutralist center had split. The Pathet Lao and their "new" neutralists had attacked Kong Le's "old" neutralists, pushing Kong Le into a tactical alliance with Vang Pao and the right. The U.S wasn't about to give up on Kong Le yet, but the Meo operation was perceived with new respect by the officials halfway around the world in Washington.

◆

A second event hastening the end of the stand-down was a changing of the guard at the State Department. Averell Harriman was promoted to undersecretary of state, which brought him responsibilities wider than Asia. He didn't have much time for Laos anymore. His replacement as assistant secretary for Far Eastern affairs was Roger Hilsman, who didn't hold the position long, and who was one of those cameo players who were always coming on stage for a short while and affecting Laos's destiny before moving off somewhere else.

As a young man in World War II, Hilsman had been a commando in Burma, where U.S. and British forces used hilltribes against the Japanese. He fancied himself an expert on guerilla war in the region. And now, when the CIA came calling on the State Department with requests, Bill Colby did not have to shout and plead with a formidable opponent like the Crocodile. He only had to sit back and listen to Hilsman's boring and repetitive war stories about Burma, though he really didn't mind. Hilsman supported what the CIA wanted to do in Laos, which was resupplying the tribal groups and going on the offensive against the North Vietnamese.

Hilsman's hawkish views on counterinsurgency were in tune with a new, more aggressive mood at the White House. Kennedy had gone from a personal low in domestic popularity with the Bay of Pigs fiasco to a high with the Cuban missile crisis, and he had a new appetite for experimenting with the use of force. The president was particularly intrigued with the Green Berets, who were already staffing the montagnard operation in South Vietnam's Central Highlands, and who were about to take over its direction from the CIA.

In June 1963, the National Security Council, which had not been much involved in Laos before, secretly began to remove the restrictions on American involvement imposed by the Geneva agreements. The regular U.S. military was still excluded from Laos, to preserve Geneva appearances, but step by step the CIA was allowed to resume its resupply flights and its trainings.

Planes started landing at Long Tieng again with ammunition and new weapons. Resupplied, Vang Pao stepped up his mosquito-sting guerilla attacks. He went off on some of the operations himself, walking with the brisk, bandy-legged stride characteristic of his people. Tony Poe and Vint Lawrence talked to Vang Pao and his commanders before and after these operations, but the Americans didn't go into combat themselves, a role restriction that stayed in place.

In August 1963, Lair received an order—a "requirement"—to disrupt North Vietnamese truck traffic into Laos by blowing up parts of Route 7, which ran east of the Plain of Jars to the North Vietnamese border. This was a much larger undertaking than guerilla attacks on Pathet Lao outposts. Lair worked out a plan with the help of CIA demolition experts at Udorn. Then he went up to Long Tieng to fine-tune the details with Vang Pao and the Paru.

The basic tool of the Route 7 mission was the cratering charge, a standard explosive device for blowing holes in the ground. The cratering charges arrived in Long Tieng in well-padded boxes. A Paru team ran a demonstration, digging pits in the ground, inserting detonators into the charges, running fuses, filling the craters with dirt, and blowing some craters while the Meo and the Americans watched.

There was a final review session by lantern light in a bamboo shack in the chilly Long Tieng valley. Vang Pao dominated the meeting, asking questions, barking orders, the excitement showing in his narrow, flat-set eyes. The Paru went over the steps again with the younger Meo officers. Tall

Vint Lawrence stood in the background, sketching the zigzag pattern of the cratering charges on the road. Tony Poe looked on benignly, a few shots of rice whiskey under his belt, not needing to do anything because the Paru had everything under control.

It was a joint operation. From an Air America plane circling overhead, Poe helped drop the charges, using parabolic twenty-four-foot cargo parachutes. On the ground, at two points east of the Plain of Jars between Ban Ban and Nong Het where the road ran along steep hillsides, the Paru demolition teams received the parachutes and radioed for more when a few of the chutes went over the cliff. The Thais supervised twelve platoons of elite Meo troops, known as Special Guerilla Units. Each platoon dug ten holes two meters deep, five meters apart. They put two cratering charges side by side at the bottom of each hole, together with booster charges of C-4 plastic explosive. They rigged the detonators and fuse cords and filled the holes with dirt. Along the road and off to the sides in the hills, other Meo provided flank security. On schedule, in the middle of an August night in 1963, the charges went off.

In the first hour after sunrise an Air America plane flew over Route 7 to take photographs. In the two cliff-like sections the road had utterly collapsed. Nearby there was a crater in a flatter section of the road. The camera caught Pathet Lao soldiers standing at the edge of the crater, gawking.

That afternoon Pop Buell flew from Sam Thong over the ridge to join the celebrations at Long Tieng. After a few drinks he got a lopsided grin on his face and he started telling anybody who would listen that he was an old ordnance expert himself, from World War II, and proud of "his" Paru boys for following "his" instructions. This was news to the other Americans at the party, who knew that Buell had had a little ordnance training in the army but that he had basically spent World War II as a supply sergeant in Kansas and Tennessee. Buell hadn't had any role in the Route 7 raid at all.

The next day Poe walked into Buell's shack in Sam Thong with a cratering charge. He set the device down on the floor and said that it was about to explode. Buell, who was painfully hung over, mumbled that he had just had a call on the radio and had to go off to a meeting.

"Yeah. Well, take this with you and get it out of here," Poe recalled saying. "I don't want it with me. I don't know how to handle it."

"Oh, well, if you don't know how to handle it, how the hell do I?" said Buell, rubbing his forehead.

"Well, you just told everybody you just blew up the goddamn road, at Route 7."

"Oh. Those were my boys. My Paru."

"Shit, Pop." Poe lowered his voice to a conspiratorial whisper. "There are no fuckin' *Paru* in fuckin' Laos. There are no fuckin' *Thais* here. All right? Why do you keep forgetting that? We want to protect their background."

"Aw, fuck it, Tony. It was the whiskey talking, you know."

The two Americans were soon quaffing *lao cao* from cups. They both liked good liquor, and neither of them was totally opposed to bad liquor, either. They had reason to celebrate. The Paru and Meo with whom they worked had carried out the operation flawlessly. That was worth something. It was definitely worth another drink.

Poe, Buell, Lawrence, and Vang Pao had no way of knowing about the Omega war games, or about the curious evolutions in thinking far away in Washington, or for that matter in Hanoi. All they knew was that the standdown was ending, and their small war was gearing up again.

# The Bureaucracy

Two doctors were in an elevator in USAID headquarters in Washington, D.C.

"Where in the hell is Laos?" the first doctor asked.

"I don't know," said the second doctor. "Is it in Africa?" Lagos, the capital of Nigeria, sounded almost the same.

The first doctor said she thought it was in Asia, maybe even in Southeast Asia.

"Oh," said her husband, puzzled.

Like the majority of their fellow Americans, the two physicians, Charles Weldon and Patricia McCreedy, had only the haziest conception of Laos. But wherever it was, they were going there, on a career path that had begun in the Deep South and veered through the South Pacific.

They had met in medical school, married, and spent most of the 1950s practicing medicine in a wealthy agricultural community in Louisiana, where the Weldon family had its roots. The long hours interfered with their family life—they had three children—and in 1960 they decided to do something different "for a year or two," as they thought. They went to American Samoa, where Dr. McCreedy hired on as a public health officer and Dr. Weldon, known as Jiggs, as a pediatrician and later as director of health.

They were energetic and resourceful, and within two years they made major inroads into Samoa's most pressing public health problems: tuberculosis, a high infant mortality rate, and filariasis (also known as elephantiasis). They liked public health work and decided to go someplace where the medical challenges were even greater.

The governor of American Samoa, who had become a friend of theirs, told them about USAID, the U.S. Agency for International Development. He said that USAID was a terrible bureaucracy but had the kind of jobs they were looking for. He told them to go to Washington and see the personnel director, and that if they didn't get results, and they probably wouldn't, to call a friend of his on the White House staff. He handed them a slip of paper with a number written on it.

They flew to Washington and everything turned out just as the governor had said. USAID was noncommittal and unhelpful.

Disgusted, Weldon pulled out the slip of paper and called their contact at the White House. The staffer set up another appointment for them at USAID the following morning.

The Weldons went back and found that the atmosphere had changed now that the right political strings had been pulled. Everybody was cordial. Both were asked if they would like jobs in Laos.

The Weldons said that they had always wanted to work in Laos and that it sounded like a very exotic and interesting place. But in the elevator on their way out of the building they found they weren't entirely sure where it was.

They went to a library and looked it up in an atlas. It was in Asia all right, with the Mekong River on one side, the Annamite mountain chain on the other. But it was still an abstraction to them. There was no historical link between the U.S. and Laos, any more than there was between the U.S. and the other countries in the region, like Vietnam and Cambodia.

They moved to Laos with their three children. When they reported for work in Vientiane, the USAID director for Laos told them that he had no job for Dr. McCreedy. Dr. Weldon started work, preparing to take over the public health program while his wife got the household set up and the children in school. He felt uncomfortable. The USAID director, Charles Mann, didn't introduce Weldon at staff meetings and didn't say anything to him.

After a few days of getting the cold shoulder and not knowing why, a stumpy, grizzled man with an incipient potbelly walked into Weldon's office and introduced himself as Edgar Buell. He explained that he was the refugee relief coordinator at Sam Thong, upcountry. He had come for some medical supplies, which he had been accustomed to getting from Weldon's predecessor, who hadn't said anything to Weldon about it.

Weldon tried to learn what Buell was doing, but without much luck. Buell didn't have a list of the medicines he wanted, and he either wasn't able or willing to offer a clear picture of his work. Finally, though, Buell asked Weldon to fly to Sam Thong to see him soon.

A few days later Weldon found himself airborne in a Helio Courier, flying above the cloud cover. To the north a mountain massif called Phu Bia jutted above the clouds. With the plane's engine droning on, Weldon let his thoughts run, wondering what he was doing in Southeast Asia, when all of a sudden the pilot found a hole in the clouds, banked, and dove down almost vertically. The pilot pulled the nose up just in time to avoid a crash into the green forest, skimmed over another ridge or two, and then descended into a valley with a cluster of tiny villages, a dirt airstrip, and a medium-size bamboo and thatch-roof building alongside. He landed and pulled to a stop. Edgar Buell was there waiting for them, unshaven, and looking distinctly unglamorous with his thick black eyeglasses and a cigarette dangling from his lips.

They went into Buell's office-bedroom. Weldon had seen better-looking shacks in Samoa. Next to the folding metal field desk with the radio was a bamboo platform, where Buell and his workers unrolled their sleeping bags at night, to get off the cold dirt floor and away from the rats. Within reach was a crossbow, for target practice on the rats. The warehouse next to it also had a dirt floor, and there were piles of sacks and supplies all over the place in no apparent order.

Then the planes started arriving—Helio Couriers and Dorniers, DeHaviland Caribou C-7A light cargo planes, and C-47 "Goony Birds." Chaos gave way to order. The pilots landed, unloaded, took on a new cargo, taxied down the strip, and took off again without wasting a second. By then other planes had pulled up to the warehouse in their places. The warehouse crew was lifting sacks and checking lists, and Pop Buell was among them, conferring with the pilots and sending and receiving messages over his voice radio. Everybody knew exactly what he was doing.

Later in the day Buell took Weldon for a quick hop over a couple of ridges south-southeast to another base. He introduced Weldon to a moon-faced Laotian soldier named Vang somebody-or-other and to a couple of Americans who were there, too. Then Weldon flew back to his job in Vientiane, a little wiser, but not much.

A month later Weldon still hadn't made much progress getting his own job straightened out and no progress at all getting the promised job for his wife. Then Buell showed up in his office again and invited the doctor to attend the opening of a new field hospital in Sam Neua. Weldon didn't know where it was but agreed to come, largely because he was frustrated in Vientiane. As his contribution to the field hospital, he brought kerosene lanterns, wash basins, sterilizing equipment, scissors, forceps, and other basic equipment.

A plane flight later Weldon was in a little scraggly village called Hong Nong, on a knife-edge ridge way off in rugged mountains in far northeastern Laos. To the west rose a striking butte-like mountain called Phou Pha Thi. To the east and at a lower elevation was Sam Neua city, shortly to become Pathet Lao headquarters for Laos. About 120 miles farther east from Sam Neua city lay Hanoi, the capital of North Vietnam. Weldon discovered to his considerable surprise that he was closer to Hanoi than he was to Vientiane.

The new field hospital had a waiting room, a consultation room, a treatment room, a surgery, and fourteen beds for patients. It was clean, light, airy, and built entirely of bamboo and thatch. A Paru medic nicknamed Sam supervised a Meo building crew, and their total construction costs were zero.

Vang Pao, Buell, Weldon, and others attended the opening ceremony. Immediately afterwards, Sam the medic and a peripatetic American Catholic missionary, Father Luke Bouchard, described to Weldon the outbreak of a fatal and contagious gastroenteritis that sounded a lot like cholera. This was serious business. Hong Nong was a strategic location in northeast Laos. Containing the disease was crucial, both for humanitarian reasons and to keep the military operation from falling apart. Weldon went into overdrive.

It was a Sunday. Weldon flew back to Vientiane and got the right embassy people there to rouse the right embassy people in Bangkok into sending eight thousand doses of cholera vaccine from Bangkok to Hong Nong within forty-eight hours. Then he flew to Long Tieng with an initial vial to vaccinate Vang Pao and any of his men who might be traveling in and out of the Hong Nong area. From there he flew up to Hong Nong again to work out the plan of action with Sam the medic and with a Maj. Thong Vongrasamy, the lowland Lao military commander in the area.

The epidemic was believed to have broken out between Hong Nong and the big mountain, Phou Pha Thi. There were Helio strips on the periphery of the affected area, but travel to the settlements between them was possible only by foot or horseback. They decided to vaccinate all the people on the periphery first and then get those in the middle.

Weldon, Sam, and Sam's Meo assistants started by vaccinating a thousand people at Hong Nong on Thursday, August 15, 1963. Major Thong kept everyone in order, assisted by Buell, who showed up with his pockets full of hard candy and balloons. The next morning, while Meo medics fanned out on foot to vaccinate some of the smaller villages, a Helio pilot took Weldon to a little airstrip and left him there alone. Nobody at the village spoke a word of English, but Buell had promised to follow in the Helio within a few minutes.

When Buell's plane didn't show, Weldon explained himself by sign language to a little Meo lieutenant who smiled and seemed to understand. By late afternoon the two of them had vaccinated seven or eight hundred villagers and Weldon had diagnosed and treated more than fifty other cases of miscellaneous medical ailments.

When they finished they sat down to a meal of porcupine stew, cucumbers, sticky rice, and Meo rice whiskey. Then they went out to inspect the village. The school was a little jewel of woven bamboo and thatch sitting on a lonely green mountainside. The grass was neatly cut, and the Lao flag flew from a towering bamboo pole raised on a dais of bamboo and smoothly packed earth. Inside, the desks were fashioned from a beautiful dark brown local hardwood. The faces of the young students at the desks were clean and bright, though some students lacked books and pencils and paper.

At 5 P.M. they finally heard the drone of an aircraft engine. The missing Helio landed and Edgar Buell got out, with a look of sharp surprise that turned to disappointment that everything had gone so well without him.

Buell gruffly explained without looking Weldon in the eye that the Helio had developed mechanical problems and had had to return to Vientiane, a story that Weldon suspected was untrue. Later he confirmed it. Buell liked putting Americans alone in isolated areas where nobody spoke their language. It was his way of testing Americans, to see whether they were worth keeping around.

The two men flew back to Hong Nong. They broke open a bottle, and that night Buell led the local soldiers, still wearing their pistols, in impromptu *lamvong* dancing around the fire with village maidens. The *lamvong* was the Lao national dance, hands waving gracefully in the air, the partners never touching.

The next morning they got up before dawn for their horseback trip to the center of the epidemic, escorted by the quiet Major Thong and a dozen soldiers. After riding all day on a rough, rocky, up-and-down trail they arrived at the epidemic's source. Twenty-six had died of a violent diarrhea from contaminated water, but since then the disease had not reappeared.

Weldon and Buell vaccinated into the evening, going to sleep with their feet to the fire with pigs, horses, ducks, and chickens all around them. The next day they rode toward their final destination, through a forest with pine trees six feet wide at the stump. Descending into a valley they passed through a triple-canopy rain forest, with big-leafed plants and shafts of light that never penetrated to the clean forest floor. At the little village on the valley floor, they began vaccinating again. Then they went into the river to soak off the grime and the fatigue of their travels. There were hot springs above the village, and they found they could take baths at any temperature they liked by moving closer to the hot springs or farther away. Watching these carousing Americans was Major Thong, sitting unobtrusively with his rifle a short distance away from the river, keeping guard.

Weldon, who had been a Marine Corps captain in World War II, took stock of Thong. While some of Thong's men took turns bathing in the hot water of the river, the others cautiously sealed off the entrances and exits to the village. Thong and his soldiers were disciplined and competent. They were also ethnic Lao, which contradicted the stereotype about lowlanders being lazy. Weldon was impressed with them, just as he had been impressed with the school and the bamboo hospital. He decided that these were people who amounted to something. They were willing to work and sacrifice for their common good.

The next day Weldon returned to Vientiane exhilarated. The trip had opened up a whole new world for him. It appealed to him because of the challenge. He belonged to the same highly motivated generation of World War II veterans as Lair, Buell, and Sullivan, and he was looking for a way to serve his country.

The trouble was, Buell's enterprise in the mountains of north Laos didn't have much to do with Weldon's work routine in Vientiane. By the time the exhilaration faded, he and his wife found they had mixed feelings about staying in Laos at all. The children loved the smelly markets of Vientiane and were already chattering away with their new friends in Lao, but Pat still didn't have a job. Though Weldon's boss, Charles Mann, seemed to dislike him marginally less than at their first meeting, the USAID director declared that any money for new programs would have to wait until the next fiscal year. Weldon didn't know that Mann hadn't asked for either of them, and that there hadn't been job openings until USAID headquarters got a phone call from the White House. Mann's treatment of him and Pat carried a sting of rejection.

Weldon flew up to Sam Thong to talk to Buell in the thatched hut at the end of the warehouse.

He told Buell that he and Pat liked Laos but were thinking of pulling out. The USAID office hadn't come through with her job, and they didn't like being jerked around.

Buell jumped to his feet, livid. "You educated fool!" he shouted.

A tongue-lashing followed. Its gist was that just when Buell was starting to think that maybe Weldon was worth a damn, the doctor was turning out to be a no-guts, no-balls fool. Weldon didn't care about anybody but his goddamn rich-ass little educated self, declared Buell, who added that he didn't want the Weldons around anyway.

Weldon was taken aback. He started to think that Buell was right, that he and his wife had cared only about themselves. He began apologizing, but Buell interrupted.

"Anyway," he said grumpily, "don't do anything for a goddamn week."

"Why a week?" Weldon ventured to ask.

"Just do it!" Buell thundered, with the wrath of an Old Testament prophet.

In Vientiane a few days later, Weldon got a call from a man named Whitehurst, asking him to come to his office the following day. Weldon was puzzled. He had shaken hands with "Whitey" Whitehurst, the CIA station chief, once or twice at embassy social functions and at cocktail parties. But they'd never had anything to do with each other.

Whitehurst greeted Weldon cordially as he entered the office. Whitehurst said he understood that Weldon had had some difficulty in starting up public health projects. Weldon said that this was so, but he wondered what the Agency had to do with it. Whitehurst said that perhaps he could be of assistance and asked Weldon to describe what he did.

Weldon began explaining his plans for training medics, for an inoculation program, for rural dispensaries and clinics. He laid out a blueprint for a public health program that dovetailed with USAID's development efforts and, though he didn't know it yet, with the CIA's re-expanding efforts to organize the Laotians of the countryside.

After a while Whitehurst led Weldon to the office of his assistant and left him there. The assistant asked Weldon if he had any immediate needs. Weldon said that if he had some petty cash, he could buy some medicines, syringes, and bandages on the local market to send to Buell. The man opened his desk drawer, took out a paper bag, and handed it to Weldon. Weldon opened the bag and looked at the contents, stacks of Laotian kip.

"Do me a favor," the man said. "Don't keep any receipts, and don't tell me how it's spent."

Soon after that Charles Mann called Weldon in and told him that it looked as if there was a job opening up for his wife after all.

Back in his office, amazed, Weldon picked up the phone and called someone on the ambassador's staff whom he had treated for a minor medical problem a short while before.

"Tell me," said Weldon, "is Pop Buell around? No? But he was here a few days ago, right? So he saw the ambassador, did he?" The voice on the end confirmed that the ambassador and Buell had met.

"Yeah, that's what I thought," Weldon said. He put the phone back in the cradle.

He had discovered that there was an outer layer to the American bureaucracy in Laos whose apparent purpose was to prevent anything meaningful from getting done. It was no different from bureaucracies anywhere. But in the very center of the Laos war effort there were a few people from different agencies who knew one another well, and who got a lot done by bending or breaking the rules if that was what it took, and it usually did.

Edgar Buell was one of these inner-circle players, the station chief was another, and Mann, to Weldon's surprise, was a third. They had asked him to join them in fighting this war, where the U.S. bureaucracy was itself an enemy, less dangerous but just as stubborn as the Pathet Lao and the North Vietnamese.

# Nation-Building

By the fall of 1963, Vint Lawrence and Tony Poe had been together a year, living in a hut in Long Tieng. They had more visitors than before—pilots daily, Buell often, Lair and other spooks, and Dr. Weldon from time to time. But for the most part they were the only white men at an isolated outpost far off in the Asian boondocks. They were not entirely thrilled with the company, and they had started to avoid each other when the chance arose. Usually Lawrence stayed at Long Tieng to cable his nightly sit reps to Udorn, and the restless Poe went on longer trips to front-line outposts. But sometimes they switched roles.

In late November 1963, they learned that the North Vietnamese had repaired the blown-up sections of Route 7 and were sending an unusual number of trucks into northeastern Laos. Vint Lawrence flew to a friendly airstrip a few mountains away from the road and then hiked to another tiny village to help organize a roadwatch team.

He settled in for the night in a dirt-floor, thatched-roof house belonging to the village chief. Though the North Vietnamese border was just a few miles away, he felt quite safe. Around him in the hut was a tough, loyal Paru team, and whoever wanted to get him would have to get through them first. He sat in the dim light of tiny oil lamps on that November night thinking that there probably wasn't another white man within a hundred miles; and if there was, he didn't want to know about it because it would be someone on the enemy side. Tired, he went to sleep around ten o'clock while his team listened to a radio.

During the night one of the Thais woke him and said, "Monsieur Vin', there's trouble," and handed him the radio. The shortwave was tuned to a Voice of America program where the news was read slowly, for listeners who didn't speak English well. There was something about Dallas and motorcades. Lawrence impatiently twisted the dial to the regular-speed VOA news, on another frequency, and heard about the assassination.

◆

A few hours later at Long Tieng, Tony Poe charged into a hut where the visiting Bill Lair lay sleeping. Poe was holding a radio.

"Well, they finally shot that bastard," Poe announced cheerfully.

Lair didn't know what bastard Poe was talking about. Three weeks before, on November 2, 1963, the South Vietnamese leader, Ngo Dinh Diem, had been shot and killed in a coup in Saigon. Diem's assassination had been on Lair's mind, troubling him a great deal, but Tony wouldn't have woken him up for that.

"Who got shot, Tony?" Lair said groggily.

"The president of the fuckin' United States," said Poe.

Lair was too stunned by the news to think much about Poe's bizarre delivery of it. He couldn't imagine why Poe was saying anything of the sort.

Later it turned out that Poe had friends in the outfit that had gotten the short end in the Bay of Pigs invasion, when Kennedy withheld air support at the last minute. Because of that, Poe hated Kennedy with a vengeful passion—abandonment of one's men in battle being the worst crime imaginable, for a marine.

◆

It was impossible then, in the late fall of 1963, to foresee the consequences of the two assassinations, of Diem in Saigon and Kennedy in Dallas—how South Vietnam would sink into greater and greater turmoil, and how the new U.S. president, Lyndon Johnson, would react. Nor was it possible to foresee how a little country like Laos would slide from its place on the periphery into the larger whirlpool of events.

Remote from the outside world, and only marginally connected to the Mekong valley and Vientiane, north Laos was a realm of its own. Lawrence and Poe had too much to do to worry about matters beyond their control. The war had resumed and there were trainings to run, sit reps to write, battle plans to review with Vang Pao.

By then, Lawrence was close to Vang Pao. Several times the tribal leader told him that Bill Lair was like an older brother and Vint like a younger brother. In Asian terms, this was a great compliment. Poe, however, was outside this family circle. He and Vang Pao had the wary mutual respect of fellow warriors who find themselves more or less on the same side. Sensing Poe's volatility and not liking it when Poe got drunk, Vang Pao kept a polite distance whenever possible.

Lawrence was wary of Poe as well. The older man was genuinely tough. As a hobby, he made hand grenades into minibombs by pulling the pins and putting the grenades in glass jars. He threw the jars out of airplanes for fun. He made crude claymore mines with nails, plastic explosive, electric caps, and detonating wires. Once in a while he made batches of home-brewed napalm, carefully stirring detergent into gasoline over heat, then letting it cool and gel.

Another hobby of Poe's was collecting enemy ears. He did it only a few times at Long Tieng, and he downplayed it later, explaining that the marines had done the same with Japanese ears in World War II. "We had 'em on our cartridge belts. The guy's dead anyway, what's the difference?"

In Laos, where the veneer of civilization ranged from thin to nonexistent, Poe's ear collecting did not seem especially significant. But to Lawrence, Poe's overall behavior was a problem. The guy was just not normal. There was something inside him, bothering him, driving him to overcompensate. Poe needed to prove that he was the best and the bravest, and when he could not be the best he tried to be the funniest or the most outrageous.

As the operation expanded toward the end of 1963, Poe went off to the farthest bases to run trainings, only to find, again, that he wasn't as effective as the Paru, who spoke the local languages well. Looking for a proper role, Poe went off on combat missions, getting closer to the action than Udorn or the Vientiane station was happy with. When he was reprimanded, Poe got drunk and obnoxious, angering everybody around him.

In Long Tieng, Poe and Lawrence had replaced their sleeping hut's leaking thatch roof with sheet metal. For nighttime heat, the two men had rigged up a wood stove from a fifty-five gallon drum, with leftover tin sheeting for a chimney, daubing the cracks with mud. Poe's bunk was on the far side of the wood stove.

By then Poe was consuming a fifth to a half gallon of whiskey a night. When he passed out, getting him to bed wasn't easy. Tony was heavy, and if he wasn't out cold he clowned around, singing and joking as Lawrence tried to carry him around the red-hot stove without burning him. He put Poe to bed every night.

◆

Lawrence had his own kind of drinking problem. Tribal leaders kept inviting him into their thatched huts and offering him their homemade whiskey, which he accepted for politeness' sake. When there were impurities in the whiskey his immune system rebelled. His eyelids swelled and his face puffed up like a prizefighter's after fifteen rounds.

It had happened to him one night in Long Tieng and the next day he was hung over and his face puffy. He felt terrible. He was sitting at his desk in his hut when, in midmorning, the light outside began to fade. He supposed that he was going blind from alcohol poisoning. It got darker and darker and he started to get scared. And then there was a burst of gunfire all around him and he figured he'd died, that being the Meo salute to the soul's departure from the body.

In the dim light the gunfire went on and he heard talking outside.

He got up and staggered to the door. In the twilight Meo soldiers in fatigues were silhouetted against the sky, aiming their M-1s at some unseen target. Something very odd was happening. The birds had stopped singing and there was a shadow across the sun.

I'll be darned, thought Lawrence.

It was an eclipse—a solar version of the event Bill Lair had witnessed in Vientiane a few years before. The hill people had adopted the lowlanders' myth of the cosmic frog and they were chasing it away with all the firepower at hand.

As the sun emerged Lawrence's vision returned, but the dislocated feeling persisted. On their own turf, in their own mountains, the Meo cosmology seemed deep and convincing and more valid than his own.

Understanding their beliefs became a crucial goal. Part intelligence officer, part anthropologist, Lawrence felt he had to understand what made the hill people tick to work with them effectively.

The tribespeople believed that every living thing had a spirit. Before they slaughtered animals the Meo talked to them, asking their permission. Before they felled trees, they told the tree they needed the wood. When outer beings died, the spirit went back to where it was born.

When an important tribesman named Ly Sao died at Long Tieng a long ceremony followed, and it brought Vint Lawrence deeper into the spirit realm that paralleled and sometimes connected with the physical world. Ly Sao's body lay in state atop a wood plank next to the bamboo wall of the hut. The body was dressed in traditional Meo finery and covered with a blanket, except for the head, which lay on a cushion, uncovered.

A chorus of wives and female relatives kept up a steady wail. Clustered about his head, mournfully rocking back and forth, they sang of Ly Sao's life, their sorrow, and their hopes that his spirit would have a good journey. Probably out of a wish to keep the flies and maggots that were already underneath the funeral clothing from working on the face as much as a wish to touch Ly Sao for the last time, the women constantly caressed the head—stroking, patting, smoothing. When one was tired another would take over. A new female would not make a sound until she was next to the body and then appear upon the point of heartbreak until she left, at which time she very quickly regained her composure. The men remained quietly in the background.

From a beam in the center of the room hung an enormous cluster of many hundred sheets of cheap paper, each with a piece of gold and silver foil pasted on either side. This was the money of the dead, purchased in the local market. This money accompanied the dead to meet expenses on their journey.

Toward the end, the body was put in a coffin carved from a special log, as the smell had become too much for even the heavily perfumed air.

On the sixth day of mourning, Ly Sao was taken to a prepared bier outside. On either side of the bier was a pole with a leafy vine attached to the top. To the sound of steady chanting, the coffin was carried around the poles dozens of times, passing underneath and finally in a figure eight. The changes of direction were to confuse the body's spirit so it would be unable to find its way back to the house of the family.

A beef cow and two water buffalo were tied to stakes in front of the bier. These had been donated by friends who wanted to ensure that the spirit had animals to cross rivers on, since spirits couldn't swim. The animals were slaughtered with an axe. Then a sharp knife to the jugulars, the dark throbbing blood filling pails. The men chatted. The women wailed. The animals were butchered, and the feast prepared.

In the afternoon the body was buried with full honors.

Contemplating what he had learned from the funeral and from other tribal practices, Lawrence decided that the Meo belief system affected, and limited, their military performance.

"By and large," Lawrence explained later, "the people never wanted to leave their villages because of their animistic attachments to this tree and that tree and this stone and that stone. You would find out that they were going to build something somewhere. Only afterwards would you find out that they'd put the building at such-and-such an angle so that Aunt Millie's tree or her stone or her grave or whatever would look at the reflected light of the building in the early morning. You'd only find out the reason long after, and they wouldn't tell you that up front. But it certainly governed how they built their house.

"They wanted to stay local, and if they stayed, the family stayed. Up to a certain point, the families just didn't want to move. A man would go off on patrol and you'd see the woman traipsing along behind, carrying his rations. He'd be strutting along in his new little green fatigue outfit with his rifle, along with his friends.

"So, it was pretty much a catch-as-catch-can army."

The local attachments of the Meo, along with their lack of education and fierce independence, limited their operations to reconnaissance and minor harassment attacks. If a roadwatch team in far Sam Neua Province spotted a truck convoy coming in from North Vietnam, Vang Pao down in Xieng Khouang Province a hundred miles away would not always be able to do anything about it. "You didn't necessarily run a raid against the trucks," said Lawrence. "The kids wouldn't go that far. You're talking about poorly trained or rather barely trained humans, who don't have a long history of working together as a unit. Asking them not to defend their own land, which is what the deal was when you gave them the old M-1 rifle, but to go out and attack somebody's truck in the land of people whom they didn't even know. They'd turn to Vang Pao like a bunch of lawyers and say, 'This wasn't in the contract. You didn't tell us we had to go out and fight somebody else.' Taking guys from the south of the plain and sending them to Sam Neua was a huge journey for them because they were so local. And so bewildered."

The nature of the challenge facing the Meo operation, Lawrence decided, was nation-building. In those years "nation-building" was a great catch phrase for Americans in Asia. Putting in roads and highways was nation-building. Setting up rural aid programs to help farmers was nation-building, too. There were nation-building programs in South Vietnam, the Philippines, and Thailand, but no nation needed as much building as the haphazard stew of ethnic groups gathered by French colonizers into an artificial political entity called Laos. Many isolated tribespeople did not know they were citizens of any country. Their loyalties were to their families, villages, clans, or tribes. To believe in Laos, to fight for a political entity by that name, took more faith than they could muster.

The people could not fight well unless they were united and had something worth fighting for. Because of this, the north Laos war, Lawrence felt, was political first and military second. Lair, Buell, and the others in the inner circle all agreed, and for all practical purposes the USAID and CIA programs were a joint operation. USAID built a house in Sam Thong for Chao Saykham, the hereditary governor of Xieng Khouang, from which he ran a provincial government-in-exile. Working closely with Saykham, Pop Buell built thatched-roof schoolrooms, ran pig-breeding programs, and dammed and stocked fish ponds. Working closely with Buell and local leaders of all ethnic groups, Doc Weldon built medical dispensaries and trained medics. Every civilian developmental project made the Laotians stronger and more aware of those larger entities to which they belonged. The stronger they were, the more they could contribute to the fight against the communists.

Lawrence's niche was the intangible political side of nation-building. He saw the need to forge connections between tiny hamlets on mountaintops, villages in a district, districts in a province, and ultimately the mountain people and their central government. He thought the Meo, in particular, had a reasonable chance of success because of the American help and the tribe's rich history in Xieng Khouang Province.

From his conversations with the elders in the evenings, he learned that the Vietnamese had invaded Laos in the latter part of the nineteenth century. They came into the Plain of Jars and the then-king urged the Meo, who were relatively new immigrants from China, to resist. The Meo created a zone-based resistance to the Vietnamese, with local chiefs as the commanders. The zones remained the same through the present day, and many zone leaders were descended from the original chiefs.

Because they had staved off a Vietnamese invasion then, the king granted the Meo of Xieng Khouang Province a form of limited political autonomy, with their own district headmen, regional headmen, and eventually a spokesman in Vientiane, Touby LyFoung. Partly self-governing, the Xieng Khouang Meo were much more politically sophisticated than Meo in other parts of the country, and more of a force to be reckoned with than any other hilltribe. They had cattle, silver, and profits from opium, and some of them had schooling. They knew they were living in Laos, and even though they did not like the lowland Lao much they had something worth fighting for.

The old connection to the king of Laos, in Luang Prabang, was a trump card waiting to be played. The king was a symbol of the country, with his likeness printed on paper currency and his portrait hanging on government walls. He was not involved in the day-to-day running of the country, and he commanded less allegiance from his people than a monarch from a neighboring nation, the king of Thailand, did from the Thais. Nevertheless, Laos's King Savang Vattana had genuine symbolic and historical stature. Lawrence and Lair decided to use him.

Toward the end of 1963, after intense American pressure, Vang Pao was promoted to the rank of brigadier general in the Royal Lao Army. Shortly after, Vang Pao invited King Savang Vattana to visit Long Tieng, where no lowland soldier or Vientiane government official had ever been before.

On December 10, 1963, the entire Long Tieng runway was lined with Meo children holding Laotian flags. When the plane landed, the king, a lean, dignified, somnolent old man wearing a white uniform, got out. He handed out promotions and received the village chiefs. There was a little parade, a *baci* ceremony, and lunch, and then he left. Lawrence stayed in the background taking photographs. He didn't hide, but the visit was Vang Pao's show.

"It was very important to Vang Pao," said Lawrence. "It provided him a cachet, that he had been recognized; that his people had been recognized and appreciated. He had been under unceasing attacks by the more political types in Vientiane, by the Lao generals. After this, in conjunction with other things he did, he became less of a liability to the Lao and more of a plus."

◆

Nobody was happier about the king's visit to Long Tieng than Bill Lair, who wasn't there to see it. He stayed away from large public gatherings, figuring that the fewer people who knew who he was, the better.

From afar, in Udorn, he drank in the details when Lawrence reported to him afterwards: How Vang Pao had had a house built for the king. How there had been an actual red carpet for the king to walk on, laid over the orange laterite dirt. How the neatly dressed children had waved the flags with the white three-headed elephant.

The king had thanked Vang Pao for enlarging royalist territory against the communists and for bringing hill people into the government fold. He told Vang Pao to continue the good work. Above all, the king had been surprised and pleased to find that Vang Pao's radio communications were in the Lao language. It proved to him that the Meo were Laotian citizens, even more Laotian, in a sense, than the lowland Lao army, which used French, the language of bygone colonialism, in their radio messages.

To Lair, the king's visit to Long Tieng was a political victory, the fruit of many years' labor, achieved by events he had set into motion and by people he had handpicked.

From a tribe scattered on the hilltops, the Meo were becoming a significant regional security force. They controlled their own territory, the mountainous northeast. And with the king's visit, it looked as though the Meo were on their way to being successfully assimilated into the larger Laotian scene. It had always been one of Lair's worries that the Meo might get too strong, that the lowland Lao would try to put the Meo back in their place, and that the Meo and the lowlanders would end up fighting each other openly.

The king's visit had righted everything at a stroke. It had conferred a royal blessing and signified that the Meo were there to stay. The lowland generals might continue to resent Vang Pao, but they wouldn't move against him; and the Meo would continue to improve their lot through military training and the American-provided nation-building programs.

It was all going very well. Perhaps, thought Lair, there was no need to set up the Sayaboury escape route after all.

# The Wedding

The king's visit to Long Tieng in December 1963 marked the beginning of the brief golden age of the Meo operation. By then Vang Pao had personally matured, and he excelled at the role that fate had thrust upon him. He was charismatic, almost messianic, and tribespeople came from all over northern Laos seeking his help.

His original tribal paramilitary force, the so-called ADCs, or Auto Défense de Choc ("Self-Defense Shock") troops, had long passed the initial ten-thousand-man ceiling approved in early 1961. Vang Pao felt, and Vint Lawrence concurred, that the ADCs had nearly reached the limits of their usefulness. They were farmers with rifles, a part-time militia. ADCs would defend themselves, but they didn't like leaving their villages to go on the offensive.

What Vang Pao and Lawrence wanted was not to increase the number of ADCs, but rather to train a better brand of tribal soldier. Small numbers of elite Meo troops already existed—the Special Operations Teams (SOTs), trained by the Paru in Thailand, specializing in reconnaissance and dangerous raids; and a battalion of Special Guerilla Units (SGUs), who were somewhere between actual guerillas and light infantrymen, and who would go wherever they were needed. Lair supported building up the SGUs, but this was a new direction for the program and required authorization from Washington.

At CIA headquarters, William Colby had been promoted to chief of the Far East division, succeeding his old boss, Desmond FitzGerald, who had been assigned responsibilities for Cuba. It was Colby's task to convince others in the government bureaucracy, including key members of Congress who were kept quietly informed of CIA operations, that the escalation was a good idea. He could not take their approval for granted. Laos was supposed to be neutral as far as the general public was concerned, and a "holding operation" as far as U.S. government insiders were concerned. What he was proposing was a departure from existing policy.

Colby set out to make his case with all the flair of an advertising executive pitching a campaign to a prospective client.

He wanted to convey "just the right impression—that the situation in Laos was extremely serious, but with a greater effort it was salvageable," a man who helped him develop the presentation for Congress wrote later. "The chart had to show an extensive threat, but one that was ultimately controllable. Factual data had little part in the briefing material. One unfortunate fellow used red on an early version of the map to indicate the government/Hmong forces. This was completely unacceptable. Colby ordered that red could be used only for Communist forces."

Part of Colby's approach, according to his then-subordinate, Ralph McGehee, was sleight of hand, asserting that the new units existed by dividing the old units on paper into the necessary number of teams. "Whether it was true or not, the briefing material had to indicate an existent force that was primed and ready to go and needed only one thing: congressional approval for the necessary funding. The thinking at Langley was that if Congress approved the program, the group could be brought quickly up to strength. So why not fudge a few details? On paper the struggling, ragtag group of Hmong fighters began to resemble a small army."

Colby instructed his staff to come up with precisely the right name for the new armed force. The staff nixed Hunter-Killer Teams for sounding like an assassination squad, and rejected Home Defense Teams and Self-Defense Units for being too passive. Finally, they settled on Mobile Strike Forces, which sounded versatile and aggressive, like a hilltribe version of the Green Berets.

After meticulous preparation of his charts, slogans, and sales pitch, Colby briefed the key politicians and got their approval to proceed.

◆

The men at Udorn and Long Tieng were unaware of Colby's slick sales job in Washington. They were field-oriented, and to them, the new Mobile Strike Forces, usually known as SGUs, gave Vang Pao a welcome ability to move troops around better than before—attacking here, reinforcing there. The new troops were better paid and trained than the old ones—overall, better military quality.

The SGU program also affected the nation-building process. Now when young men joined Vang Pao's force, they left their home villages and went to Long Tieng for training, bringing their wives and children along. The arrangement was that the families would be fed and taken care of when the men were off fighting. This relieved the men's worries, but it came with a price tag attached. As Lawrence put it, "When the families come to Long Tieng, in effect they are hostages of Vang Pao. And Vang Pao knows that. That helps him control the troops."

Another effect was on the trade in opium, the tribe's traditional cash crop. Before the SGU program, Vang Pao had made tentative moves to enlarge and consolidate his fraction of the opium shipping market. He wanted to increase his power, naturally; but he also wanted to make himself genuinely useful to his people, who needed an outlet for the opium they produced. Lawrence and Lair, however, found out about his moves in advance. Confronted with their knowledge, aware he couldn't do anything major without the CIA finding out, Vang Pao appeared to have decided that a central role for him in opium marketing just wasn't worth it. He didn't need money from opium anyway. With the SGU program, he could get whatever he wanted by skimming from the U.S.-supplied payroll, as most Laotian commanders did. In terms of tribal politics, all he required was that the opium trade stay decentralized, and that no other tribesman emerge with a dominant share of the market.

A profound change was under way in the tribal operation. At the start of Momentum Vang Pao had been a man of his people. He had no traditional power base beyond his rank in the royalist army, and he had to use persuasion and the prospect of economic gains to get the village chiefs to cooperate. With the SGU program he had a growing number of soldiers and their families under his direct control and a growing budget, too. Eventually there would come a time, in the years ahead, when Vang Pao would grow so accustomed to power that he would lose many of the qualities that had made him attractive at the start.

At the time, however, in 1964 and 1965, the SGU program made perfect sense to the Americans in the field and to the hill people themselves. Village leaders, both Meo and other tribes, walked for days and even weeks through the mountains to Long Tieng to join the cause.

Vang Pao grilled them himself. If he believed that they weren't just in it for the free rice, rifles, steel ingots, and pots and pans the Americans provided, he formed radio and training teams of about five people each. Those teams and the village leaders headed back, perhaps riding part of the way on a plane. A week or so later, when a radio message reached Long Tieng that the new airstrip was ready, Vang Pao got in a plane or a helicopter with Lawrence at his side.

Lawrence came along for face, and as proof that Vang Pao had American support. He was the white man who stood in the background and didn't say a word, which helped emphasize that Vang Pao was in charge.

One such recruiting drive took place in the far northern province of Phong Saly, which borders China rather than North Vietnam. In a foreign aid project with menacing overtones, the Chinese government had begun building a road through Laotian territory in the direction of the Mekong River. Local Meo who up to then had not taken sides were anxious for protection. Vang Pao gathered everybody around and began his speech.

The communists, Vang Pao said, were like tigers in the next valley. The villagers had to join together to defend themselves. They had to forget the old problems that caused them to fight one another and ally themselves with the cause. Only by working together could they survive. If the village gave one hundred men, Vang Pao said, he would help them in return.

By prearrangement, a hundred men stepped forward. At that point there was a rumble up in the sky and overhead flew a C-123. Out the back of the plane came a hundred weapons, floating down on parachutes.

The recruitment drives were not always that well timed, nor as successful. Sometimes when Vang Pao went into an area to scout its possibilities, he found it wasn't worth it. He told Lawrence, "The people are in the middle. They're with us today, against us tomorrow. Let them ripen."

"He didn't need coercion out there," said Lawrence. "He could let people alone who wished to be let alone, and let them 'ripen.' He could afford, then, to take the people he could trust. He had more people wanting to be armed than he could possibly arm."

◆

Lawrence had done much of the groundwork for the SGU trainings. He worked closely with Lair. His long, articulate cables on the Meo, sprinkled with insights into their culture, had caught Colby's attention and helped convince Colby of the necessity of expansion. But Lawrence was not around for the first SGU trainings themselves. He was sick.

Like most Americans in upcountry Laos, Lawrence was a little bit sick most of the time. He had a persistent cough from the smoke of cooking fires and the wood stove in his hut. He had had dengue fever, which is mosquito-borne, like malaria. Digestive tract problems like diarrhea were routine. Once he had reeled a twenty-six-foot tapeworm out of his rear end, thinking he was losing his intestines. The tapeworm went in formaldehyde in a big glass jar in the Laotian dispensary, where it stayed for years.

But these illnesses were trivial compared with hepatitis. He had lost his appetite at the beginning of March 1964, but didn't think much of it. A week later he was running a fever in the afternoons and he could not eat. A few days more and he was nauseated and his urine was the color of Coca-Cola. He flew to Udorn and then to Bangkok as the whites of his eyes began to turn yellow and his stool white.

In Bangkok, tubes were hooked up to his body to deliver food and medicine intravenously. He responded well, and within two weeks his liver functions were back to normal.

While recovering, he read a half-dozen books of history, biography, and fiction. The books gave his mind something to do while his body was still weak.

Then once he had rested and refreshed his mind, he lay in bed and thought. He looked at the big picture and tried to figure where the program was going.

Regardless of the king's visit, nation-building, and the rise of the SGUs, a clear-cut Meo victory was unlikely, he thought, if that meant the total withdrawal and surrender of the enemy. That was not going to happen because the North Vietnamese were so disciplined and tough.

Would the Meo be satisfied with less than total victory? he wondered. Probably not. Every previous agreement had been broken. "Peace," after so many breaches of agreements, would only bring a breathing space, a time to review progress and then get ready for a new tack.

On the other hand, thought Lawrence, it would be hard for the other side to "win" a total victory. That would involve occupying Meo territory, and the size of the terrain and the number of Meo would make that difficult. Tribal resistance had grown too deep and strong a root to be pulled out by anything other than a major effort.

But what if the enemy *did* make the major effort? wondered Lawrence. What then? Only a major offensive would accomplish anything, and that would permanently end the enemy's hope of winning over the minorities. The hill people would have to be crushed, and in the act of crushing the flames of resistance would be fanned.

But it was not safe to assume that the North Vietnamese accepted their own weakness. They might decide a full-scale assault was worth the gamble. Until the Meo themselves could fend off a major offensive they should remain as decentralized and flexible as possible. They had to avoid offering themselves as a target.

We are everywhere yet really nowhere, thought Lawrence. That is our greatest strength.

◆

By late March 1964, Lawrence was ready to go back to work, but the doctors told him he couldn't. There were mandatory procedures to be followed for hepatitis patients in U.S. government service. He went back to the States for more medical tests and stayed for the next four months.

His absence left Tony Poe in charge at Long Tieng during a crucial period of change.

Poe was angry and out of sorts. Part of this was the weary cynicism of the man who had seen it all before. He had seen the Tibetan Khambas hanging their butts out the window when nature called, and to him there was nothing at all special about working with the Meo; they were another bunch of Asian primitives, better than some and worse than others.

He was also angry about injustices among the Meo themselves. There were two basic groups in the tribe, the majority "white" Meo, and the minority "blue" or "green" Meo, named for the color skirts their women wore. The groups' clothing and dialects differed, and the people perceived themselves as different. There had been a few firefights between them, but the real problem was "white" Meo discrimination against the weaker group's members.

There was also discrimination between clans. The Vangs and the Lys—people from Vang Pao's clan and Touby LyFoung's clan, all from the white Meo—got the soft jobs and quick promotions. Members of other clans, above all members of the blue Meo minority, were paid less, and exposed more to dangerous combat.

Another big gripe of Poe's was corruption. Every month a plane landed in Long Tieng and the other major bases. Out came the payroll, boxes and boxes of money. Vang Pao counted what he felt was his fair share of kip, surrounded by his closest aides. The other commanders counted their shares. A 10 to 20 percent cut off the top was considered normal by Asian standards, not "graft" in the Western sense. But even with that, when the enlisted men lined up to get theirs, somehow it never came out the way it was supposed to. There were "ghost" soldiers on the payroll, kickbacks aplenty, unequal levels of pay between units, and other peccadillos.

Other knowledgeable Americans admitted that these financial problems existed, but they pointed out that hilltribe corruption was minor in comparison with the miasma of graft and greed among the lowland Lao. The tribal program was *working*. It was growing. It had popular support. It was militarily effective. Why mess with it, especially since correcting the flaws caused more problems than it solved?

The example often cited was a base north of the Plain of Jars where the pay was always screwy, the men were unhappy, and Poe had complained loudly and often. Mostly for Poe's sake, Lair sent up a financial officer to see that each soldier received every kip he was owed. After a couple of months, nobody at the base would do anything at all. Everybody was on strike. The tribesmen preferred the old way—Vang Pao or the base commander decided who would get what, on the basis of past performance, or else to motivate the men for something they would have to do in the future. The tribal pay system wasn't fair by American standards, but the men at the base preferred it to the system of the *farang*s.

This didn't satisfy Poe, whose biggest gripe was Vang Pao himself.

The two men had clashed over the upgrading of ADC militiamen to Special Guerilla Units. Vang Pao wanted SGU trainings in Thailand with Thai and American trainers. Poe, who wanted to save money, favored trainings in Long Tieng, with Paru and Meo trainers—"white" Meo from the Ly and Vang clans whose high social status kept them out of combat anyway. The two men disagreed, compromised, then clashed again over the length of the trainings and the deployment of new SGUs in the field. "We started getting in these arguments," recalled Poe. "Discussions would lead to arguments, which would lead to heated problems, and who's the leader, Vang Pao, you or me?"

With Lair in Udorn and Vint Lawrence home on sick leave, there was no one to gently guide the two men away from awkward confrontations. The biggest argument, according to Poe, was over an operation to be launched from Long Tieng. Twenty-six helicopters had landed on the runway, ready to transport SGUs on a mission. "This was something we'd planned for months. Everybody knew we were going to do it, probably including the enemy," said Poe. "We got up at 5 A.M. Choppers are ready to go. No troops. So I went down to VP's big house, and I said, 'What's going on?'" Vang Pao, said Poe, had a white doctor's coat on. He had a stethoscope around his neck and he was giving injections.

It was another one of those events beneath the surface of tribal life, beyond an American's ability to figure out. The United States had built a hospital at Long Tieng manned with Thai doctors. For some reason, Vang Pao told his people to come to his house for shots instead. Poe claimed he saw Vang Pao give a shot to a baby girl that morning, hitting her in the spine and paralyzing her legs.

"I'm laughing, kinda sad, and I said, 'VP, do you know how much we're paying for those Thai doctors down there? We build you a beautiful hospital. If I tell Bill and Pat in Udorn that you're not using that hospital, they're going to blame me for it.'

"He said, 'I want to learn about doctor.'

"That's where he broke down. He wanted to be everything," remembered Poe. "I said, 'That's not for you. You're the big man. You're supposed to fight and get my choppers going. And get the troops up there. Let's go out and kill those bastards so your people can go out and start farming again. We're not supposed to be doctors. It takes eight or ten years to be a doctor. And then you paralyzed that baby.'"

Poe said he gave Vang Pao an ultimatum: No more rice, no ammunition, no airplanes until the operation started. Vang Pao refused, angry at the loss of face, and a standoff began. Poe got Pop Buell on the radio and convinced him to cancel rice resupply flights. It took a week and negotiation by intermediaries for Vang Pao to give in. Poe rescheduled the operation and stood on the runway to inspect the troops, while the helicopter pilots gave him the thumbs-up sign.

The operation commenced and Poe resumed the rice resupply flights. "I won. They all knew it," recalled Poe. "But it was bullshit. Just bullshit. And then it got worse. Much worse."

◆

Whether the incident happened as Poe told it, with Vang Pao paralyzing a young girl with a hypodermic while twenty-six helicopters were put on hold, is unclear. Poe's colleagues shake their heads when they hear his stories and then wearily point out how they could not possibly have happened as Tony said. There couldn't have been *twenty-six* helicopters. Udorn or Vientiane would have had something to say about stopping rice shipments. Vang Pao never paralyzed anybody with a needle, and so on, and so on.

But like most Poe stories, and like most folklore about the Laos war, this one has grains and even nuggets of truth. Like many other Laotian officers, Vang Pao did give medical injections though he had no formal training. Tony Poe and Pop Buell sometimes did work together to curb Vang Pao's impulses and to try to correct what they felt were inequities, though Buell was far more subtle about it than Poe. And it is agreed by people who knew them that Poe and Vang Pao were increasingly on a collision course by 1964.

Poe's liaison with a local woman was another slap at Vang Pao. Poe had been working near the airstrip one day when an attractive Meo woman emerged from her thatched hut and hurried in front of him, leading her young daughter to school. "She had slacks on. And, geez, she had a beautiful rear end. *Real* good rear end. I said, 'Who the hell is that?' " Poe recalled years later. "I found out it was Ly Sang, Touby LyFoung's niece.

"I said, 'I gotta meet her.' The Meo I was talking to said, 'No, no, Vang Pao want to meet her. She too tough. She just got rid of husband, or he got rid of her, something li' dat.'

"Then Vang Pao said, 'Oh, that woman, don't want to know. Danger she,' " said Poe. "So then I wanted to meet her even more, because VP had his eye on her. One thing led to another, and finally I did meet her."

A relative if not an actual niece of Touby LyFoung, the Meo political spokesman in Vientiane, Ly Sang had grown up near the Plain of Jars. She had a smattering of education and religious training from Catholic missionaries. Strong-willed and independent, she became a small trader, traveling from one mountain village to the next with a donkey, buying and selling goods, including opium. By the time Poe met her she had been married at least once and had two daughters, but she was single again. She and Poe were both nominal Catholics, which helped bridge the cultural and language barriers. They got a Laotian marriage certificate, which made them legal in their own eyes, if not in the U.S. government's. Poe gave a dowry to her family, a branch of the wealthy, powerful Ly clan. "I had to give a hundred water buffalo to marry her and seventy goats. And her family still thought I was a piker."

They had the wedding at Long Tieng. Vang Pao signed the certificate but didn't attend, claiming that he had to be someplace else. Touby LyFoung was there with Pop Buell and Father Luke Bouchard, the roving Catholic priest who had helped report the cholera epidemic.

"There wasn't much ceremony," said Poe. "Just signing papers. Then Touby tied strings connecting me and my wife, just like the *baci*, and all that bullshit. Drums beating and bells and all that crap, you know.

"I was clean, you know. Loaded to the gills with *lao-lao*. Normal fighting clothes. Wore my .357 Magnum, like always. Had to. You got to keep the operation going. But that day I didn't have any hand grenades on.

"I was forty-one years old then. I have to say, I slowed down a lot after I married. I might have to say that I chickened out a lot. Having a family and a couple of children and so forth.

"And after that, Vint never carried me home when I drank. My family did. I just blew the whistle I carried, and the whole damn family came and got me."

# The Trail

Bill Lair often thought about transferring Tony Poe out of Laos, but he hesitated, hoping that his old friend would dry out on his own, or that some other position would open up for him. The secrecy of their profession, and the difficulty of making friends outside it, encouraged loyalty. As long as Tony kept the faith, as long as he didn't fall apart completely, Lair put off firing him.

At that time, in early 1964, Lair was devoting much of his efforts to Momentum's expansion, into Sam Neua in the far northeast, into Phong Saly in the far north, and into every mountainous corner of Laos. That expansion, he firmly believed, depended far more on the indigenous people themselves, and on their leaders, than on the few Americans in their midst.

Lair's superiors also believed that the tribal leadership was crucial. On a brief home leave in the States, Lair stopped in at Langley, Virginia, outside Washington, D.C., to visit the CIA's new headquarters in the woods near the Potomac River, and to see his boss, Bill Colby. Colby had always been good to Lair in a courteous patrician way, and Lair had always liked him in return. This time Colby took Lair to see the director of Central Intelligence, John McCone, in his corner office on the top floor of the striking new marble-and-concrete building.

Colby and McCone were scheduled to attend a meeting later that day of the National Security Council, which had come to set the policies for the CIA. Colby said that he'd like to bring Lair along in case any questions came up about Laos. Momentum was the brightest spot in Colby's covert operations, and one of the most successful programs worldwide. The director, a hard-boiled veteran of the Washington power game, turned to Lair and said bluntly, "If they want you to say something, stand up and say what you've got to say; then shut up and sit down. Don't stand up and ramble all day."

The meeting was attended by names and faces familiar to Lair from the newsmagazines. McGeorge Bundy, the national security adviser, presided. The conversation ranged all over the globe, and when it turned to Laos it was clear to Lair that the committee knew pretty much everything of importance about Momentum and its growth: the policies, the locations, the funding, the cast of characters.

Someone commented that the Laos operation depended heavily on this hilltribesman Vang Pao. What if something were to happen to him? Wouldn't the operation fall apart?

The CIA director replied that Mr. Lair of the Laos operation would say a few words in answer to the question.

Everyone swiveled around to look at Lair, who stood up in the back of the room and said that the operation didn't just depend on Vang Pao but on a tribal leadership.

Vang Pao, Lair went on, had several officers working under him who were extremely competent. If something happened to Vang Pao, it would be hard to say which one would step forward and take the reins. But some strong individual would emerge. There would be a period of sorting it out, but it wouldn't last long. The organization wouldn't fall apart because it was based on a large group of people who pretty much believed in what they were doing, and who had always stuck together in the past.

Heads nodded. The committee was satisfied. And after the meeting was over and they'd gone out in the hallway, McCone gruffly told Lair that it had been a good answer.

In fact, the question of top Meo leadership had never bothered Lair as much as it did others, who felt Vang Pao was indispensable. Lair had chosen Vang Pao and admired him, but he had always believed that leadership was a character trait that could grow or fade over time: While one commander was burning out from overwork and exposure to danger, another younger commander might be maturing and developing, getting ready to take his place. The Meo had a large talent pool and a long tradition of stubborn resistance; and Lair didn't worry too much about their leaders or about the Meo grass roots. He was more concerned about the other Laotian tribal groups, who were harder to organize.

After the Meo, who numbered about 250,000 in Laos, the next largest hilltribe was the Yao, who called themselves the Mien. About a hundred thousand Yao lived in far northwestern Laos, near the so-called Golden

Triangle where the borders of Thailand, Laos, and Burma meet. But the Yao didn't fight as hard as the Meo, and didn't dominate their region the way the Meo did. Bill Young had organized a force of several thousand part-time militiamen, some of them Yao, the rest from other ethnic groups. The various tribes sent their representatives to a council, which for practical purposes was run by Bill Young and the CIA.

There were over fifty other ethnic groups in Laos, with names like Akha, Lisu, Loven, T'ai Dam, T'ai Deng, and Lu, but they were small and scattered and their leaders had only local influence. Some of them were already allied with the Pathet Lao and North Vietnamese. There was even a Meo faction with the Pathet Lao, though it had little military importance.

The largest ethnic mass left for Lair to recruit was the Lao Theung, the generic name for Laotians of middle elevations—the people who lived below the hilltribes but above the lowlanders. The Lao Theung, comprised of various tribes and subtribes, were a dark-skinned race who had lived in the area long before the ethnic Lao arrived from southern China in the twelfth century and the hilltribes arrived in the nineteenth century. Both the hilltribes and lowlanders disdained the Lao Theung and called them Kha, meaning "slaves."

With the exception of some outstanding individuals, the Lao Theung as a whole tended to play their assigned role at the bottom of the social heap. They were poor. They were not clean. However, the Lao Theung of northern Laos were fierce fighters. They signed up in droves for the new SGU units. Soon they were second numerically only to the Meo, though underrepresented in the officers' ranks.

Lair focused his attention on the Lao Theung tribes of the southern Laos panhandle, who were less warlike, and who lived in a lightly populated area between the Mekong valley and the mountainous border with Vietnam. Traditionally, when these southern Lao Theung were threatened by enemies they simply moved out of danger. Lacking a critical mass, there had seldom been reasons for leaders to arise and put up a resistance. The major exception was a family of chieftains whose patriarch had rebelled against the French and whose son had been given an honorific title as deputy defense minister of the Pathet Lao.

With the help of a Lao Theung officer in the lowland army whom Vang Pao knew, Lair developed village militias and some reconnaissance teams anyway. The Paru ran the trainings, and the new southern teams were sent from the royalist-held Mekong valley through the no-man's-land foothills toward the North Vietnamese border. The nearer they got to the border, the more enemy activity they reported—some Pathet Lao, but mostly North Vietnamese.

The reconnaissance teams were afraid of the North Vietnamese and never attacked them. Lair didn't want to push his tribal forces beyond their abilities, but he knew he had a problem. Organizing the tribals had worked beautifully in northern Laos. In the mountains of southeast Laos, he didn't have good tribal material to work with, and the enemy had gotten there ahead of him.

◆

Lair's southern Lao Theung teams operated out of Savannakhet, about halfway down the panhandle along the Mekong. Farther south, from the town of Pakse, Roy Moffitt ran a similar intelligence operation with the help of a plantation owner who knew the area well. About a hundred and twenty-five miles east of both Savannakhet and Pakse, across the wild and inhospitable Annamite Mountains, another operation had grown up on the South Vietnamese side of the border. It had started as a CIA operation patterned on Momentum, and was sponsored on high by Desmond FitzGerald and William Colby. Its indigenous people, known as montagnards (French for "mountain people"), were the same racial stock as the Lao Theung. The montagnard operation was turned over to the U.S. Army Special Forces in mid-1963, and one of its key field organizers, Brandon Carlon, transferred to Udorn to work for Lair, and later moved to Pakse to take over from the departing Roy Moffitt.

These three reconnaissance operations shared a common objective, located roughly midway between them. This was a multibattalion force of North Vietnamese soldiers around the dusty little trading town of Tchepone, inside Laos but near the demilitarized zone, or DMZ, separating North Vietnam from South Vietnam. With about three thousand soldiers, this was the largest North Vietnamese troop concentration in Laos and the largest single violation of the Geneva accords.

Lair, Carlon, and others believed that this enemy force had little to do with the struggle for northeast Laos and Vientiane. Rather, it appeared to be part of a long-term North Vietnamese plan to open a back-door logistical route to South Vietnam. Hanoi's men had controlled the Tchepone area for over a decade. They stockpiled supplies in caches and caves, and small numbers of their guerillas and couriers—perhaps a few hundred men a year—were known to make the long, arduous trip between North and South Vietnam on paths through the forests, traveling by foot and occasionally by elephant.

This trickle of foot traffic through the Laos mountains wouldn't have mattered much if it hadn't been for the worrying presence of those three thousand troops, and the failure of the South Vietnamese to stop the larger movement of North Vietnamese supplies anywhere else. At that time, early

1964, most communist supplies were reaching the south either by boat along the coastline or by land through the DMZ. Whatever the route, Hanoi moved supplies with a smuggler's creativity, often at night, switching the loads as necessary from boats to foot to bicycles to elephants to trucks to avoid detection. The communists also relied on coercion, forcing local villagers to act as coolies and porters, to reduce the energy costs to themselves.

For the North Vietnamese, the costs of moving goods through the mountains of southern Laos were high because of the steep terrain, the unbridged rivers, and the torrential downpours of the rainy season. But they already had the start of a back-door motorable route. Three mountain passes led from the southern part of their country westward into the Laos panhandle. From these passes Laotian roads carried traffic farther westward toward the Mekong valley. For the North Vietnamese to then build their own roads southward through the Laos mountains and then back into South Vietnam would be a massive feat, but not impossible, given enough determination.

And if those motorable roads in the mountains of Laos did not yet exist, Lair, Carlon, and others believed that it was only a matter of time. For there, in the Annamite Mountains, the CIA and Green Beret teams found a pattern of assassination and grassroots organizing that they recognized as a standard precursor to large-scale enemy logistical operations. North Vietnamese propaganda teams were arriving in remote villages in the panhandle and killing or threatening to kill the schoolteachers and village chiefs. After neutralizing anyone in the village with any education or knowledge of the outside world, the North Vietnamese convinced the surviving villagers that the Americans had evil intentions and that the royal Lao government was a puppet of the Americans. Converted—brainwashed—these villagers then went after the U.S.-supported indigenous reconnaissance teams with rifles and machetes.

In Washington, the new president, Lyndon Johnson, and the National Security Council were also worried at the prospect of a Laotian logistical route between North and South Vietnam. Such a route, if it were improved, would mean a further deterioration in Laos's Geneva accords, and it would also spell more trouble for South Vietnam, which was losing ground to the communists. The administration issued orders. From Takli air base in Thailand, the staging airstrip for "black" reconnaissance and resupply flights over China, the air force sent U-2 high-altitude spy planes over Tchepone and the Annamite Mountains. From Savannakhet and Pakse, Lair, Carlon, and others launched more tribal reconnaissance teams in what was codenamed Operation Hardnose. From the South Vietnamese highlands, the Green Berets led their own small expeditions across the Laotian border, with the help of South Vietnamese commandos, montagnard tribesmen, and other indigenous people.

The U-2s came back with pictures of mountains and trees, with here and there a North Vietnamese barracks or an antiaircraft gun. The Lao Theung teams and the Green Beret–led teams came back with little more.

The Americans kept an eye on the communists' network of footpaths and gave it a nickname, the Ho Chi Minh Trail.

◆

In Saigon, the assassination of President Diem in November 1963 had led to one junta of generals at the top of the government and then to another in January 1964. The generals spent much of their energies scheming against one another and little on improving conditions in rural areas or on curbing corruption. American weapons given to the military vanished, and so did much of the U.S. foreign aid, then running about two million dollars a day.

The North Vietnamese infiltrators and their southern protégés, known as the Viet Cong, found it easy to exploit the Saigon government's indifference to the lives of ordinary people. In the Mekong delta, where the great river split into myriad channels before emptying into the South China Sea, peasants who had been forcibly moved into government "strategic hamlets" gladly helped communist guerillas wreck the hated buildings and fortifications. Many of the peasants were wary of communist social regimentation, but to them the guerillas seemed like the lesser of two evils and had a better claim on their patriotic support than the Saigon regime.

In Washington, President Johnson, who had little foreign policy experience, found it hard to believe that aid to the South Vietnamese regime caused as many problems as it solved. As far as he was concerned, he had inherited the Vietnam mess from his predecessor, John Kennedy, and from Eisenhower before that; but Johnson didn't want to become known as the American president who had "lost" Vietnam. Few of the people advising him on Vietnam understood Asia in depth; and most of them—from the U.S. military commanders in Saigon, to Secretary of Defense Robert McNamara, to his national security adviser, McGeorge Bundy, to the State Department's Vietnam Advisory Group, chaired by the young veteran of the Laos negotiations William Sullivan—favored further U.S. investment. A general feeling arose in Johnson's administration that South Vietnam was a test case of U.S. resolve against communist "wars of liberation" around the world.

By mid-March 1964, the U.S. advisory force in South Vietnam was up to sixteen thousand men, and scheduled to rise to twenty-three thousand. Facing an election in November 1964, Johnson decided to keep further

Vietnam escalation plans secret from the voters and from the politicians on Capitol Hill.

Without fanfare, the U.S. raised its spending on nation-building programs in South Vietnam, like hospitals and roads, and sent more and better weapons to the South Vietnamese military. Johnson's aides devised a covert program to bring increasing pressure on the North Vietnamese government, including psychological warfare "dirty tricks," sabotage raids inside North Vietnam, and South Vietnamese commando raids on North Vietnamese coastal radar installations. The U.S. Navy sent ships to detect the radar frequencies and positioned aircraft carriers in the South China Sea. The Pentagon drew up a list of bombing targets in North Vietnam. Overall, the plan was to keep applying covert military pressure on the North Vietnamese and, if the North Vietnamese struck back, to pass a resolution through Congress to serve as the equivalent of a declaration of war.

◆

Seven hundred miles up the Mekong River in Laos, during this same period in early 1964, the political situation was deteriorating nearly as badly as the situation in South Vietnam. The Laotian neutralist center had split, with nearly half of its soldiers having gone over to the Pathet Lao side. The right-wing defense minister, acting on his own authority, tried to make a deal with South Vietnam to send its soldiers across the border in pursuit of North Vietnamese soldiers. In despair, the head of Laos's coalition government, Prime Minister Souvanna Phouma, flew up to the Plain of Jars for another three-way conference with the defense minister, Phoumi Nosavan, and the Pathet Lao head, Prince Souphanouvong. They weren't able to agree on anything. On April 18, the prime minister flew back to Vientiane and with tears rolling down his cheeks announced that he planned to resign.

The surprise coup the next day at dawn was not led by the defense minister, but by right-wing rivals of his who wanted to prevent him from taking over the government. As usual in Vientiane, there was a half-baked, unreal quality to the coup. Under house arrest, the prime minister appeared on the balcony of his official residence; the U.S. ambassador, Leonard Unger, shouted encouragement to him from the garden. Within hours the right-wing generals were quarreling with one another. Western ambassadors and spies scurried about, composing long cables home for analysis by the tea-leaf readers, while average Laotians, more accustomed to coups than the *farang*s, took their regular siestas in the heat of the day.

When the dust had settled, the Laotian prime minister was back in power and the generals were out, but with a major change. The three-way coalition put in place by the Geneva accords had collapsed in everything but name. The Pathet Lao kept a symbolic office in Vientiane, but their men stopped working in government offices. And Kong Le's neutralists formally allied themselves with the right under a new joint military command.

Excluded from the Laotian government, perhaps glad for the excuse, the Pathet Lao and the North Vietnamese forced Kong Le to the edge of the Plain of Jars and into Vang Pao's protective arms. By fleeing into the foothills, and by adroit maneuvering, the neutralists and Meo were able to avoid getting overrun. But then when the communists kept pressing, an entirely new weapon in the Laos war came into play.

This was airpower. The day after the Pathet Lao kicked Kong Le off the Plain of Jars, Vang Pao sent a representative to Vientiane to persuade the high command to send three T-28 aircraft parked at Wattay Airport to help Kong Le out. The T-28s, built as trainers (hence the designator-letter "T"), were stout-bodied, single-engine propellor planes with short, stubby wings. They looked like bumblebees in the air. The T-28s flew to north Laos and dropped a few bombs and made a few strafing runs on enemy troops, who hadn't faced planes before, and were scared and ran away.

A few weeks before, additional T-28s for Laos had arrived at the Udorn air base in Thailand as an adjunct to the covert buildup in South Vietnam. They were part of a training program called Waterpump, run by a U.S. Air Force unconventional warfare unit, the First Air Commandos. Because of a shortage of qualified Laotian pilots, Waterpump took on mercenary Thai pilots and a few American pilots as backups. The T-28s were rigged with three-sided frames on the fuselage into which metal insignia plates could be slid: the Lao insignia on one side, the Thai insignia on the other, or no insignia at all.

Almost immediately, the T-28s were in great demand among Laotian ground commanders. Vang Pao asked for an air strike near his old headquarters at Padong, where an enemy force had massed. The planes carried out the raid "in classic fashion, one after the other, sweeping very low dropping their bombs and sweeping again and again until ammunition was exhausted," as a CIA report put it. To Laotians the airplanes were almost magical. Their appearance overhead cheered the ground troops and filled them with confidence. The enemy fled. Elsewhere in Laos, other officers who had been afraid to send out patrols began making plans to go on the offensive.

The T-28s were only the first step. Within a few weeks, to nearly everyone's amazement, and to the delight of the royalists, U.S. jets were also flying reconnaissance missions over Laos. The jets, taking off from aircraft carriers at sea, and from air force bases elsewhere in Asia, had been readied as part of the U.S. plans for bombing North Vietnam. They had not been intended specifically for use in Laos, but were sent over because they happened to be handy. Souvanna Phouma gave his private permission for the overflights.

On June 6 and 7, 1964, two jets were downed over northern Laos by communist antiaircraft fire. The mainland Chinese government, which kept a mission on the Plain of Jars, found out about it first and broadcast the news. In retaliation for the downings, U.S. Air Force jets attempted to strike the antiaircraft position, missed because of bad weather, and tried again.

Prime Minister Souvanna Phouma, acutely aware that his national sovereignty was at stake, said he would resign if the flights didn't stop. But he was in no position to bargain. The United States had restored him to power after the coup, and it paid his government's budget. And if he resigned, it was pointed out to him, one of his scheming right-wing rivals would take his place.

Under pressure, Souvanna gave the U.S. government a verbal blank check to fly wherever it wanted in his country and for its planes to defend themselves against antiaircraft fire. He asked only a couple of favors in return. He wanted the U.S. to use a euphemism—"armed reconnaissance"—to describe all its flights, whether they were reconnaissance missions or not. And he wanted the U.S. not to release day-to-day news of the missions. This would help to preserve the fiction that the Geneva accords were still in force.

Publicly, the U.S. embassy announced that flights would resume, and that its planes had the right to fire if fired upon.

That same day a T-28 with Lao markings flown by a Thai mercenary pilot bombed the Pathet Lao headquarters on the Plain of Jars to smithereens and turned the Chinese mission into rubble. Souvanna Phouma was not happy about that.

Airpower was like a genie, hard to put back in the bottle once it had been let out. It had materialized all of a sudden, for reasons that had more to do with Vietnam than with Laos. Washington, which had not fully planned on using airpower in Laos, decided that it wasn't such a bad idea after all. The news reports could be controlled. There were few American journalists in Laos, and they were already tightly restricted from traveling upcountry.

However, the news stories that had already appeared raised the perception in various capitals of the world that the United States was unilaterally escalating the conflict in Laos. Unless the use of the jets was better justified, the U.S. government concluded, other countries wouldn't forgive the jets' deployment, Souvanna Phouma wouldn't allow wider use, and airpower couldn't reach its full potential.

A curious process began, mostly out of sight, with occasional leaks to the news media. It tied together several trends—the U.S. diplomatic bullying of local allies' governments, the secret U.S. drive to escalate the war in Southeast Asia, and the simultaneous and equally secret North Vietnamese escalations. On May 28, 1964, less than two weeks after the flights started, a *New York Times* story revealed that U.S. reconnaissance photos substantiated charges made by Souvanna Phouma that the North Vietnamese truck convoys were supporting Pathet Lao operations in north-central Laos and the Plain of Jars.

A month later, on June 26, another *New York Times* story introduced the term "Ho Chi Minh Trail," which had not been widely known before. The article said that "U.S. reconnaissance missions have confirmed earlier reports that Communist forces have been improving their road network in southern Laos and have considerably stepped up the pace of their supply convoys there." The new network of truck roads, the article said, stretched south of Tchepone. The report came within a whisker of making the big connection of North Vietnam, Laos, and South Vietnam that the United States had been expecting to find.

On September 19, 1964—six weeks after Thai-piloted T-28s had bombed across the Mu Gia Pass in North Vietnam, and three weeks before U.S. jets started flying "cap," or escort, for T-28s bombing in Laos—Souvanna stated that the connection had occurred. The Communists, he declared, were using the Laotian corridor to send troops and supplies to South Vietnam. "We have the aerial photographs to prove it," he said.

Souvanna Phouma had not come to that conclusion on his own. The U.S. military was pushing hard for permission to expand its use of airpower, and sometime during that summer and fall of 1964, U.S. Ambassador Leonard Unger decided the time had come to use information on the enemy's activities to extract maximum concessions.

Unger proposed a new, more aggressive use of American-controlled airpower in Laos—not just reconnaissance and escort missions, but air strikes, regardless of the presence or absence of ground fire. He showed the prime minister a stack of photographs of North Vietnamese trucks entering Laos via the Mu Gia Pass, one of the three passes that led from southern North Vietnam into the Laos panhandle. Although the trucks in the pictures were traveling on existing Laotian roads rather than on new routes built by North Vietnamese, the pictures proved that Laotian territory for varying distances west of the border was essentially under North Vietnamese control. This made any notion of a Laos free of the Vietnamese struggle unrealistic, Unger pointed out. The North Vietnamese never had any intent of living up to the Geneva accords.

Souvanna Phouma already knew about the North Vietnamese intentions. At around the time of the Geneva accords he had secretly, and mistakenly, given Hanoi permission to use Laotian territory, never dreaming that the North Vietnamese would use his territory so brazenly, or for such a long time. Now that the Americans wanted to use Laotian territory in response, his distress and embarrassment were real. Reluctantly, he gave the American ambassador permission to go ahead.

From that moment on, the Kingdom of Laos kept no more than the tatters of its sovereignty. The North Vietnamese had already stationed six to seven thousand soldiers in Laos. Now U.S. aircraft were free to bomb and strafe wherever they wanted, without prior clearance from the Laotian government. And the U.S. bombing, like so much else in the region, was to be kept secret from the outside world.

# The Seesaw War

Each of the changes of 1964—the collapse of the coalition government, the introduction of airpower, and the rise of the Ho Chi Minh Trail as a separate military theater—was like a twist of a kaleidoscope. Each changed the picture, and before long a new phase of the Laos war was under way.

Politically, all the governments involved—the Americans, the Thais, and the royalist Lao on one side; the Pathet Lao, the North Vietnamese, and their backers, the Chinese and Soviets, on the other—reached the same conclusion about the Geneva accords. As much as they would have liked to publicize their enemies' violations of the accords, they had more to gain by keeping their own roles quiet. So, by tacit agreement, they all outwardly pretended to abide by the accords—cynically guaranteeing the peace and neutrality of a weak country while keeping it polarized and at war.

Militarily, both sides increased their efforts, though their internal balance of forces changed. On the communist side, the Pathet Lao role diminished and the North Vietnamese grew. The North Vietnamese planned the campaigns, controlled the supplies, and put their own advisers, or "stiffeners," in Pathet Lao units. On the royalist side, Kong Le and Phoumi shrank in influence, while Vang Pao became the kingdom's most important field commander. The Americans contributed more airpower. Neither the Americans nor the North Vietnamese pressed for total victory, however, saving their main energies for the main war theater in South Vietnam.

In Laos, the fighting assumed a seesaw pattern, with the opposing sides going on the offensive when the weather suited them best. In the dry season in Laos, from about October to May, when the ground was hard and the roads were good, the North Vietnamese sent trucks and troops into the kingdom and captured terrain. In the rainy months, roughly June to September, when the laterite roads and paths became slippery and sticky, it was the royalist side's turn to take back terrain and for the North Vietnamese to retreat. The Royal Lao T-28s and the American helicopters, cargo planes, and attack planes had advantages of maneuver and firepower the communists couldn't match.

The seesaw war began with the communist offensive on the Plain of Jars in May 1964. The communists took sole control of the plain but couldn't exploit their advantage, as Vang Pao controlled the surrounding hills. In the following months, as the interior of the Asian landmass heated and rose, drawing moist air and rain in from the Indian Ocean, pulling in the monsoon rains, it was the royalists' turn to strike back. This took the form of Operation Triangle, a large-scale offensive approved directly by Lyndon Johnson and micromanaged by the upper-level Washington bureaucracy. The target was the Pathet Lao–occupied intersection of Routes 7 and 13, connecting Vientiane, Luang Prabang, and the Plain of Jars.

As much a public relations as a military offensive, Operation Triangle's goal was to demonstrate that Laotians of different factions were working together and controlling their own destiny. The Force Armée Royale, or FAR, the conventional lowland army, was assigned the starring role, and supporting roles were parceled out to the remnants of Kong Le's neutralist army, Vang Pao's tribals, and the stubby-winged T-28 fighter-bombers with interchangeable insignias. A few U.S. military men were brought incountry as advisers but told to keep out of sight.

The operation succeeded, even though Kong Le failed to show up. The T-28s, many of them flown by mercenary Thais, softened up the opposition, which was soft to start with—panic-stricken Pathet Lao units, rather than disciplined North Vietnamese. But at the intersection of the roads itself, at the symbolic as well as military objective of Operation Triangle, one cheerfully insubordinate case officer with whiskey on his breath refused to stick to his role and tore up the script.

The tribal irregulars had been asked to support the FAR with flank security while the lowlanders took the junction. When Tony Poe appeared on the scene, Vang Pao was up on a hill nearby, casually firing a 105mm howitzer in the general direction of the junction. Poe saw that Vang Pao wasn't marking his range with smoke shells or using reconnaissance teams to report on the enemy's location, and decided to change tactics. On impulse, Poe got on the radio and diverted all available helicopters to his location. He loaded two Meo SGU companies into the arriving choppers, and flew with them into the junction itself and to a nearby village. The enemy had already gone. Poe was defusing booby traps made from hand grenades when the lowland royalist troops arrived.

News of Poe's improvisational capture of the intersection, which violated CIA rules against case officers in combat, was quickly suppressed. The Meo role was played down in State Department cables. The other Americans understood that Poe's behavior wouldn't reflect well on any of them if it became known; and besides, it would be unwise to deprive the lowland Lao of credit for a victory that should have been theirs. But nobody found out, and it turned out not to matter much anyway. Within a week Operation Triangle was nearly forgotten, superseded by far more important events in North Vietnam and Washington, D.C.

Two hundred fifty miles east of the Plain of Jars, in the Gulf of Tonkin along North Vietnam's coastline, where jagged limestone karsts tower dramatically against the sky and sea, South Vietnamese commando speedboats and a U.S. Navy destroyer had been playing electronic cat-and-mouse games with Hanoi's coastal forces, trying to learn the locations and frequencies of Soviet-supplied radar installations by provoking them into switching on their radar. On July 30, 1964, the same day that the lowland Lao conventional forces met up with Poe, South Vietnamese commandos opened fire on a North Vietnamese installation on an island in the gulf. A few days later North Vietnamese patrol boats attacked the U.S. destroyer, the *Maddox*, without success. The next night the jittery gunners of the *Maddox* and another U.S. destroyer opened fire on what they believed were North Vietnamese patrol boats and torpedoes, though afterwards the commanders were not sure that there had been any enemy boats there. Working from a list of targets prepared months before, U.S. aircraft carrier–based jets flew retaliatory raids, hitting an oil storage depot and twenty-five boats, and losing two planes in the process. On August 7, 1964, Congress passed the Gulf of Tonkin resolution, which became Lyndon Johnson's justification for the Vietnam War.

The Gulf of Tonkin incident focused Washington more than ever on Vietnam itself. Rarely would the Washington bureaucracy again bother micromanaging Laotian battle campaigns from afar. The kingdom was allowed to slip again into its customary obscurity, a place where the few men on the scene were allowed to call the shots more or less as they saw fit. However, to assist in the deepening U.S. commitment to South Vietnam, the CIA was given general instructions to build up tribal assets in Laos still further and expand as far as possible into North Vietnam and southern China. The initial goal was collecting intelligence, though it was hoped that the tribals would go on the offensive and harass the communist regimes.

Tony Poe had been the third American to join Momentum, and there was no way to keep him entirely out of the new expansion and penetration operations along the North Vietnamese border. But he was excluded from a central role. "Tony became unreliable," one of his exasperated friends explained. "When he was drinking he'd get obnoxious and start shouting. When decisions had to be made it was no good having a drunk around." The role of coordinating the buildup went to Vint Lawrence, who had returned from the States still weak from the aftereffects of hepatitis but eager to get back to work.

Lawrence felt that recruiting tribes under communist control, particularly in North Vietnam, was a highly sensitive business and that showing a white face there was out of the question. Inside North Vietnam, tribespeople were not allowed to leave their villages without official permission, or hunt near roads the military used. Informers and a system of personal responsibility for neighbors' activities made contact with outsiders difficult. But this oppressive government control also created an opportunity. If the border and North Vietnamese tribesmen couldn't come over to Vang Pao's side openly, many were willing in varying degrees to help his forces, if it didn't get them in trouble.

Ethnic groups on both sides of the border had potential for this quasi-recruitment. Most of them were of T'ai stock, distantly related to the Thai and Lao lowlanders, and named after the colors of their women's clothing: Red T'ai, White T'ai, Black T'ai, and so on. At Lair's request, Lawrence also evaluated a proposal from CIA headquarters for employing the Nung, an originally Chinese people who by deliberate intermarriage with T'ais some centuries back created a new hybrid tribe with unique customs.

The Nung were supposed to be good fighters, and several groups of them who had moved out of the mountains to Vientiane and Saigon were willing to go back to the mountains and fight as mercenaries. Lawrence firmly rejected the idea. The Nung were not motivated by the desire to protect their own territories, he pointed out. They were in it for the money. The success of the existing program, Lawrence believed, lay in its grassroots support. Though the United States was paying for the operation, the local people were fighting for their own cause. They were under the tactical command of Vang Pao, who was one of their own. The soldiers and militiamen were all related to the civilians and fought on their behalf. To change this approach by using outside mercenaries near the North Vietnamese border was asking for trouble.

Airpower had no more part in Lawrence's expansion scheme than outside ethnic groups. Up until that point U.S. jets had flown only reconnaissance missions in the far northeast border region, and it seemed unlikely to him that supersonic jets could coordinate air strikes with people still living in the Iron Age. Lawrence didn't even want cargo planes landing near or across the border. It was better, and far more subtle, to build up stockpiles inside Laos with small planes and do the forward transportation by pack animals or humans. With that low-profile, tried-and-true approach, he thought, the expansion might work. Weapons for several thousand men, household goods for several thousand families, and limited amounts of rice were all that were needed.

So Lawrence reasoned, and Lair and Landry concurred, though if anything the men at Udorn were more careful than he was, and reluctant to approve operations far behind enemy lines that were hard to resupply.

The expansion and penetration operations into the border areas of North Vietnam began, in embryonic form, in September and October 1964.

All too soon, however, the rainy season ended, the roads dried out, and the North Vietnamese seasonal offensive got under way.

◆

North Vietnam was shaped like a funnel with a dent in its side. Houa Phan Province of Laos, usually called Sam Neua after its capital city, was that dent. It was lightly populated by a mix of hilltribes and Lao Theung and by lowlanders in pocket-size valleys, and transected by a few dirt roads connecting Hanoi to the Plain of Jars.

Because of that dangerous closeness—its border with North Vietnam was eighty-five miles from downtown Hanoi—Sam Neua had always been on the periphery of Vang Pao's influence, even before the plans for expansion. The CIA had hastily armed and trained some resistance units in Sam Neua during the first burst of expansion, in 1961 and 1962, and then abandoned them when the operation shrank after the Geneva accords. When the Americans came back to Sam Neua in 1963 and 1964 for the second expansion, they were pleasantly surprised to find that many of the units had survived, and that some of them were even tougher, leaner, and more sure of themselves for having been on their own.

These Sam Neua resistance units were not so much guerillas as homegrown partisans, a force arising from the people themselves. The men who held the rifles also planted and harvested the rice. Some wore boots. Others went barefoot or wore rubber thongs. There were Meo ADCs and understrength FAR battalions and village militias of one sort or another. Nobody was fully in charge, but one man exerted more leadership than the rest. He was Lt. Col. Thong Vongrasamy, a lowland Lao who wore his hair to his shoulders and a Buddha amulet around his neck.

Thong had led the escort party for Pop Buell and Dr. Weldon during the 1963 cholera epidemic. He was a rare man, a virile mystic who prayed to Buddha for hours at a time, and who liked nothing better than fighting the North Vietnamese. He had built up an enviable combat record, with night assaults on enemy outposts and daring preemptive strikes on larger enemy forces. Buell and Weldon admired him without reservation. "There is only one other man who is probably more important to my operation: Gen. Van Pow," Buell declared in a letter home. Weldon concurred. "He had a quiet, pleasant manner," the doctor recalled later of Thong. "But in his presence you knew you were around an unusual man. It was that thing called charisma. You know it when you're in its presence. Sometimes you see it by the way the locals react."

Even Tony Poe, a hard man to please, liked Thong. "The guy was good. No doubt about it," said Poe. "But then he wasn't thinking about how much money he could make, like the rest of them fuckin' Lao bastards."

Thong had graduated from the Royal Lao Army's officers' training school, where he got to know a thin sprinkling of other Lao who were more interested in military professionalism than using high rank as an avenue to wealth. He went to the United States for advanced military training but didn't like America much. He told Weldon later that in all his months in the States not once had anybody invited him into their home. He said this calmly and without rancor. Weldon was impressed. Here was one Lao who neither fawned on Americans nor tried to steal them blind. If Thong accepted American help it was for the sake of his own country's defense.

Toward the end of 1964 and the beginning of 1965, as the clear, cool weather of the dry season got under way, roadwatch teams and reconnaissance planes all reported large convoys of North Vietnamese trucks driving into Sam Neua again. This time the North Vietnamese appeared to be nearly doubling the size of their force in Laos, from five to six thousand at the end of the 1964 rainy season to nine to eleven thousand in January 1965. In one of the first bombing raids in northern Laos, U.S. jets hit the same stretch of Route 7 that the combined CIA-Paru-Meo operation had blown up with cratering charges a year-and-a-half before, to try to slow the influx. But the jets were not available on a regular basis. Tony Poe was sent up to Sam Neua to find out what was going on and to help Thong organize the resistance on the ground.

About seven North Vietnamese battalions, or 3,500 to 4,000 men, poured out of Sam Neua city, looking for Meo and royalist forces to attack. Though they preferred traveling by truck, the Vietnamese started walking at the roads' end and made steady progress over the rugged terrain. They attacked Thong's battalion and forced him to retreat up a ridgeline. Heavily outnumbered, Thong retreated south and then west, fighting and backing up in good order and staying to the heights to maximize his terrain advantage. Thong radioed Poe, who started directing heavy 4.2-inch mortar fire over Thong's position at the enemy.

At the time Poe was at Site 86, the village of Hong Nong, where Buell and Weldon had discovered the cholera epidemic. The village lay athwart a ridge between the large, spectacular karst of Phou Pha Thi to the west and Sam Neua city to the east. His command post was barricaded and connected to a system of trenches. It looked down over the sloping dirt runway and across a valley to other mountains with the light-colored, wedge-shaped areas indicating Meo slash-and-burn cultivation. Poe had with him a five-man Paru team, whose leader spoke broken English. The rest of his soldiers were all Meo.

A portion of the enemy force chasing Thong broke off to go after Poe's 4.2-inch mortar, which was manned by a particularly capable Thai Paru. As the North Vietnamese came closer over the rough terrain and up the ridge, Poe ordered the other Thais and the Meo to fire their smaller, more portable 81mm and 60mm mortars and a tripod-mounted 75mm recoilless rifle, too.

Poe was under the standard orders not to get involved with the fighting, but as he saw it, if Udorn wanted him to get intelligence information he would have to get close to the action, and if he got close to the action he was not going to run away.

Various outposts called in to say they were under fire. Through an interpreter Poe told them to get their women and children out and then cover them with a slow retreat along the ridgeline toward him; the women and children would be okay if they got out ahead and then scattered westward toward Phou Pha Thi, the Meo stronghold and refuge.

There was sporadic firing through the night and then around noon on January 20, 1965—the day of Lyndon Johnson's inauguration as elected president—the first North Vietnamese came into sight. They were firing and advancing in twos and threes along the edges of the strip, moving in leapfrog fashion. One man got up and ran while the other fired in support, and vice versa.

Poe put a Meo soldier in position and set the man's rifle sights for two or three hundred meters. There was no wind, so no lateral adjustments were needed. While the first Meo shot, he set up a second and third and fourth, lining them behind the barricade. The tribesmen weren't hitting anything, though. They had forgotten everything they had learned about correcting for distance by adjusting the sights. Poe sat each man down again and showed him how to set the sights, explaining through hand motions.

The nearest North Vietnamese were two hundred meters away when Poe began firing at them himself with his M-1 carbine. He waited until the North Vietnamese jumped up, or else put their gun butts on the ground to help themselves up, and then he gave them a lead and aimed for their heads. He fired, aimed again, changed ammunition clips, aimed, fired. When no more North Vietnamese jumped up he figured he had killed them all. Paru looking through binoculars counted seventeen bodies on the strip. The firing around them had quieted down, although on Thong's side the firing was still heavy.

Poe decided to search the bodies, to see whether they were carrying papers, maps, and battle plans. Poe, the *chao muong* and his deputy, the Thai team leader, and some bodyguards walked down the slope in single file with intervals between them. They walked parallel to the edge of the landing strip but downhill for a little extra protection. They had no intention of walking down the middle of the landing field and presenting an easy target.

When the North Vietnamese bodies were about a hundred meters ahead and to their left, Poe's party started to cross to the other side of the strip. That was when three or four other enemy soldiers hiding in the brush opened fire.

The first bullet tore into Poe's hip. He jerked in reflex, flipping around and landing in the dirt. His legs were numb and he tried to shake them. He was lying on the ground feeling nothing in his legs when he heard the Thai team leader behind him yelling, "Tony, help me."

Ignoring the Paru, Poe took the hand grenades from his harness. He laid them on the ground neatly in a row. By then he saw the enemy soldiers rising up from the other side of the strip and further downhill. There were three of them, and they were carrying Chinese-made weapons that looked like Thompson submachine guns, with ammunition drums and perforated barrels for cooling. The soldiers all had tiger suits on, camouflage suits. He had never heard of Vietnamese with tiger suits before.

He concentrated on getting ready. Lining up the grenades, checking his rifle. When they got close enough he pulled the pin and let the spoon fly on the first of his grenades. He counted to three and lobbed the grenade in an arc. Then he pulled the pin of the next one. After he threw three or four nothing moved on the runway. He supposed he had gotten them all.

He looked around and saw the Thai team leader lying down in the bushes, dead. Everyone was dead but him. There was a big hole in his hip with bone showing and a lot of blood.

He shrugged off his pack and threw away his binoculars, not wanting the weight. He put his floppy marine campaign hat back on his balding head. Using his M-1 for a walking stick he hobbled back up to the command post. He told the Meo and the surviving Paru there to go get the bodies of their people, and some of them went down on the airstrip.

While a Meo medic administered first aid, he gave instructions to the remaining soldiers in the command post, whose leaders had all been killed.

Poe told them to maintain contact with Thong on the radio and to do whatever Thong said because he had the experience. He had trouble making them understand because the Thai team leader had been the best interpreter, and the one Meo who spoke broken English was too scared to pay attention.

Poe called Thong on the radio again. Thong was withdrawing toward Pha Thi, and Poe told him to talk to the Meo and try to make them understand that they had to make an orderly withdrawal, too. Thong talked to them in Lao, and then Poe tried again in pidgin Lao and Meo. The best thing, said Poe, was to get all the people who weren't needed for fighting and send them back to join Thong. But if they wanted to stay, they should make sure the people nearest to the enemy got out first, and then backed up in good order.

Bullets were still coming in from the east, fired at long range and making a click as they passed through the thatch, almost expended. There weren't many bullet wounds, but a lot of people had been hit in the face and shoulders by mortar shell fragments. Big wounds. Faces ripped open and teeth hanging out. Half the face blown away. They were taking a lot of fire, and Poe was wondering whether he could talk a chopper into coming down there, or whether he should even try. He didn't like asking a chopper to come under fire unless it was absolutely necessary.

He got on the radio and called a pilot flying far overhead. Poe said he was wounded but walking out and gave the pilot the location.

It was eight kilometers to the spot where a chopper could land safely. Down the hill, through a creek and then up a hill, almost due west toward Phou Pha Thi. Over a big karst ridge. He walked with the M-1 as a cane. He couldn't make it up the last hill, so the Meo put him on a poncho and carried him up from a dry creek bed. Three Thais passed him there, heading for the chopper. The other surviving Paru had stayed back at the command post, faithfully manning the big 4.2-inch mortar.

The three Thais didn't say anything to Poe, who started cursing them and told them to get back and join Thong. They told him they didn't understand, and kept on walking.

When Poe made it up the hill the chopper had just landed. It was waiting for him, the blades still turning. Inside were the pilot, a mechanic, and the only passenger, Dr. Weldon.

The three Thais tried to climb in the chopper. Poe grabbed his pistol and told them that the chopper was for the wounded and that they should go find Colonel Thong. Poe waved his pistol and told Weldon that if the Thais got on the chopper he was getting off. They were trying to desert. The chopper was going back to Hong Nong for the wounded and there wasn't room for anyone else.

The chopper pilot, Bob Nunez, said the elevation was too high to take on a bunch of passengers. Poe told him he had already promised the Meo. Nunez said it would burn out the motor and Poe told him to do it anyway.

The helicopter took off with Poe inside and without the Thais. The paramilitary officer lay on the floor, pale and with his mouth open like a dead fish and seemingly unconscious. Weldon began working on the hip wound when Poe grabbed him and pulled him down and began talking gibberish. Ultimately Poe was able to make the doctor understand that he knew where they were and that they were headed in the wrong direction.

The door of the chopper was open. Weldon dragged Poe over to where he could see, with his head at the edge, and Poe began pointing to the doctor to show him where the pilot should go, first this way and then that, back to Hong Nong on a route to minimize exposure to enemy fire. The chopper landed near the command post. There were thirteen wounded Meo in bad shape, but stoic, asking for cigarettes.

The chopper flew the wounded southwest to the provincial military headquarters, Hua Moung, where they were transferred to a fixed-wing plane and flown out for medical treatment. Weldon came along to supervise. He put Poe in a new U.S. hospital at Korat air base in Thailand, and saw his friend and patient being wheeled off in a gurney toward the surgical ward to have the fragments of bone picked out and the remnants of his lower digestive tract patched up.

Weldon had already headed back to the Korat airstrip in a military jeep when the driver got a radio message that Poe wanted him back at the hospital. Weldon went back. Tony began blabbering about wanting his fatigue trousers. Weldon told him to calm down, nobody was going to steal his pants. Poe whispered that there was something in his pockets. Eventually somebody produced the bloody, torn fatigues. In one of the pockets was a metal pin for connecting a 75mm recoilless rifle to its tripod. Poe whispered to Weldon, "You take this and give it to Vint. Be sure you give it to him. They can get that recoilless rifle running again."

When Poe was recuperating in the hospital, Pat Landry came in from Udorn to see him. Landry showed him a North Vietnamese newspaper with an article claiming that the heroic Pathet Lao had killed an American adviser. "You're dead," said Landry. Poe replied, "Oh yeah? That's good."

For Lair and Landry, and for other Americans of the inner circle, concern for Poe's health and admiration for his bravery were mixed with irritation. Poe had been told many times to stay out of combat. He had disobeyed and paid the price. But to the pilots and some of Poe's Laotian admirers, it had been Tony's finest hour.

Poe had indeed forced the helicopter pilot into a medical evacuation that would not have been made otherwise, burning out the helicopter motor in the process. He had put the Meo's concerns ahead of his own. He had kept to the code he had learned from the marines.

Poe was pleased at the outcome. He said later, "The story spread all over that these white bastards actually liked the Meo. That we're helping them fight the enemy. And that's the difference between being successful with the indigenous people and being a failure. You can be the biggest prick in the world, as long as you take care of your people."

# The Ambassador

Vang Pao was depressed.

It was nine days after Tony Poe had been shot, not that the wounded American had anything to do with his mood. Hundreds, perhaps thousands of his own people had been killed or wounded in northeast Laos since he had allied himself with the CIA. In Vang Pao's house, nobody was shedding tears for the bullying paramilitary officer.

Greater matters absorbed Vang Pao. He had been promoted again, from one star to two stars, brigadier to major general, and put in charge of Laos's Second Military Region, made up of Xieng Khouang and Sam Neua Provinces. He was now in command of both the tribal irregulars, who were funded and supplied by the CIA, and the lowland armed forces in the northeast, who were funded and supplied by Vientiane. His Second Military Region was the most important of any in the country in the defense against the communists.

That's what depressed him. He had no illusions. He knew he was being used.

The lowland generals in Vientiane, who controlled the civilian government and stole from it and kept it weak, knew that he was close to the Americans. They consulted, wooed, and manipulated him for that reason alone.

The royalist commander in chief, Gen. Ouane Rattikone, an obese, clever man from a powerful family, had proposed that Vang Pao become regional commander in the northeast. Ouane wanted Vang Pao's political support.

Vang Pao went to Luang Prabang, the old royal capital, for a meeting with the other generals. There he detected signs of another coup in the making. It was like minor tremors before a major earthquake—sharp glances exchanged across a conference table, petty arguments allowed to fester, an atmosphere of devious plans left undisclosed.

Vang Pao saw the king again, and the weak, gracious old man honored him by personally bestowing the promotion and the second star. The king made known his growing displeasure with all the quarreling, scheming Vientiane factions, who were more interested in making their fortunes than they were in fighting a war. Vang Pao was glad to find that he and the king thought alike, and sorry that neither of them could change the generals' behavior.

The king himself was obligated to General Ouane, who had the royal opium concession for Luang Prabang Province, the king's ancestral strong-hold. General Ouane got a piece of all the opium traffic moving through northwestern Laos from across the Golden Triangle in Burma. The king got a piece of Ouane's piece, and this helped keep the frayed-at-the-cuffs royal household solvent. But Ouane's loyalty was to himself. His name means "fat," and his greediness far outweighed his patriotic instincts.

And as for Ouane's immediate boss—the defense minister, Gen. Phoumi Nosavan—Vang Pao felt it was impractical to support him any longer. Phoumi had followed that familiar career parabola of the Asian strongman. He had risen through charm, ability, and attachment to mentors. At the top, he had turned his attention to his business interests, his casinos and brothels, his self-assigned monopolies on imports of gold and liquor. His own corruption as well as that of his friends and cronies aroused envy and resentment, and now he was on the way down. Phoumi's brother, the head of Laotian customs, put most of the money he collected in his pocket in-stead of in the national treasury, and this was a fortune that the other pow-erful families wanted to steal for themselves.

So Phoumi's time was running out. Some sort of coup was in the offing, either by him or against him, whoever got organized first. Whatever it was, Vang Pao wanted nothing to do with it. The best outcome, he told Vint Lawrence after returning to Long Tieng, would be if the violence grew widespread and the most corrupt royalist leaders killed one another off.

Vang Pao often complained that the Pathet Lao had better leaders than the royalists. Some of the North Vietnamese discipline and drive had rubbed off on the Pathet Lao; either that or the North Vietnamese kept the Pathet Lao leaders in line. But either way, the lowland leaders looked terrible in comparison. They never endured hardships, said Vang Pao. They were too busy with their money-making schemes to fight a proper war. From Prime Minister Souvanna Phouma on down, every subordinate kept tabs on his boss's sleazy dealings, partly out of jealousy, partly in hopes of taking over the business himself. Running opium, selling truck parts and weapons to Thailand, engaging in petty scams of one kind or another—that was the royalist government in Vientiane. Nobody was loyal. That plus the lowlanders' contempt for the hilltribes put Vang Pao in despair.

What it all added up to, Vang Pao wearily told Lawrence, was that he was fighting a war on two fronts. The lowland Lao did not trust him. They feared him. They sought to undermine him. Yet at the same time they wanted him to be their hunting dog against the Pathet Lao and North Vietnamese. His Military Region II was home to the heaviest fighting, and except for a few outstanding lowlanders like Thong his tribe was carrying the burden. His people were getting killed and wounded by the communists. And for what?

All that kept his people in the war, Vang Pao emphasized to Lawrence, was a balance. While some suffered, others held on, preserving their traditional way of life on the mountaintops. And still others were not only holding on but improving themselves through education and through opportunities the Americans created. For his people to stay in the war, Vang Pao said, the balance had to be maintained. The benefits had to at least equal the costs.

◆

That balance had been upset by the North Vietnamese dry season offensive in Sam Neua, in January 1965, which was still under way. After Poe was wounded at Hong Nong, Colonel Thong had held on as best he could. He used brilliant tactics of maneuver and delay, but he was heavily outnumbered. He slowed the enemy and bought time for civilians to escape. Nothing more was possible. He could not stop the North Vietnamese by himself.

Thong and Vang Pao had pleaded for planes to come the way farmers in a drought pray for rain. They had called for T-28s on the radio. They had called for jets. The skies were empty. Nothing came.

Seven thousand frightened and traumatized Meo poured out of their villages, heading for safety. Vang Pao flew up to see the mass of new refugees, and the sight of babies crying of hunger, of women freshly widowed, had shaken him to the core.

He had had what Westerners might call an epiphany, a flash of realization.

In that moment he doubted that what his people had been through, and would go through before the war was over, was worth it. The balance was gone, and he felt powerless to correct it.

Returning to Long Tieng on January 29, 1965, Vang Pao called Lawrence and two of his top tribal assistants, Ly Tou Pao and Tou Lu Moua, to his office. He began by praising all the Americans had done and saying that his feelings were not affected either by the personal friendships formed or by the lack of air support. He just wondered where it was all leading.

Vint Lawrence said nothing. He felt no reply would be adequate. Vang Pao went on talking, exhausted and overwrought.

Vang Pao recited the names of his better leaders who had been killed in four years of fighting. There were too few capable survivors, he said, to replace them. Rather than see his people leaderless and aimless, it might be best for him to leave, or die. Maybe he should resign from the army. He had served his country well and perhaps he should leave while things were neither too good nor too bad.

He went on for an hour. He was concerned for his people, whom he saw slowly being killed off in an unending fight. He felt responsible for getting them into this war, and when he could not get them what they needed to resist effectively he wondered what he was doing. Maybe it was time to cross the Mekong to Sayaboury. Maybe it was time for him to take a trip abroad.

Lawrence knew Vang Pao well enough not to try to reason with him when he was in the grip of his emotions. Lawrence asked him only to wait a few days before taking any action. Vang Pao promised to do that.

Afterwards Vang Pao's worried aides agreed with Lawrence that this was the blackest mood, the deepest depression, they had ever seen him in.

The following day—which happened to be the day before the coup attempt—Vint Lawrence made preliminary inquiries into sending Vang Pao to France to visit two of his sons who were in school there, and to see the United States.

But already Vang Pao was a little more relaxed, more his normal self.

◆

The U.S. government had a new man in Vientiane. He was a triple-threat player—diplomat, bureaucrat, and field marshal, all rolled into one.

Ambassador William H. Sullivan quickly took control of his domain. Each weekday morning at nine o'clock he held his daily operations meeting with his Country Team—the chiefs of the CIA and USAID, the military attachés, and the lesser barons of the bureaucracy. There was no detail too small for him to inquire about, from the number of bags of rice in an airdrop to obscure appointments far out in the countryside. He demanded to know what was going on, and he required his staff to tell one another about their plans. He forced them to avoid problems before they arose. By this strong hands-on management he maintained close control over the U.S. mission in Laos, and by extension most of the country as well.

His embassy had excellent communications equipment. When the coup of January 31, 1965 began, with the city's telephone system going out, and

the government radio broadcasting reports of more and more officials joining the coup-makers, Sullivan used a backup walkie-talkie system to contact Americans and other Westerners throughout the city.

He learned that enthusiasm for the coup was minimal, and that the
largest single contingent of pro-coup soldiers, about twenty individuals,
was gathered in the government radio station, led by a right-wing colonel
who had recently returned from a psychological warfare training course in
the United States. Though he favored the right-wing defense minister,
Phoumi Nosavan, the colonel had pretty much decided to mount the coup
on his own, to forestall the coups of other factions. At preplanned intervals, the colonel's announcer read fabricated reports of support from all
segments of society.

The colonel didn't realize that the radio transmitting tower was some
distance away from the studio, and that it was unguarded. Sullivan quickly
ascertained that an Australian civilian was in charge of its maintenance.
The Australian had been drinking heavily that night, but he sobered up after a few cups of black coffee in the U.S. embassy and agreed to do what
Sullivan asked. He went off in the dark in a jeep with rubber gloves and a
pair of bolt cutters, and fifteen minutes later the radio station went off the
air. In the broadcast studio, the rebel colonel tapped the microphones,
flicked switches off and on, and pounded his fists on the consoles, trying
to find the magic trick that would get his announcements back on the air.

The next morning, with suave aplomb, Sullivan personally brought the
pro-Phoumi colonel in to meet the leader of the anti-Phoumi faction, the
deputy commander in chief, who was a member of another powerful and
scheming Vientiane family. The two soldiers conferred privately and then
emerged smiling, thanking the Americans and exchanging the Buddhist
palms-together *wai* gestures all around. The misunderstandings were
solved. The colonel would be reassigned. There would be no reprisals. The
coup attempt was over.

Still, four months of intermittent civil war followed, like a series of land-
slides triggered by the coup's earthquake. The dozen or so extended families making up the Lao elite were jostling for power and influence, and
they used the confusion to settle scores. Phoumi was forced into exile in
Thailand, never to return. The army fought the national police, royalists
fighting royalists. Some of the best lowland officers in the country got
caught up in the factional infighting that followed, and they were impris-
oned or murdered.

Most of the victims were friends of Colonel Thong's. When the fighting
was over, soldiers of the victorious faction were ordered to arrest Thong's
mentor, Gen. Khamkhong Buddavong, in his barracks in the town of Paksane. The soldiers were afraid to make the arrest. An American from the

U.S. Army attaché's office went to see General Khamkhong and offered to accompany him abroad for a few weeks until things calmed down. The general agreed and climbed into the American's plane, which instead of flying out of the country as promised flew to Vientiane, where he was arrested. "It was the slimiest thing I've ever seen the U.S. do," said Dr. Weldon, who knew both the general and the embassy circle well.

There were other betrayals as well, and it is hard to imagine how Sullivan could not have known about them in advance, considering his detailed knowledge of events and his control over Americans serving in the kingdom. A Colonel Karpkeo of General Khamkhong's staff went into hiding in the countryside around Paksane. A young USAID field man who knew where Karpkeo was reported it to his superiors as confidential information. Shortly afterwards, Karpkeo was captured by Vientiane troops and murdered under the pretext that he had attempted escape. Another colonel, Thong's closest colleague from Sam Neua, went on the lam to avoid a similar fate, and stayed in the bush for a year.

Whatever Sullivan and his staff did or didn't do in luring Khamkhong to Vientiane, and in giving the royalist command the information that led to Karpkeo's murder, has never been clear. But even in the sordid aftermath of the coup Sullivan's press coverage was excellent. He charmed reporters in Laos, even as he limited their opportunities to cover the war. His blue eyes held the appearance of candor, whether he was speaking the truth or not. He had powerful friends in Washington and in Saigon, too. There were no revelations about him behind his back.

Sullivan's assignment in Laos was pure Wonderland: to wage a war while appearing to abide by the Geneva accords for Laos's peace and neutrality. He arrived knowing that the U.S. was planning a bombing campaign against North Vietnam called Rolling Thunder. After only three weeks in Vientiane, even before Rolling Thunder began, Sullivan set up his own secret bombing programs for Laos, called Barrel Roll in the north and Steel Tiger in the south. It was dirty, bare-knuckle warfare, but he had no regrets. The North Vietnamese were playing dirty, too.

The Soviets, who knew what the Americans were doing, kept quiet about the bombing. The Soviets realized that it cost them less to send antiaircraft guns and other military aid to the North Vietnamese and Pathet Lao than it cost the Americans to send jets; therefore, the Soviets cannily pretended to believe in Wonderland, too. Once, Sullivan attended a diplomatic party with the Soviet ambassador, Boris Kirnassovsky. A U.S. Air Force tanker plane appeared high overhead, trailing booms from which delta-winged jet fighters thirstily sucked fuel, like tiny brood jets nursing from their dam. "Are those your planes overhead?" asked the Soviet ambassador, who knew perfectly well that they were. "What planes, Boris?"

said Sullivan. "I don't see any planes." And the Soviet ambassador didn't press the point.

Laos was Sullivan's war now; and no matter how much it grew, he worked hard to keep it semisecret, behind the fig leaf of the Geneva accords. He wanted to keep the war quiet for the sake of Souvanna Phouma, the Americans, and even the Soviets. All found it easier to pretend to respect Laotian neutrality than to change their positions and gear up for full-scale war. That way everybody kept their costs down, while the main contest was escalating next door in Vietnam. Sullivan also wanted to keep Geneva as a framework for future political settlements in case the communists were beaten in South Vietnam. A return to true neutrality in Laos would be possible then, he maintained.

But Sullivan also liked holding on to the vestiges of Geneva for personal reasons. He had helped negotiate the Geneva accords himself; it was a milestone of his career. And because the accords excluded outside military forces from Laos, it helped him control his turf.

Sullivan was passionate about keeping the regular U.S. military ground forces out of the kingdom. Soon after he arrived in Laos he cabled Washington with an idea he credited to a former chairman of the Joint Chiefs of Staff, Gen. Lyman Lemnitzer. To stop the traffic on the Ho Chi Minh Trail, he wrote, why not consider a conventional invasion of North Vietnam? If the troops landed near the coastal city of Vinh, they would only have to capture a forty-mile strip to the west to cut the country in two. This was the narrow neck of the North Vietnamese funnel, north of the mountain passes that led into the Laos panhandle. Karst cliffs on the western side of this forty-mile strip would keep Hanoi's troops from going around the Americans and attacking from the rear or the side.

This cable was vintage Sullivan. He created cover for himself by insisting that the plan came from a military man and, in fact, the plan made sense. It *was* easier to block supplies from leaving North Vietnam in the first place than it was to stop them along thousands of miles of Laotian jungle trails. Less obviously, though, the idea served Sullivan himself. Such a U.S. invading force would stay in North Vietnam, without having to set foot in Laos, on Sullivan's turf. People who worked in the embassy in Vientiane found that par for the course. Sullivan was full of ideas that sounded great at first because he was so convincing, and because he was smarter than anyone else around. But the solutions he proposed always benefited him and always came at somebody else's expense.

Sullivan permitted limited, covert, U.S. Army and Marine reconnaissance missions and raids on the Ho Chi Minh Trail area in southeast Laos. He was under White House orders to do so. But the orders went no further and there he drew the line. He did not let the U.S. military station regular American ground troops in Laos or base military planes in the kingdom, either. The planes had to take off from Thailand or South Vietnam or from carriers at sea.

Sullivan's biggest headache was controlling the secret U.S. air strikes. In the early months of 1965, navy jets had hit the wrong target three days in a row. In another incident a jet missed its target by twenty miles and bombed a village where Sullivan had been just the day before on a goodwill visit. He found it embarrassing to have to send some young USAID field guy in there to apologize and hand out money for the loss of innocent lives.

Sullivan had the authority to approve or disapprove the military's preplanned bombing targets. He also could request that targets be hit. But the air force and navy, who owned the planes, could decide whether or not to send them, and the services did not want to play by Sullivan's rules. As a CIA case officer in southern Laos said of the military, "They bombed a lot of friendly villages. We screamed and yelled a lot, and they promised it would never happen again; and then it would happen again the next week."

The war was changing. Against this backdrop of a growing air campaign in Laos, the arrival of the brilliant, imperious ambassador in Vientiane, and the growth of the Vietnam War next door, Bill Lair's role would have to change, too.

# Vietnam

Lair had been thinking about Vietnam. The air war was growing, retaliatory bombing of North Vietnam had begun, and there were more and more interagency meetings to discuss what his tribal forces might do, or what the U.S. military might do, about stopping the traffic on the Ho Chi Minh Trail. He saw that as the Americans were getting more and more involved in the defense of South Vietnam, the South Vietnamese themselves were becoming less so. And that, he believed, was a serious mistake.

His thoughts always went back to a personal experience—to a training the Paru held in the late 1950s, at Hua Hin, Thailand, for a group of some forty South Vietnamese. The trainees had been handpicked by their national leader, Ngo Dinh Diem, who in turn was advised by the CIA. The training had been arranged at higher Agency levels, the protégés of one CIA station helping the protégés of another.

Though they had no military backgrounds, the forty South Vietnamese were supposed to become a sort of personal security force for Diem. Before the training they had all worked in offices in Saigon. They arrived looking, Lair recalled, like little white worms that had never seen the sun. But to everyone's surprise, the Vietnamese learned quickly, and got sunburned and grew muscular with exercise. They turned into soldiers, keen and smart and proficient. They were one of the best groups the Paru had ever trained.

They went back to their country, and that was the last Lair heard of them. But he had always wondered why it wouldn't be possible to do large-scale trainings of South Vietnamese that worked. He believed they would have worked if afterwards the Vietnamese had been left in charge, with no long-nosed Americans or Europeans for them to grow dependent upon.

By backstopping the Vietnamese, by taking over for them, the Americans created a cycle of passivity that made it impossible for the Vietnamese leaders to get the most out of their own countrymen. The Americans thought the locals couldn't do anything right, and before long that became a self-fulfilling prophecy.

Corruption was another part of the problem. Lair understood the miasma of graft and intrigue that kept even the best soldiers from being used in South Vietnam. He had seen plenty of it himself in Thailand and Laos: soldiers extorting chickens at checkpoints, officers buying their promotions, top officials committing the very sorts of crimes that they were supposed to protect their nation against. But that was Asia. Realistically, you could not stamp out those habits, but if you spoke the local language and you were prepared to work quietly with the leaders for ten to twenty years you could reduce the problems' scale. And he did not see that his own government had done that successfully.

He did not personally know that small group of CIA men who had guided the Diem regime and launched the early and futile sabotage raids and dirty tricks against the North Vietnamese—the Edwin Lansdales, the Lucien Coneins. They moved in different crowds. Saigon was a central, important posting and he had been laboring for years in happy obscurity in the far boondocks. But he worked for the same bosses, Desmond FitzGerald and Bill Colby; and he had followed the career of Ngo Dinh Diem from the time the Americans latched on to him to Diem's assassination in late 1963. The killing of Diem, he believed, had been the turning point, where a bad situation grew worse. And he knew that Americans indirectly had killed Diem, by telling Diem's rivals that he had become an obstruction, and then sitting back passively as events took their course.

Diem's successors had even less grassroots support than Diem himself. And since the new leaders were paralyzed and indecisive and could seem to do nothing themselves—like the lowland Lao generals—the Americans started taking over the war against the communist insurgents in South Vietnam. They did it the American way, without knowing or caring much what the local people wanted.

To Lair, there were many "Vietnams." It was the place on the other side of the Annamite Mountains where people didn't live in houses up on stilts the way the Thais and Lao did. The Vietnamese lived on the ground and wore conical hats and practiced a different form of Buddhism, the Greater Wheel, with ornate temples and a greater reliance on monks.

It was the name for a war, Vietnam; and for a style of conflict that even then, in early 1965, was not driven by field imperatives but by the political requirements of men in suits halfway around the world, and was commanded by generals who had never waded through muddy rice paddies. It was a place, if you were an American field man, where you were always too late to define the terms, and where you got enmeshed in something you hadn't bargained for.

But Lair was as capable of self-delusion as the next man, and in spite of growing evidence to the contrary he believed the Laos war theater was separate from Vietnam. If the Americans wanted to bomb North Vietnam, or shuffle governments like so many decks of cards in South Vietnam, well, that's what they were going to do. They could even send their jets into Laos. Whatever. They didn't really affect his ground operations.

Or so he thought until he saw the cable traffic of March 8, 1965. Two battalions of U.S. Marines had landed at Danang, South Vietnam, to protect the airfield there—the first American ground combat troops. With a sinking feeling, Lair wondered whether more ground troops would follow. It was, he felt, a terrible mistake. And one from which Laos could not stay immune.

He sat and thought in his office.

An old Thai and Lao proverb came to mind: "You cannot kill a snake by beating it on the tail."

If Americans were going to use ground troops, Lair believed, they should invade Hanoi massively and get it over with. That was the best use of conventional American military power. Hit the brain, not the tail.

Or else don't fight the snake at all. Let the South Vietnamese fight their own war.

Just walk away. Let the Asians settle their quarrels themselves. And keep the U.S. out of it.

◆

Rolling Thunder, the sustained program to bomb North Vietnam, got under way in March 1965. Analysts in the U.S. military and in the CIA peered through magnifying glasses at aerial photographs, assessing the bomb damage, a straightforward task. Far more interesting to the analysts, though harder for them to ascertain, were the secondary reactions of Hanoi's regime: Now that North Vietnam was under bombing pressure, would it change strategies? How would it continue to fight the war? The way Hanoi moved men and matériel to the south would help signal its long-term intentions.

The intelligence analysts knew that the Ho Chi Minh Trail was a shifting, growing, evolving network of footpaths and existing Laotian roads, with traffic patterns that shifted, too. They also knew that the Trail was organized into segments of thirty to forty kilometers in length, connected by way stations, where the porters and truck drivers unloaded their cargo for pickup by the next batch of porters or truck drivers. Each segment team was responsible for carrying cargoes over the same stretch, time after time. The motorized traffic segments were still rare at that time and did not necessarily connect to other motorized segments. The few trucks photographed on open roads by airplanes kept traveling the same stretches over and over, which meant they were counted many times by the American side. From those dubious truck counts, it was impossible to extrapolate valid projections of the volume of supplies and men coming down the Trail. There were just too many unknown factors.

Rivalries among the American services magnified the uncertainty about the Trail's importance. Away from the field, especially in Washington, each service had institutional incentives to tailor information to its own benefit. The U.S. Navy stood to gain by reporting that most North Vietnamese supplies came to South Vietnam via boats. If it did, the navy might get larger appropriations from Congress. The air force had an incentive to report that most supplies came by land and to claim that jets were best at stopping these supplies. CIA headquarters stood to gain from downplaying the importance of the Ho Chi Minh Trail, the better to keep the U.S. military from intruding onto its Laotian turf. Politics intruded, as it often did, on the intelligence business.

General William Westmoreland, the overall U.S. commander in South Vietnam, put new pressure on the air force, with its jet reconnaissance planes, and the CIA, with its ground teams, to clear up the matter of North Vietnamese activities in south Laos. The CIA put the pressure on the Vientiane station chief, a new man named Douglas Blaufarb. Blaufarb put the pressure on Lair.

At Udorn, in his nondescript office by the airstrip, Lair sat and thought at his desk. He lit a cigar and puffed on it awhile. He reached for his "worry" pile and leafed through the papers until he got to the most recent Lao Theung intelligence reports. They mentioned peculiar sightings of North Vietnamese trucks in the mountains east and a little north of the town of Savannakhet, where there were no known roads. Nobody had believed these reports at first. Lair hadn't either. The Lao Theung were notorious for mixing facts with imagined sightings of spirits, or *phi*.

Lair approached a big, tall Air America special-operations pilot named Jim Rhyne. He asked Rhyne to fly over the coordinates the Lao Theung ground team had supplied and see what he could find.

From Udorn, Rhyne took off in a Helio and flew east of the Mekong toward the Annamite range. He took along his personal camera, a compact, half-frame 35mm model of a type then popular with tourists. The camera produced seventy-two half-size images per roll instead of thirty-six, which saved on film and money.

When Rhyne got to the right part of the forested mountains, about thirty to forty miles south of the Mu Gia Pass, he put on flaps and slats, slowed the Helio to eighty knots, and descended to treetop level. He got ready to hold his camera out the window with his left hand. Peering down through the forest canopy he saw bulldozer tracks and nearby some bamboo trellises with vines tied to them for camouflage. Whatever the North Vietnamese were up to, they were going to a lot of trouble to hide. He put his camera out the window and snapped as many frames as he could manage. He made only one pass, knowing that he would be a target of ground fire if he returned. He banked his plane, added throttle, climbed and headed back toward Udorn.

When Rhyne landed, he brought the film to an air force photo reconnaissance laboratory that had set up shop on the other side of the runway in preparation for a larger American buildup at the base. The darkroom technicians botched the first set of prints and he had to bring them back and explain he wanted a full-size image made from each half-size negative. The second time the techs got everything right and Rhyne brought the pictures to Lair, who took one look at them and said he wanted a thousand prints right away. Rhyne went back to the photo lab with a couple of cases of beer for the techs, who made the prints overnight.

Rhyne's amateur half-frame photographs were the U.S. government's first hard evidence of camouflaged road construction on the Ho Chi Minh Trail. They confirmed that the North Vietnamese were using heavy equipment to upgrade the Trail for truck traffic, in spite of the bombing of the north, and showed that they were trying to conceal their road-building from American planes by a primitive but effective method.

In the short term, the pictures were a victory of technique for the CIA in its rivalry with the military intelligence agencies. Ground reports from tribals and amateur photography from a slow, low-flying plane had accomplished what supersonic jets and high technology couldn't.

"We thought it was pretty sensational," Douglas Blaufarb said later. "I remember showing it to General Westmoreland at a meeting. His jaw dropped, as I recall."

In the longer term, the discovery of upgraded road-building on the Trail was sobering news for the South Vietnamese, for the royalist Laotians, and for the Americans.

The lowland Lao generals made clear that they had no intention of fighting for the Trail themselves. They preferred to stay at lower elevations, in the Mekong valley where ethnic Lao lived. Their prime minister, Souvanna Phouma, didn't want the Americans or the South Vietnamese to fight the North Vietnamese in Laos either, at least in any significant number. He was holding on to the last shreds of the Geneva accords, hoping to keep any more foreign troops out than were already there.

There were only a couple of ways to tackle the problem, and one of them was airpower. Shortly after Rhyne's flight, another Air America plane flew to the same coordinates and dropped some road nails for puncturing tires. Informed of this tactic, Royal Lao Air Force T-28s flew out there the next day to hunt for easy truck kills. Sure enough, the Lao pilots found some stranded trucks and strafed them. But North Vietnamese gunners were waiting and shot one of the T-28s down. The North Vietnamese were matching the royalist countermeasures with countermeasures of their own. A pattern had been set, the two sides taking turns at upping the ante.

Another option was using Laotian hilltribes from other regions to try to stop the Trail. Bill Lair got called into a meeting with the U.S. military in South Vietnam and asked what he could do.

Lair replied that he couldn't do much. His best tribal fighting force, the Meo, wanted to protect their own territory, farther to the north. The Meo wouldn't come that far down in the panhandle. His Lao Theung teams were in the right area, but there weren't many of them, and they weren't fighters. They were good for reconnaissance, and not much more.

◆

Without publicity, U.S. Air Force jets had begun to arrive at five big airstrips in Thailand—Udorn Thani, Korat, Takli, Nakhorn Phanom, and Ubon Ratchathani—built by the Strategic Air Command in the 1950s. Thailand was a secure rear area, without much threat of enemy attacks. Supersonic jets could take off from there and reach targets in Laos or in North or South Vietnam within minutes.

The previous ambassador to Laos, Leonard Unger, had given Bill Lair permission to call up planes and direct air strikes in Laos, in emergencies. Lair, however, had never used that power until May 20, 1965.

On that day, Ernest Brace, a pilot for Bird & Sons contract cargo airline, flew his propellor plane to a site in northwestern Laos without knowing that it had just been overrun by the enemy. Shortly after Brace landed, another pilot spotted his plane in the middle of the runway with nobody around. The second pilot's radio report was monitored by the U.S. embassy in Vientiane. The new ambassador, William Sullivan, instantly asked the CIA to find out whether Brace was dead or alive.

In Udorn, Bill Lair got into the fastest plane available, a twin-engine Beechcraft Baron. En route, he requested the launching of American-piloted T-28 propellor-driven fighter-bombers from Udorn. He also got a Caribou light cargo plane circling overhead for radio relays and an Air America helicopter diverted from other duties. Lair told the chopper pilot to find out what had happened on the ground.

The helicopter pilot was reluctant to land on an airstrip that might be in enemy hands. But Lair's favorite Paru, Lt. Col. Dachar Adulyarat, who happened to be on board, shamed the chopper pilot into going in. As the helicopter hovered over the runway, the stocky Thai stood in the open door. He saw no bullet holes in Brace's plane. There was nobody in sight. The area around the landing strip was thick forest, perfect for concealment.

The sound of AK-47s erupted from the brush. As the helicopter rose, Dachar spotted a lone man in a field some distance up the valley. He told the chopper pilot to descend, and he grabbed the man, an ordinary farmer, and threw him inside. Questioning him, Dachar confirmed that the enemy had taken Ernie Brace prisoner.

There wasn't much to be done. The enemy, and Ernie Brace, were down there somewhere underneath the canopy of vegetation. Lair decided to try a long shot. He directed the T-28s to strafe the trees and brush along the edge of the runway, to see whether that would flush anybody out. At the same time, U.S. F-105 Thunderchief jets appeared. Lair hadn't asked for them, but there they were, responding to the needs of a fellow American pilot. He told them to do what the T-28s were doing but farther out from the runway. The jets strafed the trees without result. Lair returned to Udorn, disappointed but convinced that he had done his best.

Unknown to Lair, another jet had lost its bearings and bombed a friendly village in another valley, killing innocent civilians. The error was easier to make than it might seem. Depending on the model and the armaments they carry, F-105s have a top speed in the neighborhood of 1,250 to 1,500 miles an hour, roughly twice the speed of sound. Even at a slower speed, it took a pilot only a few seconds to cross from one valley into the next, and if he didn't know the landmarks he might not notice the difference. The hillsides were a blur of green. In the pilot's mind a cluster of huts in a red-orange laterite clearing had registered as "target." Bombs away.

Sullivan, unaware that Lair was empowered to call in air strikes, decided to punish him. He sent a message to the director of Central Intelligence asking him to reprimand Lair for exceeding his authority. The Laos station chief, Douglas Blaufarb, backed Lair and so did the CIA director.

No reprimand was issued, but the incident left a bad taste in everybody's mouth. Lair stayed away from Sullivan when possible, and if they met he avoided looking Sullivan in the eye, the easier to suppress his anger, in Thai style.

Sullivan, so well connected in Washington and so conscious of his own rank, dealt almost exclusively with Blaufarb. Sullivan didn't know that Lair had been the founder and architect of the tribal war. To him, Lair was just a redneck in Udorn who had been around forever and was useful for handling the Thais.

With a Thai Paru who had been captured at the same time, Ernest Brace began a long, slow painful journey of beatings and cages and failed escapes that led him through Laos and eventually to the Hanoi Hilton. He was a prisoner for seven years, ten months, and seven days. The Paru was held prisoner even longer.

◆

By the time of the Brace fiasco, in May 1965, Udorn air base was in the midst of a transformation. On both sides of the runway and along the ramps, hangars were rising, like great warehouses with curved roofs. Revetments or parking places for the individual planes were being built, with walls of concrete or pierced steel planking or dirt and a thin metal roof on top to shield the aircraft from the broiling rays of the sun.

Several squadrons of F-4 Phantom II jets had arrived. They were odd-looking craft, sleek and menacing, with a slight turn-up in the wings near the tips, and stabilizing fins on the tail that angled down. From his office, Lair couldn't hear the high-frequency idling whine of their engines over the noise of his window air conditioner, but he heard the thunder as they barreled down the runway. At first he watched them from his window as they leaned back, roaring upward, then banking steeply as they sped away like darts. Later the novelty wore off.

Soon there was an air force officer's club with hamburgers and club sandwiches and American soft drinks on the menu. Crew-cut uniformed men gathered there and over at the Air America club next to the CIA building, everybody being sociable and talking in the accents of Oklahoma, Nebraska, and Texas. It was almost like being back in the States.

Lair liked the air force men as individuals. But he felt bad for the Thai government officials on the base, who never went to the American clubs. They were being squeezed out. Whatever a Thai's rank or personality, the newly arrived Americans looked at him as though he was the same as all the others—a generic, brown-skinned local.

Unconsciously, the Americans assumed an air of cultural superiority, and the Thais played right into it with their cultural practice of not wishing to offend. And so they vanished from the base, except for the low-paid civilian men who cut the grass and the women who flipped the hamburgers. It was as though Udorn Royal Thai Air Base was not part of Thailand anymore.

For the first time in years, Bill Lair was forced to think about race. He recalled the process that he himself had gone through, growing up in a north Texas town where everybody was white, then arriving in Thailand and being amazed, believing the Thais to be strange and exotic and utterly different from himself. It had taken him awhile to realize how different the

Thais were from one another, then a while longer for individual Thais to remind him of somebody he had known back home, and finally to realize that many Thais resembled other Americans more than they resembled other Thais. He reckoned it had taken him two or three years to get to that point, where he had passed through the transparent barriers of race and where he was fully ready to deal with Asians and be effective. And he could not expect air force men to go through that process any faster than he had. On one-year tours, most would not go through it at all.

So Lair did not proselytize about race. It was not in him to lecture people anyway. But he was determined in his quiet way to blend the tasks the races were performing. He believed that Asian wars should be run by Asians, and he would do what he could to restore their ownership or at least to minimize their loss. His target was the cockpit. It was a bastion of the white man's mystique, of colonial attitudes. As if *only* white men could fly. He reasoned that the basic activity of flying was a lot like driving a truck. Thais drove trucks; therefore, they could learn to fly.

The contract cargo business of Bird & Sons and Air America depended on the CIA. Thai pilots quietly appeared on the Bird & Sons roster and later Air America. There was grumbling from American pilots that the Thais, being Buddhists, lacked the proper aggressiveness and were quicker to give up on a plane when it got into trouble with weather or enemy ground fire. There may have been some truth in this at first, but it was mostly rear-guard sniping, and not enough to stop the program. Thai fixed-wing and chopper pilots did much of the transportation and resupply of trailwatch teams on the Ho Chi Minh Trail.

Then there was the U.S. Air Force's Waterpump program at Udorn, to teach Laotian pilots to fly T-28s. Vang Pao wanted Meo pilots in the program. The U.S. Air Force turned him down and so did the Lao high command. The Meo wanted to fly before they could drive, an audacious ambition for a tribe that lacked the wheel.

Lair felt there would be an advantage to having Meo pilots support their own troops, because they knew the ground terrain and spoke the same language as the ground commanders. On one of his trips to the big CIA supply depot on Okinawa, he happened to spot a couple of old single-engine Piper Cubs in a warehouse. Nobody was using them. He started pestering headquarters for the planes and eventually got them. He went up to Long Tieng and got Vang Pao to send him about a dozen of his brightest young soldiers for a pilot program. Lair set up a flying school for the Meo at the Nong Khai airstrip, where he and Landry had lived for a few months just after the signing of the Geneva accords. The Meo began taking English lessons along with their flying lessons. It was a long-term, low-profile program. Lair didn't tell his superiors about it and paid for it out of his own operational funds.

And finally there was the U.S. Air Force itself. Lair found that the American pilots at Udorn were receptive to learning more about Laos and its terrain. Before long, pilots were going upcountry on their free time in Air America planes to study the landmarks and to see for themselves the damage they had inflicted. The pilots did it out of professional pride. Knowing the terrain better, and knowing something of the friendly ground forces, they became more accurate with their munitions. After a while nobody seemed to know how or when these aerial sightseeing trips had started. Which was how Lair liked it, and why he would never rise high in the CIA.

# The High-Water Mark

Vang Pao bounced back from the battlefield defeats of early 1965. After the North Vietnamese overran much of Sam Neua Province, he moved one of his new Special Guerilla Unit battalions to Nakhang, a base in northern Xieng Khouang that served as a jump-off point for Sam Neua. Soon afterwards, he shipped two lowland battalions farther north to bolster the defenses there. By May 1965, as the dry season was ending, he was ready to retake the land that had been lost to the other side.

It was then that Vang Pao acquired the powerful combination of forces he had only dreamed of before—his tribal guerillas, plus royalist conventional soldiers, artillery, propellor-driven T-28s, and American jets. He had no formal training in their use and it never occurred to him to care. On his first jet strike, near Nakhang, a bomb dropped short and the air concussion blew him off his feet. His advisers were horrified and began to worry about the dangerous side effects of airpower. But Vang Pao dusted himself off, laughing, and cheered as the jet went after its target a second time, with better success.

By July and August, his rainy season counteroffensive was in full swing. Air America flew ammunition directly from Thailand to Nakhang, and from Nakhang to the front-line units. Thai and American forward air controllers on the ground, and Americans flying planes with Thai and Lao markings, marked the targets with smoke rockets so the jets could make their runs. Tribal guerilla units ambushed North Vietnamese resupply and reinforcement columns, isolating the enemy in a few extremely well dug-in positions near Colonel Thong's old head-quarters, Hua Moung.

Vang Pao was everywhere at once, firing 105mm howitzers, personally directing the T-28s by radio, conspicuously staying in charge as his culture demanded of its leaders. For their part, the North Vietnamese dug deeper, patiently creating a series of interconnected trenches, tunnels, bunkers, and caves.

Vang Pao pressed on and recaptured Hua Moung on September 12. Northeast of its airstrip rose a three-pointed mountain and another hill occupied by the enemy that had to be taken before the airstrip was safe. The enemy fortifications there were the strongest yet, with bombproof earthen roofs as much as twenty feet thick.

Against them Vang Pao employed the pattern of attack he had tested and improved in the previous months. He brought his heaviest weapons, 105 and 75mm howitzers, 4.2-inch mortars, and 75mm recoilless rifles, to bear on the enemy strong points in an almost nonstop bombardment. His ground commanders marked targets with smoke shells from the howitzers and heavy mortars for the T-28 and jet aircraft. Three times Vang Pao's troops took two of the mountain's three strong points. Each time enemy counterattacks from the remaining summit forced them to retreat.

Vang Pao paused to regroup. His forces had been attacking the other enemy hilltop, known as Hong Oy Neua, from the northwest. On a sudden inspiration, Vang Pao loaded two companies of soldiers in helicopters and brought them around to the south side to launch an attack on Hong Oy Neua from there. The enemy couldn't dig new defenses quickly enough, and after several more days of punishing bombardment their resistance fell apart. The royalist and tribal forces captured both positions, ending their rainy season campaign for that year.

Vang Pao's shift in forces from the northwest to the south had been, as his American advisers liked to joke, the "coop de goose." Going head-to-head with the North Vietnamese and beating them was a genuine accomplishment, with or without the help of artillery and American airpower. Few South Vietnamese commanders had been able to do it. Few Laotian commanders had been able to do it, either. The only other officer with a record as impressive was Colonel Thong, who had always used old-style guerilla tactics, traveling on foot, attacking where the enemy was weak, and dispersing to avoid pitched battles. But Thong wasn't around to help anymore.

The expansion of tribal operations over the border into North Vietnam had undergone a change of emphasis. Fearing the creation of more refugees, the American embassy told Vang Pao that it would not support the formal recruitment of tribes in North Vietnam after all. Instead, friendly cross-border people were asked to help U.S. airmen shot down in their areas. On June 20, 1965, two Air America helicopters flew forty miles into North Vietnam to rescue two jet pilots who had been shot down. As a volunteer guide on one of the choppers rode the Lao with the shoulder-length hair and Buddha amulets around his neck, Colonel Thong, who knew the territory well. Both helicopters met with ground fire. A large-caliber bullet, probably from a 12.7mm antiaircraft gun, hit Thong, blowing a hole through his abdomen and out his back.

The two helicopters clattered back to Laos with the wounded Thong but without the two downed jet pilots, one of whom was rescued the next day. A radio call went out, and Pop Buell met the choppers with Doc Weldon's wife, Dr. Patricia McCreedy, who happened to be visiting that day. Thong was evacuated to the same U.S. Air Force hospital in Thailand as Tony Poe, who was already out on convalescent leave. By 6 A.M., when Buell left Thong's bedside, the operations were over and the young Lao colonel was awake.

The news of Thong's wound dismayed Vang Pao and his senior officers and advisers. Thong was the lowland Lao most respected by the Meo and other tribesmen. He was thus a symbol of nation-building and of the political need for all the Laotian races to work together. He had been wounded in this new kind of war, in which American jets were gaining primacy. Over the next few days, however, Thong was reported to be getting better.

Life went on. In Vientiane, restive military officers staged another mini-coup attempt. Nothing much came of it, but commanders from south Laos promised to support Vang Pao if another coup was staged. This new respect from lowland military colleagues delighted Vang Pao. Normally a light drinker, he felt like celebrating.

He got roaring drunk that night, forcing Lawrence and another case officer to put down six glasses of *lao-lao* to catch up to him. Then he started dancing the *lamvong* with his latest sweetheart, a fifteen-year-old girl whom he was thinking of adding to his roster of wives. He kept extolling her love-making ability and insisting that Lawrence dance with her. When the American obliged, Vang Pao cut in on him and danced with the girl himself again, waving his hands to the music and laughing. At dinner, he amiably discussed where the capital should be relocated, since the generals in Vientiane were obviously incompetent to run the country.

Someone mentioned Long Tieng as a possibility. Why not just take over? Why not stage a coup of his own?

Then a message came in from the radio room that Thong had died in Thailand of a massive blood clot, and suddenly the partying was over.

A lowland colonel present at Vang Pao's table began quietly talking with Lawrence about finding a replacement for Thong.

Their conversation turned to Buddha amulets of the kind Thong had worn. Joining in, Vang Pao explained that one kind of Buddha amulet protects from all bullets, and another attracts all bullets but causes them to ricochet. Thong's amulets, Vang Pao said, just hadn't worked.

◆

Pop Buell, one of Thong's greatest admirers, arranged for the funeral. He found Thong's two wives, both of whom were seven months' pregnant and neither one of whom had known about the other. He brought them to Vientiane. Buell had a coffin made and after the weather cleared he flew to Sam Thong with twenty-eight people, the body, and food for the funeral ceremony.

With the backing of his superiors at USAID and his allies at CIA, Buell pressured the embassy to take part in Thong's funeral. The embassy agreed and put pressure on the Vientiane government to do the same. In death, Thong became a celebrated figure, made larger than life because of his importance as a bridge between the lowland Lao and the hilltribes, and between the Laotians and the Americans.

On the funeral day the skies were rainy in Sam Thong. Puddles formed on the orange laterite of the landing strip, and wet mist clung to the sodden hillsides. In a corner of the giant new Quonset hut that served as Buell's warehouse, Buddhist monks with shaved heads and saffron robes chanted and prayed for Thong's soul. The monks held a white thread in their hands, connecting one to another, and connecting them all to Thong's casket, which was decorated in a loud golden filigree. There was a pavilion outside with a wooden stage and a parachute rigged above it to give the VIPs some protection from the rain. Everybody who was anybody was there: Vang Pao; the commander in chief of the Royal Lao Army, Gen. Ouane Rattikone; Ambassador Sullivan; the head of USAID; everybody but Bill Lair.

The notables gave speeches on the stage. There had been a little fuss when it was discovered that Thong left two pregnant widows, but Sullivan, the diplomat, adroitly sidestepped the question of which wife was senior by presenting Thong's father with the U.S. government's posthumous award, the Silver Star. A drum and bugle corps from Vientiane, in dress whites and red berets, marched and played on the tough grass where water buffalo normally grazed. It was a major event, the red-bereted lowlanders coming together with the Hmong on a scale never seen before. When the monks were finally done the coffin was placed on a tractor decked out as a funeral carriage with layers of gold staging. The tractor was symbolically pulled by the monks and bystanders with a long white rope to the funeral pyre. More gold, more wreaths, and then a procession of mourners carrying lighted tapers to the pyre. The wood was too wet to light until some of Vang Pao's men splashed aviation fuel on it, and then the flames took hold.

Thong had personified a belief or at least a hope that the people of northern Laos would be able to defend themselves. That out of that perilously thin layer of talent and ability, great leaders would rise, and the people would be able to defeat the enemy with hand-carried weapons while making their way around the mountains by foot. The hope—the dream—was that guerilla war would be enough, with a little help from the Americans. Thong had died just as airpower was starting to change the war's equation.

Even at the height of the operation's success—the territory grown, the people rallying to the cause, Vang Pao's army giving better than it took—the fragility of the dream had been exposed. Everything was changing in 1965. The machinery of war was taking over, and there was no turning back.

◆

At Long Tieng and Sam Thong, the two bases at the heart of the Meo operation, 1965 was the year of a major buildup. The Americans were tired of living in thatched shacks and tin huts with rats running around on the rafters. There was no road between Long Tieng and Sam Thong, which meant chartering planes, which meant spending hundreds or even thousands of dollars a day on airborne taxi rides. The dirt airstrip in Long Tieng was often fogged in, which didn't help logistics, either.

So when Tony Poe recovered from his battle wounds and came back in mid-1965 he found a transformation under way. There were more spooks in Long Tieng—six case officers now—and better housing for them, the Air America pilots, and the new U.S. Air Force forward controllers. Vint Lawrence, very much the man in charge, had laid out a road route between Sam Thong and Long Tieng, and a bulldozer was noisily grinding away at the mountainsides. Engineers had blown up some karst outcroppings on Long Tieng's valley floor and created a new airstrip, with the far end under a spot that was always free of fog in the morning and the upper end turning at right angles into a broad cargo ramp at the base of the karst mamelons, the tits. They had used some of the rubble to build a two-story stone house for Vang Pao.

Months of recuperation had not mellowed Tony Poe. Even before getting shot he had felt himself the odd man out, with his nightly drinking binges and his bullying and his constant discovery of irregularities that didn't seem to bother the other Americans, who made more generous allowances for the Meo being different from themselves.

In no time at all Poe resumed quarreling with Vang Pao. The intensity of Poe's paranoia and his drunken bellowing alienated his fellow case officers, and made it harder for them to accept that at least some of the criticisms he made of the Meo were valid, or would be in the future, if the problems that were minor then continued to grow.

Poe was an anachronism when it came to progress. He didn't see the benefit, except in upgrading the airstrip, which made life easier for the pilots. He wanted to improve the troops, not Long Tieng. He didn't want warehouses, roads, trucks, or jeeps. He didn't want civilian tribespeople moving into Long Tieng. "We needed that shit like we needed a hole in the head," he said later.

Poe was enraged when he found that Vang Pao was buying houses in Vientiane for his wives, who liked city life and had business ventures there. With Lawrence's help, Poe blocked the wives' attempts to commandeer Air America flights between Vientiane and Long Tieng. "Later VP wanted his own airplanes," recalled Poe. "When he got his own airplanes, they carried his relations and their supplies. And isn't it *funny*? Wife Number Two and Wife Number Three had to pay Wife Number One to transport supplies on his own airplane. VP didn't even want to get involved in that.

"That's where we should have stopped it. That's where we should have stopped the whole thing. Just got up and left, like I tried to do half a dozen times. We should have said, 'VP, fuck it.'

"Every Meo New Year's they were shooting up five hundred or five thousand bullets at the moon. That really blew me. I asked VP, 'What'd you give them that ammo for? You didn't tell me.' VP said, 'Vint Lawrence gave it to me.' "

Poe went to Lawrence, all steamed up, and Lawrence explained that he was honoring the Meo customs. It was a new moon, not an eclipse, but it did no harm, and maybe some good, for the Americans to show support for tribal ways. Poe was disgusted. "Shooting at the goddamn moon," he reflected. "*Bullshit*. If they were going to shoot, they should use their homemade muskets, you know. But they shouldn't use our bullets and weapons.

"Well, we had all kinds of little problems like that," said Poe, "and they added up to the big problem. Which was, I can't stay any longer, and I'm a hindrance to him, and he's a hindrance to me. So, I'm the less important, so I can go elsewhere. And it's lucky—I mean, tragically—that we had that chopper wreck with Ojibway."

In far northwestern Laos, Bill Young had quarreled with some Thai intelligence operatives whose cooperation was crucial, and Lair had replaced him with a big, slow-moving paramilitary officer named Lewis Ojibway. Ojibway was a Native American with a flattened nose who had once been a sparring partner for Joe Louis. On August 20, 1965, Ojibway boarded a helicopter piloted by Bob Nunez, who had flown the wounded Poe out of Hong Nong exactly seven months before. The monsoon clouds closed in on the helicopter while it was flying near the Mekong. The pilot used the river as a marker but eventually lost all visibility, flew lower and lower without realizing it, and hit the water. Of seven people on board, four died, including Ojibway.

Bill Lair sent Poe to take Ojibway's place, hoping never to hear from him again.

The far northwest was the quietest military region of Laos. Occasional missions into Yunnan Province of China to keep an eye on things there. A few opium caravans crossing the Mekong from Burma into the heart of the Golden Triangle.

A quiet place.

◆

The U.S. Air Force's unconventional warfare specialists, the Air Commandos, were roughly equivalent to the army's Green Berets. The Air Commandos worked in brushfire wars in the Third World, among other settings, and they had a long-standing connection to the CIA. One of their commanding officers and guiding lights was Heinie Aderholt, who had been on loan to the CIA at the start of Operation Momentum, and who had also run Operation Millpond, the covert force of B-26 bombers that had been assembled in 1961 but never used.

Thanks in part to Aderholt's good relations with the CIA, the Air Commandos had started to play a significant role in the Laos war. There was an Air Commando medic working in Sam Thong for Pop Buell. In Udorn, Air Commando instructors taught Laotian pilots to fly T-28s and flew a few T-28 missions themselves. Mostly they flew spotter planes, but they also worked on the ground as combat controllers or forward air guides, selecting targets, calling in jet strikes, and directing the pilots to their targets. Getting supersonic jets to provide close support of hilltribe irregulars—as opposed to, say, using jets to bomb or strafe trucks on an open road—was a new concept in warfare and took experimentation.

An Air Commando captain named Jack Teague was one of the first to pull a six-month tour with Vang Pao's troops. From Nakhang, where he was based, he ranged far up into Sam Neua in the area around Phou Pha Thi for the rainy season counteroffensive. The F-4 jet jockeys responded well to his directions, blasting at enemy troop concentrations and clearing the way for friendly troops to regain terrain lost to the North Vietnamese the previous dry season. It was still early in the air war and Teague would always remember later how primitive the living conditions were. He got dengue fever once, and he got sick many times from the food. He carried a roll of paper towels to remind himself that the concept of cleanliness still existed, elsewhere if not in the mountains of northeast Laos.

Once in a while Teague went down to Udorn air base in Thailand for a shower and American food. He dutifully took pictures of the base and its surroundings to send back to his wife and his parents. His cover story was that he was an administrative officer at the air base there. Being in the black, as a participant in a war that had no official existence, he was under orders to stick to his cover story even in his letters home.

Jack Teague's father was Texas congressman Olin Earl "Tiger" Teague, the chairman of the Veterans' Affairs Committee in the U.S. House of Representatives. Rep. Teague was a highly decorated World War II veteran himself and a strong supporter of the military. Lyndon Johnson had asked him to take a tour of South Vietnam as part of an effort to build congressional support for the war. The CIA, which kept files on politicians, discovered that the congressman's son was serving in the Agency-run war in Laos, which the senior Teague had not known. Seizing the opportunity, the CIA invited Rep. Teague to visit Laos, starting with a briefing from Lair.

Until that time Bill Lair had never had any congressional visitors, and few Americans of any kind outside the CIA. The congressman arrived in Udorn toward the end of 1965. It was established that the senior Teague was a graduate of Texas A&M. Bill Lair was a graduate of A&M, too. So was Pat Landry. The three old grads sat around reminiscing about their college days. It was amazing how you could meet fellow alumni out in the middle of nowhere, wasn't it? Once they had all gotten on the same wavelength, the spooks and the congressman spent a stimulating evening talking about counterinsurgency warfare in Asia. Teague was conversant with strategy and tactics and, being a politician, saw what Lair was trying to do in enlisting the support and participation of the local people. It was a new kind of war to him, but he understood it readily.

From Udorn the congressman flew up to Sam Thong, along with a colleague, Representative Emilio Daddario of Connecticut, who as an OSS veteran was also on the CIA's list of favorites. Pop Buell, their host, explained in his own earthy terms why the Laos approach made more sense than what the United States was doing in Vietnam. The Hoosier farmer threw a *baci* party for the congressmen with liquor, mysterious chanting, and the usual centerpiece of furled banana leaves draped in string. Gen. Vang Pao himself was at his most charming, tying the good-luck *baci* strings around the congressmen's wrists, and so on. Then the congressmen flew up to Nakhang and saw the area where until a few weeks earlier the younger Teague had been calling in air strikes.

The congressmen were converted. "Dad is convinced that the only thing our foreign policy needs is a few more Pop Buells," Capt. Jack Teague wrote in a letter to Buell shortly afterwards. Representatives Teague and Daddario went back to Washington, and the word spread among a select circle of congressmen and senators about this exotic program run by Lone Star rednecks and Asian hillbillies that was better and cheaper than anything the Pentagon was doing in South Vietnam.

A precedent had been set. It wasn't many months before the next VIPs from Washington came along, and the next and the next. The CIA didn't give Senator Edward Kennedy a briefing with Lair or Vang Pao because it didn't trust him, and Ambassador Sullivan kept other politicians out, including Senator Stuart Symington, who favored freeing the military from the kinds of constraints Sullivan wished to impose. But more and more VIPs stopped in at Udorn on what Lair and Landry jokingly began to refer to as "the Tour." Though the two men did their best to be hospitable, the briefings for the politicians became time-consuming, to the point where they felt it was interfering with their management of the war.

Lair began to wonder whether the good old days were over. Five married case officers whom he hadn't asked for came to work in upcountry Laos, and they'd forced an agreement with headquarters to have their wives work at Udorn. Lair had always resisted getting secretaries before, and he was devastated when the wives arrived, ready for filing and touch-typing and telling people on the telephone that the boss was in conference but they'd be glad to take a message. He had always known that once he got secretaries he would have the beginnings of a bureaucracy, and that would be the end of Udorn as a place that responded to the needs of the field.

And flat, drab, dusty Udorn was not exactly the greatest place for American wives to be. The women tried gamely for a while, but after the novelty wore off the complaints began. The office was primitive. Nice ladies' rooms did not have the kind of toilets where you put your feet on two concrete pads and squatted. There was no commissary. There were no doctors. The American men were all fooling around with cute Thai girls rentable at very low rates by the hour. There was no nightlife for the American wives, nothing for them to do.

Luckily, the Air America club built a swimming pool, and the Agency wives sat around it in their sunglasses and bathing suits, eating sandwiches and hamburgers. That stopped the complaining for a while. But everything at Udorn had changed: the thunder of jets taking off, the chatter of crew-cut Americans, secretaries typing and filing, politicians arriving to be briefed. It was the beginning of civilization, and Lair had always wanted to be at the end of the road.

# From a Country Store to a Supermarket

Around the end of 1965 a small plane landed at Long Tieng and taxied onto the oiled dirt landing ramp. From it emerged Bill Colby, the Far East chief, wearing polished loafers and a buttoned-down shirt with a tie.

Colby asked Vint Lawrence to accompany him as interpreter to a meeting with Vang Pao. The general's guttural speech—a blend of French, Lao, Meo, and English—was almost impossible for the man from headquarters to understand. Later the two Americans went off to talk together. Colby had been reading Lawrence's cables, which, besides being full of intelligence information, were written with literary grace and richly sprinkled with observations on the history and culture of the Meo. Colby knew that Lawrence had graduated from Princeton, which happened to be his alma mater, too.

In their meeting Lawrence yessired Colby like any junior employee in awe of the boss. He was unaware that the Far East chief was looking for young men to put on the fast track back in Langley.

Lawrence was then finishing his second two-year tour in Laos. He was planning to stay for a third tour, but Colby told him he couldn't. "You'll never come home," declared Colby. He meant either that Lawrence would get killed, which was possible—five of Lawrence's friends had died, most of them in air crashes—or else that Lawrence would identify so much with the hilltribe cause that he would "go native." The CIA management, by and large, looked down on officers who "went native"—even though Operation Momentum owed its success to one man, Bill Lair, who had stayed in one place, mastered the local languages, and learned how to motivate the locals. Lawrence had become Lair's top protégé.

Lawrence prepared to go back to the States with mixed feelings. He felt he had succeeded with his nation-building measures. His crowning achievement had been setting up a radio station at Long Tieng, called the Union of Lao Races radio station, which broadcast in the numerous languages of Laos Vang Pao's message that the people of the north would have to unite. But Lawrence was beginning to be worried by the changes in the war, and by airpower in particular.

Sometimes the arrival of jets overhead, dropping their bombs and firing their deadly ammunition, turned the tide of battles. But Lawrence was starting to worry that the Meo would get too dependent on air support, call for it when they got in trouble, and find themselves in even more trouble if the planes didn't come. Air strikes planned in advance were still relatively rare. Most resulted from pilots coming back from North Vietnam with unused ordnance. They needed to drop their loads before returning to their bases in Thailand. If the pilots had already dropped their loads, they couldn't help.

Then there was the issue of the Meo T-28s. Bill Lair was eager to have the tribesmen fly their own aircraft. Lawrence wasn't sure. Giving the Meo planes might make them think that they were better and more powerful than they were. "I thought we were about at the right level," recalled Lawrence. "I thought we were on the side of the angels, and I was pleased with the idea that we could get air support—but it was always with a caveat."

He was leaving behind an operation that had already seen its heyday, though the expansion of territory would continue for several more months. One sign of early decline was the food supply at Long Tieng. By 1966, there was little meat to be had. War had disrupted Meo agriculture. The farmers and herdsmen were all in uniform. But Vang Pao was still holding his own with the North Vietnamese, slipping their punches and hitting them with guerilla-airpower combinations, and there was no reason yet to think the agricultural setback was permanent.

Another early warning sign was the performance of the Thai Paru. Like Tony Poe, they had succumbed to the need to comfort themselves with local women and to dose themselves nightly with inebriants. Captain Makorn, the amiable though weak-willed Paru leader, was drinking some evenings and smoking opium others. The Paru were reacting to some kind of deep homesickness and cultural deprivation that they and the Americans felt and nobody fully understood. But the Paru were still doing their jobs, and they weren't giving up.

There was a farewell party in Lawrence's honor at Long Tieng. Bill Lair and Pop Buell showed up for it and stayed overnight. Even Tony Poe came back from the far northwest with no hard feelings, ready to have fun. The White Horse whiskey flowed. There were women and *lamvong*-style dancing at the party and everybody got drunk. Lawrence changed into a black Meo costume and gave a speech in mixed Lao and Hmong. Vang Pao presented him with three heavy silver necklaces.

And then it was over. After four years, no more tang of woodsmoke in the air, no more views from mountaintops of fog filling the valleys. No more rainstorms so heavy the ground turned silver from the water runoff. No more late nights writing cables in the Thai radio room, or watching spellbound as shamans chanted by lantern light.

Lawrence left Long Tieng for a long skiing vacation in Europe and from there to the States. Back to headquarters, and back to normal civilized life as he had known it.

◆

About a week after Lawrence's departure, in the early morning hours of February 17, 1966, the 5th Battalion of the 168th North Vietnamese Army regiment attacked Nakhang, the big staging base north of the Plain of Jars. When daylight arrived, an American forward air controller who had been staying there managed to get a spotter plane in the air and directed F-105 jets in strikes against enemy positions. In the following days, the North Vietnamese overran the base, capturing it; but the jets turned Nakhang into a wasteland, destroying the fortifications, most of its support buildings, petroleum supplies, weapons, and ammunition; and, by using napalm for the first time in the north Laos war, hundreds of the North Vietnamese attackers.

It was a new kind of battle. The Pathet Lao didn't play a significant role; and neither did the royalist and tribal troops. The real combatants were the North Vietnamese soldiers on the ground and the American pilots in the air. The war had gone high-tech.

The battle led to a curious incident between Vang Pao and the Americans. On the second day of fighting Vang Pao flew onto the strip by helicopter. When he got out to visit the troops, some enemy soldiers popped up and shot at him from a distance, wounding him in the chest and upper arm.

The helicopter took off again with Vang Pao inside and headed across the Mekong to the U.S. Air Force hospital at Korat. A few minutes after he arrived in the emergency room Ambassador Bill Sullivan, who had taken his own helicopter from Vientiane, joined him there. The air force doctors reading the X-rays told the ambassador that a rifle bullet had sheared off a chunk of Vang Pao's upper arm bone just below the shoulder socket. He would heal well, the doctors said, if they could surgically implant a metal rod to bridge the gap.

Sullivan foresaw a problem. The tribals, being animists, believed in exorcising evil spirits from the body. The body had to be kept clear of foreign objects. Sullivan suggested implanting the pin without telling the patient, but the doctors refused on ethical grounds.

Sullivan then proposed telling Vang Pao himself about the pin to obtain his consent, and the doctors agreed. In French, which the doctors didn't understand, the ambassador told the general about the operation, and then persuaded him, as Sullivan wrote later, that "the steel would eventually melt as it was warmed by the body, and would ultimately depart from the system just like bad spirits." The doctors watched Vang Pao's expression change from a frown, to resignation, to a smile. When Vang Pao said, "O.K.!" they wheeled him off to the operating room.

But the pin didn't heal the general's shoulder. Later in the year Vang Pao flew to Hawaii, where even more sophisticated Western treatment finally cured him.

◆

By 1966, Bill Lair had been with the CIA fifteen years. He was self-effacing, and his reputation lagged behind his achievements, except among a few who knew his story. "Been over there a little too long," was the comment sometimes heard at headquarters. Lair hadn't followed the usual pattern of two years in one posting followed by two years in another. Marrying a Thai woman added to the suspicion, in some circles, that he had gone "pro-Thai," which was a polite way of saying that he had gone native.

Still, he had done what he wanted, and to Lair that counted for more than promotions or hallway gossip at headquarters. He had never asked for a transfer from his obscure, exotic niche. The outfit had given him a free hand, first in Thailand when he'd organized and trained the Paru, and later in Laos with Momentum. At headquarters he'd had Desmond FitzGerald and then Bill Colby as his patrons and protectors, and he got his own money directly from headquarters, too. His budget was about $20 million a year, and Langley gave him all he wanted and offered to give him more. Lair always turned those offers of a bigger budget down.

His first two station chiefs in Laos, Gordon Jorgensen and "Whitey" Whitehurst, never questioned anything he did. Lair appreciated that. His next boss, Douglas Blaufarb, had needed winning over. Blaufarb had been wary of Momentum at first and unsure how to manage such a large, informally run program manned by people he hadn't worked with before.

A tall, bespectacled intellectual with degrees from Harvard and Co-lumbia, Blaufarb requested the classified files on the history of the opera-tion. From those, he rediscovered the use the French had made of the Meo in the 1950s. Normally, when two countries attempt versions of the same thing, one after the other, the second country can learn a great deal from a study of the first country's attempt. That had not happened in Laos. Lair knew about the earlier period, but he had not been particularly curious, and by the mid-sixties few Americans were even aware that the French had worked with the hilltribes at all. The odd thing was that it didn't really mat-ter. In spite of a lack of formal knowledge of their predecessors, Blaufarb decided, there wasn't much about the CIA paramilitary operations in Laos that needed to be improved.

Analyzing the success of Momentum, Blaufarb gave credit to Vang Pao for his leadership, and to the Americans for their understanding of local culture. These Americans responded, wrote Blaufarb, "to the needs of the tribals *as the latter saw them,* with minimal interference with tribal cus-toms—including some that to the Western mind can only appear as the grossest superstition. The aim was to encourage the tribal clients to think of the effort as their own cause, assisted but not controlled by a powerful foreign ally." For this to have worked, Blaufarb believed, the Americans had to do more than "show respect for the picturesque oddities of the tribes-men. Even at the Vientiane level, the U.S. advisory organization was obliged to place at the top of its values that of *serving the real world of the field.*"

Blaufarb allowed Momentum to remain field-driven. He also recognized that the CIA and USAID programs in Laos were interrelated. People like Edgar Buell and Dr. Weldon were crucial to the CIA's success. Once, Blau-farb called Dr. Weldon in and told him not to try that cheap-shot B.S. again. What B.S.? the perplexed doctor wanted to know. Blaufarb explained that Weldon had sent a memo to the USAID chief and the ambassador that had contained information of interest to the CIA, and it was something Blau-farb hadn't known about when the ambassador raised it at the daily meet-ing. Weldon apologetically promised to send copies of any reports that had significant political or military information, and then left, a little stung by the criticism, but flattered that they had reached this explicit under-standing, that they were on the same team and were going to help each other.

Blaufarb saw no reason to change the operation much. Through the end of his two-year tour—Blaufarb left a few months after Lawrence in 1966—he continued the practice of letting Lair call the day-to-day shots in the field.

By then, however, Lair's original plan of arming the tribals with World War II weapons, and keeping the locals more or less in charge, was beginning to look old-fashioned. The north Laos theater was changing and becoming more conventional, with more jets and other high-tech weaponry. This powerful weaponry, totally controlled by Americans, was even more noticeable in southern Laos along the Ho Chi Minh Trail, and in South Vietnam.

B-52s were dropping conventional bombs on the Mu Gia Pass, one of the entrances to the Ho Chi Minh Trail. U.S. planes were spraying the defoliation chemicals Agent Orange and Agent White along infiltration routes nearby. On the ground, a small number of Nung tribesmen, rejected for use in the north, had been hired as mercenary soldiers east of the Bolovens Plateau. More Nung were hired by the Special Forces on the South Vietnamese side of the mountains, and soon the line blurred between mercenaries and those who were fighting for their country or their tribe.

In South Vietnam, the 3,500 U.S. Marines that had landed in March 1965 had grown to 184,000 U.S. military men by year's end. General Westmoreland was asking for 459,000 troops in all. U.S. jets had been bombing North Vietnam for a year, inflicting damage, but strengthening rather than breaking Hanoi's resolve. North Vietnam, and the Ho Chi Minh Trail of Laos, acted as a conduit for a growing stream of Soviet- and Chinese-made military supplies heading to the south. What looked like eventual victory to optimistic Americans—"the light at the end of the tunnel"—was more like a freight train coming the other way.

◆

In mid-1966, Blaufarb's replacement came down to Udorn to see Lair and Landry. He was tall, blond, fair-skinned, sallow, a little overweight. An office type. He was in his late thirties, a few years younger than Lair. His name was Theodore G. Shackley. Lair's first impressions were: smart, ambitious, nervous.

Shackley announced that he was the new Laos station chief and that they reported to him. Bill Lair acknowledged that they reported to him and welcomed him to Udorn.

Shackley said that Lair and Landry had been there a long time and probably thought they knew a lot about the Laos war. But from now on he, the station chief, was going to run everything on a day-to-day-basis, and they were going to do exactly what he said. There were going to be a lot of changes. They had been running a country store, and he was going to turn it into a supermarket.

The three of them were sitting in the small unpretentious office that Lair and Landry shared. Bill Lair resisted the temptation to look at Pat Landry and shake his head in wonderment, as if to say, is this guy for real? It was as though Shackley was the new boy moving into the block and asserting his territoriality, only he was a little unsure of himself and acting extra-tough to compensate.

Shackley described how he was going to make the Laos war bigger and more modern. He was going to increase the number of Americans. He was going to require efficiency reports, to measure whether the outfit was getting the most out of its Americans and the Americans were getting the most out of their Laotians and Thais. And they were going to get more and bigger weapons and more air strikes and more kills on the Ho Chi Minh Trail.

Lair and Landry listened to the plans for improving their war. Then Landry leaned back in his chair and propped his feet on the desk. He was wearing rubber shower sandals and no socks. Tapping the desk surface with his swagger stick, Landry told Shackley that he didn't see anything wrong with the country store.

Shackley didn't like Landry's behavior, but contained himself. He told Landry that he would be transferring to the Vientiane station to run south Laos and the Trail operations from there. That way Lair could stay in Udorn and run north Laos operations while reporting to him, the station chief.

Landry had that baleful glare on his face, his standard expression. He said bluntly that he didn't want to do that.

Pat Landry didn't want to undercut his old friend Bill Lair and he didn't particularly want to spend two years running roadwatch teams, either. In effect, he was turning down a promotion that would have made him Lair's equal. Disliked by many Americans because of his brusque manners, Landry was trying to protect Lair and the operation the best he could, and doing a far better job of it than Lair himself, who avoided outward conflict, in Thai style. Lair had dropped his eyes. He was outwardly calm, though anybody who knew him well might have known that he felt otherwise.

The two men listened glumly to Shackley's presentation, which went on for several hours. He talked about north Laos, a war of position and maneuver, as he called it; and the south, the Trail, a war of infiltration and attrition. The United States was expanding its effort in Vietnam, Shackley pointed out, and from there came the drive to expand in Laos. There was no question of whether to expand farther, only a question of how; and although Westmoreland wanted to put American troops in Laos and keep them under a combined area command for Southeast Asia, the collective wisdom in Washington was to get the most possible out of some combination of the Laotians on the ground plus Lao and U.S. airpower. So there were going to be some adjustments to the mission and he wanted everybody to contribute to the best of his abilities.

Shackley was relentlessly logical. He was utterly sure of himself. Against the enemy and their proxies, he seemed to be saying, you could employ a straightforward power equation: More Americans + bigger funding + more force = better results. He completely dominated the meeting, and it was impossible for Bill Lair and Pat Landry to break through that assurance of his to convince him that over the years they had found that a different equation worked better. Fewer Americans + a deliberately lean budget = greater participation by locals in protecting their own turf. But, of course, turf was the name of the game, and it was their turf, in Udorn, that Shackley was after.

At one point Shackley backtracked to establish his credentials. In one of his previous assignments, headquarters had sent him to Miami to clean up after the Bay of Pigs fiasco. And he'd gone in, pushing a broom, digging with a backhoe. He'd cleaned up Miami, all right, and done a lot with Cuba, too.

Lair privately wondered how working in Miami qualified Shackley to run the Laos war. In Laos, without Shackley, they'd expanded the area of government control, at a tiny cost, without U.S. ground troops, by enlisting the help of the indigenous people. If there were comparisons to be made, Lair thought, compare Laos to South Vietnam. In South Vietnam, the government lost territory, with the help of U.S. troops, at a much higher price tag. Why send a man to fix what was already working well?

But as Shackley talked on, Lair spotted the flaw in his own logic. The north Laos war was going reasonably well, but not the war in the south. The outfit hadn't been able to damage the enemy's supply lines into South Vietnam, and the situation in South Vietnam was getting desperate.

And then Lair finally understood: Shackley was a purely Vietnam-related appointment. Shackley, a rising star in the outfit, had been sent to wring whatever could be wrung out of Laos, not for Laos's sake but to help the war in South Vietnam. And he would sacrifice Laos, if necessary, to do it.

The meeting lasted three hours. Shackley didn't ask a single question.

After Shackley left, Lair and Landry sat in their chairs in silence. They were drained.

Lair finally said to Landry, "I tell you one thing. That fellow will learn more in the next few years than we will."

But Lair was wrong.

◆

Theodore George Shackley Jr. was a mystery even to the CIA types and the handful of other Americans who knew of his appointment. He didn't socialize much, and he didn't make small talk, particularly about himself or his background, even to people he had known for years. His work was his life and his life was his work.

Shackley was born to a mother who had emigrated from Poland and a blue-collar, alcoholic father who worked as a house painter. When his parents split up, the young Ted went to stay with an older woman who taught him to speak, read, and write the Polish language. When Shackley's mother remarried, she brought him to West Palm Beach, Florida, where he attended high school. He did his military service in Germany after World War II, where his knowledge of Polish helped him land a position in the Army Counterintelligence Corps. After this first exposure to the world of international intrigue, he attended the University of Maryland on the G.I. Bill, and then went into the CIA.

Shackley was part of a team that tunneled under the Berlin wall and eavesdropped on the East German telephone system in 1955 and 1956. His boss and mentor there was William Harvey, a gun-toting, hard-drinking operator who was in the process of becoming a CIA legend. Shackley's assignments kept him peering through the Iron Curtain, mostly from Germany, for thirteen years. Harvey then chose him to be station chief in Miami, Florida. The Miami station, which targeted Fidel Castro's regime in Cuba, was the only CIA post located in the United States. It was in disarray after the failed Bay of Pigs invasion, and the first thing Shackley did when he arrived was to tell the staff that it had been run sloppily, that he was in charge now, that there were going to be big changes, and if anybody didn't like it this was his chance to clear out and go back to headquarters.

In Miami, one of the men listening to Shackley was Thomas Clines, then the deputy chief of covert action in the station. Clines didn't like Shackley at first, but his attitude changed to respect for Shackley's efficiency and precision. "He would say, 'I want to see you at 10:22 tomorrow morning,' " Clines recalled. "And everybody soon learned when he said that, he meant it. Not 10:25 or 10:20. I mean, that's how organized he was, almost like a machine. That's the kind of mind the guy's got." Though there were others in the station who complained that they couldn't get him to sign off on things they needed, Clines got what he wanted by going in to see Shackley at ten o'clock at night, when Shackley was still hard at work at his desk.

During Shackley's tenure the Miami station grew from thirty to three hundred officers. Much of the station's energies went into Operation Mongoose, the U.S. government's multiagency attempt in the aftermath of the Bay of Pigs to reorganize the anticommunist Cubans and overthrow Fidel Castro's regime. The overall Mongoose budget grew to something like fifty million dollars a year, more than double the size of the paramilitary budget for Laos at that time. The Mongoose money went for cars, speedboats, weapons, agents, paramilitary trainings for some 2,600 Cuban exiles belonging to various groups, and so forth. The exiles raided Cuban installations and sabotaged a few sugar refineries but accomplished nothing substantial, nothing that even began to destabilize Castro's regime.

Shackley also organized infiltration teams into Cuba, and collated and analyzed their intelligence findings. There were Soviet soldiers and technicians in Cuba, and Shackley wanted to find out what they were up to. There were many false alarms about nuclear missiles, and then in September 1962, the first credible reports were received suggesting that Soviets near the city of San Cristóbal were setting up missiles capable of striking targets in the United States.

The reports led to U-2 aerial overflights, and to photographs confirming the findings, which set off the Cuban missile crisis a month later. Though it was unclear how much credit Shackley deserved for those first crucial intelligence reports, the missile crisis got him noticed. He briefed top CIA people and others at upper levels of government, and they remembered him. He was a brilliant speaker, never at a loss for words, never needing to look at notes. A young go-getter.

In early 1963, Desmond FitzGerald, the former chief of the Far East division, came into the Cuba picture, replacing William Harvey and others. FitzGerald upped the number of paramilitary raids and sabotage operations. He also planned a number of assassination attempts on Castro, in what had practically become a CIA tradition. (Some of his ideas became famous later, like the fake seashell packed with explosives, which was meant to be placed on the ocean floor in Castro's favorite scuba-diving spot.) FitzGerald didn't make any more progress in getting rid of Castro than his predecessors, but he did notice Shackley. He became Shackley's new promoter within the CIA hierarchy.

FitzGerald became Western Hemisphere division chief in 1964, and then deputy in the Directorate for Plans, the overall boss of Agency covert programs in 1965, while Mongoose was sputtering to a close. In 1965 he sent Shackley back to Berlin, to become base chief there; and the next year FitzGerald suggested to Richard Helms, who was then deputy director of Central Intelligence and about to become director, that Shackley be given the Laos station chief's job. Helms proposed Shackley to Ambassador Bill Sullivan when Sullivan was back in Washington, and Sullivan agreed, provided it was understood that Shackley would report directly to him, the ambassador.

Once Shackley started working in Laos, Sullivan thought he ran a good operation and understood the nature and essence of guerilla war. The career CIA men Shackley brought along to Laos, like Tom Clines, respected the new station chief, too. "He's probably the most professional intelligence officer that I've ever worked with," recalled Clines. "He made every person in that station earn their keep full-time. He didn't allow for anybody to lag. He just made everybody produce." Another of Shackley's subordinates in the Vientiane station confirmed: "Ted always had strong motives, laced with personal ambition. He is not a subtle person. He is a hard charger and he's going to bend the thing to his will. He would always take a problem, analyze it, and *move*. He was a relentless worker."

But other Americans in Laos were upset by Shackley's arrival and the changes he made. They admitted that Shackley was hard-driving, but they pointed out that he had never worked in Asia before and didn't know much about paramilitary operations. He was an empire-builder—from thirty to three hundred case officers in Miami!—and here he was again, turning a country store into a supermarket.

In Udorn, where Lair and Landry continued to work, and where the opposition to Shackley centered, the initial sense was that the new station chief wasn't as much interested in effectiveness as size. Asked what effect Shackley had, an administrator there wearily replied, "There was a helluva lot more stuff to feed the statistics machines. The paperwork increased. Fitness reports on people. More roadwatch teams." A finance officer recalled, "I think Shackley used to sit up at night, thinking up ways to spend money. For a guy like Shackley spending bigger meant better. More people with arms, better weapons. More air support. Combat boots. And this costs money. The budget kept creeping up and creeping up."

In the field, the more recently arrived paramilitary officers tended to like Shackley because he had a management style that they understood from home, and because he was far more interested in Washington's needs than in those of the locals. But many longtime field men were appalled at the change. "Before he came, there would be these long reports generated once in a while," recalled one officer who worked in the southern panhandle. "Under him, it might be broken down into three or four reports issued more frequently, just so he could say he was getting more reporting. Some of it was really quite petty, in my opinion. To me, he was out to make a record for himself."

Another man who worked in the northwest recalled, "I think there was somebody who respected the guy, but I don't remember who it was. I hated the guy because he treated Bill Lair like shit. I suppose it was designed to put Shackley on the map. We became thumbtacks on his map. And that was what destroyed the *esprit de corps* of our movement."

The esprit had arisen from their dedication to the Laotians, from their belief that the Laotians ought to run their own war as much as possible, and from the close working relationship upcountry between the spooks and the USAID Refugee Relief types. They were part of a team, and when someone from CIA didn't have a plane and needed one, he could usually borrow one from USAID, and vice versa. The CIA men may have privately regarded themselves as members of a higher elite, but in practice they treated their USAID colleagues with respect.

Doc Weldon, by then a fluent Lao speaker with excellent contacts all over the kingdom, had been up north one day in 1966 when he learned what he thought was important information about the enemy. When he came back to Vientiane he went over to see Shackley at the CIA office, just as he had done from time to time with the earlier station chiefs. Shackley, however, had had a serious bureaucratic run-in with the Laos USAID chief, Joseph Mendenhall. Shackley and Mendenhall had argued loudly at meetings over rice appropriations, air costs, and other matters; and Weldon worked for Mendenhall.

Weldon was kept cooling his heels longer than he was accustomed to, and then finally he was let in. He gave Shackley the information. Shackley coolly asked why Weldon was coming over to tell him this. Weldon said he thought it was important. Shackley said that it was nice of Weldon to drop in, but it wasn't necessary.

Dr. Weldon said that he wasn't trying to take up the station chief's time, but—and he told Shackley about the episode with Douglas Blaufarb and his promise to always keep the intelligence agency informed.

"Well, I'm not like that," said Shackley, according to Weldon. "It's not necessary. You just run your operation up there, and you don't have any obligation to report to this office at all."

Weldon went away from the office upset. If the CIA didn't want his help, well, he had plenty of his own work to do. The same rift appeared at lower USAID and CIA levels, though it was partially patched by the efforts of a few individuals who saw the need to work together.

In later years the old hands of the Laos war used Shackley's arrival as the point at which everything changed—an oversimplification, perhaps, but one that they did not feel was unfair. Before Shackley, and before the Vietnam War became inextricably intertwined with Laos, they had believed in their jobs. If the Americans and the Laotians were not equal allies, neither were the Laotians simply carrying out the Americans' wishes. It was a partnership. The Meo, especially, had wanted to defend their territory against the North Vietnamese and were glad for American help. For their part, the Americans helped make the Laotians' sacrifices worthwhile, by building schools and clinics, resettling refugees, stocking fish ponds, and otherwise upgrading the agriculture. There were fewer than a hundred Americans upcountry in all of Laos. They didn't take over the country. They had to work closely and carefully with the local leaders, and as a result, the program had popular, grassroots support.

Shackley's arrival marked the point when the United States started using the locals almost purely for American ends in Vietnam, the old hands believed. The CIA lost interest in long-term nation-building and civic action programs as a means of pacification. The priority changed to using

Laotian "assets" to tie down North Vietnamese divisions in Vang Pao's area and to making the Ho Chi Minh Trail more expensive for the North Vietnamese to use.

These changes were especially conspicuous in the Pakse unit, responsible for operations on the Bolovens Plateau and on the southern portion of the Ho Chi Minh Trail. The unit chief there, Brandon Carlon, had patiently put together deals between the royalist military commanders and the local chiefs. To keep the tribal men of the Bolovens from being drafted into the lowland army, the chiefs agreed to form local militias, on the understanding that they would be used only for village self-defense. Much of the Bolovens had actually become pacified as a result, safe enough that Americans from Pakse occasionally picnicked with their families there.

When Shackley demanded results that Carlon didn't think were possible and resisted, Shackley replaced him with Dave "Pancho" Morales, a hard-drinking, irascible crony from his Miami days. Morales began turning village militias into trailwatch teams and trying to turn the trailwatch teams into offensive strike forces. It was a disaster. In one helicopter-borne assault on a communist position, only fifteen men out of a hundred-man tribal company came back alive. Formerly friendly villages, unwilling to sacrifice their men, began switching sides. The enemy started taking over the Bolovens Plateau again. South Laos had never had much indigenous material to work with; and paradoxically, after Shackley's pressure to upgrade, it had less. It was the start of a trend.

# The Taj Mahal

A few months after Shackley's arrival, a short, stocky U.S. Air Force captain emerged from a shuttle flight from Saigon at the Udorn Thani air base in Thailand. He asked where he might find the AB-1 building, but nobody seemed to know. Udorn was a big, busy field. Hangars and buildings lined the runway, which shimmered in the tropical heat. An Air Commando detachment took up part of the base with its T-28 propellor planes and the 432nd Tactical Reconnaissance Wing much of the rest, with its Phantom jets and a few A-1 propellor planes poking out of their shaded revetments.

Eventually the captain decided to try his luck on the southeast side, where Air America kept its maintenance hangar, cargo and utility planes, and helicopters. Somebody there pointed out a low, inconspicuous wooden building, which bore no markings of any kind.

He found Bill Lair and Pat Landry in their modest office at desks facing each other. They hadn't been expecting anybody. Lair was wearing glasses, his hair combed neatly back and looking rather prim and proper, like a schoolteacher. Potbellied Pat Landry, who was wearing shorts and rubber shower sandals, was tapping his desk with his swagger stick. It was, thought the air force captain, a little peculiar for the paramilitary headquarters of a large covert war.

He reported in, squaring his broad shoulders and formally stating his name in the military manner. Hesitantly, Lair asked whether Ted Shackley had sent him and the captain replied that he didn't know who Shackley was. Lair seemed to relax a bit on hearing that, and told the captain to talk to other people in the office about housing and getting settled.

The captain was thirty-four years old. His name was Richard Secord.

Secord had been in enough strange situations himself not to make snap judgments. As an Air Commando, he had flown about two hundred combat missions in South Vietnam in 1962 and 1963 in T-28 fighter-bombers bearing the markings of the South Vietnamese air force. The operation was called Farmgate, and it was secret because the Americans weren't supposed to be fighting in South Vietnam then. After that he had been sent to Iran, where he worked with the Shah's air force and U.S. Special Forces in an even more secret operation to suppress Kurdish insurgents in northwestern Iran. At the Air Commandos' Special Air Warfare center back at Hurlburt Field in Florida he had been the director of tactical operations, reporting to Heinie Aderholt, who at that time was the commander. Secord had then gone to Maxwell Air Force Base, Alabama, for midcareer training at the Air Command and Staff College; and it was there, at Aderholt's suggestion, that the CIA got hold of him and asked him to volunteer for a two-year stint in Southeast Asia.

As the AB-1 building, a former air force man on the staff briefed Secord on the Laos war, which was being run by a civilian ambassador and the CIA behind a false front of political neutrality. To Secord, it seemed like an awfully convoluted set-up: U.S. troops were forbidden in Laos because of some treaty or other. Special Forces troops crossed into southeastern Laos to raid the Ho Chi Minh Trail all the time, but other exceptions were not allowed. Did it make sense? Not entirely, he thought.

Soon afterwards Lair and Landry emerged from their office and told Secord to go see all of the military regions of Laos for himself. He went; and in that trip over the shrouded peaks and meandering footpaths of Laos, landing at most of the major strips and some of the minor ones, the red-clay STOL strips scratched out of the mountainside, Secord got a close-up view of the people and the land they were fighting for.

He discovered that the Laos war was tactically opposite of the war on the other side of the Annamite Mountains. In South Vietnam, the enemy controlled most of the countryside and the American side controlled the roads. In Laos, the enemy was confined to within a few kilometers, or "klicks," of the roads, while the pro-American locals observed and attacked roads from remote sites.

He met the various lowland Lao, hilltribes, Thais, and Americans, and gradually began to understand how the pieces fit together. Or, in the case of airpower, how they didn't fit together. A lot of different organizations were sending up planes—the Laotian royalists, the Thais, the U.S. Navy and Air Force, and even Air America with its few armed T-28s—but the ground forces couldn't always get tactical air support when they wanted it. The command and control systems were different for each organization and didn't mesh well with one another or with the forces on the ground. Secord decided to try to help change that, and to make airpower more efficient.

By the time he got back to Udorn the rainy season of mid-1966 was drawing to a close. The North Vietnamese were preparing for their dry season offensives and Lair and Landry for their countermoves. "Bill and Pat were real artists in moving forces around, and at drawing blood from the Dreaded Enemy, as we called them," Secord recalled. "They were a real pair. Calm. Cool. Reasoned. They knew the Little Guys, knew what they could and couldn't do. I saw them absorbing the shocks and calmly issuing directives to do this and do that. They had command of the situation.

"Basically, they had split the labor, with Bill managing the north and Pat the south on a day-to-day basis"—to an extent, they had accommodated Shackley—"though they cross-talked all the time and knew what the other was doing. When one was gone the other was perfectly capable of running the whole thing. They knew the terrain better than almost anybody. They had a rapport with the different groups that probably would have been very difficult to beat. Bill spoke Thai very well, and Pat was deceptive. He'd try to conceal the fact that he spoke Thai, but he did.

"So the two of them together by virtue of their backgrounds and characters and intelligence and chemistry worked fine together. We always called them the Dynamic Duo. And they truly were. Those of us who worked for them with very few exceptions—there were a few exceptions— really liked them, not only respected them but liked them.

"I learned more in my first year in Laos than I'd learned in the previous ten years."

As a newcomer, Secord could only steer events as a member of an existing team, and even then he irritated many of his teammates, for he was abrasive and condescending and had a habit, some said, of taking personal credit for group achievements. Still, he was there when airpower was growing fast; and when the ex–air force man at AB-1 was transferred, Secord created a role for himself with Shackley's support.

As the roads dried out, North Vietnamese trucks were observed coming into northeast Laos in record numbers. "We weren't stopping truck activity around Sam Neua," Secord recalled. "So I undertook to beg, borrow, and steal USAF fighter assets to interdict some of the activity up there. I explained to Bill what I had in mind, and that was deploying a Meo guy that we'd trained to be a forward air controller on the ground. He was named Tallman because he was a couple inches taller than the average Meo. He spoke fair English, and he had a lot of potential. He was a real good soldier, plus he had a lot of respect within the tribe. He'd already called in some great air strikes.

"We called it Operation Night Watch. Somehow or other we got it authorized. I wrote it up and the 7th Air Force went along with it and put together a frag order for some A-26s." A frag order, short for "fragmentary order," assigned planes daily to specific operations and targets. The A-26s were the new designation for the World War II–era B-26 bombers, the longtime favorite of unconventional air operations. Given the radio call sign "Nimrods," they were based at Nakhorn Phanom, Thailand, under the command of Secord's ex-boss, Col. Heinie Aderholt, who was making one of his periodic returns to the Southeast Asia war theater.

"The Nimrods flew to the north on successive nights to go under Tallman's forward air control and interdict the truck traffic," said Secord. "It went on for about a week, and there wasn't any more truck traffic seen for thirty days. The enemy were stunned. We just tore 'em up. Of course Bill and Pat were delighted. Anything we could do to interrupt the flow of supplies was important. Then we started putting Tallman, who could really get in tight on targets, against troop concentrations, headquarters, little bivouacs, things like this. We had a lot of success."

Soon after that Tallman died, shot under mysterious circumstances by his own troops. (The suspects were taken to Sam Thong and given a severe public beating on the runway, on Vang Pao's orders.) But Secord, working with Aderholt and other Air Commandos, had made his point. The coordinated bombings showed, said Secord, "what we could do with the air weapon if we managed it just right. You couldn't do it willy-nilly, helter-skelter, just run out there and push some buttons. They learned that there's a lot more to this air business than meets the eye. You don't just send a bunch of fighter pilots up north and tell them to kill the enemy."

Lair was worried about the guerillas' dependence on airpower, but he felt he had no choice. There were too many North Vietnamese regulars on the roads for Vang Pao's men to stop by themselves. With Secord's help he could get more out of the U.S. Air Force than before, and that was what Shackley wanted him to do.

Soon after Secord's arrival the station chief came down from Vientiane again. The visit was tense. "I didn't particularly care for the bastard either, to tell you the truth," Secord recalled of Shackley, "but he was effective. He was very precise. Very, very good mind. I regarded him as a novice in tactical matters—he had no field experience and, you know, you're not born with that experience, so I don't say it in a denigrating way. But he knew what his orders were and he was trying to carry 'em out. And he also recognized the importance of Bill and Pat or he could have easily removed them. In those days a chief of station was a god. A veritable feudal lord."

Shackley, having failed to separate Landry from Lair, made two changes in the Udorn staff. The first was to put Thomas Clines, his deputy from Miami, in as the chief of ground operations, one step down from Landry. Clines was a tall, burly, blue-eyed guy who radiated streetwise competence. At first Lair and Landry thought of him as Shackley's spy and didn't give him anything to do. Later they ignored him. Clines and Secord, however, became fast friends—"foxhole buddies," as Secord put it.

Shackley's second appointment, in December 1966, was to elevate Secord to the same level in Udorn as Clines. He was put in charge of the air liaison division—the job title being euphemistic, as most titles were. Secord was not strictly a liaison, or coordinator, between the CIA and the air force, though that was part of what he did.

The 7th Air Force—the command group for mainland Southeast Asia, headquartered at Tan Son Nhut air base outside Saigon—was led by a devout proponent of existing air force doctrine, Lt. Gen. William W. Momyer. The doctrine had been developed for a war with the Soviet Union rather than a brushfire war in the Third World, and it emphasized jets, which were perfect for reaching distant targets in Siberia but too fast for close coordination with soldiers on the ground. Rigid and conventional in his thinking, Momyer disliked Ambassador Sullivan, the CIA, and their black theater of the war, over which the regular military had little control.

As a result, Secord found getting tactical air support a battle in itself. "We were always trying to pry assets out of the air force at times and places where they didn't want to go," he said. "You had to push 'em, cajole 'em, at times threaten them. Most calls for tac air were urgent or semi-urgent. I would have to go to the 7/13th in Udorn [the Thai-based subsidiary of the 7th Air Force] to request diversion of assets in the air, or else the launching of alert forces somewhere. My people were always trying to corrupt the process because the process itself simply wasn't structured for our kind of war, in support of guerillas. It was a continual frustration."

Another part of Secord's job was arranging for helicopter transportation for tribal reconnaissance teams along the Ho Chi Minh Trail. A line had been drawn on the maps of southern Laos, running more or less north and south. To the east of that line, U.S. Special Forces teams operated. Most of the CIA's work was west of the line, where about eighty tribal teams (most of them led by men from Thailand's special forces) were at any given time, some of them always being choppered in and out or needing supplies.

A third part of Secord's job was coordinating technical intelligence for Shackley, who was spending heavily on new equipment and personnel. An Air America plane was outfitted with reconnaissance cameras to fill the gaps in the military coverage. More photo interpreters came over to Udorn from Langley. Ground teams began collecting enemy radio transmissions; and later on eavesdropping planes flew over Laos recording enemy signals. Many enemy messages were in code of one kind or another, so this meant a staff of cryptoanalysts and translators, too.

And then there were the projects of the Hobby Shop, the CIA's Technical Services Division, which sent its gadgets to Udorn for field-testing. Secord's favorite, developed by an ad hoc committee under intense pressure from Shackley, was a hand-held truck-counter for the tribal teams watching the Trail. Called the Hark-1, it was a survival radio redesigned with buttons for the trail-watchers to push. Each button had a picture of a type of military equipment—a truck, a tank, a piece of heavy artillery, and so forth. Each time one of the trail-watchers saw the piece of enemy equipment, he pushed the corresponding button. When he was finished, he pushed another button that transmitted all the data in a single "squirt." The radio signals, picked up by aircraft orbiting overhead, were relayed to Thailand, and the message and the exact position of the transmission plotted for the intel analyzers and then telexed to the air force. Now, when trucks drove from North Vietnam into the Mu Gia Pass, the air force knew about it in minutes, and jets dove in for the kill.

Secord was maverick enough to get along with his temporary CIA bosses. He picked up the lingo and the attitudes of the office in Udorn where they all worked seven days a week, dressed the way they wanted, propped their feet on the desk, and joked about the Dynamic Duo, the Dreaded Enemy, and building the war from a country store to a supermarket.

Gradually, toward the end of 1966 and in the first months of 1967, Secord became accepted as a member of the team. One of the major battles of that dry season was at Nakhang, northeast of the Plain of Jars on the road to Sam Neua. After losing it the year before, Vang Pao had taken it back a few months later and rebuilt it. Now the Vietnamese were trying to take it again.

The assault began at dawn on January 6, 1967, during a week of solid overcast weather, which made airpower difficult to use. That morning the cloud ceiling was nearly down to the ground, with some of the nearby mountaintops piercing the clouds into the clear skies above. The enemy captured a kidney-shaped hill overlooking the base, which had a .50-caliber machine-gun nest at its summit. They swung the machine gun around and fired at the command bunker and the airstrip. One of the two Americans on the base, a young man from USAID named Don Sjostrom, whom Pop Buell had been grooming as his replacement, was killed instantly when he jumped up and tried to lead a charge to retake the position. The other American, a CIA paramilitary officer named Mike Lynch, managed to radio out for air support; and this was where Secord came in, as the Agency's air force liaison.

Secord got a flight of F-105s diverted from the Ho Chi Minh Trail, and the lead pilot, who knew the area well, performed the risky maneuver of penetrating the cloud cover above the site. The pilot was going way too fast and low to be able to line up his weapons right—that was the problem with jets, of course; they were just too fast to maneuver in small spaces— but he made enough treetop-level passes over the base to slow the enemy down a bit and to cheer up the Meo defenders. When the jet left, a propellor-driven A-1 attack plane from Udorn dove through the clouds and took its place, but by then the North Vietnamese had overrun most of the compound and were firing at Lynch, who was barricaded inside a building and radioing despairingly for help of any kind.

Over that day, that night, and the next day, the planes broke the attack and sent the North Vietnamese into retreat. To accomplish this, according to a later report, the air force used 62 MK-47 bombs, 27 cluster bomb units or CBUs, four cans of napalm, 427 high-explosive rockets, 28 white phosphorous marker or "Willy Pete" rockets, 10,300 rounds of 7.62mm machine-gun ammunition, and 14,000 rounds of 20mm cannon fire, plus other conventional bombs, cluster bombs, rockets, flares, and cannon and machine-gun fire.

The air force and its overwhelming firepower had saved the day—or at least, that was what the air force thought; and it was easy to see why: Vang Pao's guerillas had gotten in trouble, the CIA man on the ground had called for help, and the air force pilots had come in at considerable risk to themselves to save the good guys and send the commies packing. It was like a Western movie, from that point of view: The fort got encircled by Indians and the cavalry came to the rescue, with commies instead of Indians and pilots instead of cavalry.

◆

Bill Lair admired the air force pilots' skill and bravery. He also admired Secord. He, Secord, and Landry stayed up nights together at the office for the fighting at Nakhang and other bases, and Lair watched Secord work the radio. For long stretches there was nothing to do but chew fingernails and drink coffee. They were far away from the fighting, and often they had no way of knowing what was happening; and when they did there were lags in getting the air force to respond. That's where Secord had come in, and Lair had never seen anybody cut through bureaucracy better.

Secord used all the right military jargon, and everything from cajoling to reasoning to bullying, to get the 7th Air Force outside Saigon to do what Udorn wanted. Normally the watch officer was some godforsaken captain or major. Did the major want to wake the general to see for himself, and risk the general's displeasure at being woken for such an *obvious* emergency? Secord demanded. Did the major have any idea what would happen to him personally if the planes were not on their way within three minutes? Did the major wish to be personally responsible for the deaths of Americans and their friendly allies? And so on. Secord didn't miss a trick, and Lair was grateful.

Which was not to say that Lair thought the air force had saved the day either at Nakhang or anyplace else. He thought that defensive, fixed-site battles of that sort should never have happened in the first place. And wouldn't have, if he were running the war, but he wasn't anymore.

If Nakhang hadn't been rebuilt the way it was, and if the air force hadn't based its Jolly Green Giant helicopters there for rescue missions, it wouldn't have made such an attractive target for the other side, Lair believed. It was the kind of target that practically invited attack by North Vietnamese infantry. And with jets to do the heavy fighting for them, the Meo had lost incentive. They had become dependent on the planes. In the aftermath of the battle, the Meo wouldn't go out on patrol around the base to reconnoiter for the enemy. It was too dangerous, they claimed.

So Lair didn't like the supermarket war. He thought its victories were defeats in disguise. But he was fascinated by the potential for the use of air, and tempted by it. His old friend Heinie Aderholt, commanding the 56th Air Commando Wing at Nakhorn Phanom, was already making plans for the end of the dry season, when some of the enemy troops returned to North Vietnam. Together he and Heinie would use the Meo to bottle up enemy battalions in valleys—hold them up just long enough to send in the good old slow-moving propellor planes, the A-26s and the A-1s. They'd do some damage then. Heinie was very good, very creative with airpower—and he said Dick Secord was about the best junior officer he'd ever seen.

So it was complicated. Lair didn't like the supermarket war, but he liked Secord, who was helping raise the war to supermarket status. While working in Udorn out of uniform, Secord had been promoted to major; and Lair surmised that Secord was heading toward a general's star, or higher—that if he kept his nose clean he was a good bet to make air force chief of staff.

If he kept his nose clean. Because there was one other thing that worried Bill Lair. On quiet nights Major Secord had taken to exploring the bawdy bar scene with Shackley's blue-eyed boy, the streetwise, underworked Tom Clines. Seeing the two of them together made Lair uneasy. He couldn't explain why, but his instincts nagged him about it.

◆

By 1967, the CIA's wooden, nondescript AB-1 building at Udorn, topped by radio antennae, with air-conditioning units sagging out its windows, was crowded and run-down. The congressmen and other VIPs who swung by on the Tour always looked around in surprise, and their expressions said it even if their words did not: You run your big, top-secret operation in Laos from *here?*

There had been a space shortage even before the case officers' wives had moved in to work as secretaries. The new staff who had come in under the Shackley regime, like Clines and Secord, made it even worse.

Lair decided to get a bigger office, not because he really wanted to, but because it was expected of him. He drew up preliminary plans and sent them to Langley. The construction estimate on his new building came in at $135,000.

Headquarters sent an engineer out for an appraisal. The engineer took a look around and went in to see Lair in the small office he still shared with Landry. The engineer made it clear that Lair didn't understand the situation. Pointing at Lair's plans, he said, "You can't start with a building like this. By the time you finish, it'll be too small."

The engineer drew up some plans of his own. He called in architects, and they worked with the elaborate specifications the Agency has to ensure security. By the time the new plans were finished, the estimated cost was a million dollars.

In the next meeting it was Lair's turn to object. It was one of the rare times he allowed anger to show on his face. He didn't want anything as grand as that. He didn't need it and he hadn't asked for it.

The engineer told him firmly, "You're obviously not the executive type. You've got to plan for expansion." The Udorn facility, said the engineer confidently, was going to expand.

The engineer went back to headquarters and won approval for his plans. The building went up. It was two-story, mostly white, near some large, spreading acacia trees to one side of the Air America repair shops. There weren't many windows, because the Agency doesn't like windows, and there were combination locks with buttons to push next to the doors. But it was a handsome modern building, radiating good taste and solidity and prestige. There were a couple of kitchens inside the new building at Udorn, even some sleeping quarters.

The new building, like the old one, was officially known as the administrative center for the 4802nd Joint Liaison Detachment, at the Udorn Thani Royal Thai Air Force Base. But Bill Lair and the people working with him called it the Taj Mahal.

As soon as they moved in, the size of the staff increased to fill the space. Overnight, the bureaucracy ballooned. Security was supposed to be tight, but before long the Thai women and some Meo girls who did the cleaning got the door lock combinations and went in and out without escorts.

Lair and Landry got adjoining offices on the ground floor near the front entrance. They had large desks, couches and coffee tables, and little placards with their names outside their doors, just like real executives in the States. Their doors opened onto a shared anteroom, where their secretary sat. They couldn't see the airfield anymore. There weren't any windows on their side of the building. But they could hear the thunder of jets on take-off through the walls.

# Commando Club

At Udorn, Richard Secord took up flying in his spare time. Men from his old unit, the First Air Commandos, ran the T-28 program, and they had extra planes. Every month or so he flew a stubby prop-driven fighter-bomber down to Bangkok to see his wife and children. More often, on slow afternoons at the office, he filled in as an instructor for Meo tribesmen learning to fly. Or else he slipped a Lao royalist insignia—a white three-headed elephant—into the frame that held any kind of insignia and buzzed across the Mekong on bombing and strafing runs, if he thought his bosses wouldn't find out, and they didn't.

Getting airborne was a welcome relief from working in an office. If Secord had to break the rules to fly, it didn't trouble him much. He had come to see that in the Laos war a lot of the rules didn't make sense. The Ho Chi Minh Trail was a case in point.

By the spring of 1967, the North Vietnamese had upgraded the interconnected routes that made up the Trail. They had more segments suitable for truck travel now, along with footpaths for porters pushing bicycles loaded with cargo. They had underwater fords, and underground bunkers, warehouses, and hospitals. They had more antiaircraft guns than before, which forced the low-and-slow-flying A-26 propeller planes to fly higher and lose accuracy. For the North Vietnamese, traveling on the Trail was a dangerous, miserable ordeal because of the bombs and because of malaria, not to mention leeches, hunger, mud, and rain. But the traffic kept growing: The infiltration rate rose from roughly thirty-five thousand in 1965 to double that in 1966, and was about to double again, according to American intelligence estimates.

The U.S. government was throwing everything it had against the Trail—except its own regular infantrymen. The human effort included Laotian tribesmen, Thais (both Paru and the special forces branch of Thailand's army), South Vietnamese, various local Asian mercenaries, and U.S. Green Berets leading teams from the South Vietnamese side of the border. The technological effort included bombs from U.S. Air Force and Navy planes and newly invented devices. The U.S. secretary of defense, Robert McNamara, had asked a group of scientists to determine whether a barrier—a sort of electric fence—could be erected across the Trail to block the traffic. Although this original concept, the "McNamara Line," turned out not to be feasible, a multibillion-dollar research-and-development effort brought new gadgets into Laos on a piecemeal basis. Many of them were field-tested at Udorn: remote sensors that relied on different operating principles—seismic, acoustic, and antimagnetic—to detect trucks; and various night-vision devices for airplanes, like low-light TV cameras and the first generation of forward-looking infrared, or FLIR, cameras. There was a rain-making project using specially equipped C-130 cargo planes to drop silver halide crystals and other chemicals into cloud formations.

Secord and his colleagues discovered that many of these inventions didn't work in the field. The rain-making project, for example, was famous for dropping torrential rains onto friendly forces—six feet of rain in one hour on a Green Beret team, according to the folklore. Another special project involved dropping about 150,000 pounds of Calgon detergent onto a Trail intersection. Scientists in the States claimed that the combination of supermarket chemicals and ordinary rain would turn the ground slippery. Secord helped test the concept, which was nicknamed Project Mud. "When we first dumped this Calgon on the Trail, and it rained, the enemy thought we were practicing chemical warfare," he remembered. "Then they discovered it was harmless and they went on their merry way. It wasn't any more muddy than any other place. It was absolute nonsense."

It was clear to Secord that nothing the U.S. government was then trying had a chance of stopping the Trail traffic. He decided that the only way to do it was an invasion of southern Laos by regular U.S. infantrymen, backed by artillery and airpower. Of course, invading Laos with American conventional forces would be a violation of the Geneva accords—or rather a violation of the curious and selective way that the U.S. government was trying to live up to the accords—but so what? The accords had never stopped the North Vietnamese from sending their troops into Laos. Why couldn't the United States?

But the U.S. government was not about to invade Laos with a large ground force. Not while Sullivan was ambassador. And so the plainclothes major took to the air. There was nothing like firing rockets into enemy positions or dropping a few bombs to work off his frustrations. He played by his own rules, and though he got along with those he respected, including both Shackley and Lair, he chafed at everybody else who tried to fence him in.

Secord's aggressiveness frequently got him in trouble with Sullivan's staff. The U.S. code of conduct for the war, the rules of engagement, kept most air strikes within two hundred yards of roads and motorable trails, and away from civilian settlements. Secord kept pushing the limits of the rules, and occasionally went over them. "I used to say that I've been thrown out of his office more times than most people have been in it," Secord recalled of the ambassador. "Air strikes on this, that, and the other outside of the rules of engagement."

One incident in particular, in 1967, had especially galled Sullivan. In the ambassador's version, Secord proposed bombing a village on the edge of the Plain of Jars, and the embassy turned him down. Secord brashly proposed it again and was turned down again. A month or so later it was accidentally discovered from aerial photos of bomb damage of a nearby target that Secord's village had been obliterated. Somebody on the air attaché's staff tried to find out what had happened, and the air force said that the CIA claimed the target had been validated by the ambassador.

Sullivan was furious. He called Secord into his office, and Secord claimed that it was a navigational error on the part of the pilots. "In the fog of war, you can't be certain of all your facts and figures, but I was certainly suspicious of Secord," Sullivan recalled later. "He was an arrogant little bastard. Maybe supercilious is a better word. He gave the impression that he knew better than I did or anybody on my team. He was a pain in the ass."

In later years Secord didn't recollect the bombing incident Sullivan referred to and said there was another one, also on the edge of the Plain of Jars, that showed what an impediment to winning the war the ambassador had become. "I recall a request that we made several times and finally got done, and argued with him a lot about, to ambush a high-level enemy meeting in a couple of small structures that he kept calling a village. I kept saying it wasn't. We were very confident of the intelligence about the coming meeting. A high-ranking NVA [North Vietnamese Army] colonel was going to be there. An NVA colonel is a power dog, let me tell you. I wanted to ambush it by air, and we did. We initiated it with an attack by a flight of A-1s and followed up by F-105s, and we were very successful. We got 'em.

"But I mean, we had to argue over this unnecessarily. He kept saying it was a village, that there were innocent civilians around. It wasn't a village.

It was deserted, really. Well inside so-called Pathet Lao territory. An important target. My second go-round with him I had to bring my photo interpreter up there and show him the row cropping in the gardens were typically North Vietnamese. He didn't believe it, and we showed him row cropping in North Vietnamese gardens identical to the row cropping scheme being used right there. And that did it. But he hated it."

Secord kept going up against Sullivan, and then Momyer's 7th Air Force, and then the ambassador, then the air force again, sometimes losing but always coming back for more. Eventually he realized that his problems were not with either man or even with their individual institutions. The problem was larger than that. Neither the State Department nor the air force— nor the CIA, in fact—had an incentive, much less a responsibility, to fight the war the way anybody else wanted to fight it. Each institution had its own chain of command with competing interests and priorities. The turf struggles brought to mind a concept that Secord had learned about at West Point (from which he graduated before the air force started its own service academy). The concept, called unity of command, held that military efficiency was impossible without all of the commanders on the same side taking orders from the same source. You couldn't have parts of your war machine competing or only reluctantly cooperating with other parts, like feuding barons and dukes in the Middle Ages.

But as Secord looked at the Laos war, that was exactly what he saw:

- An ambassador who insisted on complicated rules for reasons that didn't make sense anymore, based on a treaty that was obsolete, which he himself had helped negotiate.
- The U.S. Air Force, which didn't feel it owed much to Sullivan.
- The U.S. Army, allowed to send Special Forces teams into an arbitrarily chosen portion of the Ho Chi Minh Trail, but not into the other parts without the ambassador's permission, which it usually didn't get.
- The CIA, which didn't feel it owed much of anything to the air force or army.
- The same held true internally in Laos, with a weak central government under Souvanna Phouma and strong regional military commanders. Vang Pao didn't feel he owed much to the leaders of the other military regions, and they felt the same way about him.

Everywhere there were turf problems. There was no single headquarters for the entire Indochina war, and no strong-minded sensible generalissimo who would knock heads together when organizational squabbles arose.

It was a huge problem. It hadn't mattered so much when the war was young and small and local, when Bill Lair and Vang Pao made their decisions sitting around a campfire. As airpower came in, and as Laos became more and more intertwined with Vietnam, the size and the complexity of fighting had outgrown the old peculiar command structures. The war needed different management if the United States intended to win. At the Taj Mahal, Richard Secord and the others talked about it, cussed about it, joked about it. It wasn't the right way to run a war, but it was the way things were.

◆

One day in the middle of 1967, Bill Lair, Pat Landry, and Richard Secord were summoned to a meeting at the headquarters of the 7/13th Air Force at Udorn; Shackley had a scheduling conflict and couldn't make it. The 7/13th was in itself a chain-of-command nightmare, a bastard offspring of the 7th Air Force in Saigon, which controlled its operations, and the 13th Air Force at Clark Air Base in the Philippines, which was supposed to run its administration and logistics.

Presiding over the meeting was a four-star general, Hunter Harris, the commander in chief of PACAF, the air force's Pacific air command, based in Hawaii. Four-star generals didn't come to Udorn often, and Lair and Secord knew it had to be some kind of turf problem that went over their heads.

General Harris and his retinue of lower-ranking generals and colonels proceeded to lay out in workmanlike fashion the concept for a new piece of electronic wizardry to be placed on the top of a mountain in far northeastern Laos near the North Vietnamese border.

The mountain was Phou Pha Thi, also known by its landing site number, Lima Site 85. The CIA men nodded, not needing to be told where it was. In earlier years Tony Poe had been injured nearby and Thong had led retreats across ridges and ravines within sight of the summit. The Meo of Sam Neua had always considered it their ultimate refuge.

In the Lao language, the word *phou* simply means "mountain." At a little under six thousand feet, Phou Pha Thi was not the tallest mountain in the kingdom, but it was the most distinctive—a broad-based, ridged, limestone mass that rose first gradually and then suddenly and almost vertically up to a rough plateau on the top. There was a cliff on the western side, near enough to vertical that a skydiver could conceivably jump off it with a parachute and survive; and on the forested eastern side a slope of about a forty-five-degree angle except near the top, where the pitch was steeper. Near the highest point on the plateau there was a little sink in the limestone where the best opium in Laos had been grown. There were a few scraggly Meo huts nearby; and farther down the ridge a hazardous little airstrip that had gone into disuse as helicopters became more available.

The helicopters had started coming in around a year before, to install a navigational beacon called a TACAN, for Tactical Air Control and Navigation. The air force had come to Udorn for advice on that one, too, and Bill Lair had told them where to put it. He had always thought Pha Thi would have been the perfect place for a vacation cabin, a sort of eagle's nest with a view and lovely cool air, if there hadn't been a war going on. But there was a war and the mountain was less than a hundred fifty air miles from Hanoi.

The new piece of electronic wizardry was to be an addition to the TACAN beacon. The air force men called it a "blind bombing" device, model TSQ-81, which would carry the operational identifier of Commando Club. A unit in the Strategic Air Command had figured out a way to modify existing antiaircraft tracking equipment, feed computer data into it, and essentially reverse its original purpose. The TSQ-81 could direct fighters and bombers precisely over their targets, even through heavy cloud cover, and electronically release their bombs at exactly the right instant.

The air force men said that the Commando Club would enable them to hit the enemy right where it hurt. The equipment had been specially designed to be taken apart and helicoptered into remote locations, and then reassembled. They would man it with air force people, who would go through the formality of resigning from the military so as to be able to comply with Sullivan's requirements of bringing only unarmed American civilians into Laos.

The briefing went on, a lot of questions asked and answered. Finally somebody noticed that Bill Lair hadn't said a word and asked him what he thought.

Since Shackley's arrival Lair had grown more and more reticent. He kept his eyes averted, and those who knew him saw the smouldering anger and the depression. But he was the senior CIA man at the meeting, and some of the air force men knew him by reputation as an old timer who knew everything about Laos. So they waited for their meek Texan oracle to speak and geared down to his pace. It always took awhile; Lair was a slow talker.

Lair said, Yeah, the air force could put its new equipment on the mountain, and it would last awhile; but it would also create a high-value target. They had to remember that Pha Thi was close to the North Vietnamese border, and that Hanoi would consider it a provocation, a threat to its security. There was no question that Hanoi was going to find out about the installation and make a plan to attack it.

The first sign of Hanoi's intentions, Lair went on, would be road construction. That was how they operated. The enemy would start building a road to the mountain. Once they got near the base they'd come in with a big force, and then the air force would have to get its guys out fast.

The air force men asked whether the tribal force could defend it.

Everybody waited for Lair to answer.

Up to a point, Lair said finally. The mountain itself was favorable terrain for a conventional ground defense. The trouble was, defending fixed sites wasn't what the Meo were good at. There weren't any ground troops in Laos up to the standards of, say, the 82nd Airborne Division. The Meo would always run if the North Vietnamese attacked in force. That's just the way they were. They ran away to survive.

The meeting broke up with the air force men enthusiastic over Commando Club, and Lair and Secord unsure whether it would be installed. The spooks were uncomfortable with the idea, because Sam Neua was already shaky and because the device would benefit the U.S. Air Force with its Hanoi bombing raids at the possible expense of Vang Pao. But it was all over their heads, and Shackley and Sullivan would have to make the call.

◆

As it turned out, Ambassador Sullivan had already gotten a cable from Lyndon Johnson himself directing that the Commando Club be installed; it was one of only two or three presidential orders that Sullivan received during his tenure. So the decision was already made.

Within weeks a man in civilian clothes, with a bristle haircut and erect posture went into the CIA station and attempted to see Shackley, who refused to meet with him. He then went across the street to see the air attaché, who took him upstairs to the second floor of the embassy, where they could talk in electronically assured privacy in a new soundproof chamber known as the bubble. It was a room inside a room, with transparent walls and floor, equipped with a device that created a whirring "white" noise, up and down the frequencies of speech, to protect against eavesdropping.

Here in this cocoon of privacy the visitor, whose name was Gerald Clayton, explained that he was in charge of Commando Club and that until recently he had been a lieutenant colonel in the Strategic Air Command. He was a civilian now, with an ID card from Lockheed Aircraft Services to prove it. When he went back across the river to Udorn, where he would live, however, he would change back into uniform again, as the commander of a radar evaluation detachment that had no official existence. The air attaché, who was used to double and triple layers of identity in Wonderland, listened politely and then took the colonel downstairs to meet Ambassador Sullivan. The three men agreed that Pha Thi was precarious, and that the Commando Club men would be given plenty of time to get out when or if the enemy attacked.

Huge air force cargo helicopters lifted the metal, ribbed, trailer-like components of the Commando Club unit to Phou Pha Thi, where they were assembled next to the TACAN unit near the edge of the limestone cliff. A radar dish antenna was installed on the roof of the main building. As insurance, the electronic gadgetry on the inside was packed with C-4 explosive, and a layer of thermite was placed over the crypto gear, so that if worst came to worst part of the building would be blown into smithereens and the rest melted down into goo. The main radar building lay some distance above the old runway with its cluster of buildings, and a steep scramble above the helicopter landing zone that had replaced it. The CIA enlarged its quarters near the helicopter pad and upgraded its communications gear. Meo soldiers were flown in. Trenches were dug. Mines were laid. And sentries were stationed.

On October 20, 1967, less than two weeks before the Commando Club was due to begin operating, somebody noticed a couple of Lao Buddhist monks near the top of the mountain. Or at least they looked like monks— the bare feet, the saffron robes, the shaved heads and shaved eyebrows. The monk-like men had cameras with them, and they had also made sketches of Phou Pha Thi. They were flown out on a chopper for questioning. "They were taken into VP's tender mercy," said Secord, "and we never saw them again."

◆

While the air force was installing its equipment on Pha Thi, relations between Lair and Shackley stayed tense. But the two men buried any personal rancor under polite professionalism.

Lair had been doing a lot of thinking. He admitted to himself that part of his anger with Shackley was injured pride. He had always thought that he, Lair, would make a pretty good station chief himself. Not chief of Moscow or Rio de Janeiro or someplace he didn't know anything about; but if headquarters had wanted a good station chief for Bangkok or Vientiane, it wouldn't have had to look any further. Nobody knew more about Thailand and Laos; nobody had better contacts; nobody was better at getting the locals to do things that America wanted while keeping the locals believing that they had done it for their own sake instead.

But headquarters had sent Shackley. Lair knew that Des FitzGerald, his old mentor, had something to do with it, and that just made it worse. He went through all the usual stages, shock, denial, anger, grief, before accepting that it wasn't Shackley's fault for landing the Vientiane assignment. He disagreed as strongly as ever with Shackley's ideas for running the war, knew in his brain and his heart that they were wrong. But Lair was able to distinguish between the man and his ideas, and over time he had reluctantly admitted that Shackley had his good side as a boss and human being.

For one thing, Shackley was essentially honest. It was true that he had brought his own people in and was putting them one by one in positions that would undercut Lair's authority. But it was all done in the open. There was nothing devious about it. Shackley dealt with midlevel subordinates in the field far more than his predecessors had done; but he often brought Lair along on his field trips, and when he didn't, he kept Lair informed. And that straightforwardness counted for something, in Lair's book. Not for a whole lot, but for something.

For another, he had come to understand why Shackley was on the fast track. The two men went together to meetings with the army and air force brass in Vietnam, to discuss enemy truck movements down the Trail and the U.S. reactions. The army and air force were always proposing larger roles for themselves in Laos; and Lair watched, an admiring bystander, as Shackley fended them off.

The generals outnumbered the spooks and they looked impressive in their uniforms, with all those rows of decorations, but they were staff-fed. Whenever they needed detailed information, aides stepped forward to whisper in their ears or lay statistics on the table. The generals were never quite sure of themselves when Shackley challenged their facts, figures, and assumptions.

Shackley took them on single-handed. He seldom even referred to his notes. He had a cool, lucid mind, extraordinary recall, and an organized way of laying out his arguments, one, two, three, while looking the generals in the eye until they squirmed. He never showed the slightest doubt, even when Lair happened to know his information was suspect—claiming, for example, that CIA trailwatch teams killed a half-dozen North Vietnamese for every man of their own lost in firefights.

Even when he was wrong, a boss like Shackley had his uses, and Lair came to rely on him in the turf wars with the military, just as Shackley relied on Lair for help in running the paramilitary end of the war. Shackley needed help talking with the Thais and Laotians, who found him cold and arrogant, and wouldn't cooperate unless Lair was there to talk them around.

So the two men agreed to disagree. Lair respected and even grew to halfway like Shackley, which was about as far as he could go. Shackley, for his part, was unaware of Lair's inner turmoil, and unaware that Lair thought the supermarket war was tearing Laos apart.

◆

Around the time Commando Club became operational, Shackley asked Lair to come up to the station in Vientiane for a chat. Lair dutifully flew up to see him. That day the subject on Shackley's mind was a place eighty air miles to the west of Pha Thi, in north-central Laos, called Nam Bac.

Nam Bac was outside Vang Pao's military region and roughly north of the old royal capital, Luang Prabang. It was a rather unimportant valley that had changed hands once or twice in the war and was currently being occupied by a light force of Pathet Lao, a couple of companies, around the airstrip. Udorn had collected the intel on Nam Bac and had sent it to the Country Team as a matter of routine.

Shackley wanted to know what Lair thought about a plan the Country Team, especially the army attaché, was discussing for Nam Bac. What would happen if six or eight FAR, or Force Armée Royale, infantry battalions went in?

Lair mulled it over. He could visualize the Country Team cooking up plans in that new soundproof bubble of theirs in the embassy, Sullivan and Shackley and the others playing field marshal and loving it. (Should we move the little guys *here* or *there* on the map? How many T-28 sorties? Where's the NVA 316th Division now?) Some Lao general had suggested the idea of capturing Nam Bac, and the Country Team had taken it up, enlarging the plan. They would look good in Washington, thought Lair, if the royalists could take and hold Nam Bac.

Lair said in his quiet way that he didn't recommend it.

Why not? said Shackley. There were no real roads for the North Vietnamese to come in on.

Lair explained that Nam Bac still wasn't all that far from North Vietnam. Forty or fifty miles as the crow flew. A large, fixed Laotian force would create a target for the North Vietnamese to come in and hit with a superior force. The North Vietnamese would see it as a wonderful opportunity.

Shackley watched and waited.

There was a terrain problem, Lair went on. Nam Bac was down in a valley. Holding the airstrip was impossible without holding the surrounding hills. That meant more troops, and that multiplied the logistical problem. There was nobody in the Royal Lao Army capable of handling the logistics for a multibattalion force in combat. There was no integrated support system for the whole army. It just didn't exist because of all the pilfering. Even if supplies were flown in to the airfield, the right quantities of bullets, shells, and food would never get to the guys on the front lines. Once the ammo got used up, the positions would break and then there would be a disaster.

Shackley listened, but his expression hadn't changed. He thanked Lair for coming.

A few weeks later the royalist troops went in and took Nam Bac with little opposition. Though sanctioned and approved by the U.S. embassy, which had provided the supplies and much of the transportation, the victory belonged to the Royal Lao Army. It was the biggest lowland victory of the war.

The Udorn CIA base kept an eye on Nam Bac.

Before long, signs of a North Vietnamese response appeared. Trucks carried elements of NVA forces as far toward Nam Bac as the roads would allow. At the roadhead, the soldiers got out and walked. They reached the hills around Nam Bac, and then they got out their shovels. Patient and disciplined, the North Vietnamese had proved elsewhere that they could dig underground bunkers and infiltration tunnels able to withstand direct air strikes.

When it became clear that Nam Bac was coming under siege, Shackley leaned on Lair to lean on Vang Pao to help out. Lair flew up to Long Tieng to talk to the Meo commander.

Vang Pao himself had gotten into set-piece battles, starting with Padong, back in 1961. He had done it again a couple of times in Nakhang in 1966 and early 1967. His blind spot was defending fixed sites. But like most human beings, Vang Pao could see other people's errors more clearly than his own. He told Lair that the lowland generals should never have allowed themselves to be trapped in a position like Nam Bac.

Lair agreed. But perhaps there was a way to ease the pressure. What did he think about some kind of diversionary attack to give the NVA there something else to worry about?

Vang Pao said that he was sorry, but his people were already under great pressure. No SGUs could be spared. Sorry.

Lair, of course, had known the answer before he asked the question. There was no love lost between the tribals and the lowlanders, nation-building or not. When push came to shove, the people of the mountains were really only interested in defending their own territory.

And when Lair got back to Udorn and thought about it, he wondered what the hell was happening. In the old days, he wouldn't have had to sit and watch while a disaster was being planned. He wouldn't have had to make empty gestures, such as going up to see Vang Pao when he already knew what Vang Pao's response was going to be. It wasn't how he would have used his time. Or Vang Pao's.

Lair sat at his desk and thought, then pulled up a typewriter and began to type. He pulled together everything he knew about Nam Bac—the planning, the troops, the terrain and logistics, the enemy deployment, the thinking at the Vientiane station and at the embassy. He dated and signed the memorandum, then put it in his safe.

He couldn't think what else to do with it. Nobody was all that interested in his opinions anymore.

# Branfman and Lawrence

In the United States, by the middle of 1967, neither the main-stream politicians on Capitol Hill nor the editors of the major news media had actually turned against the Vietnam War. But the facts of the war, and the images brought home on the evening television news, had started to create a realization that the U.S. might have blundered in sending troops into Vietnam, and in any case would have a tough time finding an honor-able way out. American troop levels in South Vietnam had risen to 431,000, and a further ceiling of 543,000 had already been approved by the Defense Department. In the fiscal year ending in June 1967, the U.S. spent about $21 billion dollars on the war, which was far more than it had planned (and roughly seven hundred times the cost of the CIA's Operation Momentum in Laos). When President Johnson proposed a 10 percent surtax on cor-porate and private income taxes to pay for the war, businessmen began to see that Vietnam would affect them personally. College students had al-ready begun questioning the war, for it was their generation that was be-ing called up by the draft system and sent over to South Vietnam to fight. About fifteen thousand Americans had already died on the battlefield.

Among the very early war protesters—he had demonstrated outside the White House back in April 1965—was Fredric Branfman, a young gradu-ate of the University of Chicago and Harvard University's School of Edu-cation. The son of a New York Garment District executive, he had grown up materially comfortable but otherwise ill at ease in suburban Long Is-land. Highly idealistic and strongly influenced by the civil rights movement, Branfman was attracted to the causes of brown and black people in the United States and to those of indigenous people of less developed countries. To Branfman, the peasants of the Third World seemed to possess a wisdom and an understanding of life that was conspicuously lacking in America. The Vietnam War—dropping bombs and napalm on peasants—was proof of America's alienation from itself.

To postpone induction into the military, Branfman worked out a deal with his local Selective Service board freeing him to teach in Tanzania, in eastern Africa. He taught school, wrote studies of the Tanzanian school system, and had just gotten an offer to work as an educational adviser to the nation's president, Julius Nyerere, when all of a sudden a telegram from home notified him that his draft board had just reclassified him 1-A, eligible to serve. Branfman rushed back to Long Island and presented his draft board with his fallback plan, an offer to join International Voluntary Services in Laos. Most of what Branfman knew about Laos came from reading *Newsweek* magazine. He didn't know the United States was bombing there, or that the CIA was running a covert war, because *Newsweek* had not mentioned it. Laos was supposed to be a "neutral" kingdom. Branfman imagined it to be a charmingly backward place, full of Buddhist temples, rather like Nepal.

In April 1967, the height of the hot season, Branfman stepped off a plane at Wattay Airport in Vientiane and into the blast furnace of tropical heat. Somebody from IVS was there to meet him and they drove off in an open jeep. They were no sooner out of the airport than a Lao man ran up and poured an entire pail of water over Branfman's head and then walked away laughing. Tired and disoriented, Branfman had arrived in the middle of Phi Mai, the Lao New Year, which was celebrated with ribald jokes and water dousings on the street. A few blocks later he got another pail of water on his head.

Branfman had been told that he would be working as an IVS volunteer for the USAID department of secondary school education, writing a report on the Laotian elementary school system. Once in Vientiane he found that his job didn't exist. The layers of bureaucracy had proliferated along with the growth of the war, and his assignment was in some kind of limbo that his USAID bosses couldn't or wouldn't explain.

Branfman didn't know quite what to do—except that he couldn't quit. Being in Laos kept him out of the U.S. Army, and out of Vietnam. He had two years to go until he reached his twenty-seventh birthday, after which his eligibility for the draft would expire.

He was neither the first nor the last young American who was in Laos to stay out of the war next door. A number of Pop Buell's assistants were either IVS or former Peace Corps volunteers who wanted to avoid military service for one reason or another. But most of them became extremely devoted to the American program and a few of them upcountry even carried guns. Branfman was different.

With his assignment to study the Laotian school system on hold, he got permission to visit a village east of Savannakhet to learn about lowland Lao culture. This little village fulfilled his fantasies of lost horizons in Asia. The houses were all built on tall stilts in traditional style. Monks with shaved heads and saffron robes collected alms at sunrise and then returned single file to the *wat,* the Buddhist temple. Little boys tended water buffalo, and teenage girls in sarongs languidly threw fishing nets that sparkled in the sun.

Branfman attended *boun*s, or festivals. He sat in on classes in an elementary school. He worked on improving his Lao language skills. And he began to hear from the local people and from other Americans about the Laos war, the war that hardly ever made the news. He began to collect stories about the royalist and Pathet Lao sides, about Pop Buell and the role of the Americans who wore civilian clothes. He heard rumors about General Vang Pao throwing prisoners in pits and buying and selling opium. Branfman was only about a hundred miles from the South Vietnamese border. He was even nearer to the Ho Chi Minh Trail. It dawned on him that maybe he hadn't escaped the mess of the Vietnam War after all.

He was totally absorbed with his life in the village when he received a message to go back to Vientiane. His congressman, of all people, wanted to see him.

Representative Lester L. Wolff, of the 3rd District, New York, had come to Laos on the Tour and was looking up one of his constituents. Branfman met Wolff in the office of Joseph Mendenhall, the USAID director. The congressman asked Branfman how he was doing. Branfman said he was involved with an AID education project that had turned weird, and since the congressman asked, the United States really wasn't helping out in Laos the right way. Just then, Mendenhall and a second congressman entered the office and said that the plane was ready. They were going to Sam Thong. Branfman asked if he could come along.

As they neared their destination, the pilot announced that there was a problem with the Sam Thong runway and that they would land at a nearby airstrip and take a helicopter to Sam Thong. The plane landed, turned around, taxied, and stopped at the bottom of an incline in a bowl-like mountain valley. American men, every one of whom wore sunglasses, escorted them onto the tarmac and into the waiting helicopter. The chopper took off and then landed a few minutes later in Sam Thong, and there in a line on the runway were Meo women in full tribal regalia with Hawaiian-style floral leis. They draped the leis around the congressmen's necks.

Branfman grew suspicious. He sidled over behind a man who had accompanied them on the helicopter, who was talking with a short, balding man with glasses. Branfman knew without being told that this was the famous Pop Buell.

"How did it go?" Buell was saying out of the side of his mouth.

"Fine," the other man answered in a low voice.

"Do they know anything?" asked Buell.

"Oh no, they got the usual briefing," replied the other guy. "They were told all about Sam Thong and what you people are doing here. There was no mention of Long Tieng, and they were very, very impressed."

"Good," said Buell.

Branfman realized that the plane had landed at Long Tieng, the so-called secret air base. He had met lots of Americans in Laos who talked about Long Tieng, but never anybody who had been there.

As the congressmen's tour continued, they saw the tribal soldiers and the weapons captured from the communists. They saw the schools with woven-bamboo walls and the medics being trained and all the good deeds USAID was doing. Finally, they had their audience with General Vang Pao in a small, crowded room. In broken English, Vang Pao gave his talk, which seemed well rehearsed, about leading his freedom-loving people in a fight against the communists. Vang Pao asked whether he could count on Congress for continued support. Representative Wolff said yes, that the American people admired what he was doing and would never let him down. The other congressman was a bit more cautious and said getting money out of Congress wasn't always easy.

Each time Vang Pao got up to say something in his own language Branfman leaned forward to whisper in Wolff's ear that the general was a warlord, that he didn't really have the support of his people, that he dealt with opponents by throwing them into pits and letting them starve to death. Another American in the room overheard this and glared at Branfman, who became suddenly self-conscious and afraid.

Branfman and Wolff spent that night in another base in a kind of trailer with *Playboy* pinups on the walls. The congressman listened to Branfman's spiel about the injustice of America's war in Laos while looking increasingly uncomfortable. The congressman finally explained that he and many of his colleagues owed their election to Lyndon Johnson's coattails, and they couldn't afford to confront the president directly on the war, whatever they thought in private. The next morning they flew back to Vientiane together. The USAID director, Mendenhall, politely asked Branfman for a copy of anything he wrote on education in Laos, promising to read it.

On his own initiative Branfman then produced a series of reports on the Laotian school system, which had been set up in French colonial days. He proposed a radical overhaul. The primary schools should focus on producing better, prouder Laotian farmers, he wrote, rather than teaching a small gifted minority Western languages and skills. Secondary schools should be de-emphasized in favor of primary schools. He sent a copy of his final report to Mendenhall.

Branfman was summoned to the office of his USAID boss, the secondary school man. His boss showed him a letter he had written to Mendenhall rebutting every point Branfman had made. The letter, which was dated the day before, concluded that Branfman had had second thoughts about his report and voluntarily withdrew it.

His boss gazed across his desk calmly and launched into the story of another IVS volunteer who was a wise guy, too. Who was also, like Branfman, trying to get out of the army. Who hadn't fooled anybody, who got thrown out of IVS and out of Laos and into an infantry unit in Vietnam. And got killed in combat.

His boss told him to go teach English at a teacher training college outside Vientiane. Any more trouble, and he would lose his draft deferment.

Scared but still rebellious, Branfman went to his IVS supervisor and pointed out that he knew his congressman. IVS didn't want a big fight and neither did he. He said IVS could list him as an English teacher at the teacher training school, but he was going to be living in a little village nearby and setting up his own project on agricultural education. He had only eighteen months left and they didn't need to bother each other.

With the deal approved, Branfman moved to a little lowland village north of Vientiane with a *wat,* houses on stilts, and wattle fences around the vegetable gardens. He was the only *farang* there. He rented a room from a seventy-year-old peasant man who had been a *samlor* driver much of his life, operating a three-wheeled bicycle-powered taxi. Now he was retired. Most days the old man sat on the smooth wood floor of his house holding a piece of wood with a pin in the end, engraving tales from the life of the Buddha onto palm leaf, a traditional form of temple book. The old man hand-copied these religious stories hour after hour, in a trance.

Branfman loved the villagers. They were everything that had been missing from his own upbringing. They were gregarious and he had been a loner ever since he was a kid. They were spiritual and he was secular. They were gentle and he came from the country that dropped bombs and napalm. So he was drawn to them as a people, though he was finding that their society was deeply flawed with venality, corruption, and greed.

Examples were easy to find. The name of the place where he lived, Ban Xa Phang Meuk, means "The Village of the Deep Pond." The pond was off to one side of the dirt lane leading to the paved road. It had some lily pads and floating weeds in the wet season when the water was high, and a fence around it. Nobody in the village was allowed to use it for drinking water or for their draft animals. Why not? he asked. Because some big man years ago had bribed all the right officials in Vientiane and then had claimed the pond was his.

The Village of the Deep Pond—every village in Laos—had big problems. People were half sick a lot of the time with intestinal ailments from drinking dirty water, which reduced their enjoyment of life. There was no legal system to speak of, which meant that rich people could steal land. It was implicitly understood that the main incentive for working for the government was being able to steal with power behind you. The people of the village had few prospects. Young men became either peasants or soldiers. Young women were leaving to become prostitutes in Vientiane.

Branfman himself spent a lot of evenings in the bordellos of Vientiane, as many *farang* men did. The two best-known establishments were the White Rose and Madame Lulu's. At the White Rose, the women took off their clothes and did bump-and-grind dances for the customers having drinks. For a few dollars more they would do things with amazing muscular control on bananas and coins, or take the men to little rooms upstairs. Madame Lulu's specialized in oral sex. Branfman usually arrived on his black Honda motorcycle after toking up on the ganja sold openly in the Vientiane market and left the same way.

He was smoking a lot of ganja then, which was of no great consequence—the tolerant Lao had never gotten around to passing a law against it, and it was the drug of choice for his peer group. Sometimes he smoked opium, too. Being stoned helped him tune into Laos. It amplified his dislike of the war and of the inequities of the American presence. The drugs opened all kinds of physical, spiritual, and esthetic leads, and if they didn't tie them back together and make sense of the place, some of the moments were worth it in themselves. He became a familiar figure putt-putting around on his motorbike, always dressed in black, a vague sartorial statement of sympathy toward the Viet Cong—black sandals, black chinos, a black peasant's shirt from northeast Thailand. On his wrists were scores of thin white strings from attending *boun*s and *baci* ceremonies.

His main preoccupation was his self-assigned Lao-language agricultural textbook. He believed that teaching European languages in schools way out in the countryside wasn't giving average Laotians knowledge they could use. It was trying to make peasants into little versions of Westerners rather than helping them become better versions of themselves. He went into the USAID office one day and happened to see some Pathet Lao textbooks that the Meo had captured and that had been brought back to Vientiane for translation.

He had no way of knowing that Edgar Buell, Bill Lair, and others of the inner circle had been aware of these Pathet Lao textbooks for years, had studied them carefully, and had modeled their own nation-building educational programs on similar principles. Nor did he have any way of knowing how upset the old-timers were at the changing course of the war, at the Shackley-era innovations. The layers of bureaucracy had multiplied, and Branfman was in the outermost layer, far from the core.

Branfman began reading the Pathet Lao textbooks. He was stunned. The textbooks were everything he had thought of doing and more. The whole curriculum was in the Lao language, not the language of *farang*s. They taught about Laotian history, not French history. And they taught about different crops, the seasons for planting and harvesting, and other agricultural topics.

The Pathet Lao, Branfman decided, were already doing what he had been trying to do, only better. So why am I doing it? he asked himself.

Staring at the Pathet Lao textbooks, Branfman discovered that he felt no intrinsic loyalty to the American program in Laos. Why are we fighting the people who know more than we do about educating the peasants properly? he wondered. He had hoped to educate himself in Laos, but he was only getting more confused.

He knew something about Lao culture and village life, but next to nothing about the Laos war. There were more news stories about Vietnam in the papers every day than about the Laos war, even in Vientiane. Nobody knew what was going on because it was supposed to be a secret war. There were rumors of colossal battles up north, of CIA air bases, and of bombing, but they existed in a strange atmosphere of information deprivation. Nobody seemed to know anything.

Vint Lawrence's new job at CIA headquarters, as Bill Colby's special assistant, sent him zooming upward on the fast track, over the heads of men who were considerably older. He was jumped in grade and given a medal that he had to give back as soon as he got it. The award itself was classified, Lawrence recalled later. "They couldn't let me have a medal that said I was working for the Agency when I was supposed to be working for some godforsaken airline."

In his first few months back, he was often asked to go around and lecture. People in headquarters wanted to believe that there were lessons to be learned from Laos, and that those lessons could be encoded in some sort of generalized theory of counterinsurgency. Lawrence told them that although it was useful to understand what had worked in Laos, and what had worked in other situations, the best solutions were developed in the field by operatives who understood the indigenous people, and who were given maximum authority to act. Aside from that, he had no doctrine to propose, to the disappointment of his audience.

Working for the Far East chief, Lawrence got a wider view of operations throughout eastern Asia, particularly Vietnam. It struck Lawrence that though the scale of involvement in South Vietnam was much larger than in Laos, the overall quality of its work in Vietnam was lower. "The whole business of the hamlet evaluation system in South Vietnam always struck me as the most bizarre form of computerized horseshit, even though the Agency was responsible for doing it," Lawrence recalled. "And I was very concerned that we were not on the side of the angels in South Vietnam. I just became increasingly aware that what we had done in Laos was something unique and special."

As Colby's special assistant, Lawrence got to meet the other special assistants around town, young smart guys like Tony Lake, who was then a special assistant to Nicholas Katzenbach, the attorney general; and Richard Holbrooke, a special assistant to Robert Komer, then on the White House staff. (Years later, under President Bill Clinton, Holbrooke would become assistant secretary of state and Lake the national security advisor.) "The three of us would have power lunches, and I'd always lose," Lawrence said, laughing ruefully at the memory. He didn't want to compete at the business of being a power-exuding Washington upstart.

"And there was a lot of jealousy at the Agency, I subsequently learned. Because the foreign intelligence people did not like the fact that this young kid goes off and gets involved with paramilitary operations and not only gets his name mentioned in dispatches but gets promotions. So there's an awful lot of people waiting to prove to me that I am not nearly as good as I think I am. Drop-dead comments in the men's washroom, etc. And I knew I'm not as good as I'm alleged to be. *I know that.*

"Within a year, I start to wonder whether, if I had been back there, I would have had the balls to say no to pushing the Hmong into these types of operations. And would I have had the balls to resign. I worry whether I would have had the courage to do that.

"Then some old guy took me aside. He was a nice man, and he'd been around a long time. And he said, 'Vint, you're a good kid. You want my advice?'

"I said yessir.

"He said, 'You've had the best tour that anyone in the world could ever have. You're twenty-seven years old, and you had a 27,000-man army. You'll be looking for that for the rest of your career, and you'll never find it, ever again. And not only that, the rest of them are all waiting to take you down.'

"He said, 'Go out when you're on top. I've been wandering the halls looking for something like this for years, and I've never found it.

" 'You won't find it,' he said. 'Not again. Not ever.'

"He was very high. The deputy chief of the Far East division. Colby's deputy. Highly respected, and a wonderful operator."

Colby himself signaled that he knew that what was going on in Laos was not all to the good. "Bill Colby actually once said that we have a terrible track record of destroying the people we try to help," Lawrence recalled.

"Colby was very good to me. He said, 'Don't quit. You've got to get yourself another career. You need another career. You need another profession that you can fall back on so that you're not beholden to the government for everything you are, and can be. You've got to maintain your independence, unless you're terribly wealthy.' " Colby himself had a law degree, a fallback profession in case he ever wanted to leave government service. Lawrence began applying to graduate schools.

"These men were terribly loyal to the Agency, but they realized that a bureaucracy is a bureaucracy is a bureaucracy. And that you have to protect yourself.

"I wasn't that wealthy, so I went off to do something, with the idea that I'd take a leave without pay.

"Colby, I think, was hoping I'd come back."

# Ted Didn't Know Shit About Tactical Warfare

Commando Club was working. From the summit of Phou Pha Thi, where poppies had grown and flourished and waved gently in the breeze, electronic signals now sped out through the ether.

High above and out of sight, the dart-like jets of the U.S. Air Force and Navy rode the invisible signals toward their targets in the cloud-covered Hanoi valley. On cue, the bombs fell twenty thousand feet through the thick winter cloud cover and onto their targets—railroad yards, airfields, barracks, and marshaling yards. The bombs were accurate within areas the size of a football stadium, thanks to the electronics that guided their release from the planes. No nation had developed that kind of all-weather, high-altitude bombing capability before.

There was another unit like Commando Club in northeast Thailand for strikes against the Trail, and others in South Vietnam for bombing the southern half of the north. Their range was roughly two hundred miles, which did not allow them to guide planes as far north as Hanoi. Only Commando Club could, because of its location high on a mountaintop in North Vietnam's backyard.

The technology worked without a flaw. During its first two months of operation, however, November and December 1967, American planes used it for fewer than a sixth of the sorties (40 out of 247) they flew against North Vietnam. The problem was human. The pilots hated surrendering control of their planes to anybody, much less to a computer. They complained that the final minute before releasing the bombs, when they had to hold their planes straight and level, while the computer ran its final calculations of position, speed, and distance, was the worst. That minute seemed like an hour, and all the while the pilots wondered when a SAM missile would pierce the clouds and come right up at them like a flying telephone pole. They also didn't like not being able to see their targets beneath the clouds, or to learn whether they had hit them. The bureaucracy hadn't caught up with the program, and the follow-up reporting on the raids was poor.

But if the American pilots disliked Commando Club, the North Vietnamese military leaders disliked it even more. It is likely that the Soviet technicians who set up Hanoi's antiaircraft defenses warned them of the new threat first; and probable that the North Vietnamese saw the radar as a first step in a dangerous buildup on their border—a buildup that could lead to an American invasion of their country through the Laos back door.

Three North Vietnamese Army battalions entered Laos in early November and started clearing Meo outposts near the roads. In mid-December they mounted their first probe of the mountain's outer defenses. A small force attacked a Meo position a few miles to the east. The Meo melted away, counterattacked, and retook the position. The enemy came back again, then scattered when American airplanes arrived.

Far to the south in Udorn, Richard Secord studied those first North Vietnamese attacks closely. He was in charge of day-to-day coordination of defense of the mountain, reporting to Lair and Shackley. The basic pattern of enemy intentions was easy enough to spot; all it took was marking little crosses on a map where contact had been made. The biggest cluster of crosses was east of the mountain, the side facing its climbable slope; he and others thought the enemy attack would come from that direction.

The photo interpreters kept peering through their magnifying glasses at the reconnaissance pictures, looking for new roads and ways to stop traffic on the existing roads. Sometimes jets came back from North Vietnam still loaded with bombs and looking for a place to drop them; and once in a while Secord got sorties planned in advance for Phou Pha Thi. But he couldn't get them as often as he liked. The air force, which had pushed for installing the special radar, didn't seem to care much about protecting it.

What neither Secord nor anybody else expected was that the North Vietnamese would use their own air force against the mountain. Early in the afternoon of January 12, 1968, four dark green planes were seen flying in formation southeast of Sam Neua city. Two broke off and circled, and the other two kept on going slowly toward Phou Pha Thi. They were old-fashioned biplanes, with double wings, one stacked above the other in World War I style. The biplanes made three passes over the mountain, one of them dropping bombs and the other firing rockets and strafing with machine guns.

A new, shiny tin roof on the CIA building near the helicopter pad attracted much of the biplane pilots' attention. They fired only one rocket at the radar itself, and it missed, passing overhead. The North Vietnamese pilots also fired on the Meo village, killing two women and wounding two men.

From the ground, one of the CIA officers, Jerry Daniels, opened up with his M-16. He claimed he hit a biplane, and maybe he did, because one of them crashed and burned near the back side of the mountain. An Air America helicopter happened to be on the chopper pad at the time. The chopper pilot took off and found that he was going faster than the remaining biplane. He began to chase it toward the North Vietnamese border. Inside the cabin a crewman switched the safety off an automatic rifle he wasn't supposed to be carrying. When the chopper pulled alongside the biplane, the crewman opened fire out the left side door. The biplane lost altitude, then crashed, breaking into pieces. The other two planes of the original four got away.

The biplanes were AN-2 Colts, products of the Soviet Union's Antonov aircraft factory. With their cloth-covered wings and wooden propellors, they looked like antiques. Souvenir hunters took a piece of one of the crashed planes with the tail number and hung it in the Air America bar at Long Tieng. The biplanes' bombs, it turned out, were mortar shells dropped through holes in the floor of the plane—a crude, Tony Poe–like improvisational weapon that had nearly worked.

◆

The North Vietnamese had never attacked anything with biplanes before; and the CIA's best guess, taking into account Hanoi's limited airplane inventory, was that they wouldn't try it again. This proved to be correct. The biplane attack continued to be a subject of wonderment, but the focus of American attention shifted westward to the siege at Nam Bac, which was then in its final days. The royalist victory there was turning into a catastrophe.

The North Vietnamese had surrounded the royalist battalions in the valley. They took the heights, and kept on digging until they had tunneled under the royalist lines. As Lair had predicted, the royalist front lines ran out of ammunition, even with airdrops directly overhead from Air America. It also didn't help morale when Lao officers on the ground got their coordinates mixed up and called in T-28 strikes on their own positions.

Under Shackley's relentless pressure, Vang Pao finally sent some units east of Nam Bac to harrass North Vietnamese troops there. But they didn't affect the final outcome. When the base fell on January 14, 1968, American helicopters picked up units fleeing in all directions. Two thousand lowland soldiers vanished, some of them turning up later in Pathet Lao ranks, fighting for the other side.

The reversal at Nam Bac was devastating to the fragile self-esteem of the lowland army. In Vientiane, the U.S. embassy tried to absolve itself of blame. Nam Bac, declared Sullivan, had been a Lao plan all along, not a Country Team plan. It had been pursued, he said later, "in full recognition that it was going to be a fiasco, which it was." This raised an obvious question: If he had known it was going to be a fiasco, why hadn't he stopped it? The U.S. ambassador's permission was required for the Lao government to mount large-scale operations needing American transportation and resupply.

As the finger-pointing continued, Ted Shackley took the position that the military attaché at the embassy deserved much of the blame for what had been, after all, largely a Royal Lao Army operation. Shackley had a point. But at the Taj Mahal, the ranking people believed that Shackley himself had played as great a role as anybody else. Bill Lair thought so, and Landry, too; and, more tellingly, so did Secord and Tom Clines.

Clines, a Shackley protégé, had decided to work under Lair and Landry, even though he knew they really didn't want him. For all his genuine loyalty to Shackley, Clines had begun to side with Lair and Landry on paramilitary planning. He kept quietly cutting the size of the forces in the field that Shackley wanted to deploy, trying to slow the growth of the supermarket war. Years later, when he was asked who was to blame for Nam Bac, he admitted, "Yeah, Ted had a lot to do with staging it."

Clines's friend Secord put it more simply. "Nam Bac was a loss we didn't need. It was predictable, on a grand scale," he declared. Or as he said in another context, "Ted didn't know shit about tactical warfare."

◆

The capture of Nam Bac was only part of the North Vietnamese general dry-season offensive. They pushed outward from the Plain of Jars, and their mortar fire was clearly audible at Pop Buell's headquarters, Sam Thong. Buell reported: "The situation as a whole can be listed as critical, the people themselves and the troops are more worried and morale at the lowest I have seen it in the past five years. I myself feel that if we Americans who are here continue to work hard with the people, giving moral support, plus assurance we will remain with them, continue to give commodity support as we have in the past, eventually we will pick up the pieces and start over. If there was ever a time for us to put out it is now. It is surely no time to cut down. If we do, the whole works could go.

"V.P. himself is a worried man. As he has many times in the past when there are big problems, he comes to me to pour his troubles out. He is again in the mood that he asks, 'When it happens are you going to North Thailand with me? How long do you think my people can stand it? How much longer will they have confidence in me?' "

Local tribal leaders told Buell of mass desertions to the enemy side. They asked when reinforcements were going to come in, and whether the U.S. government would send its own troops to Laos. They also started asking when, or whether, the U.S. would be pulling out of Southeast Asia.

Buell didn't have any answers to their questions. He and his staff went into high gear, arranging for refugee airlifts and emergency supplies. A couple of weeks later, when Vang Pao's men retook some of the outpost they had lost, the crisis eased. But in terms of territory held, wrote Buell, "We are now back to where we were four years ago. The difference between now and then, over 25% of our fighting men have been killed, others captured, and everyone worn out and tired of war. It is all up to how far the enemy wants to come and just how much Gen. V.P.'s troops have left to put out."

◆

The U.S. government had a defense plan for Phou Pha Thi, but the official version, at least, made sensible people tear their hair out by the roots and bang their heads on the wall. It was an elaborate political compromise between the embassy and the air force, which had tiptoed around each other in a jurisdictional minuet and conceded as little as possible for fear of setting precedents.

"The key role in the plan," a classified air force study declared, "was played by the Local Area Defense Commander (LADC), the local Meo commander." This was an odd statement, since the air force was unlikely to trust its top-of-the-line bomb guidance system to a non-American. In fact the LADC was a euphemism for the top CIA officer on the mountain, who worked in the shiny-roofed shed near the helicopter landing zone, downhill from the TSQ-81 radar site. The air force history goes on to say:

> The concept was that if the enemy threatened the site, the LADC would co-ordinate with the Embassy in Vientiane and get authorization to call for airstrikes. With authority given, the Embassy would then notify 7AF that execution authority had been given to the LADC. When the enemy attack was imminent, the LADC would contact the Embassy and receive final execution authority. Thereupon, the LADC was authorized to notify the TSQ-81 commander of the requirement for the strike and supply him with the target coordinates (hopefully precomputerized, otherwise a 10-minute delay ensued).
>
> At this point the TSQ commander was to contact 7AF via secure voice and request the strike force. Seventh Air Force was then to provide the strike forces as circumstances and time allowed.

In other words, if the mountain came under attack, which seemed virtually certain after the biplane incident, a sequence of at least a half-dozen radio calls and permissions had to be made in order for the 7th Air Force in Saigon to send out planes, if it felt like it—"as circumstances and time allowed."

Nobody on the mountain itself or at the Taj Mahal had any intention of sticking with such a cumbersome plan. The tribal soldiers couldn't be relied on to defend the site, and the air force couldn't be counted on, either. Secord and others felt that American ground soldiers were needed on the mountain itself, and that they should probably come from the U.S. Army Special Forces—not a lot of them, just a few highly experienced veterans of combat in Vietnam, some sergeants and an officer or two.

Secord didn't think this was asking for much. Green Beret teams operated in southern Laos on the Ho Chi Minh Trail every day and night. He got Landry, Lair, and Shackley to agree with him, but not Sullivan. The ambassador might have gotten the order from the White House to install Commando Club, but it said nothing about Green Berets, and Sullivan didn't want to give the military any more footholds in north Laos than it had already.

Undeterred, Secord then looked into the backgrounds of the Americans on the mountain. What he found was not particularly encouraging. There were four CIA men based at Nakhang and only sometimes staying on Pha Thi overnight. Two of them were ex-smokejumpers—part of a contingent of ex–forest fire fighters that the Agency had recruited from around Missoula, Montana. They were all young, healthy guys, but they didn't have professional military training.

Next he looked into the men staffing Commando Club. They were a mixed bunch, ranging from veterans of air strikes over North Vietnam to pure technical types. None of them had combat experience with infantry weapons. Secord decided to arm them. He sent a proposal through CIA channels to Sullivan. When the answer came back negative, he went up in person to Vientiane to plead his case. He was already in Sullivan's bad graces and the ambassador turned him down again.

Secord didn't take the rejection personally. It bothered him, though, that his government had put the hardware on the mountain without adequately protecting the men running the installation. It was, he thought, another one of those problems resulting from separation of command. The war was divided up into little boxes, and the commanders of the little boxes were busy keeping everybody out of their own little squares.

"So I went to the commander of the 7/13th" at Udorn, Secord recalled, "and told him and his deputy that I had decided to put on my military hat. I was in a unique position: I had been assigned by the Agency the responsibility of the defense and the emergency evacuation of Lima Site 85. And since I was a serving military officer at the same time I was a CIA officer, and under the law a commander's first responsibility is for the security and safety of his troops, I made the determination that *they would be armed,* in contravention of the ambassador's directive. Therefore, I wanted M-16s."

Secord hand-received and signed receipts for some M-16 automatic rifles, a relatively new weapon and one the CIA hadn't been using much in upcountry Laos. And he helped arrange for weapons practice for the men on Phou Pha Thi, who were also given large quantities of ammunition and grenades.

Eventually the site's defenses were upgraded further. The Agency got an eighty-man Thai unit sent up as stiffeners for the Meo. It got an Air Commando forward air guide to help call in air strikes. There were trenches and bunkers everywhere, sensors and mines on the approaches even on the back side, in case the enemy tried scaling the cliff. The largest weapons helicopters could carry, 105mm howitzers and 4.2-inch mortars, sat near the summit. But when all was said and done even the new improvements didn't correct the old weaknesses. No first-rate infantry soldiers experienced in defending fixed sites had been assigned to the mountain. And nobody had untangled the lines of responsibility and command.

The radar installation belonged to the air force, but the CIA was supposed to defend it. The CIA couldn't defend it as it chose, because the ambassador didn't want "unauthorized" weapons on the mountaintop. Kept from direct accountability for its own men, the air force lost interest, even though it had proposed the installation in the first place. Nobody was really in charge, which didn't help when the photo interpreters found a new thin line through the trees, the light-colored soil contrasting with the dark vegetation. It was the start of a road, heading right toward the base of Phou Pha Thi. In the Taj Mahal, they named it Route 602.

"I had my PIs, my photo interpreters, watching it daily," said Secord. "I tried and tried and tried to interdict the construction of that road. I could never get enough striking assets. It was catch as catch can. If you're going to stop anybody from building a road you've got to be on 'em every day. And the 7th Air Force wouldn't allocate the air necessary to do the job. It was very frustrating to watch that road grow."

Road construction had begun on January 31, 1968, which was brilliant timing for Hanoi and terrible timing for the 7th Air Force. In South Vietnam, for the first time, the North Vietnamese regulars and their local guerilla allies, the National Liberation Front, or Viet Cong, burst into the open in force in what came to be called the Tet offensive. A sapper squad got inside the U.S. embassy compound in Saigon. The Viet Cong took over the old city of Hue. The communist soldiers seemed to be almost everywhere, and the U.S. Air Force, working overtime to get them, paid even less attention than usual to a limestone mountain way off in northeast Laos.

Between February 2 and February 14, planes made no air strikes on Route 602. By February 11, trucks were rolling down it, though the road itself had not yet reached the mountain.

By then, Vang Pao's spies reported propaganda meetings in villages nearby, where the Pathet Lao and North Vietnamese openly bragged about the coming assault and told the villagers to stay clear. The North Vietnamese confiscated food and conscripted men for coolie duty. They brought two more regiments into the area, one of them an artillery regiment never before used in Laos. They occupied an arc of territory from the north and through the east and around to the south of the mountain, and had begun to swing around to the west. And the road pushed in.

The new regiments were from the Homeland Forces, Hanoi's finest. An artillery survey party went out in advance of the main force, and one of Vang Pao's patrols got lucky and trapped it in an ambush. Map pouches found on the dead surveyors were flown down to Udorn. The charts were exquisitely drawn, with the standard symbols for weapons laid out and surveyed in; one of them had a bullet hole right through it. Another captured notebook used the word "TACAN" in its English spelling and showed that the enemy knew the navigational beacon's exact location.

At the Taj Mahal, Secord brought the air, ground, and electronic intel people together and put their findings together on plastic map overlays. Their conclusions tallied with the enemy survey charts: Artillery was going to be a major component of the attack, and on a scale never seen before in the Laos war.

With a sinking feeling, the intel people also realized that the assault on the mountain was just one step in a dry-season offensive much larger than in any previous year. The North Vietnamese had never committed huge, blockbuster forces in Laos, partly because Vang Pao's guerilla forces had never offered a stationary target and also because, until the radar installation, nothing in Laos had directly threatened the security and the existence of North Vietnam.

By mid-February, in South Vietnam, the Tet offensive was sputtering to a halt. The communists, by fighting in the open and exposing their troops, had taken casualties they could scarcely afford. But their military defeat was a political victory: The Pentagon, and the U.S. commanders in South Vietnam, lost their credibility at home in America, the result of years of official denial and evasion about the aims and means of the war.

With the end of the Tet offensive, the 7th Air Force's planes were free again. And so the jets flew back to northern Laos in respectable numbers, about thirty sorties a day. Sullivan relaxed his rules for air strikes near the mountain. A forward air guide directed them to their targets in fair weather, and Commando Club directed them when the cloud cover was thick. The problem was, Vang Pao's men weren't going out from the mountain to fight the North Vietnamese on the ground.

By late February, the enemy was close enough to be seen through binoculars. From the CIA shack near the summit, an enemy warehouse was visible in the distance. The Americans figured the coordinates, called for an air strike, and electronically guided the jets to the right spot above the clouds. They watched as the bombs fell through the clouds and down around the warehouse. The muffled percussive sound of the explosion reached them a few seconds later. The warehouse was still standing; ballpark bombing wasn't accurate enough to finish it off. Tiny figures emerged, waving in their direction. Better luck next time, the North Vietnamese soldiers seemed to be saying.

Meo forces ran a few ambushes. The warplanes hit troop concentrations, truck parks, and artillery, whenever they could find them. The pilots dropped conventional bombs, napalm, cluster bomb units, and the antipersonnel mines known as gravel. Through binoculars, the Americans saw North Vietnamese officers beating men to get them to work. Bulldozers came in, and the road inched day by day toward the base of the mountain until finally it arrived.

Now even Lair and Shackley agreed that the time to blow up the radar site and get out of there was approaching fast. Several messages carrying Shackley's name but drafted at Udorn were transmitted to the military and to the CIA director. One of those memos, dated February 25, 1968, read:

> It is clear that the enemy will continue to attempt to consolidate his gains in the Phou Pha Thi area during the next two weeks while making arrangements for his final assault by three or four battalions. If . . . aircraft continue to strike enemy concentrations in and around Phou Pha Thi and in the area east of Sam Neua, the TACAN and other sites at Phou Pha Thi will continue to be viable for the next two weeks. It is not possible to predict, however, the state of security at Phou Pha Thi beyond 10 March because of the enemy's willingness to continue to escalate his commitment in this area.

Shackley had learned caution from the Nam Bac defeat. He was less inclined to risk, more inclined to listen. March 10 was the latest safe pullout date, he repeated in other cables; after that, forget it.

Secord said, "We had more evidence than any person ought to need to get the hell out of there, or get reinforcements. But we couldn't do either. The 7th Air Force and the director told us to 'hold at all costs'—those words were used—that it was so important, that it had a tremendous effect on the enemy with the nighttime raids. They said, 'We're willing to take that risk because you're saving lives every day.'

"And so we strapped on our seat belts and said, all right.

"We had already written emergency evacuation plans. It was thought by many that we'd be able to pull 'em out by chopper, if we had to. But when we saw the artillery regiment coming down—anybody who has any battle experience knows that that's bad damn news."

The demolition charges in the radar and the TACAN were checked and rechecked. Nobody wanted the top-secret equipment to fall into the hands of the Soviets, who were advising the North Vietnamese on electronic air defenses. Elsewhere in Asia an American spy ship, the *Pueblo,* had been captured by North Koreans a short time before, a disaster for U.S. intelligence; and the Americans on the mountain knew that there was more at stake than their own base—that beyond the northeast Laos war and the Vietnam War loomed the struggle between the superpowers.

Another crew of technicians carrying ID cards from Lockheed Aircraft Services came up from Udorn to work the radar around the clock. More than a third of the February air strikes in northeast Laos were Commando Club–controlled; in early March that figure jumped to over 90 percent. As the enemy drew in closer and closer, the air force men on the mountain wondered just whose lives they were supposedly saving. They hoped they could save their own. Commando Club had never been much used in guiding planes over Hanoi. Instead, the radar itself had become a target. The technicians began to realize that the site's greatest use was in *aiding its own defense*—an ironic perversion of the original goal.

There were sixteen plainclothes air force men on the mountain in addition to the forward air controller and two CIA men. They met to work out the details of the final evacuation plan, which in spite of efforts to simplify would still require Sullivan's approval to begin. They agreed that after blowing up the radar the air force men would walk down the steep path to the helicopter pad by the CIA buildings for the helicopter pickup, if possible. If not, they would wait near their own buildings for the pickup.

The radar, the crew quarters, a sandbagged bunker, and some other buildings were all clustered together on a little rise on the long western ridge, just a few yards from the cliff. From there, when the clouds hadn't reduced visibility to zero, the Americans had a dreary, somber panorama of wild jagged mountains, dark green and bluish gray, the treetops looking like tufted objects far below. The western cliff had many shallow ledges, including one protruding just ten feet down from the top. The air force men set out a cargo net to help them scramble down to it. They figured it would make a good emergency fallback position, protected by the mountainside from the shelling, which would come from the east.

In Udorn, the top Agency men bunked in the small sleeping quarters on the second floor of the Taj Mahal while waiting for the attack to start. Lair postponed an important meeting with Thai officials in Bangkok. A local barber came in to give a haircut to Secord, who didn't want to leave. They waited and waited. On the night of March 9, Phou Pha Thi reported enemy contact. Planes flew up. But it was not a full-scale attack and the planes came back again.

Lair couldn't put off his business in Bangkok any longer and he went down on the morning of March 10 to take care of it.

Later that day Meo patrols reported villagers fleeing the Phou Pha Thi area. The weather was heavily overcast. On an airborne tour of the airstrips and the chopper pads that afternoon, a few of the locations did not display the letter of the alphabet assigned to them as the drop signal, and in other stops the local people were noticeably nervous.

The senior case officer on the mountain then was Howard Freeman, a short, bearded man who had worked with the Meo since Vint Lawrence's time. Immediately after the early gloomy sunset on the tenth, Freeman radioed Udorn to say that he was taking heavy casualties from artillery and rocket fire. The line went dead. A little while later he called back using a portable radio with a link to Long Tieng. He reported that the artillery barrage had hit the generator cables, the 105mm howitzer position, the living quarters for the air force techs, and their sandbagged bunker. The bunker had taken a direct hit and there was nothing left of it, but luckily it had been empty at the time. He was still in contact with the air force men, who had abandoned their radar for the ledge on the back of the cliff. They had a couple of portable radios, and they were all right.

With Lair away in Bangkok, Pat Landry was in charge at the Taj Mahal, supported by Secord and Tom Clines and what seemed like a cast of thousands. They radioed the air force for planes and got some propellor-driven A-26s that were already airborne for Trail work diverted north to the mountain. They arranged for flare ships to provide illumination, and a tanker to refuel some F-4 jets that were taking off from another base in Thailand. But heavy cloud cover blanketed the mountain and made the muzzle flashes of the enemy artillery impossible to pinpoint. With the techs away from the radar, the attack planes had no guidance. They couldn't see anything on the ground except for artillery flashes, diffused like light behind thick frosted glass; and they couldn't risk ducking under the clouds without running into the mountain.

In no time at all the Taj Mahal was chaotic, with staffers rushing in and asking questions and trying to help while getting in the way. The phone was ringing every minute from the CIA station in Vientiane.

Pat Landry's moment had arrived. First he ripped the phone out of the wall. Then he conferred briefly with Secord. The two of them went around the Taj Mahal, through the hallways, into the offices. With the glare on his face more baleful than ever, Landry walked up to every air force man and told him to get the hell out, this was a classified Agency operation. Short, broad-shouldered Secord did the same with Agency people by telling them Phou Pha Thi was an air force installation being supported by air force strikes and their presence wasn't needed or wanted. They booted everybody out and then it was down to three of them in the inner sanctum of the operations room, Landry and Secord and the blue-eyed ground chief, Tom Clines.

They had stayed up many other nights directing other battles, but it was always a nerve-wracking business and the stakes had never been this high before. They were on the far periphery of the action, more than 230 miles away, and they could only hope that what they accomplished by radio could make a difference.

Secord got the 7th Air Force at Tan Son Nhut on a secure telephone line. He asked for a C-130 gunship, a cargo plane converted into a weapons platform of enormous deadly force. Banking and circling over their targets, gunships could fire 20mm cannon so fast that the illuminated tracer rounds made a golden hose of light from the plane to the ground. The C-130 gunships were also equipped with infrared spotting devices, which gave them a chance of discerning where artillery flashes were coming from even through cloud cover. The 7th Air Force put Secord on hold, telling him they would see if there were any available. Landry and Clines worked another frequency, organizing a counterattack with Agency staff at Long Tieng, mustering Vang Pao's understrength reserve battalion.

On the mountain, when the artillery barrage ended after about an hour and a half, the air force men emerged from their ledge on the back side of the cliff and went back to operating the radar, which was still functioning. The forward air guide on the site had been trying to direct two propellor planes and four jets through the cloud cover. He had an aerial traffic jam on his hands, and some of the airplanes still on their way toward the mountain were ordered to turn back.

A lull fell over the mountain. A 9 P.M. heavy fighting flared at a Meo village a half hour's walk downhill from the radar, and then quieted again. Most of the Meo outposts were reporting to be holding. The Thai stiffeners were still in place. Near midnight when the deputy commander of the 7/13th Air Force in Udorn contacted the air attaché's office in Vientiane, Vientiane said evacuation would happen only as a last resort.

In Udorn, Secord begged and pleaded for a gunship from Saigon. His telephone went dead, and he crossed the runaway to the 7/13th in search of another secure line.

At Long Tieng, Vang Pao's commanders were assembling their troops. Helicopter pilots were on standby.

About one-thirty in the morning, after intermittent shelling and mortaring started again, Ambassador Sullivan decided that some of the Americans would be evacuated at eight-thirty in the morning. The situation was marginal but had not totally deteriorated; everyone was still in radio contact.

At 2 A.M., the senior air force officer on the mountain, a Lt. Col. Bill Blanton, exchanged messages with his boss, Lieutenant Colonel Clayton at Udorn. Clayton said that as far as he was concerned, the men on the mountain had his permission to blow up the site and leave. Blanton replied that the radar was still working and they might as well get back to work. A radio operator, Sgt. Melvin Holland, added his own postscript to Blanton's message: "See you later, I hope."

About three-fifteen in the morning, the CIA man by the helicopter pad called Udorn to say he had lost radio contact with the technicians at the top. "I heard A.W. fire up there," Freeman added, referring to automatic weapons.

Landry grabbed the mike. *"What?"* he yelled. Automatic weapons, like machine guns and M-16 rifles, have a much shorter range than, say, the artillery the North Vietnamese were firing from the bottom of the mountain. If automatic weapons were being fired on top of the mountain it meant that the enemy was near. Which meant the North Vietnamese had somehow gotten past the defenders. Where were the Thais?

"Yeah. I hear it," Howie Freeman confirmed.

Landry said, "You get some of those goddamn little guys and get your ass on top of that sonofabitch right now."

From a secure telephone at the 7/13th in Udorn, Major Secord was threatening the duty officer of the 7th Air Force, a brigadier general, with court martial if he didn't get a gunship up to Site 85.

The sequence is a little unclear, but it appears Freeman couldn't go anywhere just then. The area around the helicopter pad came under atack from both shelling and automatic weapons fire. In the meantime, the twenty-man squad of North Vietnamese Dac Cong commandos who had run up the northeast slope of the mountain and around the Thais without being detected hunted for the American radar operators. They knew exactly where to go.

It is believed that Blanton and half a dozen others who were inside the radar building heard the gunfire and grenades and went outside, where they met the enemy commandos face-to-face. Blanton tried to explain that he was an unarmed civilian. He reached around to his back pocket for his Lockheed ID card, and that was when the commandos shot him and two other Americans dead at point-blank range. A fourth American hid in the bushes, and the others inside the radar building ran for their lives from another exit without setting off the demolition charges.

With their sandbagged bunker destroyed by shelling, the off-duty shift of radar operators had been trying to get some sleep on the ledge a few feet down from the cliff. One of them was a master sergeant named Richard Etchburger, an electronics whiz who had been encouraged to apply for officer training school. When the North Vietnamese appeared at the top of the cliff and fired down at the ledge, Etchburger fired back with bursts of his M-16. The North Vietnamese began rolling hand grenades down onto the ledge. The Americans frantically kicked the live hand grenades over the cliff. Some of the grenades exploded before they could get to them, wounding them with fragments of metal and pieces of rock. Another sergeant was blown up by a grenade while kicking it and he fell over the cliff. The men on either side of Etchburger were wounded, and they handed him ammunition clips as Etchburger tried to keep the North Vietnamese at bay.

In Vientiane, Sullivan had been told that there was small-arms fire at the summit, but he didn't know the outcome. At five-fifteen in the morning, he decided to pull everybody off the mountain.

Meanwhile, Howie Freeman had taken his semiautomatic shotgun and some grenades, and started up the steep path to the top with a squad of Meo. They didn't meet any enemy. By the time they got to the top most of the Meo had melted away. The first light of dawn had arrived on the mountain peak and the cloud cover was lifting.

Freeman came around to the west side of the dozen or so buildings on top, just a few yards from the cliff. He saw a North Vietnamese soldier and fired his shotgun. After the first shell his shotgun jammed. He managed to free it and they exchanged shots without hitting each other. Running around the corner of a building he saw a machine gun emplacement ringed with sandbags. Inside a North Vietnamese was firing a machine gun at A-1 propellor planes buzzing around the summit. The CIA man shot the machine gunner and then limped and ran back down the path to the helicopter pad. He was wounded in the left leg below the knee but not badly.

Helicopters clattered in an hour after sunrise—civilian Air America helicopters, not air force helicopters, as the survivors bitterly noted. The helicopters pulled off the two CIA officers and five technicians. The last to climb aboard was Etchburger. As the chopper rose, a North Vietnamese emerged from behind a generator and sprayed fire at its underbelly. A round passed through the metal and into Etchburger, who went into shock.

The choppers flew to Nakhang, and the men transferred to a Caribou light cargo plane for the flight to Udorn. When it landed Lieutenant Colonel Clayton met it and rushed inside the plane. At first he didn't recognize Etchburger, lying down on the floor, his open eyes turned milky white. There was not a mark on him, not a drop of blood. It took an autopsy later to reveal that the enemy bullet had entered directly up Etchburger's anus and that he had died of internal bleeding. Clenched in his right hand was a pair of wire clippers. It was as though Etchburger had planned to go back to the radar shack, snip some wires, and start the demolition sequence.

Except for the summit, the Meo still held much of the mountain, and the Thai force was nearly intact. But the decision was made to abandon Phou Pha Thi without a full-fledged counterattack.

"The weather improved dramatically," remembered Secord. "We got tremendous numbers of fighters up there, everybody up there milling around looking for something to shoot when it was too late. We had one A-1 shot down and the pilot killed, early that morning. We had only a short period of time to get in and get out of there safely.

"We never planned it that way. We had always planned an orderly withdrawal. We had mined the site. We had demolitions in place. We didn't get to blow the site. It was a helluva mess.

"It was a shattering experience."

# TWENTY-THREE

# Sayaboury Time

Of the nineteen Americans on the mountain that night, eight were helicoptered off. They included the two CIA men; five of the radar team, including Sergeant Etchburger, who died within an hour; and the Air Commando's forward air guide, who had been overlooked in the initial evacuation and was the last American to leave on that fateful day.

That left eleven Americans dead or missing on the mountain. Their bodies were never recovered. Stories arose later that three of the Americans were led off the mountain as captives. These Phou Pha Thi prisoner stories, which were never conclusively disproved, marked the start of a larger phenomenon—a prolonged confusion over the fate of American prisoners of war and missing in action (POW/MIA) in the Laotian theater of the Vietnam War.

It is likely that the Soviets ended up with the hardware from the top of the mountain. The day after the site fell, the cloud cover closed in again. According to intelligence reports, Soviet or Soviet-bloc technicians were spotted on Pha Thi not long afterwards. American planes bombing the site to prevent the gear from being taken had no way of aiming through the clouds, with Skyspot itself out of commission. The planes bombed for a week without hitting the radar—plenty of time to remove anything of value.

The fall of the site and the failure to blow up its secret radar technology exposed the deepest flaw of the American management of the Laos war, the lack of a unified command. The individual most responsible for the fiasco, Ambassador William Sullivan, had refused to allow properly trained soldiers on the mountain to help in site defense, and then had waited too long to give the order to evacuate. However, since the entire episode was classified, the institution most at fault—the air force—favored a cover-up rather than a serious investigation. Sullivan, a master of bureaucratic maneuver, escaped serious blame, and soon he was given important new duties by the Johnson administration.

Three weeks after the installation's capture, on March 31, 1968—in the same speech that he declared that he would not be a candidate for reelection—President Lyndon Johnson announced a halt to the American bombing of northern North Vietnam. The bombing halt applied to roughly the same area that Commando Club had covered. Johnson, motivated primarily by domestic discontent over the Tet offensive, wanted to open peace negotiations with the North Vietnamese. Since Laos was one of the few countries outside the communist bloc where both the United States and North Vietnam had ambassadors, the White House asked Bill Sullivan to arrange a site where the negotiations could take place. Sullivan met secretly with his North Vietnamese counterpart, and eventually they agreed on Paris.

The U.S. negotiating team in Paris was led by Averell Harriman, Sullivan's boss from the Geneva negotiations of 1961–62. Harriman summoned Sullivan to Paris as negotiations were about to begin. Sullivan knew one of the lesser members of the North Vietnamese delegation, and Harriman thought that if the formal negotiating sessions became blocked, the two of them might be able to establish an informal channel of communication.

While Sullivan was in Paris, during this spring of 1968, political disturbances broke out on the Left Bank. Students from the Sorbonne and other universities, abetted by experienced leftist agitators, were calling for revolutionary changes in society. Fifty thousand tough, working-class police were called in to Paris and stationed on the Right Bank for the showdown, which was repeatedly delayed.

At the time there was no accredited American ambassador to France, and Sullivan was asked to represent his country at a performance of the Paul Taylor dance troupe. The dinner party after the performance, a few blocks from the barricades on the Left Bank, was interrupted by an announcement that the students were coming. Sullivan and his party got in their car just as the students flooded into the surrounding streets nearby. The demonstrators rocked the car from side to side and yanked a door open. The director of the theater, who knew some of the students, climbed on the hood of the car and interceded. Shaken but unharmed, Sullivan and his party drove away.

Sullivan's North Vietnamese diplomat acquaintance never came forward for quiet chats. The peace negotiations stalled and then deadlocked over the shape of the negotiating table.

◆

"April 5, 1968   Bangkok

"Well as you see I finally made my Xmas vacation. Finally made it back to a city where everyone you see is not scared to death. Only of cars, but not afraid tonight they will be killed, homes burnt or taken over by the communists.

"I knew for two months I was wearing down, but just could not leave the people and the terrable mess they was in and still are," Edgar Buell wrote to his family. "I was nearer to the breaking point than I have been for a long time. Got here about noon. I went to bed, got up at 4:30, bed at 8, got up 7:30. Laid down again this fornoon. Feel pretty good but just need a lot more of that stuff. Sleep, rest, read.

"I think without me telling you and it would be impossable to write, what all has happened up north the past 3 months. It has been *literaly Hell.* We have now completly lost Sam Neua Provence. When I left we still had only 2 small airstrips left. 25,000 people lost to the other side, not counting what we lost in Xieng Khouang Provence. We got out app. 10,000, some more will make it through the months and years providing we don't loose everything. Getting these people out was some of the most Heroic work I have ever saw, by all my Americans, my local staff, Dr. Weldons staff, pilots of all type, some of the greatest piloting and heroism from them in my life. We got at least 50% out from behind enemy lines, under air cover. For 6 days we had nearly all of Laos' airfleet, Porters, Helios, all the Carabos, 14 choppers at times.

"One way or another we airlifted all these people into Sam Tong. What a sight, and mess. For the first time since 7 yrs ago Sam Tong is a refugee center. Parachutes, Tents, tarps, what have you. Sleeping living everywhere, much sickness.

"At this point I have no idea what the President did [the announcement of the partial bombing halt over North Vietnam, and the opening of peace negotiations] will have an effect on Laos or not. It may. Right now up in my area they feel if an agreement is reached, where I have worked would be turned over to the Reds. God I hope not, after all these people have did for the U.S. and Free World. But I am afraid. It looks real dark.

"The Reds are just like flies they are everywhere. They have man power plus best armed and equipted of any army *ever.* God only knows where they are going to stop if they do. At least I am not facing them right now, and I am going to try to forget it for a couple weeks or more.

"Love to all, Your Dad."

◆

In a room on the Princeton University campus a tall graduate student was typing a paper. "There is a pattern to the fighting in north Laos," he declared. "The weather clears towards the end of October. The rains stop, the roads dry up, and the first wave of Communist attacks begins. The objectives are usually reached by January and the fighting drops off. The anti-Communist government forces wait for the second shoe to fall in May, just before the rains begin again. The Communists, known as the Pathet Lao, try to hold their newly won territory during the monsoon season when American air support and better supply lines favor government operations. Pushing out from the Mekong valley, the Government forces usually retake much of what had been lost.

"This courtly contest has been going on since 1954 and each side controls about as much now as it did then," he continued. "But there has been a gradual escalation in the last five years. The fighting has become more bitter and more costly."

Vint Lawrence had returned to his alma mater for a master's degree in anthropology. He loved being back. There were no subjects deemed unworthy of study, even remote, little-known countries like Laos. But it had been two years since he returned from the kingdom and he did not have access to classified cable traffic anymore. A recent copy of a magazine lay next to his typewriter, opened to an article. He looked at it and brought his fingertips back to the keyboard.

"In the 'New Yorker' magazine of 4 May 1968," he wrote, "Robert Shaplen has filled in some of the details of the 1968 offensive, the most serious year so far. In January, the North Vietnamese spearheaded an attack on Nam Bac, an upland valley town sixty miles north of Luang Prabang, the royal capital. The attack on Nam Bac was a prelude to the offensive in Sam Neua (or Houa Phan) Province in the northeast corner of the country. The principal objective of the Vietnamese attack, according to Shaplen, was an American communications station on top of a 6,000 foot mountain, Phou Pha Thi. It was placed there presumably for its proximity to North Vietnam and because Phou Pha Thi has been the center of the anti-Communist resistance in the area.

"Shaplen quotes two Americans who have been intimately connected with this resistance movement, Dr. Charles Weldon and Edgar 'Pop' Buell. In their bitter comments, both men underscore the dilemma of the American position in Laos. The national resistance has become subordinated to what the United States sees as its best interest on the international level of the Southeast Asian conflict. To quote Weldon:

> The whole northern region is falling to the Communists. They are fighting harder this year than ever before, and they are using their first team. The situation is hopelessly mixed up with the Vietnam War, and these poor people are taking a beating. Once we Americans had assumed an obligation to help them, we shouldn't have allowed them to suffer because of the situation in Vietnam. We should have defended them for their own sake.

"What these two men are condemning in an emotional and perhaps slightly exaggerated way is the main failure of American policy in this small and sometimes forgotten country. This failing is insensitivity. It is the insensitivity to the varied and complex forces by which a people becomes a nation. It is the insensitivity to consequences of our actions. It is the insensitivity to. . . ."

He scanned across a quote from Buell in *The New Yorker* piece. "A few days ago I was with Vang Pao's officers when they rounded up 300 fresh Meo recruits," Buell was quoted as saying.

> Thirty percent of the kids were fourteen years old or less and about a dozen were only about ten years old. Another thirty percent were fifteen or sixteen. The rest were thirty-five or older. Where were the ones in between? I will tell you, they are all dead. Here were these little kids in their camouflage uniforms that were much too big for them, but they looked real neat, and when the King of Laos talked to them they were proud and cocky as could be. They were eager. Their fathers and brothers had played Indian before them, and now they want to play Indian themselves. But V.P. and I know better. They are too young and are not trained. In a few weeks ninety percent of them will be killed.

Princeton had changed profoundly since Lawrence's undergraduate days. The smartest young people, the children of the elite, were questioning the status quo instead of trying to join it. The same phenomenon occurred at other colleges. A mysterious pipeline of belief seemed to connect the Princeton campus to the Sorbonne and to Harvard Yard and Sproul Plaza at Berkeley and scattered individuals, like Fred Branfman, around the world.

On campus, Lawrence avoided making himself a target. When anybody asked, he claimed that he had worked for USAID in Laos. He did not mention knowing Buell and Weldon, or that he had helped run the north Laos war for the CIA. When people asked him about Vietnam he changed the subject. He did not, and felt he could not, renounce the Americans or the tribespeople he had worked with. He did not join the antiwar rallies. But he did not agree with what his government was doing in Vietnam, and he no longer agreed with much of what it was trying to do in the kingdom next door.

◆

The fall of Phou Pha Thi was the turning point of the Laos war, according to many of the old hands, including Bill Lair and Edgar Buell. According to their thinking, the United States, by presenting the North Vietnamese with a fixed target—the radar device that threatened Hanoi's security—goaded the communists into crushing the Laotians rather than fighting seasonally and distractedly as in previous years.

A different theory held that the huge North Vietnamese escalation in northern Laos in 1968 was just part of the general gearing-up that also produced the Tet offensive in South Vietnam. Ted Shackley believed in this second theory, and if he had a broader perspective than the Laos hands, and possibly better information about Hanoi, he also had personal and career reasons for trying to shift the blame away from the bungling at Phou Pha Thi.

In any event, after capturing the mountain, the North Vietnamese invaders pressed on south toward Vang Pao's strongholds. The U.S. Air Force went all-out to stop them. The warplanes and the invaders met at Nakhang, the big base north of the Plain of Jars. The Laotian defenders never needed to get outside the perimeter of the base. With a ferocity born of vengeance and pent-up frustration, the U.S. pilots broke and scattered the North Vietnamese regiment that had captured Phou Pha Thi. One enemy battalion was believed totally destroyed, with no survivors.

A curious factor enabled the U.S. Air Force to send far more planes into Laos than ever before, far more than it had used in defending its radar installation. When Lyndon Johnson announced that he was suspending bombing north of the 20th parallel to help start peace talks, it was unclear whether he meant all of Indochina or just North Vietnam. As Richard Secord put it, "We took the position that that didn't include Laos, because we were denying that we were fighting in Laos anyhow. How the hell could we stop bombing when we weren't bombing to begin with? You follow me? So that was the bureaucratic battle that we waged.

"Finally we prevailed. I was requesting B-52s. The compromise was that they gave us three hundred outer-limit sorties a day, open-ended. So we went at it very methodically and crunched 'em."

If until then Secord had had a hard time getting enough air strikes out of the air force, the opposite problem now arose. There weren't enough targets to go around. The jets went into holding patterns, like passenger planes over a busy airport, circling and circling and demanding traffic control. (An even bigger swarm would arrive in November of that year when Johnson put the rest of North Vietnam off-limits for bombing, too.)

The excess of planes—"an embarrassment of riches," as one CIA man put it—created an opportunity. For several years Secord and others had been trying to close the gap between fast-moving planes piloted by men who spoke only English and the so-called Little Guys on the ground. A rudimentary system of forward air controllers, or FACs, had already existed, but they weren't being used systematically.

Secord helped the embassy air attaché set up a program for full-time forward air controllers with tribesmen sitting in the back seats to help with the radio communications with the ground. They got their proposal approved easily enough by the CIA and by Sullivan, and eventually by the 7th Air Force, which initially had balked at doing something as unconventional as putting Asian hillbillies in planes with American pilots.

The new forward air controllers, introduced on a large scale after the Nam Bac and Pha Thi disasters, were known as the Ravens, after their radio call sign. They were volunteers who had already flown in Vietnam; and they were brought into Laos under Project 404, the embassy program that provided plainclothes military men to the war under various guises. The Ravens flew single-engine Cessna propellor planes, which were cheap and readily available, and slow enough to bridge the speed gap between supersonic jets and the men on the ground. Vang Pao and the other local commanders provided the interpreters, who were known as backseaters.

"They got some real warriors up there," Secord said of the Ravens. "Guys not too concerned about discipline or about promotions. Loose enough to work in a guerilla-type war. You gotta be half crazy to do that work, or half ignorant, because you can get killed easy."

And so another phase of the war began in the spring of 1968. On the ground were more North Vietnamese than ever—between forty and fifty thousand. They built roads and burned hilltribe villages, laying waste to everything around; and if they had been stopped at Nakhang they would soon be back, driving toward the Plain of Jars and beyond it to Long Tieng. The tribal irregulars weren't beaten yet, but they were cracking. What kept Vang Pao's army from falling apart was help from the air. Up to three hundred American jets flew sorties each day, roaming the skies, looking for targets to attack, and guided to them by tiny, slow-moving single-propellor planes.

◆

Bill Lair was amazed. He could raise his arm, and the sky turned black with airplanes.

He had piston-driven planes galore—T-28s, big A-1s, and A-26s for night work. He had jets of many models, their loud whooshing belying their small size, which belied their enormous destructive power.

He could send them wherever he wanted. His government had given him and his subordinates the privilege of directing that power, subject to a few permissions, which it nearly always gave.

If this was a supermarket war, he decided, it was not all bad.

If, say, a tribesman hidden in the forest near the Napé Pass saw trucks coming into Laos and pressed the button on his hand-held counter once for each truck, the signal went out, and pretty soon someone walked into his office 170 miles away and asked, Should we launch? Lair would nod, and jets would take off from Udorn or Nakhorn Phanom, and the ground near the pass would shudder with explosions.

Or if, say, Long Tieng reported new paths leading to a cave in the limestone karst, Lair sat and thought about it for a while and then quietly gave the word. The next day, weather and electronics permitting, a Bullpup guided missile sought the mouth of the cave and exploded inside, killing all the occupants.

Of course, there was more to it than the exercise of that nearly magical power. There were requests to make, red tape to cut, failures due to weather and faulty technology. The enemy had antiaircraft weapons on the ground and there were complications everywhere. But to Lair's surprise, the war machine was more or less geared to carrying out his wishes. Thousands upon thousands of young American men were working on air bases in Thailand and South Vietnam, reading the reconnaissance photos, loading the weapons, and tinkering with the jets and flying them. And as though it were the most natural thing in the world, guys came into his corner office saying, Well, Bill, let's look at tomorrow's frag list. What do you want to hit?

It was hard to believe that he had been given this gift, after all he stood for, as an apostle of locally supported, small-time guerilla war. He could do things with airpower he had never even dreamed of before.

It was gratifying. It was humbling.

He was elated, sometimes, at the thunderous blast of the planes barreling down the runway.

He felt the power. It was his to use.

Or misuse.

Because for a long time now—he'd forgotten how long—Lair had allowed himself to half believe that supermarket war would work. He had wanted it to work because his government wanted it to work, and because he needed to believe in his government. But his visits to the field always reminded him that it wasn't working and that the whole strategy was wrong.

His problems had started with Shackley's arrival, and at first he had thought Shackley was the problem. But Shackley was just a representative of the system. The system assumed that if you threw money at a problem, it would have a positive effect. If you could do well with X number of men and Y dollars, just think how well you could do with 2X men and 2Y dollars, or 3X men and 3Y dollars.

The thing was, thought Lair, Laos had been doing well with X and Y. The tribals' war had been running at pretty close to peak performance, especially in the north. There were a quarter-million Meo, fully mobilized, with grandfathers and twelve-year-olds in the ranks. You couldn't get to 2X or 3X, to a half million or three quarters of a million, with them.

If you couldn't get more X, more tribesmen, you could do what the U.S. was doing, spend more Y, more money. If you used expensive weapons, like jets, you would kill more North Vietnamese, but not enough to stop them from coming. North Vietnam had nineteen million people. Nineteen million versus a quarter million—a ratio of seventy-six to one.

Nor was money going to improve the performance of the tribal people. You would get people who were only in it for the money. You would make them more dependent on air strikes. And maybe, if you weren't careful, you would take away the tribal people's motivation, which was to defend themselves. You would change it from *their* war to *our* war, and keeping it their war had been the secret of success.

Even if Washington's objectives for Laos had changed, thought Lair, even if the new goal was to tie down as many North Vietnamese as possible, to keep them out of South Vietnam, it could have been done the old way, by spreading out the guerilla forces and not giving the enemy big targets to attack. That way the Laotian casualties could stay low. But the pitched battles and their high casualty rates were starting to destroy whole ethnic groups, particularly the Meo. It was a vicious cycle: Vang Pao had teenage company commanders leading troops who were little more than children. Less experienced leaders meant more battlefield deaths, which meant more and more tribesmen pressed into service. And as the tribe lost its young males, the women were having a hard time finding husbands.

From the very start, when he had proposed the operation to Desmond FitzGerald, Lair had thought the Meo would lose eventually and that the solution was to send them to Sayaboury Province. He had let the idea slip in the middle years of the war when everything was going well, but it had never entirely left his mind. Sayaboury was the province on the safe side of the Mekong, a place where thick mists drifted through rugged valleys, but it was more than that. Sayaboury was a whisper of hope, the way out to safety, and Thailand.

Now Sayaboury time had arrived. It was time for the Meo to prepare for the day when they would have to fight on without American support. But what he saw instead was Vang Pao becoming less and less a guerilla leader. Spending more time in headquarters, less with his troops. Meeting bigwig Americans on the Tour, and believing their flattery. Building Long Tieng up even more, and making a bigger target for the enemy. His people needed to stay light on their feet and resist becoming dependent on the Americans or on luxuries. They didn't need more T-shirts or transistor radios or motorcycles on the Long Tieng runway. They didn't need Xieng Khouang Airways to haul goods to the Long Tieng market. But Lair couldn't tell Vang Pao any of that because it was not his place to, because he worked in a chain of command and it would have gone against U.S. policy to tell Vang Pao anything the embassy didn't want him to hear.

The Thai Paru already knew the game was over. The year before, in 1967, in a tragedy that broke morale, the most widely admired individual Paru, Lt. Col. Dachar Adulyarat, had been in a plane wreck. Dachar had walked away from the crash and run back to pull an American out of the wreckage. He got away, then returned to help a second trapped American when the plane exploded, killing them both.

From there it had been downhill. With all the new CIA paramilitary officers coming in, many of them Special Forces veterans, the Paru's authority had been taken away bit by bit until there was little left for them to do. They had already been drinking too much, and this gave the Americans an excuse to say that the Paru ought to get out of there, which they did quietly, because there wasn't much to say. Pranet, the Paru leader, went back to Bangkok to a career in the regular Thai police. A few stayed on in Laos to train tribal officers, but their main role was taken over by the Americans, and by Thais from the regular Thai army, led by an ambitious general named Witoon Yasawat, a Thai version of Shackley.

About a third of the Paru serving in Laos had died there. The organization Lair had built up from scratch was nearly gone. And he wondered whether it had been in a worthy cause or all for nothing.

Most of the Americans he had respected the most from the old days were deeply frustrated with the way the United States was fighting in Vietnam and the way the system was taking over in Laos. His oldest friends, like Ron Sutphin the pilot and Heinie Aderholt the Air Commando, were all in favor of fighting the communists, but they wanted to fight smart, and they had long ago despaired of the futile and counterproductive approach the U.S. government had taken. They didn't speak out in public because they were loyal, or because they were afraid of losing their security clearances and their pensions, or because they didn't want to give any help to the long-haired demonstrators back home, who seemed to them not only antiwar but antipatriotic. And so these disillusioned veterans seldom acknowledged one another and never reached critical mass—these quiet men of the center right and far right, who had so much more experience, and such better reason for despair, than those who shouted the slogans and waved the placards at home.

The one man Lair would have given anything to talk to was Desmond FitzGerald, who had sent him in to build up the tribals' war and later Shackley to tear it apart. But FitzGerald never sent Lair a signal, even an indirect acknowledgment, about the changes in Momentum. In 1967, FitzGerald had been next in line to become director of Central Intelligence, when he died suddenly of a heart attack.

Lair brooded for months after FitzGerald's death, trying to decode the silence. He finally concluded that FitzGerald had been operating at a higher strategic level and knew exactly what he was doing all along. FitzGerald thought there was a chance that Shackley could squeeze more out of Laos and make a difference in Vietnam, while Vietnam still hung in the balance. But even beyond that, Lair believed, FitzGerald knew that Vietnam would come and go, that Laos would come and go, but that what ultimately mattered was the perpetuation of the Central Intelligence Agency. He needed a guy like Shackley, a hard-hitting guy to take on the generals, because he wanted the outfit to keep its place at the table.

And now Momentum was up to thirty thousand armed men. Udorn was an open secret. A congressman from Texas had shipped Vang Pao a Brahma bull as a present, and when you got to that point in a covert program it was time to get out. And so in 1968, a few months after Phou Pha Thi and the big air force buildup, Bill Lair requested a transfer.

When the word spread that he was going, Lair got a message from Bill Colby, who was then on leave of absence from the outfit, helping run the pacification program in South Vietnam. Colby asked whether Lair was interested in running something called the Phoenix program in South Vietnam that had something to do with taking out the Viet Cong leadership. He thought about it and sent a message back to Colby that he would do it if requested.

But the more Lair thought about it the less he wanted to go to Vietnam. It was too late to fix anything there. And Colby never got back to him, perhaps because he had learned that the next station chief in Saigon was going to be Theodore G. Shackley.

Shackley had looked like a genius for predicting the fall of Pha Thi on March 10 in his memos to headquarters. The knowledge of his wider failures like Nam Bac and the terrible attrition of the tribal forces had not percolated to the top. Shackley was known for taking on the military single-handedly and winning, and headquarters valued men like that highly. And so he was getting promoted to the most important station chief's job in the organization.

Before Lair left there was one more big meeting at Long Tieng. It was held in the house that Vang Pao built for the king of Laos way up on a hillside overlooking the airstrip and the sprawling city of tin roofs. The king was there along with Souvanna Phouma, Vang Pao, Shackley, Landry, some of the younger case officers, and even Tony Poe, who was pretty nearly sober. Doc Weldon was there with one of Pop Buell's refugee relief men. The Americans stood indoors in an L-shaped line, and everybody got the Order of the Million Elephants and a royal handshake from the old gentleman. Photographs taken at the event show the Americans in dark suits with narrow ties. Shackley looks jovial and cerebral, the egghead intel man with the black-framed glasses accentuating the high-domed forehead. Bill Lair appears stiff and uncomfortable, and about as charismatic as wallpaper. His slicked-back hair, glasses, and downcast eyes make him look like a weak-willed clerk rather than America's answer to Lawrence of Arabia in World War I—another odd and gifted man who organized an irregular force in a peripheral theater of a war. In the photographs Lair looks prematurely aged and defeated.

He went back to Udorn and packed his bags. He went into his office in the Taj Mahal and cleaned out his safe. He discovered the long memo he had written predicting the Nam Bac disaster. He stared at it, then burned it to ashes.

He flew to Bangkok, then left on the same transpacific flight as Maj. Richard Secord, who was returning to the States and to regular air force duty at the end of his CIA tour.

Lair had always liked Secord, who had done as much as anyone in the bureaucracy to escalate the air war. And that was Lair's dilemma. He despaired of the war, but he had helped start it himself; and he liked and respected almost everyone who had sent it sliding down the tubes.

# The Opium Trade

Bill Lair's successor, Pat Landry, believed in the original philosophy of small-scale, grassroots-supported guerilla war, but nearly lost his job for trying to turn back the clock.

Soon after taking over as CIA base chief in Udorn, Landry wrote a major paper for Shackley's successor as Laos chief of station, Lawrence Devlin. In it, Landry stated that spending more money and hiring more Americans had not resulted in any improvement in the Laos war effort. In fact, the bigger the budget, the less territory the friendly side controlled. Not liking Landry personally, and suspecting an Udorn power grab, Devlin dismissed Landry from his post. Landry had packed his bags and was ready to leave when he got help from a wholly unexpected quarter: Richard Helms, the director of Central Intelligence, who was visiting Thailand at the time, personally reinstated Landry in his Udorn job. It turned out that Helms had been pressured to keep Landry by the prime minister of Thailand, who in turn had been pressured by the commander of Thai forces in Laos, Gen. Witoon Yasawat. The Thais didn't like Landry as much as they had liked Lair, but they trusted him; and because the Thais were allies in the Laos war effort, they had influence with the CIA.

Chastened, Landry did what was expected of him. He acquiesced in turning Laos into an increasingly conventional war. He coordinated air strikes with the U.S. embassy in Vientiane and with the U.S. Air Force. He hired capable staffers, most of them ex–Green Beret officers, to help him with training and tactics of the Laotian tribal forces. Landry worked hard, and he ran Momentum to the best of his ability. But Landry often found himself being compared unfavorably with his friend and predecessor.

Part of Landry's problem was his personal style. He was grouchy and sarcastic. His swagger stick and his exaggerated Texas-style speech, full of "y'all" and "howdy" and crude references to local women, did little to create the impression that he was, in fact, experienced and shrewd. He did not attract strong loyalty from his paramilitary officers, or from Vang Pao, or from most Thais. But even if he had, it mightn't have made much difference. The importance of the Udorn base chief's job had shrunk over time.

The part of the war that had been his and Lair's at the beginning—the tribal paramilitary irregulars—had merged and blurred with other armed forces in Laos. By August 1968, when Landry took over, the tribal forces fought alongside the regulars of the Royal Lao Army. Regional commanders loaned units to one another, although grudgingly. Outright mercenaries worked on the Ho Chi Minh Trail; and "volunteer" units of Thais were soon to join the Thai Paru remnants and the Thai special forces already on the Laotian side of the Mekong. The U.S. Army's Green Berets crossed the border from South Vietnam daily and the air force flew in from South Vietnam and Thailand. Air sorties rose to about 450 a day after Lyndon Johnson declared a total bombing halt over North Vietnam in November 1968. With its jets roaming the skies in greater number than before, the air force pushed for more control over the Laos war theater, claiming, with some justification, that the CIA didn't understand airpower well enough to plan how and where it should be used.

Meanwhile, more North Vietnamese troops poured into Laos. Casualties rose on both sides. There were more than a half-million refugees. The scale of fighting and of human misery made everything that had gone before look puny and insignificant. Everything was eroding in Laos—the terrain under royalist control, the pretense of compliance with the Geneva accords, royalist confidence, American self-esteem, the operations' secrecy. But everything had been eroding for some time, and for the old hands what changed the most in 1968 and 1969 was the realization that they were powerless to do much about it. The shift that had started when Shackley arrived in Laos was complete. The war had become institutionalized.

What this meant for individual Americans was that they counted for less. They were cogs in a big, expensive war machine. On the Ho Chi Minh Trail, the war machine was a system of hardware, software, and weaponry, not just a figure of speech. Remote sensors dropped from planes had started replacing the trailwatch teams and their hand-held truck-counting gadgets. The electronic sensors, which detected North Vietnamese trucks and troops, sent their data to an IBM-360 computer in Nakhorn Phanom,

Thailand, which spat out targets for the U.S. planes to hit. None of this technology slowed down the North Vietnamese much. Even under heavy bombing, the North Vietnamese built a mile of road a day, with multiple routes, so that if one road became heavily cratered or mined, they could shift over to the next road, and the next.

In the rest of Laos there were fewer than two hundred CIA officers in the field, a remarkably small number when compared to the more than half a million U.S. military men in South Vietnam. Nevertheless a feeling had arisen among them that their mission had gone offtrack. It just wasn't working. The other side was doing better. As the number of paramilitary officers being hired on contract for Laos rose, their quality dropped; and even those who tried the hardest learned that they could make only a temporary difference.

◆

And yet there was one American in Laos who was still his own man, and not just a cog in the war machine. He was not particularly good at his job, but he had been a founder of the CIA's Laos war, and the usual standards did not fully apply.

In the remote military backwater of the far northwest Tony Poe had about six thousand irregulars. He had Lao Theung units—his best fighters—and Lahu, Meo, Shan, Wa, and T'ai Dam units; plus odds and ends of lowland Lao, Thai Paru, and Thai special forces. His largest single ethnic group was the Yao, or Mien, whose women wore a sort of red yarn ruff on the collars of their blouses. The Yao soldiers sat in their bases in their uniforms, collected their paychecks, and did as little as possible.

In the near-absence of combat with the enemy, Poe's main job was to keep his own tribal groups, Thais, and Lao from fighting with one another. When Operation Unity—as the program was wistfully called—failed to minimize the ethnic quarreling and the occasional knife stabbings, he built each group its own mess hall in his main base, Nam Yu. He tried to cut down on the supplies and the weapons that vanished and reappeared on the black market, but he didn't have much luck with that, either.

Restlessly, Poe charged around in helicopters, landing at little bases, inspecting weapons and equipment, and bullying the commanders. He set up training exercises and made the men go out on maneuvers. He told the commanders, "Go take Kunming [the nearest big city in southern China]. Go take Nam Tha [a town on the Laotian side of the Chinese border]." Poe had a humorous side, and sometimes it was hard to tell whether to take him seriously.

In 1967 his men took Nam Tha by mistake. Apparently, some T'ai Dam units on maneuvers in the hills above Nam Tha had relatives in the enemy-held valley. One afternoon Poe told them they could sneak down into town in the dark and visit quietly for a few hours. The next morning when he returned he found that they had not only visited their families but set up their command post in Nam Tha town. The light Pathet Lao defense force had vanished.

When Poe landed in his chopper his men were dancing the *lamvong* with their relatives, waving their hands around in the air to the music, and drinking homemade whiskey through straws from common jars. Poe joined them, in his gaudy Hawaiian shirt with the tails out to cover his gut and the greasy marine floppy-brimmed hat to cover his receding hairline. They were using hollow water buffalo horns as whiskey cups and, of course, he tried some of that, too.

The occupation of Nam Tha lasted six days—long enough for relatives who wanted to leave to hike out on foot and for Air America to organize ferry flights for ton after ton of captured equipment, everything from shovels to Chinese-made antiaircraft guns to rusted French weapons left over from colonial days. Poe's troops pulled back just as an ominously large Chinese force was assembling at the border, twenty miles away.

China was an eternal threat, the giant that could crush Laos like a gnat. The Chinese and American governments were fully aware of each other's presence in the region and were making hostile, if careful, moves. To the east of Poe's domain in Laos the Chinese already had started building a road from their southern border to the Mekong River. The Chinese road, nominally a foreign aid project, looked like preparation for an invasion route, particularly since the Chinese military guarded the road heavily and shot at American reconnaissance planes that flew overhead.

Other U.S. reconnaissance planes had discovered that the Chinese maintained ordinary telephone lines north of their border for military communications. Before Poe arrived in the northwest, a system had evolved of tapping into those telephone wires inside China and radioing the conversations back, using the CIA's hilltribe teams. Most of the CIA's base camps for the tribal wiretapping operation were in a lawless area of northern Burma. Many of those camps were shared with the Kuomintang, or KMT, a fragment of Chiang Kai-shek's old rightist-nationalist army that, under the guise of keeping up pressure against the communist Chinese regime, ran a lucrative business in the opium trade. Freelance opium traders returning to the region carried much of the CIA tribal teams' supplies. Cheap and effective, the tribal wiretapping operation was considered a model of dirty pragmatism by the CIA. But the information wasn't particularly valuable since the Chinese threat never materialized.

All in all, Poe had an army whose ethnic groups were on the verge of fighting one another more than they fought the enemy. He had a hand in intelligence operations that others had started and nobody paid much attention to. He had cases of beer and whiskey on the floor of his office near the big radio and no rules against drinking them. He had believed for many years that his country was going to lose in Laos and South Vietnam, and he could feel, smell, and taste the failure of the whole enterprise. So why not drink? He could find no reason.

The addiction of alcohol, the craving that is supposed to override free will, had no meaning to him. He was engaged in a sort of voyage of self-actualization, finding himself through booze, even though whatever he gained he lost by the next morning and had to start all over again. He drank because he wanted to, because he was bright and bored and wanted to see how close he could get to the edge.

Once a month he visited his Meo wife and her children, who had moved to Udorn. More often Poe took a plane to Ban Houei Sai, the nearest town on the Mekong, and from there to cities in northern Thailand like Chiang Rai, where if he was sober enough and his fellow Americans hadn't locked him inside his hotel room to keep him out of bar fights, he brought five or six whores back to his room to prove his virility. The morning after generally found him bleary-eyed and unshaven near the USAID warehouse in Ban Houei Sai. If there wasn't a plane flight back to his base at Nam Yu right away, the Americans working there laid him down on a stretcher in the shade. They joked about "reverse medevacs" while Tony just lay there appearing to sleep. But the next time Poe saw them, he repeated their conversations word for word.

Poe became legendary in the northwest for his drinking, for his crude behavior toward women, and for interfering with pilots by grabbing the controls or else by simply passing out and slumping over onto the instrument panel. The bar stories about him multiplied—how Tony had conducted a serious conversation in a calm level voice while strangling a cat with one hand. How when he didn't have bombs he dropped smooth river stones out of a Pilatus Porter onto an enemy position. How he carried brass knuckles and a rubber boxing mouthpiece in his pockets when he went into bars. How he kept enemy heads in a jar in his house in Nam Yu.

In later years Poe dismissed most of the stories as being exaggerated or untrue. He insisted that he had never collected enemy heads and pickled them in whiskey. Or even hung them from the rafters. He allowed that he might have spent evenings with his T'ai Dam troops, men tattooed from the waist up, who themselves had cut off enemy heads, stuck them on stakes, and thrown stones at them while dancing around the campfire—but that was *traditional* for the T'ai Dam, he insisted. They'd been doing it for centuries.

Ears were another matter. He paid a bounty for enemy kills. "I used to collect ears, you know," Poe admitted cheerfully. "I had a big, green, reinforced cellophane bag as you walked up my steps. I'd tell my people to put 'em in and then I'd staple 'em to this five-thousand kip notice that this was paid for already and put 'em in the bag and send them to Vientiane with the report.

"Sent 'em only once or twice, and then the goddamn office girls were sick for a week. Putrid when they opened up the envelope, you know. Some guy in the office, he told me, 'Jeez, don't ever do that again. These goddamn women don't know anything about this shit, and they throw up all over the place.'

"I still collected 'em, until one day I went out on an inspection trip with my Lao Theung, and I saw this little kid out there, he's only about twelve, and he had no ears. And I asked, 'What the hell happened to this guy?'

"Someone said, 'Tony, he heard you were paying for ears. His daddy cut his ears off. For the five thousand kip.'

"I said, 'That's the end of this program, right now. It's supposed to be enemy ears, not this little guy.' And I reached in and gave this little guy ten or fifteen thousand kip. Oh, that pissed me off." But the corruption of his bounty system angered Poe at least as much as the injury to the boy.

For better or worse—generally for worse—Poe dominated the far northwest. He chafed against authority; and nothing grated on him more than rivals, whether American or Laotian.

There was only one other CIA officer in the region whose stature and notoriety approach his own, and that was Bill Young, who had returned as a contract employee to report on Mekong River traffic from the town of Ban Houei Sai. No other American was as gifted at collecting intelligence information, and no other American had so many women parading through his bedroom every day, for free. The handsome, virile Young was usually late in filing his monthly intelligence reports, and unreliable in many other ways, but it was unclear whether Poe fired him for reporting failures or because Poe was jealous and needed to be the dominant male *farang* in the region. "Everybody's criticized me for years on this," Poe sadly admitted later. "Some of my biggest problems was dealing with Americans."

The Laotians were far less threatening to Poe. In the northwest there were no tribal leaders as powerful and charismatic as Vang Pao was in the northeast. The Yao, or Mien, were led by two brothers, Chao Mai and Chao La, who wore gold surrounds on their front teeth as signs of their prosperity. Chao Mai was the military leader, with his headquarters in Poe's base, Nam Yu; Chao La was the civilian leader, with his headquarters nearby in Nam Thouei. The two bases were modeled after Long Tieng and Sam Thong, but smaller.

When Poe arrived, a complex power struggle was already under way between the brothers, who were more interested in war profits than in military gains. Poe found that the leaders were not only taking their custom-ary cut of their troops' salaries but selling their equipment on the black market, usually to Burmese opium traders.

In April 1967, the military leader and older of the brothers, Chao Mai, died of a heart attack. Poe claimed he caused the heart attack by con-fronting Chao Mai publicly with accusations of his graft. Few other knowl-edgeable Americans supported this claim, but they were almost unanimous in agreeing that Poe wrecked the indigenous leadership structure. When Poe upped his demands for reform, Chao La, the civilian leader, simply pulled out his base at Nam Thouei and moved to a village on the Mekong River a short distance downstream from the point where Laos, Thailand, and Burma meet. Chao La did not renounce his role as civilian leader, but he spent most of his time running a private sawmill and a series of refiner-ies that transformed raw opium into purer derivatives, first a high grade of smoking opium and eventually heroin.

It was Poe's fate that northwest Laos was to become much better known for the drug trade than for the fight against the communists. Large economic forces were at work, and Poe had neither the power nor the in-clination to stop them.

His employees normally avoided collecting information on the drug trade. (At the time that was a job for the Bureau of Narcotics and Dan-gerous Drugs, or BNDD, a predecessor of the Drug Enforcement Admin-istration.) In Laos, the CIA's old hands believed that the trade in unrefined opium was a local economic reality predating the war, a strand of the lo-cals' economic reality that couldn't be removed without unraveling every-thing else. You could have a war against the communists or a war against the drug traders, they said, but you couldn't have both.

Being married to a tribeswoman who had traded in opium earlier in life, Poe had a special sympathy for the hill people who grew and used the stuff themselves. He had seen the land-clearing fires set toward the end of the dry season—by day the air thick with smoke, by night the fires glowing on distant mountainsides like red snakes. Normally the poppies were planted as a second crop between the stalks of corn and bloomed after the corn harvest. When the petals dropped from the poppy flowers, the tribal women scored the remaining seedpods with a special three-bladed knife and scraped off the milky sap that seeped out. "It's almost like latex, brown and pliable," Poe recalled. "A Meo or Yao man would take a ball of this putty wrapped in something like banana leaves, put it in his pack, and take his donkey down to town and buy everything he needed for a year with that one ball of opium sap. It's a means of exchange. Every store has a scale, and you take a chunk of that ball and put it on. They had these goddamn beautiful little weights, shaped like ducks and other animals. Weigh 'em out and give 'em the goods. The tribesman would put everything on his donkey and go back to the farm, and he'd have enough to last for a whole year."

Only a minority of the tribal people who produced opium smoked it themselves. Only a minority of those tribal smokers became addicted, and emaciated, and lost all ambition, just as some fraction of those who drink alcohol become alcoholics. Poe and other CIA veterans didn't think that opium posed much of a social threat in Laos, and they had seen that the unrefined drug had many uses in these hills. Shamans smoked it before they went into their trances. People with stomach ailments swallowed little opium pellets, like homegrown paregoric. Wounded tribal soldiers wetted raw opium, worked it into a consistency like putty, and applied it externally as a painkiller, like morphine, which is one of opium's derivatives. Old people, and those who feared death at the hands of the enemy, swallowed larger amounts to commit suicide, like a deliberate heroin overdose. It was the most useful and versatile drug in the hilltribe pharmacopeia.

At first, when Poe went out to the northwest in 1965, he had only been asked to keep an eye on opium shipments on civilian cargo aircraft. There had been occasional instances of American pilots moonlighting for opium traders, but most only carried the stuff unintentionally when ferrying hilltribe people from one airstrip to another. The pilots didn't have enough time to open up and inspect the baggage of everyone getting on the planes; and most of what these tribesmen carried, in little balls wrapped in parachute cloth or banana leaves, was for their own personal use anyway.

What changed everything was the war in Vietnam. The half-million American troops in South Vietnam presented a huge potential market to Asian entrepreneurs. The American soldiers bought legal intoxicants like liquor and beer, and marijuana grown in South Vietnam and Cambodia. In the mid-sixties, they began to buy smoking opium in the shantytowns outside the military bases, followed by low-price, high-quality heroin. Most of the opium from which the heroin was refined had been grown in Burma, but the rest was from Laos, and almost all of it was transshipped through Laos by America's so-called military allies.

In Laos itself the key player was Gen. Ouane Rattikone, the royalist commander in chief. He and others like him made no particular distinction between making money from drugs and making money from skimming payrolls, selling military equipment, granting monopolies and favors, and other kinds of graft. They belonged to power pyramids, where those at the top needed income to spread around to their subordinates, so their subordinates would have reason to support the man at the top.

Earlier in his career Ouane had received the opium concession for Luang Prabang Province from the king, who traditionally controlled and taxed the opium business there. When General Ouane became commander in chief in 1965, he sought to expand his share of the drug trade. His first move was to increase his supply. He appears to have left the Meo alone even though they were the largest opium producers in Laos. For one thing Vang Pao had his own power pyramid going, allowing his subordinates to sell opium in exchange for loyalty and other favors; and for another, the Meo already had their own decentralized trade channels established with Thai merchants. (These channels included, but were not limited to, two old C-47s the CIA gave to Vang Pao. Renamed Xieng Khouang Airways, and nicknamed "Air Opium," the airline went out of business after a couple of years.) The Meo were poor businessmen, and they were stubborn and well armed, so Ouane looked elsewhere.

The Yao of the far northwest did not grow as much opium as the Meo of the northeast, and General Ouane appears to have left them alone, too, as far as their own opium production. What he did instead was to take away the much larger volume of Burmese opium that previously had traveled through their territory. The Yao had held an annual trade fair for merchants and their caravans, from which they got a percentage of the take. Ouane canceled the trade fair and began to purchase directly from the major Burmese sources, including the semirenegade army of Kuomintang ex–National Chinese soldiers and an up-and-coming half-Shan, half-Chinese trader whose name was Chan Si-foo.

Next, Ouane focused on improving his transportation. It was six hundred miles from the Burmese to the South Vietnamese border and he needed planes. He and two other generals from old elite families approached the royalist air force commander, Gen. Thao Ma, who was based in Savannakhet in the southern panhandle. They suggested he rent them two C-47 transport planes in exchange for a generous weekly fee. To their surprise Ma turned them down. He wanted to use his planes for supporting and fighting the war. Ouane transferred General Ma to Vientiane and took the transport planes away from his control. Trapped, Ma staged a brief revolt in October 1966. Pilots from his old unit bombed the army headquarters, then Ma and ten others flew out to exile in Thailand.

After Ma's departure, Ouane got more control over aircraft. He used royalist planes to transport his products, and eventually royalist helicopters to haul fifty-five-gallon drums of ether to a string of thatched-roof heroin refineries along the Mekong River, for there was more money to be made from opium's derivatives than from opium itself. But General Ouane still had not straightened out his opium supply problems. His Burmese sources were in friction with one another.

In July 1967, a caravan of armed men and about three hundred mules carrying sixteen or more tons of opium crossed the Mekong River from Burma into Laos. Its leader, who stayed behind in Burma, was Chan Si-foo, a young man destined for greatness in his trade. The caravan's armed guard skirmished with a group of rival opium traders from the Chinese Kuomintang, or KMT. The caravan then hurried toward an orange grove and lumber mill on the Mekong directly across from the point where Burma and Thailand meet, in the so-called Golden Triangle. The owner of the lumber mill was General Ouane.

With the KMT in pursuit, the caravan made it to the lumber mill and erected barricades from the logs on site. The local villagers fled into the forest and across the river into Thailand. About a thousand KMT soldiers arrived and firing commenced, mostly with small arms, though both sides also had .50-caliber machine guns.

On July 30, 1967, after a couple of days of sporadic, desultory fighting, a half-dozen stubby-winged T-28 fighter-bombers appeared overhead. The men around the lumber mill came out of hiding and waved at the pilots, whose planes bore the royal Lao insignia, the white three-headed elephant.

In the air, the lead T-28 pilot checked by radio with the airfield at Ban Houei Sai, where General Ouane was waiting. Was the general sure he wanted to go ahead with it. *Bo pin yang,* said the general. Sure, no problem. The T-28s were carrying 250-pound bombs and CBUs, or cluster bomb units. The CBUs did the most damage to the men below of both armies, and to the mules, which broke free and ran around braying and bleeding. "For two or three days," said Tony Poe, "you couldn't even go in there, it smelled so bad from the putrified dead mules."

When they got back to the Vientiane airport, General Ouane gave the pilots a reward worth more than one and a half times their normal monthly salary. He could afford it. Irritated with his suppliers for fighting, he had seized the sixteen tons of opium for himself.

The Opium War of 1967, as the newspapers dubbed the incident, was one of the few times that drug transactions emerged into the open. It resulted in sensationalist and inaccurate reporting, and later in some serious studies. Eventually the Opium War forced the Americans to realize that the Laotian opium trade had lost its innocence, and that they couldn't ignore it anymore, mostly for the sake of the American war in South Vietnam.

At some point after the Opium War, Poe was asked to report on the higher levels of the drug trade in addition to carrying out his regular duties. He really wasn't sober enough, or analytically minded enough, to do a comprehensive job of it himself. The trade was far too large and shifting for any one man to understand completely. From poppy to powder, the opium and heroin trade covered a thousand miles of territory, from northern Burma through Laos and then forking into South Vietnam and Thailand for shipping overseas.

Poe had hazy, drunken memories of chemists sent into Burma by the Taiwanese government—"they were in it for the intel, not the money"—to help the Kuomintang set up heroin labs near the China-Burma border. Poe's own tribal trailwatch teams radioed positions of caravans far off in the boondocks, he said, "to get the timing down." For the Thai route he spoke of flaming Ts in the waters of the Gulf of Siam, marking the drop zones for heroin in canisters, wrapped in Styrofoam for the freighters to pick up. For the South Vietnamese route, he speaks of flights to Dalat and Pleiku, on which good-looking Laotian women served as stewardesses, bringing the receipts back to the cabal of Laotian generals and providing sex to the South Vietnamese generals if asked. Long after the war, Poe told American journalists that Vang Pao took part in the heroin trade; but he appeared to have made this up to injure Vang Pao's reputation, for the Meo never had any chemical processing facilities, according to people who worked with them much more closely than he did; and Poe himself had nothing to say about the trade in raw opium while he was stationed in Long Tieng.

The main target of Poe's boozy reporting in the northwest was General Ouane. Rumors and folklore notwithstanding, Ouane was genuinely the big man of the Laotian drug trade, the chief of a cabal that met monthly to straighten the accounts. The center of logistical activity was the airport at Ban Houei Sai in the far northwest, where Burmese drugs in various stages of chemical refinement were stored prior to reshipment.

Whenever Ouane came up to the far northwest Poe went with him as his minder. Ouane seldom invited anybody else to come along with them, Poe said, and once they arrived at Ouane's private property along the Mekong, which had a private airstrip, the general sent him off. He asked Poe to go inspect another airstrip for possible upgrading, or to perform some chore or other.

Poe obediently left General Ouane for two or three hours. But he said he had teams already in position in concealment, ready to take photographs of the drug traders coming across the river from the Burma side, or the Thai or Lao military helicopters landing on the sandbars in the river. "All my special teams had these Pentaxes with 240mm lenses. The photos showed this Colonel So-and-so in a door, working. He's there, and the pilots are his boys. Guys he could trust. And he's doing the work, shoveling out the guns himself. They give *our* guns, that we didn't have the fucking guts to collect after we gave 'em *new* guns. They'd clean 'em up a little bit and trade 'em to the Burmese for processed heroin," Poe said. "That was one way they did it, and there were others. Ouane thought I was stupid, but I knew what was going on. He wasn't getting away with shit."

Poe kept a loose eye on the man the U.S. embassy had no intention of arresting. They played host for each other at parties, during which Ouane discreetly discussed business deals out of Poe's hearing. Later they went off carousing together. "I'd take him to Chiang Rai to get laid. I'd get him some real beautiful women," remembered Poe. Sometimes they took a gang of Thai, Lao, and American colleagues along, traveling by Air America helicopter, Ouane thinking he was hoodwinking Poe, Poe keeping an eye on Ouane's drug trade activities, and the two of them and their pals going off to the bars and whorehouses together, as the war ground on.

# My Favor

In the middle of 1968, Vang Pao wasn't thinking much about opium. He hardly ever did. He allowed raw opium to be sold in the Long Tieng market. He didn't attempt to control or centralize the Meo opium trade, and he didn't punish anyone who was caught at it in Vientiane. When occasional problems of crops and shipments came to his attention, he solved them quickly and discreetly, behind the Americans' backs. The Americans got upset about it, but there was no helping that. They came from a strange culture, with mystifying and contradictory rules.

What Vang Pao thought about—all the time—was war, though politics ran a close second, because fighting the war required political support. In 1968 everything about the war was changing—the enemy's strategy, his own tribe's will to fight, the Americans' antiwar movement, the Paris peace talks. He decided to take a vacation, to clear his mind and decide where he was leading his people. In September he accepted an invitation to visit the continental United States, where he had never been before.

It was an enormously important trip for him and he was faced with a problem of protocol: Which wife should he take? They all wanted to go to America, to the fabled, inconceivably rich country that lay somewhere beyond the horizon, even farther than the Mekong. They all knew it was going to be the trip of a lifetime.

By then he had six wives and about two dozen children, by general reckoning. His current harem didn't include his "original" first wife, who had died in the 1950s; his brother's wife, whom as tribal tradition required he had taken as his own after his brother died, though he later discarded her; or another fourteen-year-old girl whom he had married and then abandoned a week later, after he had a car accident and the shamans told him that she was the cause of his bad luck; or numerous other maidens he had bedded here and there on his nights outside Long Tieng. His people were more tolerant about such matters than their civilized brethren in the West.

That tolerance, however, did not extend to the relations among his wives themselves. Whatever his prowess on the battlefield, Vang Pao was unable to stop the fighting and squabbling under his own roof. At the end of a long session reviewing the North Vietnamese order of battle one evening, Vang Pao reluctantly got ready for the domestic tensions that awaited him. "Now my war really begins," he remarked to a CIA adviser, indicating his wives upstairs.

Each wife had a tiny room on the second floor of his house in Long Tieng. He slept with them in rotation: the first night with Wife Number One, from the Thao clan; the second with Wife Number Two, from the powerful Ly clan; and so on down the list, and then started over again. Three was a homely and unhappy member of the Lor clan. Wives Four (the Field Wife) and Six, both from the Moua clan, were his favorites. Five was an ethnic Lao woman who had caught his eye; he had married her as a nation-building gesture, and both of them were starting to regret it. The stories of the wives' spats had become minor legends in Long Tieng, such as the time Wife Number Two got sick and asked for a shaman and Wife Number One refused to arrange it, saying that she hoped Two would die instead.

The most serious, life-threatening quarrel happened after a picnic in which the general had left Number Three at home. Three, who often declared that she just slept with him for the money, sulked and fumed the whole time everybody was away. When the general and the other wives returned home from the picnic she grabbed an M-16 left lying around the house, aimed it at her husband, and pulled the trigger. The rifle was loaded but luckily for him she hadn't switched the safety off. The general slapped her and threw her down on the floor, then ordered her to get out of the house. She came sulking back a few days later. Nobody thought much about it because spats and quarrels were part of the routine.

After thinking it over carefully, Vang Pao chose Wife Number One to accompany him to America. She was a smart, good-hearted woman who delivered him a child every year, and who also ran the food end of his household, a complex logistical operation including cargo flights to Vientiane, stalls in the Long Tieng market, and gardens tended by the bodyguards. Sometimes for relaxation she smoked an opium pipe but she was by no means an addict, for addicts are thin, and Wife One was distinctly stout around the middle.

As a gift for the leader of the Americans, Vang Pao decided to bring a Meo muzzle-loader rifle, the kind the pilots were always buying as quaint souvenirs. He flew to the United States with Wife One and four aides. In Washington, D.C., the CIA laid out a special tour, but there was a mix-up when they arrived at the White House. The guards at the West Wing entrance didn't have his name on the list. He was just a short little Asian in a poorly fitting suit with a dumpy little wife and some other people and a guy who claimed he was from the Central Intelligence Agency.

The entourage trooped obediently around to the East Wing and stood in line with all the other tourists for the usual White House tour. The short moon-faced man with the musket shuffled along next to blue-haired ladies from Florida and freckle-faced kids from the Midwest. About halfway through the tour, Secret Service agents with bulges under their jackets finally noticed his musket and pounced on it. A brief panic ensued while the CIA man tried to explain that Vang Pao was an important freedom fighter from a kingdom west of Vietnam. Finally it was all straightened out and Vang Pao was whisked off to meet with one of Johnson's foreign policy aides.

Vang Pao gave the rifle to the aide, who said he would pass it on to the president. But Vang Pao could not see the great man himself, who was busy that day. It was not really a matter of being snubbed, since he had never been explicitly promised that he was going to meet President Johnson, and Vang Pao took it in stride. Johnson had announced he wasn't seeking re-election anyway, and Vang Pao's permanent connection with the U.S. government was with the CIA.

From the White House, the entourage went across the Potomac River to CIA headquarters at Langley, for a meeting with the director, Richard Helms. Helms asked Vang Pao what he wanted to do in the United States. The general replied that he would like to see where the cars were made. The entourage flew off to Detroit, where the Ford Motor Company showed him through the automotive works. Vang Pao liked that, so they went to a tractor plant next. There he decided he wanted to bring the king of Laos a souvenir tractor from America. The CIA escort, who had no intention of putting a tractor on his expense account, replied that sending a tractor to Laos couldn't be done. Vang Pao was very good about it, very polite and well behaved.

Around this time, in the Midwest, Wife Number One developed a female health problem of some kind. The escort arranged for a gynecologist, a patriotic doctor who after learning that Gen. Vang Pao was at the vanguard of the fight against communists insisted on treating her for free. The tribal custom was that when a wife went to see a male doctor, the husband went in with her, for propriety. Vang Pao tried to follow his wife into the examination room. The doctor held up his hand and said, "General, you command over there. Here, I command. Stay here. She comes in." Vang Pao halfheartedly saluted, and sat down glumly in a chair in the waiting room.

Soon the gynecologist emerged. He said that Wife Number One was in basically sound health but would have to abstain for a while until her problem healed completely. The general asked, what exactly was it that the doctor wanted her to do? His wife emerged and echoed, why does he want that? There was an awkward pause. The doctor and the CIA escort were unsure whether there was a language problem or whether, even after having all those children, the Laotian couple didn't understand that conjugal relations sometimes resulted in minor medical problems and other times in pregnancy. Embarrassed, the doctor restated his advice, the general and his lady listened with polite if blank expressions, and soon the tour resumed, with a change in escorts.

The U.S. Air Force figured, correctly, that it had as much claim on Vang Pao as the CIA did. So Vang Pao flew down to Hurlburt Field, at one end of Eglin Air Force Base near Tallahassee, Florida, where the Special Air Warfare Center was located. Col. Heinie Aderholt, the Air Commandos' patron saint of low-cost, low-tech warfare, was there to show Vang Pao around. Aderholt, Vang Pao, and Maj. Richard Secord, who had returned from Udorn not long before, went out deep-sea fishing in the Gulf of Mexico. Vang Pao had never been on the ocean before, and he got seasick.

The tribal entourage bounced around the East Coast from one stop to the next: Cape Kennedy, to see a rocket launch—the Americans were getting ready to go to the moon; Fort Bragg, North Carolina, the home of the Green Berets. The Meo men wore suits wherever they went because it fit their notion of dignity. It was a matter of face. They never complained because that would have been bad manners. They saw the sights and nothing registered. Everything was a blank. Nothing fit in with what they already knew from home, until they got to Williamsburg, Virginia, the rebuilt showpiece town from the colonial era.

Williamsburg was the first place in America that made sense to them. They saw blacksmiths' forges similar to the forges in the mountains of Laos. They saw horses larger than their own shaggy ponies, but otherwise the same. They saw crude iron plows at Williamsburg, just like the plows at home. The colonialists even cooked over open fires, just as hill people did. They found they could make the mental jump from Laos to the Williamsburg of the colonial era, and then from Williamsburg to the United States of the late 1960s. Vang Pao was ecstatic.

He returned to Long Tieng enthusiastic, wanting his people to become educated, to work hard, and to make that jump themselves into the twentieth century. The story of his epiphany in Williamsburg quickly spread among the Americans in Laos. It aroused Americans' paternalistic fondness for the Meo—for the hardy little freedom fighters aspiring to follow in America's ancestral footsteps.

Militarily, Vang Pao was outgrowing his people, which was the reason he wanted them to develop, to catch up. He was personally ambitious, and he equated power with weapons, artillery, and planes. The Americans were the source of his power now. He was eager to please them and this changed the way he ran his war.

As soon as he got back Vang Pao threw himself into a campaign already under way to recapture Phou Pha Thi. Since the loss of the mountain and its bomb guidance system earlier in the year, there had been several plans to take the site back, but they had come to nothing. In the midst of getting organized an American plane would get shot down someplace and immediately all of the other U.S. aircraft would swarm off to help, no matter what they had been doing before. It was always the Americans whose lives were considered terribly valuable, or whose bodies were important to recover.

By his own account Vang Pao organized Operation Pigfat for this reason. He said he wanted to bring back the bodies of the American airmen who had been left on the mountain slope. "Not the *raddah*," he explained, years later, in his broken English. (Not the Commando Club radar, he meant.) "*Raddah,* America have many. Our friend American in there. I have to take them back home. I need to attack and take everybody home, even they die or they get wounded. I am the leader in that part of Laos. I have to responsibility and bring everybody home. Everybody work with me and they have good *morale.* Even they die, or they get wounded, or we have victory, we have to bring everybody home. We not leave one in the jungle, say he already die, not care."

Vang Pao pressed his attack with U.S. Air Force planes and Laotian T-28s, some of them flown by his beloved Meo pilots. The relatively slow, propellor-driven T-28s had to fly all the way north from Vientiane and then go back to refuel and pick up more ordnance to give him the air support he wanted. His favorite Meo pilot, Ly Lue, a clanmate of Wife Number Two, could manage at most four round trips between sunrise and sunset. The mountain was heavily defended by well-dug-in North Vietnamese. By using his ground force as conventional infantry, and by urging the T-28s to dive-bomb protected enemy fortifications, he recaptured part of the mountain. "But the last minute, we cannot take Pha Thi," the general remembered sadly. "The *météorologie* [weather] too bad. Better we stop."

He pursued this unsuccessful operation with a curious disregard for his own men. Out of a force of 1,800, about 300 were killed, 500 wounded, and 400 were missing. This was a total casualty rate of over 50 percent. His soldiers had never taken losses remotely like that before. Another 10,000 bedraggled Meo refugees were airlifted out from the area.

As the beaten, demoralized remnants of Vang Pao's force withdrew in early 1969, the North Vietnamese drove south right on their heels. The North Vietnamese captured Nakhang again, and this time they killed the Lao military commander of the base, who had doubled as the civilian governor of Sam Neua Province. In one stroke they wiped out the civil as well as the military leadership of Sam Neua. It was a major loss. Nakhang was gone and Vang Pao never took it back.

Small, movable patches of Sam Neua Province still belonged to him. Tribespeople kept emerging from the forested hills after the North Vietnamese moved through. But the program in the far northeast was finished. Only one major base north of the Plain of Jars, Bouam Long, survived. Supplied by air and commanded by the father of Vang Pao's Wife Number Four, it was like an island in the communist sea.

Surrounding Bouam Long and pouring past it, the North Vietnamese sent more troops than ever before into the Plain of Jars, and farther south in the hills toward Long Tieng and Sam Thong, the twin headquarters of the Meo operation. Enemy detachments reached within six miles of Sam Thong and foot patrols got in even closer, threatening the base. All the civilian males in Sam Thong old enough to carry guns became instant soldiers. Fearing a night attack, most of the women, children, and elderly slept in the woods each night. Pop Buell evacuated the American women on his staff.

The enemy troops soon left the area, and the worst of the crisis passed. But the tribe was badly shaken, and another turning point had been reached.

◆

"The following is not my thinking," Pop Buell reported in March 1969. "It is only what the people have told me." On lined paper, in his schoolboy's script, with the usual errors in spelling and grammar, he wrote out a confidential memo for the USAID chief, the ambassador, and the CIA.

Around the beginning of the year, Buell disclosed, various Meo and Lao Theung tribal groups started holding secret meetings. The hill people had discovered that their men were being slaughtered for no apparent reason in the attempt to retake Phou Pha Thi. They wanted to know if there were fallback plans to go to Sayaboury or some other location. They wondered whether they should make a break for safety or go over to the enemy side.

Before long, they came to Buell, asking him to get a decision from Vang Pao. The naibans, clan chiefs, and other notables had told Vang Pao that they had packed their rice and cooking pots, and that they had chosen routes for scattering into the hills. They had organized themselves, but they wanted to hear Vang Pao's plans, too. Did he want them, the civilians, to help him fight, to take the Plain of Jars? His army could not do much without them; the army had broken down. Did he want them to become prisoners of the enemy? Did he want them to go to Sayaboury? Did he want them to go to Vientiane? All they were asking Vang Pao was to give them a plan. Not to tell them each day that he did not know, or that they should wait and he would know soon, or that he would go to Vientiane and find out. During these meetings, Buell wrote, Vang Pao would get very tired, put his hands to his head, and ask his listeners to let him rest awhile.

Buell went to Vientiane and then out of the country on vacation. During his absence more territory was lost, and there were more meetings and more demands on the leaders. When he came back to Sam Thong he got in a jeep, went around to talk to people, and didn't get to his office until the following day.

"If I am not out somewhere, my house my office is a question box," wrote Buell. "Many people, worried people. I never had so many questions fired at me in my life. Many I could not or dare not answer. Should we join the communists? Should we walk? Are your people going to help us? If I told the truth I would say no. They know for sure we are going to let them down.

"In the past 3 months have lost at least 1/3 of our area. Over 50% of my schools have been lost or closed. Have lost many people to the other side. It looks like we will loose more. They may let up when the rains come, but I have my doubts. Looks like they are out to win it all, at any cost.

"We are really hemmed in. Our fighting men have all been killed. People are tired, real tired. We are running out of land and cannot see gaining any more in the near future, where people can live and be safe. I am working my brain to decide what to do with people. No more mountains to go to. God have mercy on them.

"I personally am all right. How I stay togeather I will never know. Cig. and corn whiskey."

◆

It was during this bleak period, with most of his territory lost and his social compact with his people unraveling, that Vang Pao conceived of his audacious plan. He had lost face with the Americans, and with the royalist government, for the consecutive defeats at Pha Thi and Nakhang. He needed a major victory to consolidate his hold over his own people, who were talking of giving up the fight.

He decided that the only way to stop communist attacks was a preemptive attack of his own. If he could keep the other side off balance, he could buy time and maybe even weaken them at the negotiating table. The Americans and the North Vietnamese were already talking in Paris, and Laotian negotiations were sure to follow. He needed to be in a strong position. Already, in Washington, Bangkok, and Saigon, there was talk of withdrawing American soldiers from South Vietnam.

He told the Americans about his plan to capture the Plain of Jars. The new unit chief at Long Tieng, Tom Clines, said no. The Vientiane CIA station said no, at first. Ambassador Sullivan had just left and there was an interregnum before the new man, G. McMurtrie Godley, came in, and some of the people at the embassy didn't think it was such a good idea. For years the U.S. policy had been to leave the plain alone, except for selected targets. A guerilla force shouldn't be trying to take territory that the enemy held and would sacrifice virtually anything to keep. Why up the ante? The tribal force was already on the verge of falling apart.

Vang Pao had gotten a fixed idea into his head and nothing could shake it. He went to see Prime Minister Souvanna Phouma, who mulled over the plan and didn't absolutely forbid him. The general then went to see the king, who wasn't sure but allowed that it might be a good idea. Over time, by his stubbornness, and by the passion of his certainty, Vang Pao got the Thais and the Americans to come around to his thinking. The new U.S. president, Richard Nixon, was formulating a policy that eventually became known as Vietnamization. Nixon wanted Asian ground commanders to go on the offensive more, and he was willing to increase U.S. air support to help them. Vang Pao's plan fit in with Nixon's emerging strategy.

In later years Vang Pao remembered this campaign as a pure, sweet victory. It was his "favor," as he put it—his favorite memory, the high point of his career. "Because we had small force. We no have tanks," he explained. "We no have big force to compare with enemy force. But we have victory. Very important. Very important. Because the Plaine des Jarres strategic terrain. Very good favor for myself."

The first U.S. bombing campaign directed against the Plain of Jars, Operation Rain Dance, began on March 17, 1969. In the first four days U.S. and Laotian planes flew three hundred sorties against enemy targets. On March 23, after further bombing softened up the enemy, Vang Pao moved the main body of his troops out. A month later, after three hundred more sorties, Vang Pao approached Xieng Khouangville, in a valley off the southeast side of the Plain of Jars proper. The bombs had turned the buildings into rubble and empty shells. The walls of some of the larger houses were still standing, ghostly and roofless. The civilians who survived the bombing had fled and were living in caves and forests nearby. A few North Vietnamese soldiers, all that were left, depressed the muzzles of their antiaircraft guns and opened fire on Vang Pao, who was walking up and down in front of his troops to demonstrate his bravery. A CIA officer grabbed the general, threw him on the ground, and sat on him for most of the afternoon as forward air controllers in their little propellor planes called in the jet strikes that took the guns out.

A few days more and Vang Pao and his men walked unopposed into the rubble. There had already been numerous secondary explosions of ammo and fuel dumps, and everyone was surprised to see how much matériel was left: antiaircraft guns, jeeps, trucks, ton after ton of ammunition. A ruined bank was heaped with Pathet Lao and North Vietnamese money, and the Chinese cultural mission was full of mainland Chinese propaganda leaflets. What looked like a town had been a warehouse in disguise.

When the enemy counterattacked, Vang Pao pulled out of Xieng Khouangville and into the hills. During April he mounted numerous skirmishes for maneuver and position in and around the plain, but did not try to take the plain itself. Then a North Vietnamese defected with a satchel full of battle plans for an assault on Bouam Long, the remaining base north of the Plain of Jars. The enemy maps were beautifully drawn and magnificently detailed down to the individual foxholes.

For a couple of weeks in early May, Vang Pao concentrated on trying to prevent Bouam Long's capture. Knowing the enemy attack routes and supply caches from the maps, he targeted his air strikes precisely. Meo T-28 pilots went into steep dives, releasing their 250-pound bombs onto the heads of the attackers, pulling up and away just ahead of the exploding fragments. Meo interpreters, "backseaters," also rode in the little observation planes flown by the Ravens. Ground patrols in contact with the enemy radioed the coordinates to the backseaters, then ran as fast as they could to get away before the jets swooped in for the kill. The tribal ground forces had grown used to working with the planes, and if they could help it they didn't do much offensive fighting of their own.

During May and June, Vang Pao did not try to take the Plain of Jars. Instead, the North Vietnamese went on the offensive even as the rains began. They attacked Muong Soui, an old neutralist base west of the plain. The neutralists were a vestigial force by that point in the war, abandoned by Kong Le, their old leader, who had gone into exile, and outnumbered by the royalists and the tribal guerilla forces. The base had a long, flat airstrip that Laotian T-28s had started using to save flying back and forth to Vientiane for bombs and fuel. However, the T-28s couldn't hold the airstrip by themselves. The neutralist ground troops ran away as soon as enemy tanks appeared. A Thai artillery unit, part of a continuing Thai military buildup in Laos, ran because the Lao infantry wasn't around to protect them.

The loss of Muong Soui shook the normally torpid Vientiane government to the core. Suddenly, there was nothing to keep the communists from pushing farther west and recapturing the road between Vientiane and the old royalist capital, Luang Prabang. America wasn't going to help much; President Nixon had just announced the first phased U.S. troop withdrawals from South Vietnam. As much as they mistrusted Vang Pao, the lowland generals knew that he was their best hope. They were ready to deal, and after intense negotiations Vang Pao wrenched eight stubby-winged T-28s and their Meo pilots away from General Ouane, the corrupt commander in chief. The planes had landed at Long Tieng occasionally, but from now on they would be based there, under Vang Pao's personal command.

He was delighted. It was a Williamsburg air force, small and primitive by American standards but wildly advanced by his own. Even if the runway was too short and the altitude too high, Long Tieng was where they belonged. Within view of his two-story stone house, home to his bickering wives, they took off fully loaded, the bombs attached to the underside of their wings, barely clearing the ridgeline to the south. They banked, dropped their loads a few valleys away, came back to Long Tieng, loaded up with more bombs, then took off again. The pilots each flew as many as a dozen quick sorties a day.

In July, Vang Pao's favorite pilot, Ly Lue—a graduate of Bill Lair's original class for Meo flyers, a man whom Secord had given checkout rides, a veteran of a few thousand short-hop combat missions—was killed by enemy gunners near Muong Soui. The American embassy arranged for a three-day funeral and period of mourning. General Ouane and other Lao bigwigs came up to Long Tieng to feign their respects and to look at the operation they feared only slightly less than the communist enemy. Vang Pao was overwhelmed by grief. He wept as the coffin was lowered into the ground in Meo style. The pilot had been like a right arm to him, an extension of his own power. He got into one of his periodic black moods when he thought the world was falling apart.

But within a day or two Vang Pao was making battle plans again. It occurred to him that the enemy was overextended. The Vietnamese had stayed in Muong Soui even though the rains had begun. He had cut their rear supply lines, with air force help, along Route 7. He decided to finish what he had started.

He began talking to a circle of intimates about an operation called About Face. It would begin, he said, on August 15, when the weather cleared. Nobody believed him. If there was ever a people on the verge of collapse, it was the Meo. Widows and orphans were everywhere. Amputees hobbled around on sticks, and the soldiers were demoralized.

Even the weather was gloomy. In the heavy rains of mid-1969 few planes flew. There were no massed bombing flights because the targets were invisible under the clouds. A few T-28s and spotter planes went out from Long Tieng and looked around, and then had to fly lower and lower as the clouds descended and rain fell. They flew under the clouds, through canyons in the blinding rain, veering to avoid the black looming shapes of mountains.

When August 15 dawned bright and clear, the first sunny day in months, it was as though Vang Pao himself had parted the clouds like a shaman controlling the spirits. Operation About Face began. The tribesmen from Bouam Long harassed and attacked behind the enemy's lines. Wave after wave of jets swooshed overhead in formation, and the bombing went on, some of the heaviest north Laos had ever seen.

The first targets were mountains on the edge of the Plain of Jars that the other side held as observation posts and artillery bases. Tribal forces from Long Tieng assaulted two of them on the south and west sides of the plain, took heavy casualties, and then finally swarmed over the summits. Another force of lowland Lao from Savannakhet, led by a paramilitary officer named Will Green, took another mountain overlooking Route 7 in heavier fighting. Green, who had been a major in the Special Forces before joining the CIA, had undertaken the mission at Tom Clines's request. Though leading indigenous forces in combat continued to be against official policy, Green was setting a precedent that other American paramilitary officers, most of them also ex–Special Forces, would follow.

On September 12, Vang Pao re-occupied Xieng Khouangville. The enemy tried to react but couldn't—demoralized, confused, afraid, out of fuel. The tribal forces swept across the plain. On September 28 they re-took Muong Soui. It was all theirs from one end to the other, the undulating grasslands, the landing fields, the shattered towns, the clusters of giant, lichen-covered stone urns—the horizontal emptiness.

The capture of the Plain of Jars was, an American at the embassy declared, the first major victory in the history of the royal government. Congratulations rained on Vang Pao from everybody who mattered. He took the praise gratefully. It was his favor.

Those who knew him best, both Laotian and American, had long sensed the immense scope of his ambitions. Vang Pao didn't *just* want to be a great general, the insiders said. You could see it in the way he strutted about. Or the way he handed out fistfuls of kip to people who humbly petitioned him. Fistfuls of money, scattering in the air, skimmed off from the American-supplied payroll.

He always wanted to be the big man of Laos. Nothing less. It was an astonishing ambition for a man so feared and despised by the lowland elites who ruled the political establishment, but he was starting to succeed. Congressmen and generals had told him how great he was, and he had no reason to doubt their word. American warplanes bombed where he told them to bomb. Did any other Laotian general get that kind of support? No. And now he had achieved the greatest military victory imaginable for a local man with little education. He had captured the Plain of Jars.

Vang Pao and Tom Clines entered a cave that the North Vietnamese had enlarged and equipped with ventilation holes. In awe, they walked past operating rooms with East German medical equipment. One corridor opened up into the next, and the next. They left without reaching the end of the cave and called in air strikes with guided bombs. The entrance collapsed in a hail of rubble. The secondary explosions went on for days inside, black smoke rising from the vent stacks.

They found supplies everywhere. Trucks, jeeps, a dozen or more tanks, 150,000 gallons of gas, three million rounds of ammunition. Not having drivers themselves, they copied a North Vietnamese practice and chained communist drivers to the tank controls. They marveled that the North Vietnamese hadn't spiked their guns—hadn't blown them up.

With the capture of the Plain of Jars, the Western international press corps flew up to Sam Thong for a staged media event. Vang Pao appeared before the reporters with North Vietnamese prisoners in handcuffs and under guard. One of the prisoners was a private named Nguyun Van Co, who said he had been shot through the shoulder a few days before and left behind by his retreating unit. Vang Pao explained that the private hadn't cooperated with his interrogators after being captured. True, the private, declared; in fact he had gotten no food for four days, he had been beaten and given shocks through electrodes attached to his fingers. Vang Pao matter-of-factly concurred. The private, he said, hadn't cooperated and because of that torture was necessary.

Vang Pao was too innocent of Western ways to understand that hypocrisy would have made for better public relations. In was one thing to torture the enemy, another to let the American people read about it in their morning papers. Luckily for him, the reporters didn't know much about Laos, and didn't ask him about his torture center at Pha Khao, or about the spies he used among his own people at Long Tieng, or about the ugly, heavy-handed methods his organization was using to recruit teenage boys, now that his army was running short of soldiers.

Vang Pao had another public relations problem with the civilians who had been living on the plain before the bombing began. These people had made their accommodations with the Pathet Lao and North Vietnamese years before, and had been paying taxes to the communists before the planes came along and bombed their houses to rubble. For several months they had been living in caves and in deep ditches propped up with lumber, afraid to go out except at night. Being unarmed, they were too innocent to kill, but they were too guilty by association to be allowed to stay.

On short notice, and at gunpoint, these civilians were made to walk with whatever they could carry to one of the dusty airfields where the American cargo planes were landing and taking off from dawn to dark. There, the involuntary evacuees walked up the ramps of the cargo planes and sat dazedly on the floor for the flight south, first to Sam Thong and then to the Vientiane valley.

Behind them, on the plain, Meo tribesmen appeared, looting the abandoned Lao houses. They confiscated water buffalo and other livestock and began herding them back toward Long Tieng, doing a brisk business in the meat trade.

The air force, meanwhile, continued bombing.

When Fred Branfman finished his two-year IVS tour in mid-1969, he went to France. Behind him, in Laos, the agricultural textbook he had written gathered dust on USAID shelves. He didn't care. He was a free man, and now that he had reached his twenty-seventh birthday he was free of the military draft. He had moved on to the next stage, an assignment from himself to understand the Laos war.

An article in *Le Monde* had caught his attention. A journalist named Jacques Decornoy had visited the Pathet Lao "liberated" zones in Sam Neua and reported firsthand on the U.S. bombing. Decornoy had even interviewed the dashing, pencil-moustached Prince Souphanouvong in the prince's home in a cave. It was the first eyewitness report by a Westerner of the people on the receiving end of the bombing, and though largely ignored by the American media, it shocked and inflamed Branfman, who was instinctively convinced that the bombing was immoral. There was a Pathet Lao delegation in Paris, and Branfman traveled to see them in the summer of 1969, to try to convince them to let him travel in their liberated zones. He wanted to see for himself whether the bombing story was true, and to do something about it if it was.

To his great disappointment the Pathet Lao delegation in Paris would not let him in the door. Probably he looked too weird, with his black peasant clothing, *baci* strings on his wrists, and bush of wiry hair. Perhaps they had also heard the rumors from their Soviet-bloc friends in Vientiane that Branfman was a CIA operative in antiwar disguise, for he had often been seen entering the U.S. embassy in Vientiane to speak to the younger political officers there. He had also befriended some Soviets in Vientiane, and some Americans were convinced he was KGB, but that was the price of talking to everybody—nobody knew how to categorize him.

He got passed on from one Laotian to the next in Paris, until he met Kong Le, the tiny neutralist soldier who had started the coup that began all the trouble back in 1960. Kong Le was living in exile without much to do, except to think about his glory days. He was glad to meet a Lao-speaking *farang*. Branfman asked Kong Le whether it was true that he could make himself invulnerable to bullets. Kong Le replied that he had led his men in many battles and never been hit by a bullet, so Branfman could draw his own conclusions. And then Kong Le launched into other stories of his magical powers while Branfman listened attentively. Kong Le's superstitions were typical of the Lao villagers whom Branfman had gotten to know outside Vientiane.

The two men got along well, and they went together to a bar on July 20, 1969, the day American astronauts landed on the moon for the first time. They watched the historic event on TV, the descent to the lunar surface and the feet climbing down the ladder to touch on lunar soil.

Kong Le, who was sitting on a barstool next to Branfman, said, "Now they'll believe me."

"Who will?" asked Branfman.

Kong Le said, "When I was the leader of Laos, I visited the NASA Space Center in your country. I told them that there was life on other planets. They were very polite to me, but they didn't believe me. I could tell they didn't believe me. But now they will."

Fred Branfman nodded to show agreement. But he decided then and there to leave Paris to pursue his investigation into the war.

He went back to Vientiane and found that the Saigon press corps had arrived there, hot on the trail of the so-called secret war and eager to confirm the burgeoning reports and rumors of heavy American bombing. It was the largest American media presence since the Geneva accords of 1962, and some of the younger journalists belonged to the new breed, angry at the U.S. government and determined to expose its misdeeds.

In response to their queries about the bombing, the press attaché at the U.S. embassy in Vientiane replied, "At the request of the Royal Laotian Government, the United States is conducting unarmed reconnaissance flights accompanied by armed escorts who have the right to return fire if fired upon."

This bland announcement had been in use since 1964. Not one word had changed over the years. And even though it was an open secret that the United States was bombing in northern Laos, and the bombing had been mentioned in news stories, the lack of official confirmation by the embassy created a doubt that was hard to resolve. Even for Branfman, the U.S. government's denial that it was bombing created confusion. It gave him the oddest feeling, to be back in the capital of Laos and not know what was going on out in the countryside. It was the same old problem of information deprivation.

The Laotians themselves were not much help, since he couldn't get permission to travel to the war zones, and the people from the war zones were kept upcountry in refugee camps. Then in late September 1969, a young journalist friend of his, Tim Allman, who was stringing for *The New York Times,* came to him and said that some refugees who had been living in the Pathet Lao zones had been brought to Vientiane. Allman wanted to know if Branfman would come along and help interpret.

They got on Branfman's black Honda motorcycle and putt-putted as though on any other normal day through the streets of Vientiane, past the American embassy and then past the Pathet Lao compound nearby, then the police station on their right, up Lan Xang Avenue ("The Avenue of the Million Elephants"), Vientiane's Champs-Elysées. They negotiated the traffic circle around Vientiane's ersatz Arc de Triomphe, known as "The Vertical Runway," because it was made with the concrete stolen from a project to lengthen the airport; and they went off on a radial avenue toward That Luang, a national religious monument with an oddly shaped blue spire surrounded by white crenellated walls.

Before the monument spread a huge parade ground where public ceremonies were held. Near the center of this open space stood a *sala,* a large open-sided building with a multitiered roof like a temple. They saw several hundred Laotian peasants sitting and standing inside, holding little bundles. Branfman parked the motorcycle and he and Allman walked up the steps.

Branfman went up to the first man he saw and said, in Lao, "Hello, how are you? And where are you from, by the way?" The man said he came from the Plain of Jars. "How long have you been here?" Branfman asked. "You just got here this morning? Oh." And then he asked whether the man had ever seen any bombing. The man said he had seen bombing every day and drew an L in the dust to show how he and others had entered a cave, hiding there from the planes. Branfman thanked him and passed on to the next man. "Hello. How are you? Where are you from, please?"

It wasn't the words that got through his defenses. It was the facial expressions of the people there, the tones of voice. The horror crept up on him slowly. A man mentioned almost casually that his son had been killed in the bombing. His quiet expression of pain was more piercing than if he'd screamed.

The people in the *sala* said that their families had lived on the Plain of Jars a very long time. Generations. Their time frames were vague, and so was their accounting of the oxen and water buffalo that they owned. They were imprecise, but that was typical of their culture and it was obvious that they were telling the truth. Now they were in poverty and had nothing except what was in their burlap bags. They'd been wrenched out of their environments and they were subdued and terrified.

Branfman asked, "When did you start seeing planes?" The answer came, "In 1964, but we didn't know what they were. We didn't know who was dropping bombs on us or why." When Branfman asked what the bombs were like, the refugees explained that there were many kinds. Some bombs made fire on the ground, others made big holes, and there were *bombis* like this—a man produced a dud antipersonnel bomblet the shape of a pineapple, with hundreds of little pellet holes in the side. "Oh," said Branfman, still moving around the *sala,* interpreting for Allman, who was taking notes.

A barefoot young man dressed in white shorts and a white undershirt began to walk beside them, listening and sometimes adding comments in Lao. He had narrower eyes and lighter skin than most—an ethnic Chinese. He said his name was Ngeun and he was a trader who had traveled around the Plain of Jars. Everything Ngeun said tallied with what the other refugees said, but the others looked to him for corroboration on specific dates and factual details. Ngeun spoke knowledgeably of T-28s, F-4s, A-1Es, and other models. He said the bombing had begun in May 1964 and had built up gradually until August 1969, when the bombs had started falling like rain.

"Were there North Vietnamese around?" Branfman asked. Ngeun said no. "How did you feel about the North Vietnamese?" asked Branfman. Ngeun answered that they were the reason the bombing was happening, and for that reason, he didn't like them. Ngeun added, "But when these villages were bombed there were no North Vietnamese or Pathet Lao around. The soldiers know how to hide in the forest. The villagers who lived in the open clearings got killed."

Branfman kept himself under tight control. So did Allman, who was nodding, scribbling notes, taking it all in, and staying detached.

Branfman gave Allman a ride back into Vientiane, dropped him off, then drove to the Lao-style house he rented, where he let Western longhaired travelers stay for free. The house was full of young backpackers touring the temples, buying dope in the marketplace, and catching the scene at the White Rose and Lulu's. It wasn't until that evening, when he sat and thought about it, that the enormity of his government's deception hit him in the gut. The bombing was still going on. Laotians alive that day would be dead by tomorrow. As his anger rose at the thought of villagers being blown up by bombs, he felt his old identity, the old confused Fred Branfman, blowing up too.

Beginning that evening, and over the succeeding days—when he brought an ABC television crew to That Luang, and then a procession of

other journalists, interpreting for them, forcing them to bear witness—
Fred Branfman went through a crisis of transformation. His sense of who
he was, of what he knew about the world, his understanding of reality and
his sense of what it meant to be an American, changed. He didn't care what
happened to him anymore. He identified with the Laotians in the war zones
as though he was on the ground looking up while the bombs were raining
down.

All he wanted to do was stop the bombing. That was all. If that was how
the world worked, if America had lied about the bombing for five-and-a-
half years, dropping bombs on Laotian villagers, not just bombs but napalm and cluster bomb units, slicing and dicing and frying and burying
people alive in caves, he didn't want to belong to America anymore. No
more giving the embassy the benefit of the doubt, no more pretending that
the Americans were the good guys. He had to stop the bombing.

But then he realized he couldn't stop the bombing until he understood
where the bombs had come from. Who dropped the bombs? he wondered.
The U.S. Air Force? An F-4, that must be a jet, he thought. Where would
that come from? Who decides how many bombs to drop? Who decides
where to drop them? Who ordered this? Does Congress know? Does
Nixon know?

He was completely bewildered. It made him feel stupid and inadequate,
being in Laos and not even knowing the basics of the war. He felt as help-
less and as innocent as a newborn child.

# No Commitment

Halfway around the world from Vientiane, in a high-ceilinged room in Washington, D.C., the classified, closed-door session of the Senate subcommittee came to order. Four veteran politicians—Senators Stuart Symington, J. William Fulbright, George Aiken, and Mike Mansfield—faced a crowd of invited witnesses, of whom the chief was William Sullivan, formerly the ambassador to Laos and now deputy assistant secretary of state for East Asian affairs.

This meeting of the Foreign Relations Subcommittee on U.S. Security Agreements and Commitments Abroad came at an extraordinary time. Just five days before, on October 15, 1969, a quarter-million Americans had peacefully converged on Washington in a "moratorium" protest against the Vietnam War. Coordinated demonstrations had been held in other cities simultaneously, and more were planned for the future. President Richard Nixon insisted that demonstrations would not affect him. But he had already announced his second troop withdrawal from South Vietnam, and he was adjusting his policies to minimize the public discontent.

Adding to the drama of the Senate meeting was the polite loathing the two principals felt for each other. A few years earlier the subcommittee chairman, Senator Symington, had come to Asia expecting to visit Laos on his tour. Under the pretext that Symington was also a member of the Senate Armed Services Committee, and that his very footfall in Laos would signal new violations of the Geneva accords, Ambassador Sullivan hadn't let him in. They met at Udorn air base in Thailand instead, and Sullivan told him next to nothing. The senator had been furious at the high-handed treatment.

On Symington's subsequent visits to the region, Sullivan tried to make amends. He gave the senator full access, including briefings from Lair and Shackley and a visit with Vint Lawrence and Vang Pao in Long Tieng. After being treated well, Symington became friendly with these men who were running the Laos war—until he discovered that it would be easier to get re-elected if he were believed to be against the Vietnam War. Thereafter the senator pretended that he had known nothing about the Laos war and was horrified when he found out about it.

For his part, Sullivan was just as slippery as Symington. In a previous hearing before Symington's subcommittee, in 1968, Sullivan gave the senators the distinct impression that the Lao air force, rather than the U.S. Air Force, was doing all the bombing. He didn't actually lie, but he didn't feel obliged to tell them the whole truth. After all, he worked for the State Department, which was part of the executive branch, not for Congress.

For this hearing, on October 20, 1969 and succeeding days, the senators were better prepared. Their staffers had been to Laos to gather information. The newspapers were full of Laos stories, about refugees and heavy bombing on the Plain of Jars, about corrupt generals and the CIA. All of a sudden this obscure country was beginning to sound alarmingly like South Vietnam, with the less desirable features of Central America banana republics thrown in for good measure.

"Today the subcommittee begins hearings on Laos," announced Symington. "If there is any area where the American people need and deserve more information, it is with regard to U.S. commitments and involvements in this small, distant kingdom.

"After several trips to Laos we have become convinced that the secrecy surrounding our relations with that country has gone on far too long. Speculative news stories, Communist propaganda, irresponsible political charges, are poor substitutes for reliable information on a subject of such importance. If whatever it is that we have done there is right, the American people deserve to know it. If whatever has been done is wrong, secrecy can only compound that wrong rather than right it."

The witness with the bushy gray hair, black eyebrows, and the facsimile of candor in his clear blue Irish eyes was sworn in. In his opening statement Sullivan declared that the U.S. government had no defense commitment, "written, stated, or understood," to the Royal Lao Government. That got the senators' attention.

Sullivan then embarked on a long-winded description of the Laos war focusing on diplomatic history and the 1962 Geneva accords. He droned on at length, laying out an intricate justification for the war. Politicians, even crafty veterans, can keep their minds sharp for only so long before they lose concentration. Beneath the surface of his statement Sullivan was telling them that America was fighting a war to protect Laos's peace. Violating the Geneva accords in order to restore them.

Prompted by the senators' questions, there was little Sullivan didn't cover, or pseudo-cover, on the subject: levels of military assistance; U.S. air operations; the Chinese threat; the North Vietnamese threat; the Pathet Lao and Soviet threats; war on the cheap. "It involves no stationing of U.S. combat forces, no commitments and, in comparison with Vietnam, a fairly modest and inconspicuous deployment of personnel and resources," Sullivan said. American servicemen killed in the kingdom—about two hundred killed and two hundred missing in action so far, he said, with three quarters of those in the south along the Ho Chi Minh Trail. Vang Pao and opium. The Lao king. The relationship between Prime Minister Souvanna Phouma and his half brother, Prince Souphanouvong, the front man for the Pathet Lao.

Whatever the senators asked, Sullivan had a glib answer. He fenced with them, sidestepping and deflecting their queries, redirecting thrusts, retreating behind the protective cover of semantics. Seldom has a man talked so much while revealing so little, even on Capitol Hill. But every once in a while Sullivan circled back to his original declarative point. "I do not believe we have any legal obligation nor do we have any commitment that requires us as a nation to insist that the independence of Laos must be preserved," he emphasized. ". . . We have no commitment."

Initially this assertion pleased the senators. It was just what they wanted to hear in that era of mass antiwar demonstrations and attempts to extricate the country from the bog of Vietnam. Furthermore, it was partly true. In the early years in Laos, at least, the operation was supposed to be reversible. Easy-in, easy-out, do nothing to make the Laotians dependent. That's what all the Americans agreed, and nobody had made any commitments to Vang Pao or to Prime Minister Souvanna Phouma. At least not in writing.

But the senators were skeptical. Surely there was more to Laos than that, they pointed out. Surely on other levels there were plenty of commitments. The war in Laos had grown far larger than the Laotians themselves could sustain. Vang Pao was largely dependent on the Americans, the lowland generals wholly. The U.S. total contribution to the war was over a billion dollars, not including the bombing; and its annual contribution—the exact figure was secret—was greater than Laos's gross national product. The war had created 600,000 refugees out of a population of three million. The war had changed Laos overwhelmingly. Wasn't a commitment at least implied? the senators asked.

Sullivan defended his logic with practiced ease. The United States was in Laos to uphold the Geneva accords, he declared. It was there under the president's power to conduct foreign policy. Again, Sullivan limited his answers to what he was asked. He certainly did not reveal what he felt most deeply, which would have astounded the senators and made headlines in the newspapers had it been leaked to the press.

Senator Fulbright, chairman of the larger Committee on Foreign Relations and a renowned dissenter of the Vietnam War, was not reassured by Sullivan's answers, particularly the argument for keeping the war covert.

"Is it in our interest to continue this activity in this *secret*—I guess, I am not quite sure of the right word to call it, it is not really secret, it is well known in the press—unacknowledged, *officially unacknowledged* activity?" asked Senator Fulbright. "Is this really in our interest to continue it? It certainly is not disassociated from the Vietnam war."

Sullivan blandly replied, "I think the President has made it quite clear that he would very much wish to be able to disengage U.S. forces from Vietnam under appropriate conditions."

"That being so," said Fulbright, "it seems to me it would be wise to begin to liquidate the activity in Laos. Wouldn't you think so?"

Sullivan threw the dust of polite obfuscation in the senator's face. "I think that the two are interrelated, as you said earlier, sir," Sullivan said. "And I think the action with respect to one would have an influence with respect to the other."

Fulbright blinked and bore in. "If that is true," said the senator, "it would be in our interest to discuss this matter publicly. You talked about its effect on the Russians. [Sullivan had claimed that one of the reasons for keeping the war secret was to avoid antagonizing the Soviets, who were cosignatories to the Geneva accords.] What in the world would the Russians *do* if you acknowledged tomorrow morning exactly what you are doing?"

Sullivan replied, "I think our concern would be primarily with the attitude of the Soviets toward continuing a respect for the Prime Minister of Laos as a neutralist." More dust in the face.

Fulbright paused. "He's not really a neutralist, is he?" the senator said of Souvanna Phouma.

"He is a nationalist," Sullivan said evenly, "and nationalists would not wish to be aligned with either system."

Fulbright had had enough. "You know," he said to Sullivan, "there is something about this pretense that is a little offensive to me. You undoubtedly have heard about the credibility gap which has afflicted us for a long time, and I do not like to be a party to it. He is not a neutralist. He is an ally except we do not have a treaty with him. We are giving him *money*. He is not neutral as between the North Vietnamese and ourselves, is he?"

Sullivan was saved from having to evade this sensible question by Fulbright's colleague Senator Symington, who interrupted. "If the senator would yield," said Symington in frustration. "Why is it that we do not allow bombing in North Vietnam, preferring to work it out with ground troops in South Vietnam, but do not have ground troops in Laos, preferring to work it out with bombing? We are losing money and lives in an unpopular war, and our losses are far greater because we refrain from bombing in North Vietnam. Why is it proper to bomb the enemy in one place where your people are fighting, but not in another?"

Senator Fulbright ignored the outburst. A new thought had occurred to him on Laos's neutrality, a way to pin Sullivan down. "Let me review this just a little more," he said. "Doesn't Souvanna Phouma accept aid from Russia and China?"

"Yes, sir," Sullivan replied. "It is mostly technical assistance and primarily, I think, in terms of working with his meteorological services. And they do provide scholarships and assistance for students."

"Yet the Russians," said Fulbright, "at the same time, are supporting the North Vietnamese and say they are not there."

"Yes, sir."

"Doesn't this ever strike you as sort of an absurdity?" asked Fulbright. "They are pretending *they* are not there and we are pretending *we* are not there. What does it all lead to? We give the impression not only to foreign people but to many of our own people that we are mad. Why isn't it better to go and say what we are doing and give a reason for it and say the only possible reason, that we have just gone in and are doing what we think is assisting the war in Vietnam. That makes some sense. I do not quite see the persuasiveness of your reasons."

The man from Wonderland threw up another smoke screen. "Well, my answers might not be persuasive," Sullivan replied. "But I go back and state our concern has been, and it still is, to try to establish those conditions which would permit the 1962 neutrality agreement to apply, and in doing that I think it was incumbent upon us to maintain that initial understanding we have had with the Soviets—"

"In the meantime you are deceiving the American people and the Congress," Fulbright said sharply. "They do not know what to think, and I think you have created a situation which could become very difficult. I am very, very reluctant to accept the decision that this activity has to be secret, that we cannot talk about it out in the open in the same way we do other matters that involve our troops."

Sullivan was silent but composed.

The mention of "troops" stirred a recollection in the senator's mind. What was it? With a sigh, Senator Fulbright said wearily, "You have already gone over, I guess, how many troops we have there and how many we have operating in Laos?"

"Yes," said Sullivan at the witness table.

Senator Symington announced that the subcommittee counsel had a great many questions to ask that afternoon.

"I will desist," Senator Fulbright said, waiving it away. "I have a man from Cambodia who wants to see me, I do not know what about. Have we got any agreements with Cambodia?"

None of the senators had an answer to that question, and so they recessed for lunch.

The hearings resumed after that, but Sullivan had already won his battle.

There had been farewell parties for Pop Buell before he took home leave in the summer of 1969, before the capture of the Plain of Jars. He wasn't entirely sure he was coming back. Fifty-five years old, he'd had heart trouble, dysentery, and malaria more times than he could remember. He had washed down quinine and nitroglycerine pills with whiskey. He had played billygoat with Laotian women. He had made friends with Laotian men. He had been to many funerals. It had been a full life, with unexpected sorrows and joys. Maybe it was time to quit while he was ahead.

He returned to his family's farm, in Steuben County, Indiana, near the Ohio line. In that not-quite-flat countryside, fields alternated with deciduous woods; a few miles away lay Appalachian-style hollers. It was an area of small rural holdings, and farmhouses within sight of one another. His 220-acre farm had been his father's before him and now belonged to his son, Howard. The other Buells in the neighborhood welcomed him back, but he was just plain Edgar to them. They had never felt he was a hero, and they never understood his going off to Asia and leaving his son behind. How did your corn do last year? How many bushels?

To Buell, the farm was permanence in a changing world. Most days he drove down the driveway, turned right onto the dirt road, then left at the stop sign and onto the paved road. A mile north he crossed the old Wabash railroad track. Farther up the road in Edon, Ohio, the bank and the post office were on the corner where they belonged and the pool hall was still next to the bank. Amish wagons often stood by the hardware store, the horses waiting patiently. South of the town center and the railroad tracks, on the grassy rise within sight of the grain elevators, lay the cemetery. He stood before the headstone with his wife's name on it, Mattie Lorene Buell. There was room on the headstone for his name, too, when he came back home for good.

He thought about his wife, and how his grief at her death had driven him to the other side of the world.

Gratefully, and then restlessly, he played with his grandchildren. Showed them his favorite fishing holes. He watched the American astronauts land on the moon. He went off to visit his daughter and her husband and children in Ohio and then came back. Summer turned into fall. He didn't know what to do. He sat in the farmhouse and looked across the dirt road at a field he had plowed for decades. At the far end of the field, hardwood trees stood, like a tall hedge. Like a fence. The expanse of sky above, offering its possibilities. He looked up at the sky and decided to go back to Laos.

He wanted to be Pop Buell again. To live the bigger life. To call for planes the way city dwellers call for taxis. To play poker with the ambassador, and to have chief's wives in bamboo huts wash his feet. To have the CIA pick his brains for advice.

He flew to Bangkok and this time he barely noticed the view from the plane. He went to Vientiane and then on up to Sam Thong. In place of his old warehouse on the edge of the runway, a big Quonset hut stood, with REFUGEE GOODIES painted on the side in block letters. Nearby, a one-bedroom house with a big living room and fireplace had been built for him, over his initial objections, because he didn't want to live better than the tribal people. Now it felt like his real home, and he was grateful. The kitchen was empty of food but well stocked with beer and booze. His American staff and some of the ranking Meo came in tired and dusty at the end of the day, to talk and drink in front of the fire and ward off the chill of the mountain air.

At the end of October 1969, he wrote to his family, "The unblevable has been done, we do have all the Plain D Jarres area. I flew all over the Plains yesterday. There is nothing left in the whole area, blown up or burnt. Nothing left but shell holes. Maybe can make fish ponds out of them.

"The enemy is still strong. I do think they were hurt, but they can re-supply and strike back in force and if they do I am sure V.P. cannot hold them. V.P. was real glad to see me. He is a worried and tired man but still goes day and night."

By mid-November, Buell's workload was as busy as ever. The long, flat airstrips on the Plain of Jars were crowded all day long with supplies and refugees being shuttled about, airplanes landing in clouds of dust and un-loading and loading and taking off again. He met Laotians he had known from Lat Houang nine years before. Most were elderly. Their school-age grandchildren had barely heard of the royalist government but they knew all about Uncle Ho Chi Minh. Missing were the young adults, an entire generation gone over to the Pathet Lao side.

He noted in his letters that the U.S. had landed on the moon for a second time and wondered whether it seemed exciting or like old hat to the people back home. Maybe walking on the moon could be as boring and ordinary as anything else once you had been there awhile or tried it before. He was right in the middle of a war and he didn't hear much news himself. All the radios were tuned to operational channels, on standby. The dry season had begun, which meant that the North Vietnamese would soon launch their counteroffensive.

To keep the enemy off balance the U.S. Air Force was bombing heavily from the eastern Plain of Jars to the North Vietnamese border. The new U.S. ambassador, Mac Godley, had removed some of the earlier restrictions on bombing, and the jets struck right next to the North Vietnamese border where supplies for the enemy's 312th and 316th Divisions had been stacked with impunity. Every so often the planes got lucky and their bombs set off secondary explosions of fuel or ammunition—instantaneous fireballs blossoming to a thousand feet in diameter, buildings disappearing down to the foundations.

By then the American air machinery was operating at peak capacity. A glint of reflected sunlight from North Vietnamese equipment hidden in the trees was all it took for seasoned forward air controllers to spot the opportunity, get on the radio, and call for air strikes; and for practiced jet pilots to swoop in for the kill.

The air force being what it was, this genuine expertise was accompanied by sloppy excess. There was said to be a farmer's shanty—just four poles and a thatched roof with no walls—out in the middle of the Plain of Jars with a double line of craters leading up to and over it in the shape of a cross. The shanty was the target of two strings of bombs, both of which had missed. Eventually, however, not a single structure was left standing on the plain anywhere. At least three hundred Meo friendly to Vang Pao were killed by American planes, along with an unknown and hotly debated number of civilians. It was some of the heaviest bombing anywhere since World War II.

◆

In Vientiane one morning in December 1969, Fred Branfman picked up a copy of the newspaper and read that a billionaire from Texas had loaded a chartreuse-colored jet with canned turkey dinners and was flying to Laos. The billionaire, whose name was H. Ross Perot, was stopping off at the North Vietnamese embassy in Vientiane to get a visa and landing rights, and planning to fly on to Hanoi to deliver mail, gifts, and the turkey dinners to American prisoners of war in time for Christmas.

Dumbfounded, Branfman accompanied a bunch of journalists to the press conference the night the plane arrived.

Perot turned out to be a short, folksy, dynamic fellow who called the newsmen by their first names as soon as they'd been introduced, like a Ro-

tary Club president. The regular reporters lobbed easy questions to him—
what kind of Christmas presents was he bringing to the POWs, what were
his chances of getting permission to fly in to Hanoi, and so on. Nobody focused on what Branfman perceived was the central mystery, and that was
why he found himself standing up and saying to Perot, "Sir, my name's
Fred Branfman. I understand we should care very much about the American pilots being held prisoner in North Vietnam. As an American I can
understand that concern. But what I don't understand is that there are
thousands of Asians being killed right now, and you don't seem to have any
concern for them."

Testily, Perot answered, "Fred, of course we should share concern on
that issue, but that's not what this trip is about. This trip is about our boys,
the POWs in North Vietnam. Next question, please."

Perot and his people kept a wary eye as Branfman followed them around
Vientiane. He wasn't exactly hard to spot, with his black Viet Cong–like
outfit, bushy hair, and *baci* strings around his wrists.

Perot went to the Pathet Lao office in Vientiane, and from there to the
North Vietnamese embassy, where he was told that his plane wouldn't be
allowed to land in Hanoi. The Pathet Lao and North Vietnamese didn't
believe that Perot could be serious about helping American prisoners of
war when their own prisoners of war were being mistreated, too. This led
Perot to make a brief visit to a prison camp for North Vietnamese soldiers
in Laos toward the end of December 1969.

Branfman went along with the reporters to the prison camp for North
Vietnamese soldiers. The gates opened and there was a big yard inside with
a bunch of prisoners in the hot sun. Perot made a beeline for the prisoners and the journalists all followed him. Perot walked right up to them and
stopped, and everybody gathered around him. The North Vietnamese prisoners were all looking sullenly at the ground.

"Howdy!" Perot exclaimed in a loud voice. None of the prisoners
looked up. He turned to his interpreter and said, "Tell them I'm Ross Perot,
an American citizen. We come here as friends."

Perot wasn't able to convince the North Vietnamese prisoners that he
was their friend, and over time some of the Americans in Laos started
wondering about him, too. Perot claimed—truthfully—that he had paid
for the plane and presents himself. What he did not advertise was that
President Nixon and his national security adviser, Henry Kissinger, had
asked him to make the trip. He was coordinating his mission closely with
the government to embarrass Hanoi into improving conditions for U.S.
POWs. But this did not stop him from speaking his mind. When the
U.S. embassy in Vientiane obligingly rolled out the red carpet and held
a party in his honor, Perot made disparaging remarks about U.S. gov-

ernment officials in South Vietnam and Laos, to the surprise of the other guests.

Perot liked being a VIP with top-level government connections, but he had no intention of doing exactly what his government told him. Though the evidence is sketchy, it appears that his stated goal of putting Hanoi on the defensive for its treatment of American POWs was not all he had in mind. Without Branfman or anyone else from the press following him, Perot paid a private call on Edgar Buell, in Vientiane. The meeting lasted three hours. From Buell's letter home about their meeting, and from what is known about both men, it seems likely that Perot was entertaining the idea of rescue attempts on prisons where American POWs were held, using Vang Pao's tribal soldiers to free them.

Perot's idea was not as far-fetched as it seemed. Earlier that year, under great pressure from Tom Clines and the CIA, a team of Meo commandos reluctantly made a successful raid on enemy depots across the North Vietnamese border in Dienbienphu, with transportation from U.S. helicopters. If the tribal soldiers raided Dienbienphu, in theory they could raid North Vietnamese prisons. The flaw was that Vang Pao already had too much on his hands in and around the Plain of Jars to mount rescue missions inside North Vietnam without embassy backing, not to mention pressure. Going around the embassy with a private-sponsored rescue mission was against Vang Pao's interests.

But Perot didn't give up easily. In April 1970, he hired another passenger jet, filled it with reporters, and came back to Southeast Asia on another media tour. This time Perot visited the prisons for North Vietnamese soldiers in South Vietnam. He filmed the conditions there and took letters from the North Vietnamese prisoners addressed to their families. He took the films and letters to the North Vietnamese embassy in Laos, in an attempt to embarrass them into providing regular mail to the U.S. prisoners in Hanoi. When the North Vietnamese diplomats, who refused to accept the films and letters, told him the United States destroyed their schools and hospitals with bombs, Perot offered to pay for rebuilding them out of his own pocket if Hanoi would release all American prisoners. This startled the North Vietnamese, who weren't used to dealing with billionaires, but they didn't budge.

On that April 1970 visit, the U.S. embassy arranged for Perot to get a briefing on the 150 or more Americans then believed to be prisoners in Laos. The briefing seems to have been given in the soundproof bubble on the second floor by people from the CIA. Standing by a wall map, one of the spooks pointed out the locations of the limestone caves in Sam Neua Province near the North Vietnamese border where some of the prisoners were being held—twenty-seven in one cave, for instance. The CIA man explained that his agency had broken the Pathet Lao's radio code and regularly learned where U.S. prisoners were being moved by monitoring radio transmissions. The problem with mounting a rescue mission, he explained, was the risk-reward ratio. The odds of success were poor. If twenty-seven Green Berets were killed rescuing twenty-seven pilots, for example, nothing would be gained. Perot said he could understand their point.

But Perot did not give up on the idea of a rescue attempt. Back in the United States the following year, he telephoned a Raven forward air controller who was about to return to Laos, asking him to visit his Texas office en route. When the Raven dutifully showed up, Perot handed him a gold-plated .45 revolver to deliver to Vang Pao as a present. "I want to get the general's attention," Perot said, according to the Raven's later account. "I've got a fix on some guys who are in a POW camp in Laos. See if VP knows anything about it and I'll finance a mission to go in there and pluck some guys out." The Raven delivered the gold-plated revolver to the general in Long Tieng, but Vang Pao wasn't in a position to mount rescue expeditions in far Sam Neua Province without U.S. government help.

◆

On New Year's Day, 1970, shortly after Perot's first visit to Laos, Edgar Buell returned to Sam Thong with his good friend Dr. Weldon, USAID's chief of public health. As soon as they landed Buell felt a chilly bite in the air, which he figured was due to the mountain elevation. As they drove around in a jeep together the temperature dropped further and he stopped in his house to put on his long underwear and a jacket. He asked Weldon whether he thought it was cold and the doctor replied that the wind was brisk. The two men got in a plane for a short flight to a Meo village celebrating Western New Year. When they landed Buell felt hot again and there was something wrong with his eyesight. He told Weldon that he didn't feel good and went off to lie down in a hut, sweating. By nightfall he was back in Vientiane. He had malaria, of the falciparum strain, which doesn't respond readily to medication.

He recuperated in the Weldons' large and comfortable house overlooking the Mekong River, while monitoring the news from the Plain of Jars. The news wasn't good. Some North Vietnamese commandos had infiltrated the main air base, killing forty-two of Vang Pao's troops, and blowing up millions of dollars worth of ammunition and fuel. Then nearby bases started falling. Four thousand Meo were lost to the other side, and Buell's staff at Sam Thong was trying to get permission to evacuate by air another eleven thousand who were surrounded.

Air strikes in the north dropped to a hundred a day, down from their peak and only a third of the number flown at that time in south Laos against

the Ho Chi Minh Trail. It was like rush-hour traffic on the Trail, and trying to stop communist supplies from arriving in South Vietnam had a
higher priority for the U.S. Air Force than helping Vang Pao's tribal forces.

When Buell felt better, he went to the U.S. embassy in Vientiane. He
was told that the Plain of Jars was expected to fall.

By the end of January, Buell was back in Sam Thong. Everywhere, people were digging trenches and making bunkers. Four-engine C-130 cargo
planes flew overhead to the Plain of Jars, where they filled up with refugees
and took off again. It was the dry season. Sneezing from the dust, chug-
ging pills to fight the malaria, Buell helped direct a total exodus of the people of the Plain of Jars.

> Feb. 23, 1970 Sam Tong
> Yes I know I havn't wrote. O.K. Reason: Shit hit the fan but good.
> The enemy hit us hard east of P.D.J. Lost many positions and *many* men.
> Then they hit us at P.D.J. proper. P.D.J. is mostly all gone. We still have
> Muong Soui and Xieng Khongville but they will be gone in a couple of days.
> We are now trying to regroup the soldiers, who are scattered all over Hell.
> It will take days. Until then we are in trouble everywhere and the enemy is
> everywhere and lots of them. It is getting tight, the morale has droped, bad.
> We are on 100% alert here. All women & kids, 80% of the people here sleep
> in the jungle. Worried to death where do we go from here.

◆

The outside world was receiving plenty of news coverage of Laos, thanks
in part to Tim Allman, who was now freelancing for a number of major newspapers and magazines, and Fred Branfman, who hired himself out as an interpreter to incoming newsmen and provided them with ready-made stories.
With the press clamoring for greater access, the embassy set up one of its
scripted visits to Sam Thong—"dog and pony shows," as Buell called them.

Branfman and Allman were on the planeload of reporters that showed
up. While Buell gave the reporters his usual pep talk, which was more optimistic than his letters home, Allman and two other reporters hiked over
the road Vint Lawrence had built connecting Sam Thong to Long Tieng,
the so-called secret air base. No newsman had gone there since 1962, before the Geneva accords. They stayed in Long Tieng for an hour before
Tom Clines, the base chief, caught up with them and had them flown out
to Vientiane. To the journalists, the breaching of Long Tieng's secrecy was
a milestone in the coverage of the war. Clines and Buell didn't give it much
thought. They had more important matters on their minds.

Vang Pao's army was on the verge of disintegration. Xieng Khouangville,
the site of his initial victory in taking the Plain of Jars, fell when his young

soldiers saw enemy tanks coming and took to their heels. They abandoned their artillery in place for the other side to capture, just as the North Vietnamese had left unspiked artillery in place for the Meo to capture before.

Everything was gone now on the Plain of Jars, except for Muong Soui on the western edge. To try to save the base the U.S. used B-52 bombers for the first time in northern Laos, at the specific directive of President Nixon, who was monitoring the situation from the White House. Buell and the other Americans in the field knew about B-52s but were told to keep it from the reporters, since it was top secret. Their hopes for the giant eight-engine planes turned to disappointment. Because of red tape, it took twenty-four hours from the time of requests for the B-52s to arrive over their targets, and by that time the North Vietnamese had moved on. Jet fighter and night gunship attacks slowed the enemy advance on Muong Soui but didn't stop it from falling.

With the plain fallen, Vang Pao was back where he had been a year before, with one base to the north of the plain and most of his people concentrated to the south and southwest of it. He had bought himself a year, at a price of heavy casualties. Tribal elders denounced him to his face. They told him he was destroying the Meo race for the sake of his own power and for the sake of the Americans. His people were demoralized and scared, and his army was falling apart.

Vang Pao went to Buell with tears in his eyes. He told Buell that his head, neck, back, and leg hurt. "This is the times he calls me Father and I become just that," wrote Buell. "Most times talk strong to him, pat him a little and get him moving. But I saw a sick man, mentally sick. I took it easy."

Buell steered the conversation toward Sam Thong's security, which had deteriorated. They decided to station guards at night and to dig more foxholes, including some outside Buell's door.

For various reasons Buell believed that Sam Thong would be the enemy's main target. Vang Pao thought that Long Tieng, his own base, was the enemy's goal. With its population swollen to forty thousand, Long Tieng was a prize he would not forfeit. It had become the second-largest city in Laos, after Vientiane. San Thong had only five or six thousand.

Vang Pao regrouped his remaining soldiers around Long Tieng. He asked the Vientiane government for reinforcements and the Americans for more air support. If he got help, he told Buell, he could hold Long Tieng until the rains came, and the rains would slow down the enemy.

Buell wrote:

> This is the dry season, is it dry. At night there are big mountain fires everywhere, burning off to plant rice, really pretty at night, if it just wasn't for the guns cracking.

The enemy keeps pounding away, has not come closer in force. People are moving everywhere. They don't know where to go, to the hills, to Vientiane. Just running. We have moved thousands of people the past 2 months, we have lost a lot of territory. Our soldiers are either dead or dead tired. We have taken a bad beating. It is going to be hard to fight back. The only thing that can save us is more bombing planes, and the big rains, which are still 6 wks away. May it rain.

Sam T. itself is now only half the size it was one month ago. It can easly become a ghost town. Many decissions rest on my old shoulders. A big one is when do I evacuate the Hospital.

We are having many newspaper people. Every day someone. Tomorrow I have forty. It is hard to talk to them. They want you to lie so they can tell you people more lies back home, to upset you worse than you are.

Vang Pao's pleas for reinforcements were finally answered in early March 1970. Under pressure from the U.S. embassy, the Laotian commanders of other military regions in the kingdom grudgingly sent units they felt they could spare. From the far northwest—Tony Poe's fiefdom—came SGU companies of mixed ethnic composition, mostly Yao, who were sent to Sam Thong. The Yao could not speak the Meo language, and vice versa. Old ethnic rivalries flared. A few mortar rounds—warning shots—from Meo soldiers panicked the Yao, who had never been out of their home region before and who were bewildered. The Yao turned their weapons outward and aimed at anybody within range.

Buell radioed his old friend Tony and told him to get down to Sam Thong fast. Poe arrived, and like a cartoon of his old self advanced toward his Yao troops holding a .30-caliber Browning machine gun in his bare hands. He pointed this oversize weapon right at them and told them through an interpreter to put their weapons down, or he was going to kill them. Put the rifles on the ground right fuckin' now.

His Yao SGUs put down their weapons and surrendered. When it was over they filed sullenly past Poe toward the plane for the ride back to Nam Yu. It was a low moment for Poe. He had lost face, and he learned that he couldn't make a lasting difference in Laos any more than any other *farang.*

◆

As the North Vietnamese attackers neared Sam Thong and Long Tieng, the remaining Meo soldiers began to melt away, taking to the hills with their families to hide from the enemy. These quasi-desertions left Sam Thong almost totally unprotected and Long Tieng with fewer soldiers than it needed. Feeling endangered, the tribal elders who normally bent their will to Vang Pao's now spoke out vehemently against him.

Faced with mutiny, Vang Pao flew to Vientiane and told Prime Minister Souvanna Phouma that his people had to be evacuated to Sayaboury by air at once. All of the women, old men, and children, a hundred thousand in all, immediately. From Long Tieng and Sam Thong, from major bases and tiny outposts and villages behind enemy lines. Everybody had to be evacuated at once. Today. Now.

Souvanna Phouma was flabbergasted. So were the Americans at the embassy when they learned of it. They had not had any advance warning whatsoever. To them, being new to the scene, the plan seemed like Vang Pao at his most half baked. They put it down to his mercurial temperament—manic-depressive, wildly optimistic and depressed by turns. They didn't recognize that Vang Pao's poorly presented plan grew out of the original strategy for Meo participation in the war.

Logistically, Vang Pao's request was impossible to fulfill, which gave the embassy an easy excuse for turning it down. USAID and the civilian air charter companies were already going all-out to provide for over half a million refugees in Laos. The airlines couldn't drop everything else they were doing and mount an airlift five times larger than the evacuation from the Plain of Jars. Besides, the tribal forces were too useful militarily where they were, as a screen between Vientiane and the Plain of Jars, to be allowed to move. If the Meo civilians left, the rest of the Meo soldiers probably would too, and there would be nobody to stop the communists from marching into downtown Vientiane.

◆

The day after Vang Pao's Sayaboury request, March 12, 1970, Edgar Buell wrote:

> It is Thurs. night 11:30. Things are so quiet around Sam Tong, you could hear a mouse run away where, the only noise I hear is dogs barking in distances.
>
> I am in the warehouse as I am every night. I have laid down but can't sleep, fall off a little while, wake up thinking.
>
> We are in deep shit, belive me, we are backed to the wall. People are or have gave up. 50% have left for good, towards Vientiane, mostly Lao. The Meo are in the jungle. Many will stay there. The only ones here are people who have worked for us, have been so loyal, but they can leave anytime. Soldiers are leaving the fronts to join their families. To where they don't know.

Among those who left Sam Thong was Vang Pao's old mentor, Chao Saykham, the Lao prince who served as the governor of Xieng Khouang Province. Saykham believed that further fighting with the communists was hopeless; and with his departure any notions of ethnic unity and nation-building crumbled.

Buell continued his letter:

> I am as calm as I ever was, but worried bad. It may not be the last stand, but it is or may be the last real stand. I am sure they will never fight again like they have in the past. They wonder what they fought and died for. What they will do God only knows, but eventually most will be under or with the other side.
>
> I am going to Long Tieng in the morning to talk to my fellow Americans, get their idea as to my thinking. Then will send a message to the Ambassador. I have no idea what the enemy has in mind, but the enemy can and could take anything they want.
>
> I think the time is close at hand when most of these people will say, fight your own dam war.
>
> This letter is not for publication or even discussion. I am only telling you, and I do want it keep, just in case I need it sometime.
>
> It may interest you or a surprise, I have not touched alcohol for over 3 months.
>
> Love to all,
>
> Your Dad

Then Sam Thong fell.

From Vientiane, where he had been evacuated, Buell wrote that everything had happened on March 17. During the morning he had gotten word that the enemy was coming. He started evacuating the hospital patients, nurses, and medics. By noon Sam Thong was in uproar with people clamoring for air evacuation or walking through the valley and out on foot. The embassy ordered all Americans to leave, and Buell was the last one out, as darkness fell. The enemy attacked at midnight, blew a few buildings up, left, and came back next day.

> It would take hours to tell you about the last two months, so we will just call it memories now and some night in your little house I will tell you the story, it would have to be all night, because its like a nightmare.
>
> Many people here thought I would come out bitter, broken, etc. They were supprised to not see that. Inside I am sad, but in this game you don't stop. I set up the next day SW of Sam Tong. Started picking up our workers on trails, we now have every one but one. The next day in full swing dropping rice, picking up sick etc, on trails with small aircraft. We are now operating full scale, not easy. Where we are working is a real hot wet hole.
>
> In all the past 6 wks. 178,000 have become homeless, walking or sleeping in the jungle. They now have most all reached a place to rest and wait

the outcome. We are helping, rice, plastic for shelter, blankets, but so little. Was never geared up for this many people. The chances are great they will have to move on. Where I dont know.

Long Tieng is still holding, got additional help. Took Sam Tong partly back yesterday, maybe more today, but enemy still everywhere around. Sam Tong has been pretty well all destroyed. Even if we can hold it, I wouldn't be going back for some time. I again lost the works.

There are some peace talks among the Lao's themselves. But the VC wants it all.

◆

The Kingdom of Cambodia was another obscure Southeast Asian nation that many Americans had heard of but few could place on a map. It lies south of Laos, east of Thailand, and west of southern South Vietnam. The United States had no treaties for the defense of Cambodia and no commitments there.

Until March 1970, Cambodia stayed officially neutral in the war, under the leadership of Prince Norodom Sihanouk. It was a weak country, and in practice Sihanouk let the North Vietnamese operate out of bases there and let Nixon secretly bomb the North Vietnamese with B-52s.

On March 18, 1970—the day after Sam Thong fell—a right-wing pro-American general, Lon Nol, replaced Sihanouk in a coup. Lon Nol promptly realigned his government with the U.S. Prince Sihanouk, who had been traveling abroad at the time, joined a Cambodian communist group, the so-called Khmer Rouge, who were aligned with Hanoi and Beijing, and who were led by a secretive man named Saloth Sar, whose nom de guerre was Pol Pot.

Until then the "war," to most Americans, had meant the war in Vietnam. Cambodia hadn't been part of the war and Laos was just an obscure secondary theater, basically the Ho Chi Minh Trail, that few Americans understood or cared much about. A few weeks before the Cambodia coup, Nixon had released a long statement claiming that no American stationed in Laos had ever been killed in ground combat there. That was a mistake and news reporters jumped all over it, but the brief flare-up of news coverage failed to change the domestic perception that the war was, in fact, about Vietnam.

The Cambodia coup was followed about two weeks later by an American-led invasion, termed an "incursion," of the regions of Cambodia nearest South Vietnam. And with that invasion it suddenly became clear to many people for the first time that the "war" was not just a Vietnam war with miscellaneous add-ons. It was a larger entity, a regional war. Five Southeast Asian countries were directly involved: North Vietnam, South Vietnam, Laos, Cambodia, and even Thailand, home to American air force bases and also to a nasty little communist insurgency. The conflicts in those five countries were directly connected. The same outside powers provided the money and equipment, China and the Soviet Union for one side, the United States for the other. Hanoi had links to communist movements in the other four Southeast Asian countries, and all the right-wing regimes had links with the U.S.

Outwardly, the regional war was an ideologically driven contest between the communists and the noncommunists. But beneath the surface it was not so neatly polarized. There were so many ethic groups that it was hard to tell who was doing what. On the noncommunist side, South Vietnamese nationals of various ethnic denominations worked for hire in Laos on the Ho Chi Minh Trail. A couple of battalions of Cambodians came to Laos for training. A force of ethnic Cambodians who were South Vietnamese nationals was trained in South Vietnam for use in Cambodia. There were regular Thai army battalions in South Vietnam, along with South Koreans, both of them paid by the United States. Roughly a battalion of regular Thai security forces was airlifted to Long Tieng, and they helped keep the base from falling, along with ethnic Lao units from southern Laos regions like Savannakhet.

Many of these allies hated one another only a little less than they hated their enemies. They had despised and feared one another for centuries, and the common soldiers weren't going to change their beliefs overnight just because somebody new was paying them. Sam Thong was an example of that ethnic hatred among nominal allies.

There was no battle for Sam Thong. The lowland Lao had already left, and once Pop Buell decided to evacuate the hospital, everybody else left as fast as they could. The North Vietnamese killed a few Meo civilian police guarding the road to Long Tieng but couldn't find anyone else to fight. The tribal soldiers identified Sam Thong with the Americans, and they had decided not to fight for the Americans anymore.

The next morning—the same day as the Cambodia coup—Royal Lao Air Force T-28s from Vientiane appeared over Sam Thong. The big new Quonset hut warehouse with REFUGEE GOODIES painted on the side was already a crumpled mass of sheet metal. With few enemy soldiers in sight, the T-28s bombed what was left of Sam Thong instead. The air strikes by "friendly" planes led Vang Pao to install captured communist antiaircraft guns on the ridge above Long Tieng for his own protection. Vang Pao wanted to ensure against bombing raids by lowland Lao, and also against raids by Meo T-28 pilots, in case any of his own pilots went over to the enemy side.

The nightmare Buell referred to in his letter had begun. With the influx of Thai and other non-Meo troops, Long Tieng held and Vang Pao began

to try to take Sam Thong back again. He succeeded, but the soldiers supposedly under his command looted what was left of Sam Thong and nobody could stop them. The looters took mattresses and cots from the
hospital. They went through Buell's house and the houses of the other
Americans, spilling out the contents of bureau drawers, helping themselves
to clothing, and liquor, wrecking furniture. While the looting was going on
Buell stayed in his new base, Ban Xon, Site 272; the mob was too ugly and
dangerous for him to confront. What hurt him most was the loss of two
jeeps used to transport patients to the Sam Thong hospital. He found them
in Long Tieng, their ignitions hot-wired. The Meo who had taken the jeeps
refused to give them back, claiming them as legitimate war booty.

After the fall of Sam Thong, Buell went through the motions, but he was
never the same. The embassy decided to move the USAID warehouse and
supply hub from Sam Thong to Ban Xon, which was nearer to Vientiane
and connected by better roads.

In Ban Xon the system caught up with Buell, with its requisition forms,
committee meetings, and the "educated fools" whose apparent mission in
life was to keep anything from getting done. Buell's health was also deteriorating, and he became increasingly irrational, given to fits of sudden ve-
hement anger. It took old friends' intervention to keep him from getting
into serious trouble with his employers. Dr. Weldon spent time nearly every
day soothing and negotiating on Buell's behalf. Ambassador Godley, a
drinking and poker-playing buddy, was an ally of last resort, to be called
upon when all else failed.

Buell was burned out. His usefulness, and his role among the hilltribes,
had nearly ended.

# TWENTY-SEVEN

# The Invasion

After the loss of Sam Thong, the focus of the Laos war turned to the central and southern part of the country. The North Vietnamese stepped up their drive to widen the Ho Chi Minh Trail corridor, especially after the May 1970 U.S. invasion of Cambodia deprived them of sanctuaries and supply routes there.

The fighting followed the familiar seesaw pattern, the communists advancing in the dry season, the royalists taking territory back in the rainy season. Progress was unsteady, but overall the royalists lost more territory than they gained.

On the ground, the royalists employed what the CIA men called dust agitators—mediocre-quality, battalion-size forces of lowland infantry. The CIA provided ex–Green Beret advisers to the battalions, but most of the muscle came from the air—from the U.S. Air Force, and to a lesser extent from aircraft belonging to the navy and army.

Though the Pentagon wasn't releasing country-by-country statistics, a sense began to emerge that this U.S. air effort in southern Laos was getting very, very big. Bigger than the bombing of South Vietnam and far greater than the bombing of Cambodia. Even when the figures became available, and comparisons became possible, it was hard to picture what this bombing really meant. For example, 440,000 tons of munitions were dropped on Laos the following year, which was nearly twice the amount dropped on South Vietnam and twenty-five times the power of the atomic bomb at Hiroshima. It was simply impossible to imagine. There weren't twenty-five mushroom-shaped clouds rising east of the Mekong, and the kingdom did not appear twice as cratered as South Vietnam, although parts of the Ho Chi Minh Trail looked like a moonscape, craters everywhere, all the leaves and branches blown off the trees.

In Vientiane, Fred Branfman was trying his best to understand the air war but without much success. His main problem, still, was U.S. government secrecy, which kept him from witnessing the bombing and convinced that his government had much to hide. His anger at the U.S. government, and his deepening friendship with Ngeun, the Lao-Chinese refugee from the Plain of Jars, radicalized his feelings even further. By then Ngeun had dropped his earlier criticisms of the Pathet Lao and North Vietnamese and was starting to praise them, apparently from direct experience. To Branfman, the lack of credible information from his own government made it easier to believe Ngeun, and to believe that the so-called enemy were actually heroes, liberators. If his own government was doing wrong, it made a certain kind of sense to assume that the other side was doing right.

But of course nothing was simple, and Branfman knew it. He decided that he couldn't find out much more about the bombing by talking to refugees. The next step was to talk to pilots. The American planes were based in South Vietnam and Thailand, and the Thai bases were off-limits to the press. On a freelance assignment for Dispatch News Service, an agency that represented an antiestablishment alternative to the regular wire services, Branfman went to the Danang air base in South Vietnam.

At Danang, he began to learn about different aircraft and munitions, and about the air war's many-layered deployment of planes. Roughly speaking, there were light spotter planes at two thousand feet; propellor-driven bombers, attack planes, gunships, and gunship helicopters at five thousand feet; jet fighters and reconnaissance aircraft at ten thousand feet; B-52 bombers at thirty thousand feet, and airborne communications planes coordinating the bombing of Laos circling overhead all day and all night even higher than that.

Branfman was starting to understand the technical aspects of the bombing, but he had not escaped his moral abyss. He stayed up on evening drinking beer with a bunch of friendly pilots. They were nice young guys, sincere and dedicated, and he couldn't help liking them. The next morning, on the runway, one of them said, "Well, I'm off to bomb Laos. Wish me luck." He stuck out his hand. Numbly, Branfman shook it.

◆

Whenever the war was going badly, Vang Pao declared that next week he would take all his people across the Mekong River to Sayaboury Province and then over the border into Thailand.

That made sense to anybody who knew the area. The Mekong River was wide and it had no bridges, offering some protection as a boundary. Sayaboury was mountainous and underpopulated, and on the back side lay Thailand, the ultimate refuge if all else failed. But Vang Pao was always threatening to do it "next week" and never did. In fact, he had never done much to prepare the escape route. He had never set up arms caches or sent advance parties or maintained bases or made clear plans with the U.S., Lao, or Thai governments.

There were several explanations for this curious lack of planning. One was that Vang Pao was a talented but uneducated man who had risen to an organizational level beyond his competence. He excelled at short-term tactics—at capturing a hill from the enemy—the kinds of skills majors and colonels needed. But he had never been good at long-term strategic planning, which is part of what major generals are meant to do.

Another explanation is that Vang Pao's promotion to command of the Second Military Region removed him from the pan-tribal, Laos-wide guerilla responsibilities originally assigned him by the CIA. After 1965, this line of reasoning goes, he no longer had any business meddling about in Sayaboury. His job confined him to Xieng Khouang and Sam Neua Provinces in the northeast.

The Americans, including Bill Lair, were also to blame for Vang Pao's lack of planning. Back at the operation's beginning Lair had failed to get the U.S. embassy and the Thai and Laotian governments to take a firm position on the Meo tribe's future. The station chiefs and ambassadors to whom he reported all agreed that a Sayaboury escape route was sensible, but they were not eager to go to the lengths of negotiating formal agreements among three nations. As a result, the Sayaboury plan had never become official policy. It was never put on paper. Gradually, with the rotation of ambassadors and station chiefs, and the growth and change in direction of the war, the original Sayaboury plan had receded in American institutional memory. By the beginning of the 1970s, few people in senior positions in the embassy and the CIA station had even heard of it.

The Meo themselves had not forgotten, though. When the war started turning against them, one of the clans from northeast Laos sent some of its young men to Sayaboury on a private reconnaissance, without American support. What they found was discouraging. The mountains of Sayaboury were a little lower and hotter than the mountains of northeast Laos. The rice seeds they brought with them didn't thrive there. The scouts got sick from the heat and from malaria. Worst, Sayaboury had a road network. The enemy used roads for trucks and heavy weapons. The Meo wanted to be as far beyond the roads as possible. They were hill walkers, and their ability to move rapidly on foot through hundreds of miles of rugged wilderness was their best defense. The more isolated they were in the high backcountry, the safer they would be.

Word of this failed expedition filtered back to Long Tieng, and Vang Pao seems to have agreed that Sayaboury was not a realistic option anymore. But he didn't have any better plans to offer, and neither did the second- and third-tier tribal leaders.

They had allowed themselves to be seduced. Whenever the threat from the enemy receded, they forgot the dangers facing them. The wartime economy and the support of the Americans brought luxuries that they were unwilling to abandon. Nobody needed to farm anymore. Airplanes dropped rice from the sky. Doctors healed the sick with medicines far more effective than opium. Children were learning to read and write in Lao, and a few of the luckiest and brightest were studying in universities in France and the United States.

Without an escape route, or even an escape plan, the Meo were trapped in a crescent of bases to the south and southwest of the Plain of Jars. With no way out, they were doomed to take part in their seasonal cycles of war.

In the wet season of the middle months of 1970, Vang Pao launched another offensive on the southern edge of the Plain of Jars. It was a diversionary attack to throw the enemy off balance, later followed with harassment raids on enemy troops and supply depots. The T-28s, and the American air force did most of the work; and Vang Pao focused his own efforts in rear areas, retraining what was left of his army and recruiting new troops, which required threats, intimidation, and other strong-arm tactics. Few new Meo families were willing to have their sons fight for him now. All he could do was recruit men from outside the tribe to join his force of irregulars.

Soon, the dry season came and North Vietnamese struck back, wiping out his temporary gains and driving toward Long Tieng. On January 16, 1971, while he was at the bottom of one of his up-and-down emotional cycles, Vang Pao met with about four hundred tribal elders. He admitted to them that they were losing the war. There could be no more talk about returning to their own villages once the fighting was over. The enemy was gathering once again and would probably capture Long Tieng. Maybe it was time for everybody to move, Vang Pao said glumly.

He proposed moving to an area southeast of Long Tieng and just north of the Vientiane plain. It was still within the Second Military Region, which he commanded. He thought it might be possible to make an accommodation with the local people there and even with the other side.

One American, Pop Buell, strongly supported the move, but he had lost influence with the CIA and the embassy. At a previous meeting with Tom

Clines, Buell had spouted off suggestions in Lao that went against the wishes of the intelligence agency. Clines brought a Laotian stenographer to the next meeting to record what Buell said, and Buell kept his mouth shut from then on. A few months later Buell had a serious, near-fatal heart attack, and his visits to Long Tieng became few and far between.

Since neither the U.S. embassy nor the Vientiane government wanted Vang Pao to evacuate Long Tieng, the Meo stayed. In January 1971, about six thousand North Vietnamese soldiers attacked. The enemy swept away the outposts, clambered up Skyline Ridge, and sent a rain of artillery shells down onto the valley floor.

What saved Long Tieng was the arrival of Thai SGUs, a force that eventually grew to twelve battalions. These Thai "volunteers," as the U.S. embassy liked to call them, or "mercenaries," as Prime Minister Souvanna Phouma inadvertently referred to them in a speech, were armed, trained, and paid by the United States, but led by officers from the regular Thai army. Vang Pao discovered that if he put them in exposed forward positions under heavy fire they would fight hard to save their own lives. "Good on defense," was his verdict. Vang Pao threw the Thais into the worst meat-grinder battles up on Skyline Ridge, where one battalion took 60 percent casualties.

Meo T-28s dive-bombed the enemy positions. U.S. Air Force jets swooped in, strafing and bombing. At night, gunships rode tight circles in the sky, their tracer bullets spewing toward the ground in a molten stream. In the early hours of February 14, 1971, after successive nights of North Vietnamese rocket attacks, small-arms fire broke out on the south side of the base, and mortar and recoilless rifle rounds exploded around the headquarters buildings. The North Vietnamese had reached the valley floor.

A Cessna observation plane took off in the darkness. Inside it were Vang Pao and Jerry Daniels, the longtime field man who had become his personal adviser.

First light came, and an American Raven forward air controller trapped in the Long Tieng headquarters compound called in an air strike. The signal from his handheld survival radio reached Cricket, the daytime airborne radio relay and command center circling at high altitudes, even higher than the B-52s.

Two Phantom F-4Ds finishing a night escort mission to the south peeled off and streaked toward Long Tieng at faster than the speed of sound. The Phantoms' radio call sign was Killer. The radio signal from Long Tieng was too weak to reach Killer clearly, and Cricket had to relay some of the transmissions.

The visibility was poor and the pilots were tired. The Raven on the ground directed the air strike toward machine-gun tracer fire ricocheting

off a hillside. The pilots assumed this meant they should drop their ordnance where the machine-gun fire was coming from.

"Am I cleared?" asked Killer One.

"We don't see you," said the Raven, "but if you see everything we're
talking about you're cleared."

Killer One dropped six CBUs, or cluster bomb units, which opened in
midair like elongated clamshells, spilling thousands of bomblets onto the
headquarters compound itself.

The CBUs set the operations shack and several of the Americans' sleeping quarters on fire, and ripped holes in vehicles, buildings, and human
flesh. Some of the bomblets were time-delayed and didn't finish exploding until two hours later. News reports later estimated that about 170
tribespeople were wounded and thirty killed.

◆

As a caravan of human misery made its way through the foothills outside Long Tieng—thousands and thousands of Meo fleeing the scenes of
war, carrying their babies in cloth slings and their pots and pans in baskets
with shoulder straps—a procession of a different sort was under way in
southern Laos, in the rugged terrain east of Tchepone.

Preceded by B-52s, whose 2,000-pound bomb explosions rumbled and
shook the ground, and sent up geysers of red laterite soil that rained uselessly back on the ground again, long strings of Huey helicopters ferried
battalions of South Vietnamese soldiers toward the Ho Chi Minh Trail.
Never in the Indochina war had so many helicopter transports been used
in a single operation.

The North Vietnamese knew the invasion was coming. They positioned
antiaircraft guns and other weaponry around the few natural clearings of
southeast Laos, which they correctly figured would be used as landing
zones. As the big helicopters landed and then slowly rose again, exposing
their vulnerable undersides, the firing erupted. The chopper tilted crazily
and crashed into the ground, and the firing continued until there were few
survivors. The U.S. military replied by napalming and carpet bombing the
massed concentrations of peasant soldiers from North Vietnam.

For years the U.S. military command in South Vietnam had proposed
to cut the Ho Chi Minh Trail by using American ground troops. As long
as Bill Sullivan had been the ambassador to Laos, the military had never
gotten the White House's permission to proceed. Sullivan was gone from
Laos now and Lyndon Johnson was no longer president. With Mac Godley in Vientiane and Richard Nixon in the White House, the U.S. military
might have invaded Laos with American troops if it hadn't been for the
enormous political uproar set off by the invasion of Cambodia.

At Kent State, in Ohio, National Guardsmen opened fire on student demonstrators, killing four; and about four hundred college campuses across the country went on strike. In reaction, Congress had passed an amendment forbidding the use of American ground troops in Cambodia and Laos. The 1971 invasion of southern Laos was therefore an operation guided by political rather than military considerations—a compromise that pleased nobody.

There was no unity of command. The South Vietnamese prime minister, Nguyen Van Thieu, sent about half the number of troops the Americans had asked, and these troops went into combat without the U.S. advisers to whom they were accustomed. They Royal Lao Army sent no troops at all. The U.S. Army didn't seek advice from the U.S. Air Force on helicopter landings along the Ho Chi Minh Trail, though the air force had had far more experience. Somewhere between a hundred and two hundred helicopters, most of them belonging to the army, were lost in the operation and more than six hundred damaged—the army withheld the actual figures—along with fifty-five Americans killed, 178 wounded, and thirty-four missing in action. Owing to American airpower, North Vietnamese casualties were extremely heavy, about fourteen thousand killed, five times the number of South Vietnamese deaths, according to the U.S. government.

A major goal of the operation, which was known as Lam Son 719, was the capture of the town of Tchepone inside Laos. Southeast of Tchepone rose a flat-topped, butte-like mountain where a South Vietnamese firebase name Sophia was built. Sophia had that blasted look of the front lines—sandbagged bunkers, trees blown up or cleared away for better visibility, raw red laterite soil exposed. A young American freelance journalist who spoke Vietnamese talked his way onto a morning resupply flight. He found the base commander, a full colonel in one of the better South Vietnamese units, in his tent. The American asked him what he thought about the operation and by way of reply the colonel walked him to the edge of the mountaintop.

The colonel pointed his finger and said, "You see that dusty spot on the plain?"

Beyond the shoulder of the mountain, the young American made out a light-colored smudge on the valley floor.

"That's Tchepone," said the colonel.

"Is it going to be difficult to take it?" asked the reporter. "Do you expect a lot of casualties?"

The colonel laughed bitterly. "Your air force has bombed Tchepone off the face of the map. There is nothing at Tchepone but that dusty spot where two roads come together. There's no traffic there now. The North Vietnamese don't use it now. But we've been told to take it.

"So, I'll take it early tomorrow morning," said the colonel. "I'll go in there. And then we'll get out."

◆

In his quest to get at the heart of the air war, Fred Branfman went to Bangkok, to look up a man named Jerome Brown, who had helped choose bombing targets for the U.S. embassy in Laos. The targeting officer, who had retired from the air force, agreed to talk as long as Branfman didn't use his name in print.

Brown sketched a reasonably accurate portrait of the air war bureaucracy, and of the institutional reasons a secret program with bombs to spare and planes that flew too fast was turning parts of Laos into rubble. He also explained why such powerful weaponry wasn't wining the war, even though it was doing a lot of damage: the overreliance on expensive, fast-moving jets instead of practical, low-speed propellor planes; the futility of trying to stop trucks in heavily forested terrain. He explained the tendency of pilots to drop bombs where craters already existed and to hit civilian villages because they were far easier to spot than enemy troops hiding in the forests. Based on the interviews, Branfman wrote a three-part series on the U.S. air war for Dispatch News and sent it off in November 1970.

By then Branfman had been a catalyst in most of the major exposés of the Laos war. He had been a source of information and a goad to action to his friend the freelancer Tim Allman, who helped break open the story of the covert war. (Subsequently, Henry Kamm took over the Laos story for *The New York Times* and became the war's most insightful reporter.) Branfman interpreted for Sydney Schanberg, who would later win a Pulitzer Price for reporting from Cambodia, and he gave help informally to Seymour Hersh, who had already won a Pulitzer in South Vietnam; both men came through Laos looking for leads. For the three major television networks, Branfman suggested story ideas, set up appointments, and translated for their correspondents, including Ted Koppel and Bernard Kalb. He fed information on the bombing to Jack Anderson, the muckraking columnist in Washington, and to the staffs of Senate committees. He befriended, and got encouragement from, antiwar activists who passed through Vientiane en route to Hanoi, such as Daniel Berrigan and Noam Chomsky.

Branfman also helped blow Tony Poe's cover. A former USAID Refugee Relief officer who had worked with Poe had been ostracized by Pop Buell and others after testifying candidly to Congress on the problems of the war. Branfman introduced the man to Mike Morrow, the founder of Dispatch News Service. Morrow wrote the first story on Poe, published in September 1970. It was accurate on the major points, such as the CIA's intelligence forays into China, even if it did claim that Poe was married to a Yao princess. The story, together with Poe's loss of effectiveness from drinking, resulted in his being transferred out of Laos.

Inevitably, Branfman came to the attention of the U.S. embassy in Vientiane. Ambassador Godley became convinced that Branfman was an agent of the Soviet Union. During December 1970 and January 1971 events occurred that left Branfman feeling isolated and afraid. A U.S. embassy official paid a menacing call on Ngeun, who had been quietly collecting refugees' drawings and stories about the bombing of the Plain of Jars. By then, Branfman knew that Ngeun had been trained as a Pathet Lao soldier and political cadre. Branfman was careful not to ask whether Ngeun was still working for the Pathet Lao, and he decided he'd rather not know.

The walls were closing in. Other acquaintances were called in for questioning, and strange characters showed up at his door. A Tass correspondent in Laos offered Branfman assignments for Soviet magazines. Branfman said no. A shady South Vietnamese sought him out for information on the antiwar movement. Branfman rejected that, too.

He had never felt so worried before, nor so powerless to control his own destiny. All he could do was to try to ensure that nobody else got in trouble because of him. He moved into a bungalow by himself near the Lan Xang Hotel, where most of the journalists stayed. As the South Vietnamese invasion of southern Laos got under way, he held forth every evening in the bar at the Lan Xang for the newsmen who had flooded into Vientiane hoping to cover the invasion from the Laos side.

He talked for hours every night, and the newsmen listened. They didn't know much about Laos, and he knew the cities, towns, and villages, their population size, which side they were on. He knew the names of military units and the air bases in Thailand and South Vietnam from where the planes were launched. He knew the names of the spirits in the body and the names of Buddhist holidays. There were Americans who had more breadth and depth of knowledge about Laos than Fred Branfman, but none of them was so aggressively accessible to journalists; and there was nobody else so single-mindedly determined—so fanatically obsessed—to stop the bombing.

At eleven o'clock on the morning of February 12, 1971, four days after Lam Son 719 began, Laotian government security police found him at the Lan Xang Hotel. They were friendly and apologetic. As they drove with him to the central police station, one of the policemen turned to him and asked, "Why are the Americans angry at you?" Branfman replied that he could guess, but he wasn't sure specifically.

The policeman said, "The Americans told us to go over and pick you up."

"Did you know where I was living?"

"Yes, Bungalow Number Nine." The policeman said he had gone there earlier in the morning, but hadn't gone in because Branfman wasn't home.

Climbing the stairs inside the police station, they passed the USAID Public Safety Office. Branfman pointed to the door and raised his eyebrows quizzically. One of the policemen smiled and nodded assent.

In midafternoon they brought him down from his cell. They showed him the order of expulsion, Arrêté Ministériel No. 25, which was directed to officials throughout royalist Lao government areas and said that he was forbidden to enter Laos. The order, which was written in French, was signed February 4, 1971, and stated that his expulsion had been announced at a government cabinet meeting on January 20. It identified him as "Predery" or "Predy" Branfman, of the International Voluntary Services.

Branfman took the ferry across the Mekong to Nong Khai, Thailand, and then the train to Bangkok.

A week and a half later he stood at a lectern on a stage at Yale University, in New Haven, Connecticut, at an antiwar teach-in. He had never spoken in public before but found that the words came easily.

> In thinking of the air war, [he said] one image to keep in mind is that of the typical Laotian village. Ten to twenty bamboo huts, a Buddhist temple, a school, a few hundred head of cows, buffalo, pigs, rice farmers, their wives and grandparents, kids; that's about it. Tonight, as for the last seven years, hundreds of millions of dollars of the world's most sophisticated weaponry hover over these villages.
>
> Laos is automated warfare. Laser-guided bombs striking water buffalo; three-million-dollar jets bombing bamboo houses, infra-red scopes and complete radar sets tracking a man plowing his field. Life for the villagers is very simple. The oriental subtleties which have traditionally delighted Westerners do not apply. Life becomes a cliché: You live through it . . . or you die.
>
> They're hiding in holes in the ground or caves, or trenches dug in the hills. They sit there unless they have to leave. Only they have to leave fairly frequently because they have to work enough to survive; they have to try to grow enough rice to eat at night.
>
> Refugees have lived under this bombing for five years. Tonight hundreds of thousands of rice farmers of Laos and Cambodia are still living under the bombs, still huddling in holes, still being killed when they go out, still praying, as one old refugee man told me he did, "Oh please, don't

let the planes come anymore, don't let the planes come anymore, oh please." This bombing is militarily indecisive. It doesn't stop the guerillas; it doesn't kill the guerillas. It's true that it hinders the Communists, as any total war would. It does divert resources, it does kill potential porters, destroy food supplies, demoralize civilian population and create refugees. It does slow the guerillas down. But the question that has to be asked is, what happens in the years to come when the bombing does not bring victory?

I think we must oppose this war, for moral reasons. If any of our concepts of decency, morality, humanity have any meaning at all, we must not rest until this is stopped.

But also we must oppose this war for what it reveals about out own society. We are a people schooled in the belief that authoritarianism is the greatest threat to our way of life.

It is an irony of fate that the most recent wielders of totalitarian power are our own leaders.

By raising the subject of the automated air war, Branfman injected a new vigor into the antiwar movement, which had been losing steam with the steady announcements of troop withdrawals from Vietnam. Pleased and surprised at the reaction to his speech, Branfman moved on to Washington, D.C., where Dispatch News Service gave him a desk and a telephone in a corner of a basement room. He slept on a couch in the office. He called up all the antiwar people he had met in Vientiane. He wrote pamphlets, articles, and op-ed pieces. He briefed journalists and congressional staffers.

He was in the audience on April 22, 1971, for a hearing of the Senate Judiciary Committee's subcommittee on refugees. The chairman, Ted Kennedy, had gotten the runaround from then-Ambassador Bill Sullivan back when the senator had taken the Tour. Now it was payback time. Kennedy's staffers had been talking with Branfman, and they arranged an ambush.

At the hearing Kennedy asked Sullivan why the State Department had obstructed the committee's efforts to get information on the bombing of civilian villages in Laos. Sullivan offered an artfully constructed excuse for the delays and denigrated the accuracy of the bombing surveys Kennedy was citing. When the senator broke in to ask whether he was familiar with Mr. Fred Branfman, Sullivan said yes, he was. Kennedy called out, "Mr. Branfman?" Branfman stood up, wearing a cheap suit, the only one he owned. "Yes, sir?" he said.

NBC-TV carried the exchange on its evening news that night. Kennedy was the star of the segment, challenging the executive branch to start telling the truth. Sullivan's frustration showed on his face. Branfman seemed quiet, polite, and reserved, but there he was, on TV screens in living rooms across the country. ". . . There is good evidence the United States has been carrying out the most protracted bombings in history in Laos," Branfman declared.

He had been a fringe character in Laos. At home, in the States, Fred Branfman was rapidly becoming a major opposition player.

# Cat and Mouse

Working in Washington, D.C., was not easy for Sullivan. He tried to keep a low profile, but his past as a quasi-spook ambassador to Laos clung to him like an odor. His new job, as an upper-level bureaucrat in the losing Vietnam War effort, and as an occasional briefer and deceiver of Congress, made him automatically suspect on all sides—assumed to be guilty until proved otherwise.

In Laos, Sullivan had served Democratic administrations. In Washington, Nixon's Republican aides kept him out of the planning loop for the South Vietnamese invasion of the Ho Chi Minh Trail, guessing—correctly—that he would be opposed. When the invasion went ahead, and a few weeks later the South Vietnamese invaders retreated, and the retreat turned into a rout, the TV news carried the unforgettable image of South Vietnamese soldiers desperately hanging onto the skids of overcrowded American helicopters. Sullivan kept his mouth shut, knowing that his reactions were being watched, but the failure of the invasion offered grim satisfaction of the I-told-you-so variety.

It was just as well for Sullivan that he was circumspect. As he would learn later, the White House had placed secret wiretaps on his home and office telephones. The national security adviser, Henry Kissinger, wanted to know what Sullivan was thinking about Vietnam policy so he could out-maneuver State in the turf wars. Other Nixon aides wanted to know whether Sullivan was "loyal" or was leaking stories to the press.

The press suspected him, too. With the image of heartless, high-tech U.S. bombing of innocent peasants prevailing in the media, Sullivan became one of those government spokesmen that journalists love to hate. "U.S. AIDE DENIES LAOS BOMBING IS A MAJOR CAUSE OF REFUGEES," ran a newspaper article headline the day after Sullivan clashed with Fred Branfman on Capitol Hill.

At that hearing Sullivan tried to explain that Branfman had extrapolated from the experience of a small number of pro–Pathet Lao refugees to reach the wrong conclusions about the bombing and the evacuation of the Plain of Jars. Narrowly, technically, Sullivan had a point, but the political tide had turned against him. The enormity of the refugees' suffering made his arguments seem petty and legalistic and untruthful.

He even began to suspect those arguments himself. A congressman from California, Pete McCloskey, went to Laos, where the he got hold of an internal embassy study of the bombing that roughly confirmed what Branfman was saying about the widescale destruction of civilian targets. McCloskey then pushed the air force into giving him aerial photographs of some of the bomb damage. He sent copies to Sullivan, who was taken aback by the images of landscapes that he recognized.

Tracking the photos through military channels, Sullivan established for his own conscience that those bombs had been dropped after he left, in raids he probably would not have allowed. But in exonerating himself, he conveniently overlooked the role in the growth of the bombing that he himself had played. If bombing was Pandora's box, his predecessor, Ambassador Leonard Unger, had broken the lock on the lid. Sullivan had pried the lid open a bit—and then more and more, while denying that he ever wanted to do anything of the sort—and then his successor, Ambassador Mac Godley, had yanked it open the rest of the way.

Sullivan's own son, a student at Stanford, was showing up at antiwar rallies. Sullivan's former mentor at the Geneva accords, Averell Harriman, had turned against the war and suggested that the way to end it was to elect a new president.

In public, Sullivan supported the government party line on Vietnam, with an exquisite talent for saying what was expected of him and no more. In private, behind closed doors in classified hearings, he was artfully vague about the administration's flexibility, how far it was willing to go, and what "no commitment" really meant.

Sullivan didn't reveal his inner thoughts to anybody, even his wife.

◆

The widening realization that the United States was at war in Laos, without the authorization from Congress that the Constitution requires, began to take effect. With a new urgency, dovish senators resumed their struggle with the executive branch over Laos policy. Senator Stuart Symington, Sullivan's most determined enemy, decided that the way to bring the Laos war under control was to make the "black," or secret, budget for Laos public. He wanted to channel the money to the CIA and USAID through the regular U.S. military appropriations, and to put an annual ceiling on it of $200 million. The current appropriations were running around $240 million a year for the same categories.

Symington gathered support for his proposal on Capitol Hill. But it was one thing to announce lofty intentions in Washington and another to change the course of a war in the Southeast Asian boondocks. The tangled nature of the political system and of the CIA and military bureaucracies changed the plan for fiscal dieting into a strange, bloated beast of a program that Symington had not envisioned.

A CIA financial officer working on the Laos program in Asia watched the process unfold with cynical amusement. "We got a cable from D.C.," he recalled, "asking, how much do you think you need? We said, three hundred fifty million," and that was the amount, rather than two hundred million, to which the so-called Symington ceiling was raised and passed into law in 1971. The ceiling was raised again the next year to 375 million. "A million dollars a day. We were almost given a blank check," said the accountant. Unintentionally, the senators had given Laos a raise.

The Symington ceiling covered economic and military assistance to Laos for USAID and CIA, but not the costs of American bombing and close air support in northern Laos, which in 1971 were estimated at another $140 million a year. This put the cost of the Laos war at a little over half a billion dollars a year in 1971 dollars—exclusive of the bombing of the Ho Chi Minh Trail, which Symington guessed what in the ballpark of another billion dollars a year. (If that is true, which is conjectural, the total U.S. expenditure for the Laos war was then running about 1.5 billion dollars a year in 1971 dollars, or well over five billion dollars a year in 1994 dollars.)

The Symington ceiling money, the finance officer explained, included funds for the lowland army, the Force Armée Royale, or FAR ("We called them the Fastest Army Running"). It paid for the thirty thousand Laotian irregulars and their support, including fixed-wing and helicopter transportation costs, weapons, artillery, communications, medicine, food, rice, dry rations, and death benefits. It went for about fifteen thousand Thai SGUs. "It went for more troops, more air support, more Air America, and U.S. military shit. Helicopters. Four spider cranes, six Chinook forty-two-man transports. The army attaché in Vientiane decided he needed his own helicopter, which came out of the Symington ceiling, too."

The money went for the ammunition that poured through rapid-fire automatic weapons in defense of fixed positions. "They'd shoot at night even if there's nothing out there," remembered the accountant. "A rabbit runs through concertina wire and they start firing. First thing you know, you've spent ten thousand dollars shooting at a rabbit. Or shooting a frog off the moon. They had another lunar eclipse up there. They used four-deuce illuminating rounds. Four-point-two-inch mortar, the biggest the U.S. has. They shot off a hundred rounds at forty-five dollars each. They stopped when they ran out of ammo, or maybe when they chased the frog off the moon."

The budget paid for Vang Pao's official salary as a major general in the royalist army and for his CIA expense account of about a thousand dollars a month, most of which went for the large dinners he hosted every night. It went to rolls of black cloth Vang Pao handed out to tribal people, and to the flimsy, cheap gold rings he gave to visiting dignitaries and departing case officers.

The CIA budget included an account to cover irregular costs. "We needed to know if assassinations were planned—that kind of thing," the CIA man recalled. "As much as we like to say we run things, there's a lot of people we don't run. You've got to buy 'em off. Make 'em part of the team. Diapers for their little kids. Cigarettes. Transportation to Vientiane." The typical Laotian general, the accountant said, "doesn't need the money. He's stealing plenty of that from his own troops, you know. But what the fuck can he buy in Laos? Occasionally, when they'd get sick, we'd fly a doctor up. That was a real heart-warmer. We even imported some books on antiques out of Paris. The bill was just a couple hundred dollars, but I guess they thought it was a stupendous thing."

The finance man had seen the budget go up from less than $30 million early in the Shackley era to $375 million. "Did we get our money's worth? No," he said flatly. "Because we had outside forces telling us how to spend our money who didn't understand what we were trying to accomplish.

"We *did* have a shortage of funds. Just ran out of money sometimes. We'd sit down and try to determine the average number of combat days in, for example, Savannakhet. Try to establish rates of fire of different weapons. Whatever. Then if the rains were late, and the bad guys didn't back off until it got wet, we'd send messages to headquarters to put ordnance out in the field, or our guys'd be back to rocks and slingshots."

These temporary shortages were of an administrative nature. "I always laugh when people said that Air America or the Agency was selling opium for money. Where did the fucking money go, guys? I don't give a shit if they sold millions of tons of opium up there. You think they're going to give that money to me to buy ammo? I'm sitting in the financial office tearing out my hair, with Landry saying, "Okay, they're going to fight an extra month and we're going to give 'em a bonus.' I'd say, 'With what money?' He'd say, 'That's your goddamn problem.' "

For the most part, the ground troop costs of the Laos war were a bargain, from the American point of view. The lowest-ranking Thai SGUs were paid the equivalent of a hundred dollars a month plus about two dollars a day extra for combat pay. The Laotian SGUs got a base pay of about twenty-five dollars a month, plus bonuses and combat pay. The money for the Thais arrived in Udorn in the form of U.S. Treasury checks, was converted to Thai baht, and then held in accounts in Udorn until the Thais were ready to go on leave. The money to pay the Laotian irregulars came from a large-scale black-market dealer in Vientiane. Every month a truck belonging to the CIA's Vientiane station drove to the dealer, loaded up with five hundred–kip notes worth about a dollar each, and drove the truck back to the office. The station's moneymen made a bundle count and sent a cable to Langley requesting a deposit to the black marketeer's account somewhere, probably Switzerland.

Because soldiers had casually walked off to visit their villages or help harvest crops, and also because of "ghost soldiers," or fictitious names on the rosters, no Laotian SGU unit was up to full strength. The accountant recalled: "The unit finance officers handed the money over to the case officers, who were under pressure to make sure there weren't too many ghost soldiers. The case officers would have to have troop rosters and get the thumbprint of the recipients. Some could sign their names, but most of the dust agitators—the infantrymen—were basically illiterate. Laotian officers made the actual payments. But I'm sure those sonsofbitches figured out a way to get some of it back. We got reports that the Laotian officers were going into the mess halls and getting some of the pay back from their troops. We're talking about the Asian system."

Every once in a while the accountant went out in the field on payday to see American tax dollars at work. It was a humble, small-time scene. "The little guy puts his thumb down, they put some kip out, and off he goes. The Laotians didn't have saving banks or savings plans. They had their families living nearby, that's how they saved. Their families were camp followers. Four poles on the corners and thatched roofs. That's home. They built their houses near streams for water, and in the shade if possible."

And so the great gusher of money apportioned by the U.S. Senate divided into streams and rivulets and finally trickled off into the Laotian bush.

◆

By late April 1971, Long Tieng was safe enough for Vang Pao to bring his wives back. Soon he began planning for his annual rainy season offensive.

He knew that time was running out. In South Vietnam, U.S. troop levels had fallen from 543,000 in 1969 to less than half that, and the numbers were going down steadily. Worse, the U.S. Air Force was planning to cut back on sorties in Laos, owing to combination of budget shortages and the lack of political support in the United States. With characteristic boldness, Vang Pao decided to recapture the Plain of Jars. If the Paris peace talks broke out of deadlock, the plain would be a useful card to hold in negotiations with the communists.

He had not reckoned on the Americans making moves behind his back. On July 15, 1971, two weeks after U.S. Air Force sorties in his part of Laos dropped to a maximum of thirty-two a day, and after several North Vietnamese MiG jet fighters had been spotted in Laotian territory, Vang Pao learned that Henry Kissinger had been to Beijing to meet Jou Enlai, Mao Zedong and the other leaders of mainland China. To Vang Pao, this was a slap in the face. For his sponsor to be holding friendly meetings with one of the main sponsors and suppliers of the North Vietnamese was a betrayal of everything he had been fighting for.

The tribal elders thought so, too. In August 1971, they came to Vang Pao again with another request that he pull the Meo civilians out of the Second Military Region. They said that if the children, wives, and elderly were safe in someplace like Sayaboury, a smaller force of volunteer soldiers would be freer to stay and fight the enemy. Vang Pao went to see Souvanna Phouma again, and the prime minister told him to be patient, to wait; and that is what Vang Pao told his people to do, too.

By then, in the closing months of the rainy season, Vang Pao controlled most but not all of the Plain of Jars. Lacking the massive air superiority of previous years, and knowing from hard experience that the plain could be swept as easily by one side as the other, he set up artillery support bases in the hilltops surrounding the plain. He manned the bases with Thai SGUs, and situated the heaviest weapons in his arsenal, 105 and 155mm howitzers, to both cover the plain and support the other hilltop bases if they came under attack. He put tribal ground troops into blocking positions near the eastern and northern edges of the plain, to be ready for the inevitable North Vietnamese attack. And then he waited for the rains to end.

Through October and November 1971, all was quiet. U.S. Air Force reconnaissance photographs showed new Soviet-made 130mm artillery pieces in a marshaling yard near Hanoi or Haiphong. These weapons, which had tremendously long barrels and were made to be towed behind heavy trucks or tanks, were previously unknown in Southeast Asia. Their shells, 130mm in diameter, were narrower than the U.S.-made 155s but much longer and carried a larger charge. But there was no evidence the North Vietnamese planned to bring them into Laos. The Soviet-made MiG jets were a greater worry. There were always rumors about jets, tanks, and other weapons that the North Vietnamese were going to use.

In mid-December a few skirmishes broke out on the Plain of Jars, but there were no reports of unusual enemy activity. On December 17, smoke from farmers clearing fields in the surrounding mountains obscured the air and many plane flights were called off.

Just after sunset, the enemy opened a totally unexpected and ferociously heavy attack on the Thai hilltop bases with 130mm artillery. The 130s had a range of twenty-eight kilometers, about one-and-a-half times as far as the American-made artillery, which fired back from the hilltops but could not reach them. In Udorn, according to his staffers, Pay Landry monitored the news in the radio room, impatiently slapping his swagger stick against the side of his thigh. From Long Tieng, Vang Pao launched his little propellor-driven T-28s, the only warplanes available, to try to knock the communist big guns out. North Vietnamese antiaircraft guns positioned near the 130s opened up and shot two of the T-28s down—a sixth of Vang Pao's air force.

The North Vietnamese offensive was superbly planned. The 130mm barrage was so heavy and so lethal that the Thai crews hid in their bunkers below ground. Without anybody firing back at them, North Vietnamese infantry units, which surrounded the hilltops, had the 130s suspend their fire and then moved in. Even if Vang Pao had wanted to save the Thais—he had never shown much sign of it—he had no way to resupply them by air, and no way to defend them adequately with tactical air strikes.

The next day, for the first time in the Laos war, a North Vietnamese jet, a MiG-21, shot down an American jet, an F-4 Phantom. Two other Phantoms ran out of fuel and crashed chasing the MiG back toward the North Vietnamese border. On the following day a fourth Phantom was shot down by antiaircraft fire near the border of northern Laos and North Vietnam. All available U.S. jets were diverted to the location to support the search and rescue mission for the pilot, and all unarmed planes were ordered out of the area. In all likelihood, this diversion of U.S. planes was part of the North Vietnamese plan.

With the Americans fixated on the loss of their planes and the Thai artillery bases taking a terrible pounding, a North Vietnamese sapper team penetrated Long Tieng's defenses at night and got onto the valley floor again. The sappers pinned the Ravens down in their quarters with rocket-propelled grenades. The Ravens radioed that Long Tieng was under ground attack, and then shut off the radio and got ready to destroy it to prevent the encryption gear from falling into enemy hands. Soon after, a Lao gunship pilot managed to fly over the airstrip, dropping flares that enabled the Meo troops to see the enemy. At three o'clock in the morning, the attack broke off.

At first light, the Ravens found that two of their planes had been blown up and a third damaged. Meo soldiers had killed two enemy commandos near the parked T-28s. The tribals had cut the heart out of one of the North Vietnamese and were draining gasoline from their planes to cremate the other on the ramp.

Later in the day it was decided to evacuate almost all the Americans and all the sensitive equipment from Long Tieng.

By then the North Vietnamese were swarming up the artillery bases and sweeping across the Plain of Jars. The U.S. Air Force tried to stop them with B-52s. The cloud cover was thick and heavy, and the B-52s had nothing like Commando Club to guide them over their targets. Since the North Vietnamese were always on the move, the bombs did not have much effect, except to crater the plain.

After four days of heaving fighting, the Thai firebases were overrun. The Meo forces that had been meant to block the approaches had scattered, and the North Vietnamese were unopposed.

Civilians streamed into Long Tieng, some of them refugees from the recent fighting and others celebrants for the Meo New Year, which was already in progress. The traditional double lines formed with females dressed in their best tribal finery on one side, and males in olive green fatigues on the other—the lines of females being longer because so many males had died in battle. They threw the balls back and forth, flirting and singing improvised courtship songs, and then in the middle of the celebrations Vang Pao told them the party was over. The women went back to their bamboo huts, changed out of their finery, and trudged southward to greater safety. All the women and children left. The men either vanished with their families into the hills or else took up rifles for the defense of Long Tieng, which suddenly looked more vulnerable than it ever had before.

The valley's population dropped from forty thousand to about five thousand Meo and Thai soldiers. The Meo T-28s flew off for greater safety. Of the hundred or so Americans, almost all left—the paper pushers, the advisers, the mechanics, the men who drove the forklifts in the warehouses, the Air America pilots, even the Raven forward air controllers. The paramilitary officers bunked in Vientiane in what they called the "TV house," which was under perpetual camera surveillance from the nearby Soviet embassy. Only a few flew up to Long Tieng during the day, and then they left for the night again.

Some six thousand North Vietnamese regulars were closing in on Long Tieng in a tightening circle. When the weather cleared, pilots discovered that the North Vietnamese had been reinforcing their bridges and widening the radius of turns in the roads to get their long artillery pieces in. From the terrain and the known range of the gun, the Americans deduced that there were only three or four valleys where the 130s could be hiding. But the big guns were so well camouflaged the pilots couldn't find them.

On the last day of 1971 the few remaining residents of Long Tieng heard a whistling sound few had heard before. The 130 shell took a very long minute to travel its arc and then landed with a boom. Then the next whistling sound commenced and people scrambled to get in the lee of the karst outcroppings for shelter while Air America planes somehow took off and landed as the shells came raining down. The last Raven left, and the only American at the base was Jerry Daniels, the lantern-jawed ex-fire-fighter from Missoula, Montana, the general's personal adviser.

As darkness fell, muzzle flashes from the enemy's 130s highlighted the ridge to the northeast and momentarily illuminated the undersides of the clouds. A shell landed on the warehouse where the bombs for the T-28s were stored, setting off secondary explosions that lasted throughout the night, like a chain of time-delayed firecrackers. Another landed on one of the 105mm howitzers, and others blew up the Raven building and cratered the ramp off the runway.

The next morning Vang Pao began a desperate game of cat and mouse. He began moving his own artillery around faster than the North Vietnamese gunners could adjust their coordinates. He fired his guns, doing what little damage he could with their relatively short range and then hauling them to different spots along the valley before the shells came whistling back in reply.

Vang Pao got a valuable tip from Pat Landry's intelligence analysts in Udorn, who had discovered a telltale flaw in the North Vietnamese tactics. Before an attack, all the North Vietnamese commanders would be called back in turn to review the plan, first the battalion commanders, then the company commanders and on down to the squad leaders. The final sign of an attack would be when the North Vietnamese ordered their medical teams to the front line. It was a very rigid and predictable routine, and after being told of it Vang Pao found that just by re-deploying his men, he could throw off the enemy's timing. He bought himself a week or two by keeping the North Vietnamese off balance and making them go through the planning sequence again and again.

The problem was that even with moving his men and guns around, Long Tieng was still underprotected. Staying in a damp underground bunker for safety, Vang Pao caught a chest cold that turned into pneumonia. He flew to Padong on a recruiting mission, but at the sight of the amputees, widows, and boys who were already toting M-16s, tears streamed down his face. He wept uncontrollably. The CIA threw him on a chopper and flew him to Udorn to the air force hospital and pumped him full of antibiotics, to try to get him well again and give him a pep talk. By the time he got back a week later, the North Vietnamese were dug in on Skyline Ridge, over-looking the valley floor.

In January 1972, lowland reinforcement units arrived from Savan-nakhet. They were some of the best troops in the country, well led by their own officers and advised by ex–Green Berets. When Meo troops made a halfhearted effort at taking Skyline Ridge and then fell back, the Savan-nakhet troops took their place. Bunker by bunker, grenade by grenade, the lowland Lao fought their way along the ridge. When they finished taking the ridge and they were rotated back to the valley floor, a Meo unit fired a 105mm howitzer shell in their direction. One of the lowlanders' American advisers came over to the Meo unit and told its commander very politely that if such a thing ever happened again he was personally going to come over and shoot the colonel between the eyes. Grudgingly, the Meo held their fire.

At the beginning of February, the North Vietnamese started building a road from the edge of the plain to the road connecting Sam Thong and Long Tieng. At this shorter range, the big guns could fire with greater ac-curacy and on a higher trajectory, sending the shells in closer behind the karst that previously offered protection. So the cat-and-mouse game con-tinued, with a new twist: The North Vietnamese fired on Long Tieng with 85mm guns; Vang Pao fired back with his 105s and 155s, and then tried to move them before the 130s zeroed in, and sent up planes, hoping to spot the 130s by the muzzle flashes. The U.S. Air Force sent up planes to hunt the 130s and destroyed a few, but never all.

Then the North Vietnamese sent in tanks, the tribal soldiers' worst night-mare. With their turret hatches closed and no human drivers in sight, the tanks seemed like metal creatures that clanked and crawled along and spat fire from their snouts. North Vietnamese PT-76 tanks, which had not been detected crossing the Plain of Jars, rolled out of Sam Thong, Pop Buell's old base. The tank commanders made the mistake of coming out before dark, and American planes nailed them. Then ten more T-34 tanks rum-bled toward Long Tieng at night and three of them made it to Skyline Ridge overlooking the valley. The lead tank hit a land mine, and the other two fired their guns and then withdrew.

Soon after the tank scare, on February 21, 1972, Vang Pao learned that President Richard Nixon had made his own trip to Beijing. From the Meo commander's perspective, the leader of his sponsor country had paid a friendly visit to the sponsor of his enemies. At that moment, Vang Pao said later, he knew he was going to lose the war.

He started fighting with greater desperation. In late February, during a lull in the 130 barrage, he brought his T-28s back from Vientiane. When the chief Raven went over to his house to report that planes were ready and the crews about to load bombs by hand—the regular bomb-loading equip-ment had all been destroyed—Vang Pao ran upstairs and came down with a set of Allen wrenches he had bought himself. He went out to help the loading crews, using his wrenches to tighten the fins, which had to be manually attached to the bombs. He was a bundle of manic energy, compulsively involved in every phase of combat.

A few days later, when the 130 shelling resumed, the T-28s flew back to Vientiane for safety. The North Vietnamese closed in on the valley again and took Skyline Ridge in foggy, cloudy weather that hampered air strikes. About a thousand of the lowland Lao troops mutinied, commandeering trucks at gunpoint to take them to Ban Xon, the USAID base. They didn't want to fight for the Meo anymore, and the Americans flew them back to their home base in Savannakhet. The B-52s came back, and Pat Landry in Udorn dug deep into his pockets and came up with more Thai SGUs as reinforcements. This time it was the Thais who took back Skyline Ridge, bunker by bunker.

It took until the beginning of May 1972 to clear all the North Vietnamese from Skyline Ridge, and even then there were enemy left in the vicinity of Long Tieng. Rashly, against all advice, Vang Pao decided to take the southern and western fringes of the Plain of Jars again. He helicoptered troops onto the edge of the plain, where they got hit hard and had to pull back into the hills nearby. Now his force was split, with some of his men tied up in the woods miles away from Long Tieng and the rest trying to defend the base from the North Vietnamese.

The CIA and the air force did everything they could to help him. The B-52s made new craters on top of the old craters on the plain. The jet fighters and the T-28s came in; and a brilliantly faked transport of additional ground reinforcements planned by Landry's staff—a so-called cover and deception mission—threw off the enemy's plans and bought more time.

Then in South Vietnam, the North Vietnamese Army mounted their so-called Easter offensive. Most of the American ground troops had already left South Vietnam, and the U.S. airplanes that had been helping Vang Pao flew off to help the South Vietnamese. Luckily for Vang Pao, the rains came early, turning the hard clay to sticky, slippery muck. The new North Vietnamese–built road washed away.

Throughout May enemy troops marched up and down near Long Tieng and their radio traffic levels remained constant. An intelligence report claimed that one of the North Vietnamese divisions had pulled back, marching toward the main battlefield in South Vietnam, but Vang Pao didn't believe it. Two weeks later, after the bulk of the enemy forces had gone, he finally realized it was true, and that the North Vietnamese had pulled a cover and deception ploy of their own.

He was exhausted.

It had been the biggest battle of his life.

He had held Long Tieng against two front-line divisions of North Vietnamese. He beat them back for his own sake, but in engaging them so tenaciously he had kept those enemy divisions from contributing much to the Easter offensive in South Vietnam. Since the South Vietnamese and U.S. Air Force won that offensive by a narrow margin, it was possible, if unprovable, that Vang Pao made a difference in the survival of the South Vietnamese government.

But if he had won his greatest battle, and if he had done everything his American sponsors dreamed he could do and more, he also had lost. The CIA and the U.S. Air Force pulled most of their men and equipment out of Long Tieng. The Americans never came back in large numbers. Some of his own tribespeople did, and the base partly refilled, but it never regained its old bustle and importance. Empty bamboo and scrap-metal shacks spread far up the hillsides—a half-abandoned squatter settlement.

The tribal elders came up with more proposals to move the elderly and the children to Sayaboury, but Vang Pao bushed them aside. He wanted to see what the American leaders had to say.

In June 1972, in secret, without even telling his staff, Vang Pao flew to the U.S. and met with Pop Buell. They went to Washington, D.C., to talk with politicians, and across the river to the Pentagon and the Langley headquarters of the CIA. Though no public records of those conversations exist, it was obvious to both men that the U.S. government was committed to pulling out of Southeast Asia. In Thailand there was a temporary airpower buildup, and for the first time U.S. manpower there was higher than in South Vietnam. But the troop reductions in South Vietnam had continued; and the Paris peace talks went on.

Vang Pao and Buell flew to Missoula, Montana, which was Jerry Daniels's hometown. Daniels had arranged for three of Vang Pao's younger sons to attend school in Missoula, a small city set in broad, gentle mountains vaguely reminiscent of the Plain of Jars.

Pop Buell wrote: "My time in Missula was real fine. The house was about 10 miles out at about 3,500 ft., real pretty. They liked it but a little too cold for the Meo. I hope it got warmer. The day we rode out in the country down into Idaho was sure beiutiful, much much timber and at the top snow. I really thought they all including V.P. would go nuts when they saw and touched the snow."

The Meo had never seen snow before.

◆

Given what happened later, it is reasonable to ask whether Vang Pao sold out his people then and there, on his first trip to Missoula in 1972, or whether he waited until later.

It is not an easy question to answer, and it may be that the question itself is framed wrongly—that Vang Pao was caught in a complex situation from which he had no alternative except to escape.

The Meo had an old tradition of running away from lost battles. Vang Pao had run away from plenty, though nobody who knew him well ever accused him of cowardice.

He knew if the enemy took over Laos, they would kill him. He had six wives and twenty-five children to think of, and his own life, too.

By the standards of Laotian generals, he was a relatively honest man. He is not known to have opened Swiss bank accounts or purchased villas in France, or even in the United States. The house that Pop Buell referred to, outside Missoula, was rented for their visit, and was not purchased by the general or anyone in his family.

More to the point, Vang Pao did not give up on the Sayaboury option when he came back to Laos. He made exploratory trips to Thailand, asking and probing for resettlement opportunities for his people. He didn't tell anyone that he had made up his mind to go to Montana. In all likelihood he hadn't, yet. He was the kind of man who kept his options open until the last minute.

But a few Americans who had known Vang Pao for a very long time and understood him without idealizing him sensed the change in Vang Pao's outlook when he came back from Montana. Nothing specific was said, and nothing needed to be said. They assumed Vang Pao had arranged for his own private exit from the Laos war, and that if need be he would abandon his people. And they couldn't see why he shouldn't.

After all, the U.S. government was preparing to abandon them, too.

# Peace Was at Hand

Beyond the reach of senators and wiretaps, in the privacy of his own mind, Bill Sullivan, the deputy assistant secretary of state for East Asian and Pacific affairs, was a heretic.

At first, when he had returned to Washington, he had thought that getting out of Vietnam was a matter of cutting losses and choosing the least bad solution. That was what his "no commitment" statement to the senators meant. But around late 1971 or early 1972 he began to believe that losing the Vietnam War would be healthier for the U.S. than winning it. That losing was in the national interest. That it was a plus. And that Laos, as an afterthought, would have to be discarded along the way.

It was a radical notion at the time, that by losing the war and by abandoning our Southeast Asian allies to their fate we would be doing the right thing. It was so novel an idea for a highly placed government servant that it was unsafe to utter aloud, lest it seem too cynical and Machiavellian or even treasonous.

And yet Sullivan was not entirely wrong, from a geopolitical point of view, and perhaps he was even prescient.

He had always kept an eye on the big chess game, the struggle between the superpowers. The North Vietnamese couldn't destroy America in half an hour, flatten the cities, kill half the population, but the Soviets could, with their nuclear missiles. Communist China was not a global threat on the order of the Soviets—China didn't have many nukes—but it threatened the rest of Asia with its hard-line ideology and its huge population.

Because of this, Sullivan and his peers believed that their highest calling was to change the balance of power between the U.S. and the USSR and to a lesser extent China. Ever since the communist takeover in China in 1949 the U.S. had been at a disadvantage, particularly in mainland Asia. There the contest was, at its starkest, two against one—two communist giants at home on the Asian landmass versus one noncommunist giant operating far from its own shores. Vietnam was a subset of that Cold War dilemma. Laos was a minor subset of Vietnam, and nothing more. To "solve" Vietnam, and Laos along with it, would be easier if there were realignments on that higher, geopolitical plane.

The first crack in the solidarity between China and the USSR, the so-called Sino-Soviet rift, appeared back in 1950 when the Chinese canceled a treaty of friendship and cooperation with the Soviets. Beneath their shared Marxist-Leninist ideology lay centuries-old mutual mistrust. But the two communist regimes papered over their differences, first with one set of ten-year agreements and then with another.

Sullivan believed that the failure of a Chinese-sponsored communist movement in Indonesia in 1965 started a deep-seated process moving. In reaction to the Chinese-financed threat, a combination of civilian mobs and the Indonesian military slaughtered about 300,000 Indonesians, the innocent along with the guilty. Though the Americans had little or nothing to do with the Indonesian bloodbath, Sullivan surmised that from Beijing's point of view the U.S., by taking a stand against the communists in Vietnam, had given the Indonesians the confidence to make a stand of their own.

Certainly in Vietnam the U.S. government was no paper tiger. It had sent a half-million troops to South Vietnam, and the U.S. military was fighting hard and taking casualties. It was bombing North Vietnam and Laos heavily. The very scale of American investment required at least grudging respect from the Chinese, who had a practical as well as a fanatical side. The Chinese respected force.

As long as the Americans were fighting in Vietnam, Sullivan and others believed, the cracks between the Chinese and Soviets could not widen to a break. And yet even their joint support for North Vietnam had limits. China did not allow Soviet planes carrying military supplies for Hanoi to fly into Chinese airspace, fearing Soviet spies. The Soviets had to ship supplies to North Vietnam by sea or rail instead. Politically, the Soviets were closer to the North Vietnamese than the Chinese were, for beneath the recent Chinese–North Vietnamese solidarity lay a record of wars and subjugation dating back a thousand years.

Toward the end of the 1960s, events in distant parts of the world drove China and the Soviet Union further apart. In 1968, when the Soviets invaded Czechoslovakia, Leonid Brezhnev warned that the USSR could intervene in the affairs of any Marxist-Leninist country. The Chinese regime took this as a threat. In March 1969, and in the following months, Chinese and Soviet border forces clashed. Then in 1970, another set of agreements between the communist powers expired.

Because the outcome of the Vietnam War was not yet decided, a Chinese-U.S. accord was premature. Nixon, Kissinger, and others in Washington were re-examining U.S. government assumptions about Vietnam, and it was unclear to them whether Vietnam was salvageable, whether there would be a payoff for the blood, effort, and money already invested. Nixon's decision to Vietnamize the war meant withdrawing American troops while at the same time escalating the air war and matériel support and going after communist sanctuaries as never before, in the hope that a strengthened South Vietnam would be able to defeat or at least hold its own against a weakened North Vietnam. The 1970 invasion of Cambodia by U.S. and South Vietnamese troops was part of that strategy.

After Cambodia, the largest remaining sanctuary for communist forces was the Ho Chi Minh Trail of southern Laos. Roughly forty-five thousand North Vietnamese soldiers and civilians ran what amounted to a heavily defended dirt freeway system there. To Sullivan, the failure of the South Vietnamese invasion of southern Laos, particularly at its end, when the South Vietnamese soldiers fled, had paradoxical benefits. It proved to those who had been unwilling to perceive it before that Vietnamization was based on a faulty premise. Even with massive U.S. air and matériel support, South Vietnamese soldiers had been beaten badly. Without even more assistance, they had no chance of beating the North Vietnamese in the main war. Since the U.S. government was already phasing out its own forces in Vietnam and re-escalation was politically unfeasible, it then became easier for the policymakers to conclude that South Vietnam was a hopeless cause and that trying to save it was just throwing good money after bad.

Around that time subtle feelers began to reach Washington from the mainland Chinese via third parties, mainly Pakistan. Were the Americans interested in talking? The messages went to Nixon and his national security adviser, Henry Kissinger. Kissinger didn't tell the Foggy Bottom professional diplomats, not trusting the State Department with anything so important. But Sullivan had sensitive antennae, and he had many of the same instincts as Kissinger. He was predisposed to reach the same conclusion, that it might be worthwhile to sacrifice South Vietnam. Rather than squander more American lives and billions of dollars trying to prop up South Vietnam, with little chance of succeeding, why not accede to its failure in exchange for an opening to China, in order to weaken the real enemy, the USSR?

"So I came to the conclusion, and this may sound thoroughly cynical to you," recalled Sullivan in his plummy cultured voice, "that we would be better off not to win this war. Particularly because the Chinese had made a breakthrough to us, and it was far more important to get the Chinese broken off from the Soviets and leaning to one side in our favor than for us to win in Vietnam."

◆

The breakthrough—in the Cold War, in the Vietnam War, in the Laos war, in Sullivan's own career—had come when Nixon announced that Kissinger had just visited China secretly and that he himself would make a presidential visit to China before long.

The chance to develop and build on the China contacts meant that it was more important than ever to get Vietnam out of the way. Settlements on Laos and Cambodia would be mere footnotes to a Vietnam agreement. Though the formal U.S.–North Vietnamese peace talks in Paris were as deadlocked as ever, President Nixon had put Kissinger in charge of a secret and parallel track of peace negotiations. Kissinger needed an assistant who was discreet, good on details, and experienced at negotiating—someone to help him lose the Vietnam War ably and gracefully. Nobody was better qualified than Bill Sullivan, a veteran negotiator who knew Vietnam, and who was almost desperately eager to get out of Foggy Bottom and revive his career. The wiretaps on Sullivan had proved that he could be trusted to keep his mouth shut, and in late 1972 Sullivan joined Kissinger for the final, hectic rounds of peace negotiations.

Kissinger and Sullivan left for Paris together at night in a small, inconspicuous, government-owned passenger jet. The cabin had two Pullman-like bunks with curtains. Kissinger slept in one bunk and Sullivan across the aisle in the other while Kissinger's younger aides from the National Security Council stretched out on the reclining seats. They landed at a French military base in the middle of the night and taxied to the end of the runway, where they transferred to another small jet loaned by the French president, Georges Pompidou, which flew them to an airfield near Paris. Their original plane, in the meantime, flew on to West Germany, to throw reporters off the scent. Journalists discovered the site of the secret meetings anyway, in the Paris suburb of Gif-Sur-Yvette.

Because of Kissinger's mania for avoiding leaks, the American delegation was small and overworked. Sullivan and the others spent days and nights drafting negotiating positions, writing long cables to Washington, briefing the South Vietnamese and other allies, flying off to Washington and Saigon and coming back to Paris again, rewriting the drafts, and sitting down to haggle with the North Vietnamese.

Throughout this period Sullivan played the hard-working, self-effacing loyal supporter to Kissinger. The perfect second fiddle. Photographs of the time captured the relationship between the two men with uncanny accuracy. On the day *The New York Times* headline screamed "KISSINGER ASSERTS THAT 'PEACE IS AT HAND'; SAIGON SAYS IT WILL AGREE TO A CEASEFIRE," the photo beneath shows Kissinger at the microphones, gesticulating with his hand to make a point. Partially obscured by his raised index finger, in fuzzy focus in the background, stands the former ambassador to Laos. The next day, when Souvanna Phouma visited Washington to find out what peace had in store for Laos, the prince, Nixon, and Kissinger appeared in another news photo—along with the back of Sullivan's head. In yet a third news photo from Paris with the North Vietnamese negotiator, Le Duc Tho, half of Sullivan's face was cropped by the picture editor, being judged of insufficient interest to the newspaper readers back home.

The pictures told the truth. Sullivan was always the gray-haired man in the background whose face was obscured by the principals. Perhaps this was inevitable for any man working for the thin-skinned, insecure Kissinger, who didn't want his assistants gaining stature of their own. And perhaps it was in character for Sullivan, who had also been the number two to Harriman at the Geneva negotiations in 1961–62. But it was also true for almost everyone associated with the Laos war. They may have been important while they were there, but the kingdom exuded a sort of mist of obscurity that cloaked its players as soon as they left, and relegated them to anonymity when they re-entered the outside world.

For all that, Kissinger appreciated Sullivan's labors. Sullivan was a demon for minute details in the draft agreements—the fine points of future South Vietnamese elections, for example—that nobody else on the negotiating team really wanted to become an expert in. Sullivan also fully understood the geopolitical issues and the long-term objectives. Where he and Kissinger were weakest was in actually getting Hanoi and their own Asian allies to cooperate. Sullivan had worked in Asia, but he was like many Americans who live in the Orient for years without learning to speak the local language, and who never get to the wellsprings of the local culture. Kissinger had never worked in Asia and had no "feel" at all for the people they were negotiating with.

The tentative agreement announced near the end of October 1972 called for a nine-point plan to be signed by Washington and Hanoi. There was to be a cease-fire in place, withdrawal of American forces within sixty days, a total prohibition on new troops, repatriation of prisoners, supervised elections, and so on. There were no provisions for peace in either Laos or

Cambodia, but it was hoped that those agreements could be worked out and put in place soon. Saigon's participation was also unsure because the Americans hadn't bothered to tell the South Vietnamese what they were supposed to be agreeing to do.

Within days everything fell apart. The South Vietnamese refused to sign an agreement legitimizing the presence of North Vietnamese troops on their soil. The North Vietnamese stalled on the few issues still in dispute, hoping to obtain better terms after the U.S. elections in early November. After the election they stalled some more. Nixon was re-elected president, defeating an antiwar Democrat, Senator George McGovern, but the Watergate affair was a growing black cloud on Nixon's horizon, and the incoming Congress was more war-weary than the Congress before. The number of U.S. troops in South Vietnam kept decreasing toward the zero mark. The North Vietnamese knew that the longer they waited, the better terms they could obtain. The South Vietnamese were furious at Kissinger for being kept out of negotiations on their own future.

By December 1972, Nixon warned that he would bomb North Vietnam unless the negotiations resumed. (His real audience was the South Vietnamese government in Saigon, which was still feeling jilted.) The North Vietnamese were unimpressed. For a couple of hours in a cold December drizzle, Sullivan and Kissinger walked around and around the garden outside the house in Gif-Sur-Yvette, talking through the implications of renewed bombing. Then they flew back to Washington separately. Sullivan landed just as the B-52s were arriving over Hanoi.

The Christmas bombings, as they were called by the press, ran for twelve days, except for Christmas Day. With nearly three thousand plane sorties over North Vietnam—there were none over Laos—it was the most concentrated aerial campaign of the war. In the United States, the Linebacker II campaign, as it was known in the military, aroused anger and outrage in the antiwar camp, gloom in the war-weary population at large, and elation in the Pentagon.

Among the bombing's most ardent supporters was Colonel Richard Secord, head of the Southeast Asia branch in the Office of the Assistant Secretary of Defense for International Security Affairs, a key position in the intragovernmental politics of the Vietnam War. He and others in the branch had helped choose the targets for the Christmas bombings on Nixon's behalf, as part of an end run around the chiefs of staff.

Secord represented the Pentagon on an ad hoc interagency committee reacting to the Paris peace negotiations. Bill Sullivan chaired some of those meetings, and the two men found themselves on opposite sides once again.

They had always disagreed. They had started with different underlying assumptions about the war, and it always led them to different conclusions. When Secord analyzed Lam Son 719, the invasion of southern Laos, for example, he thought it proved what he had been suggesting all along. Just think what could have happened, Secord maintained, if the U.S. had used adequate numbers of battle-hardened American troops instead of poorly trained South Vietnamese troops, and had backed them with the right artillery and air support, particularly gunships. It would have shut down the Trail and reduced the war in South Vietnam to a lower-level conflict.

Sullivan and Secord had always disagreed on bombing and that wouldn't change now, either. Nixon had given blanket permission to bomb the shipyards and docks, power plants, railroad yards, and other targets that lay in a populous corridor between Hanoi and the port of Haiphong. It was the kind of bare-knuckle warfare Secord had advocated for years. "During the Christmas bombing," Secord said later, "I think it was fairly demonstrated what we could do had we decided on a strategy of bombing them back to the Stone Age. Because by the end of that short campaign there was no opposition. Our aircraft were roaming up there like hungry sharks looking for something to bite. There was a great shortage of targets. They were screaming bloody murder. They couldn't get back to the table in Paris fast enough. We had 'em on their knees."

From Secord's point of view, it was the first time that bombing had actually lived up to its potential, and he didn't want it to be the last. He believed to the depths of his warrior's soul that it should have been the beginning of a new phase of the Vietnam War. But William Sullivan disagreed, and Sullivan spoke for Kissinger. It was time for the Vietnam War to end.

◆

Sullivan went back to Paris, and there, on January 27, 1973, the United States, North Vietnam, South Vietnam, and the Provisional Revolutionary Government, or Viet Cong, signed the cease-fire accord at a large circular table in an ornate room hung with crystal chandeliers.

To force an agreement on Laos was in the nature of a follow-up chore. Sullivan and Kissinger's deputy, Gen. Alexander Haig, flew to Vientiane, but found Souvanna Phouma unwilling to sign his name on the dotted line.

Over the years the prince had allowed himself to be co-opted away from neutralism and over to the American side. Now that he had been put in a precarious position with the communists, he didn't want to be sacrificed like a pawn in the Americans' chess game.

In this meeting, according to an account leaked to the press, Souvanna Phouma asked what the guarantees were that the North Vietnamese would withdraw their troops from Laos. The Americans, he pointed out, had nothing specific and concrete in writing.

Sullivan and Haig answered that it was certain the North Vietnamese would withdraw because they had given their word. However, since the North Vietnamese had never acknowledged having troops in Laos, they were not in a position to announce their troops' withdrawal. Instead, they had simply agreed that all foreign forces would leave Laos.

Then why not have international supervision to make sure they do leave? Souvanna Phouma asked.

Sullivan and Haig replied that that was unnecessary. North Vietnam was exhausted by war, especially after the pounding given them in the Christmas bombing. Peace was their only option.

The Laotian prime minister countered that Gen. William Westmoreland, the former U.S. commander in South Vietnam, used to tell him the same thing all the time. The Americans had been talking about Hanoi's exhaustion for years.

Haig and Sullivan said pointedly that American air support of Laotian troops would not last much longer, a few weeks more at the most. Without air support, royalist troops could not survive.

Souvanna Phouma said he understood that, but he had deep misgivings. The North Vietnamese had never abided by the terms of any treaty before.

Sullivan and Haig had no response to that observation, and Souvanna Phouma put off agreeing to the U.S. proposals for a little while longer, as the sand ran out of the Laotian hourglass.

◆

Ever since he had been kicked out of Laos, Tony Poe had been living near Phitsanulok, in northern Thailand. In Pits camp, as the base outside Phitsanulok was nicknamed, he was the head of a training program for Laotian SGUs. He had landed the job for old times' sake and because his boss, Pat Landry, had never gotten around to firing him. The embassy in Vientiane, however, had barred him from going back to Laos without special permission.

In Pits camp, Poe had gotten into the habit of calling Landry on the radio when he was drunk, which was most of the time. Sometimes he talked in the open, without using code words, and one of Landry's assistants would take the call, tell Poe to hold on, and then put the receiver down and wait for Tony to forget all about it and go back to sleep.

Poe's radio call to Udorn, on about February 4, 1973, was an emergency. While Souvanna Phouma dickered with the Americans about cease-fires, the North Vietnamese and Pathet Lao were trying to capture as much territory as possible, including Poe's old headquarters, Nam Yu. The attackers were a small force, numbering only about a company, but they took the base without opposition. "Two thousand fucking troops in Nam Yu, and they all ran away," Poe said later. "What kind of bullshit is that? Christ, we had the troops. We could've outflanked 'em. We could've caught 'em at the ridgeline. I had mortars. I had fucking recoilless up on the hills."

This time Poe got through to Landry. Poe remembered Landry telling him. " 'You get the fuck off the radio right now. You don't listen to it.' "

" 'You fat sunofabitch,' " Poe said he told Landry. " 'Change the fuckin' dial down ten.' "

They changed the frequencies and got on another radio channel where fewer people would be listening in. Poe said, "Goddammit, I want you to honor me for all the years we've been together. Let me get up there."

Landry said, "Goddammit, if you go up there that fucking Ouane'd have your ass."

"I'm not afraid of Ouane," Poe said of the drug-dealing Lao commander in chief. "I'll fly right in."

"They're all gone. Nobody's there."

"I'll get somebody. I'll get somebody," Poe pleaded. "I'll go down to Houei Sai 'n' pick 'em up and walk in."

"Forget it, Tony," Landry said, and signed off.

Landry had an easier way of dealing with Nam Yu than sending in a drunken, broken-down paramilitary officer. In his corner office in the Taj Mahal he told a briefing officer to find aerial photographs of Nam Yu in the files and bring them across the runway to the 7/13th Air Force so the pilots would know what to hit.

An hour later the jets took off from the runway at Udorn and bombed Nam Yu, destroying it.

Tony Poe's long war was over.

◆

In Vientiane, where he lived in semiretirement, Pop Buell grumpily noted that Nam Yu had fallen, and that a camp outside Ban Xon—Sam Thong's successor base— had been attacked the night before. "Long Tieng gets mortared regular," he wrote. "They are talking about a cease fire here at any time. If they don't hurry, there will be no need."

Buell had a part-time job as a general-purpose troubleshooter for the U.S. embassy. Once in a while he went upcountry to try to talk tribal chiefs into growing crops other than opium. ("It's all a bunch of S. I sure as hell wish we would clean up our own problems in the U.S. before preaching to these people. Right.") He accompanied wives of POWs and MIAs on fruitless information-gathering tours. He felt sorry for the wives, but as far as he could tell most downed airmen died or were killed when their planes crashed, and most of those who survived were taken to North Vietnam to be prisoners there.

In his free time, which was plentiful, Buell was a regular patron at a bar called the Purple Porpoise, near the Mekong riverfront. His pilot friends hung out there too, drinking and playing a dice game called cameroons. Buell had been in Laos since the beginning of the war and he was respected for his longevity, though some younger people made fun of him behind his back. After a few drinks in the Purple Porpoise, Buell would start sounding off in his gravelly baritone against the goddamn communists, the goddamn long-haired hippies, and the goddamn bureaucrats in Washington who didn't understand anything about anything, especially that Henry Kissinger.

"God this thing of the buracrats drives me to drink," Buell wrote his family. "I am tired and fed up. If it wasn't for the money and insurance I would quit tomorrow. I am so fed up with the whole U.S. policy here now that it is hard to take."

◆

On February 9, 1973, with Souvanna Phouma still holding out against a settlement, Henry Kissinger arrived in Vientiane. It was less than two weeks after the signing of the Paris accords, and he was hoping to wrap up the Laos negotiations in a quick stopover before going on to Hanoi.

Kissinger soon found that the North Vietnamese had broken the promises made in Paris. The North Vietnamese Army had just introduced a new division into southern Laos. Like Sullivan and Haig, however, Kissinger was prepared to overlook anything that would keep him from reaching his objectives. He urged Souvanna Phouma to sign an agreement with the communists, even though Hanoi was violating its Paris obligations. In his memoirs Kissinger merely notes with understatement that Souvanna Phouma's attitude toward the peace process was one of "hope overshadowed by foreboding."

The next day Kissinger and his entourage flew off to the North Vietnamese capital. There they found their adversaries reneging even further on the earlier promises. North Vietnamese troops wouldn't withdraw from Laos and Cambodia after a *cease-fire*. Instead, they would withdraw only after a cease-fire led to a *new government being put in place*—meaning that even though the Americans were pulling out, the North Vietnamese were staying to help install the kind of government they wanted, new army divisions and all.

Kissinger claims he did what he could. ("Needless to say, my response to Pham Van Don was sharp.") But he was impotent without military power to back him up. The U.S. government was down to about twenty-seven thousand troops in South Vietnam, and with the Paris accords signed American warplanes had stopped bombing North Vietnam. All Kissinger wanted was American prisoners of war returned. He could do nothing for Laos itself and the North Vietnamese knew it.

It was hard for the American delegation to admit how badly they had been taken, either in the Paris negotiations or in the long-term course of the war. The Laos war went back even further than the Vietnam War, to 1960; and here they were in Vietnam's aftermath, still trying to find a way out of Laos.

To save the Americans' face, Hanoi agreed that Laos should return to the neutrality of the Geneva accords. That was what Sullivan had always been pushing for. But there was a catch: The U.S. would actually be pulling out its forces, and North Vietnam would only be pretending to—just as it had back in 1962.

Sullivan would claim later that it had all been for something, that the loses in Indochina helped bring about an eventual victory in the Cold War. But at the time, in Hanoi, it was hard to see what had been accomplished since the earlier and equally flawed Geneva agreement, which Sullivan had also helped negotiate. After more than a dozen years of aiding the royalists and the hilltribes in the obscure little kingdom, and conducting a massive secret air campaign, the U.S. was throwing in the towel.

On February 21, 1973, the Vientiane government and the Pathet Lao signed an Agreement of the Restoration of Peace and Reconciliation in Laos. With a last nod to Wonderland, neither the Americans nor the North Vietnamese signed the new agreement. To sign it would have meant admitting publicly that they had been fighting there. As it was, the B-52s bombed in Laos until nearly the last minute and then returned to their bases. Half an hour after the cease-fire began, the North Vietnamese captured the town of Paksong on the Bolovens Plateau and kept on advancing.

The communists controlled most of Laos, except a narrow strip along the Mekong River, the Long Tieng valley, and a few other small enclaves.

# The Second Withdrawal

When Bill Lair left Asia, he went to the Army War College in Carlisle Barracks, Pennsylvania, for a year's course of study. He wanted to change careers within the CIA, and the service colleges were an accepted way of broadening professional horizons.

When his course was over he was summoned to CIA headquarters. Any idea he had of starting over, of working in Africa, say, or Latin America or the Iron Curtain countries, ended promptly. He was made deputy branch chief for Southeast Asia, a turf division that included Laos and Thailand but not Vietnam.

In his new job, Lair put his initials on routine paperwork. He sat in on meetings in poorly ventilated conference rooms. He had plenty of time for coffee breaks and lunch. He was given little authority by his boss, the branch chief, who didn't have that much himself. He was just one of fifteen thousand employees, most of them engaged in noncovert activities, who flashed ID badges as they drove in the gates, then flashed the badges again at the bored guards in the high marble entrance foyer. Inscribed in the marble foyer was the famous phrase from the New Testament's Gospel of John: "And Ye Shall Know the Truth and the Truth Shall Make You Free."

It became clear to Lair that whatever truth headquarters was seeking did not originate in the field. CIA headquarters responded to the White House, and to a lesser extent Congress, which provided its funding and had to be given just enough information to keep the programs funded. But for the most part, it was a bureaucracy whose main purpose was to per-petuate itself. The people in the field who thought otherwise might as well have been pounding their fists on a bulletproof plate-glass window for all the impact they made. Lair had been on the outside for years and nobody had heard him. Now he was on the inside, along with a generation of other case officers who shared his disillusionment.

They were a brotherhood of Cold War idealists, these men who had joined the CIA in the 1950s for the excitement and in the belief that they were helping create a better world. Many of them were Ivy League gradu-ates who considered themselves liberals. On their first assignments they'd learned a local language, or had come to know and deeply care about the country to which they were posted. They'd taken risks, been creative. Then they came back to headquarters; and when they went out again on their next posting they didn't invest as much, for by then they had realized they weren't going to change the world after all. Gradually, as they recycled through headquarters, they became part of the furniture, serving out their years until they could retire and collect pensions. Bill Lair was just one of them, a time-server and nothing more.

When he was offered a job at the Bangkok CIA station he grabbed the chance. He knew by then that he would never make station chief and that he would always be pegged as a Thai or Thai-Lao hand in the outfit. But if he had been defeated in running his own war, and if he had not realized his ambitions to start over again somewhere else, at least he could be com-fortable in the low-lying city along the Chao Phraya River, where rice barges chugged past Buddhist temples and monks made their morning rounds barefoot in the exhaust of automobile fumes. His wife's family was from Bangkok and that clinched it. He bought a Mercedes diesel sedan as a balm for his pride, and because he knew it made the right impression on the sta-tus-conscious Thais.

His new job was assistant station chief for special operations, which meant that he did odd jobs for his boss. When the exiled king of Albania came through Bangkok on an arms-buying trip, Lair was the one who worked very quietly with the Thai police to seize the weapons, and to cour-teously show the Albanian king the door.

Mostly, however, he collected information on the narcotics trade. Like a great number of other government employees who have seen the drug law-enforcement system from the inside, Lair concluded that the system would never stop the drug trade and instead helped perpetuate it by rais-ing prices and thus profits for those who were willing to take the risks. Nev-ertheless, if his boss wanted information on the opium or heroin trades in Thailand, Bill Lair would try to get it, because getting information from Thais was something he knew how to do better than anybody else.

From privates to generals, from clerks to cabinet ministers, Thais in the military, police, and other parts of the government were working both sides of the drug trade, enforcing laws at the same time that they ran dope deals themselves. Until Lair's arrival, the CIA station had tried gathering information by recruiting and training local agents and planting them in place. It was a time-consuming and expensive process and didn't work very well, besides irritating the Thais. Now, if the station wanted information on a particular individual, Lair drove over to the man's office in his Mercedes and simply asked. He almost always got truthful answers. What made it possible was that he had trained many of these colonels and generals back when they were lieutenants, and if he hadn't trained them himself he knew their families or their classmates, and they had heard of him or knew his wife's family or knew he was a favorite of the Thai king. They also opened up to him because they knew they wouldn't be punished. Unlike the war against the communists, the drug war was mostly rhetorical. They told Lair what they were doing, Lair told the chief of station, and everybody went about his business.

He kept tabs on poppy crops and mule trains, chemical shipments and heroin refineries. On the Kuomintang remnants and on the Shan and Karen rebels and on a fellow named Chan Si-foo, also known as Khun Sa, who was emerging as the biggest heroin warlord in the world. But it was all Burmese-grown stuff, even if a lot of it came out through the so-called Golden Triangle of Burma, Laos, and Thailand, and then through the Thai pipelines. Hardly any of his reports dealt with drugs that originated in Laos, which was a job for the Vientiane station.

It was an easy job for Lair, and by drinking more than was good for him he could go for days or even weeks without admitting to himself that he didn't believe in what he was doing.

◆

With an intensity that alarmed even his closest friends, Fred Branfman had devoted every waking hour since returning to the States to the antiwar movement. He started his own organization, Project Air War. He wrote dozens of articles and was the source of information for dozens more. He made the antiwarrior's obligatory pilgrimage to North Vietnam with Tom Hayden, a founder of Students for a Democratic Society and one of the defendants at the Chicago Seven trial. Branfman married within the movement, to the sister of a South Vietnamese student activist. He edited a book of refugee accounts from the Plain of Jars, making use of drawings of the bombing collected by his friend Ngeun.

So when the Paris peace accords and the agreement between the Laotian factions were signed, and the bombing ended in Laos and Vietnam, and most people thought his job was over, Branfman disagreed. The U.S. bombing of Cambodia was still going on, and he didn't feel that he had fulfilled his promise to himself to understand why the bombing had occurred in the first place.

He flew to Bangkok, where he was oblivious to the nearby existence of Bill Lair, a man whose identity was unknown to the press and to the antiwar movement. On the bombing, however, Branfman quickly learned that the 7th Air Force had moved its headquarters out of South Vietnam to Nakhorn Phanom air base in northeastern Thailand. Its command and control apparatus, the equivalent of a war room, known as Blue Chip, controlled the remaining air sorties in the Indochina war—a couple of punitive air strikes in Laos in retaliation for communist violations of the cease-fire, but for the most part, the ongoing U.S. bombing of the communist Khmer Rouge guerillas in Cambodia.

From Bangkok, Branfman went to Phnom Penh, the capital of Cambodia, where the rightist regime held out against the encircling Khmer Rouge. Borrowing a radio from a civilian pilot he had known from his Laos days, Branfman tape-recorded the radio conversations U.S. military pilots were having on their Cambodian bombing missions. The recordings showed that, contrary to U.S. government assertions, the pilots weren't checking to make sure that civilians weren't in the way before dropping their ordnance. Branfman gave the tape recordings to Sydney Schanberg of *The New York Times,* whose front-page story appeared the morning that the Senate met to vote on prohibiting further bombing in Cambodia. The Senate motion passed by one vote, and it cheered Branfman to think that the information he had uncovered might have made a difference. But Phnom Penh was getting to be a frightening place. The government security apparatus was starting to arrest people he knew; and the murderous Khmer Rouge communist guerillas were closing their vise grip on the city. Branfman went back to Bangkok and up to Nakhorn Phanom, on the Thai bank of the Mekong, within sight of some dramatic karst ridges on the Laos side.

Until the war Nakhorn Phanom had been a sleepy town with a few thousand people and some shops around a central square. Now with the American air base nearby, the central square pulsated with rock 'n' roll from the King Diamond, the Shindig, and other go-go bars. The Honey Massage Parlor sold raffle tickets: first prize, a woman and a room for the night, both free; second prize, a free woman for the night but the client had to pay for the room; third prize, a two-hour massage. In other red-light establishments crew-cut American airmen viewed through one-way mirrors a roomful of the available women and chose them according to the numbered tags they were wearing. Hard drugs—heroin—contributed to the degradation.

Branfman, who was freelancing for Jack Anderson's syndicated column, decided to get on the base, which was off-limits to journalists, and into Blue Chip. An American Peace Corps volunteer acquaintance took him to a dope house where airmen passed off-duty hours. On a table inside were a pile of marijuana and some pills. Everyone was sitting around quietly being stoned. Branfman sat there with them, getting high and talking a little but not being intrusive. Everybody was deferring to one airman who didn't say much but was obviously the unofficial leader. On his second day in the dope house, the guy asked him who he was, and through a stoned fog Branfman gave his rap about Project Air War and trying to expose the bombing by getting into Blue Chip. The off-duty airman said he worked there.

On a quiet Sunday morning they went on the base, which was surrounded by a chain-link fence with barbed wire and guarded. The airman knew the outer gate guard, who waved them past, even though Branfman was wearing civilian clothes. They signed into the building that held all the electronics. They walked down a hall, and then a security policeman came up and asked Branfman where he was from. The airman told the security policeman to stop being nosy. The cop, who was about their own age, apologized. It turned out that he bought his own dope from the airman and didn't want to alienate his source.

They went into a room with console after console. There was hardly anybody around. The airman pushed a switch, and out came the live sound of birds twittering a hundred miles to the east on the Ho Chi Minh Trail. Then the airman put on a tape recorded earlier that morning from another location. Branfman heard voices speaking Vietnamese. With all its acoustic, seismic, and magnetic sensors, the U.S. Air Force had a good idea where the North Vietnamese were on the Trail. It just had never been able to do much about them.

They went into another room, where Branfman was introduced as a new man just in from Saigon to a pleasant and courteous elderly officer. This man was the "bombing officer" for Cambodia, who verified targets for the pilots. Branfman asked whether the pilots ever called in before they bombed the villages. The bombing officer said, Yes, sometimes. Are they worried about bombing civilians? Branfman asked. Oh no, replied the coordinator. They just want me to check for Agency ground teams. We care about them. We don't know anything about civilians down there.

They went into a big room two stories high with a map of Indochina on one wall, showing the sorties and bombing missions under way. This was the command center, Blue Chip. Rows of consoles faced the wall map and people sat in front of the screens talking quietly and intently on telephones. Nobody was talking loudly and they were all intent on what they were doing. Over in the corner stood a ramrod-straight air force general, watching.

The command center was a quiet place. There were no screams. There were no bodies being blown apart. There was no blood, or passion. And yet in his mind's eye Branfman saw bodies and people dying. To the uniformed men sitting at their consoles, bombing was just a pencil notation or two, a set of coordinates on a map. He was sure that it had never occurred to them that real people with wives and children died in the forests because of their decisions. He stood in the control room with the eeriest feeling that he had gotten to the very heart of the mystery, only to find nothing there.

There was no evil magician. There was no all-powerful man pulling strings. Blue Chip was just one more part of some vast network. The air force people were polite and hardworking. And the work they did was somehow not all that different from work that everybody else did. Just like Wall Street. Just like the Garment District, where his own father worked. They were doing their jobs, and nothing more.

As Branfman stood there, an air force supervisor turned around, looked at him, pointed his finger, and said, "You, who are you? What are you doing here?"

"New troop, sir," said the airman. "Just in from Saigon. I'm showing him around."

"All right," said the supervisor, with barely concealed annoyance. "Would you guys just mind? We get an awful lot of visitors in here, and it's awfully hard to work. Would you just move over there?" He indicated a spot in the corner.

They shuffled off to the corner, watched for a couple more minutes, and then sauntered out of the building.

◆

In Hanoi, during Henry Kissinger's visit, it had been agreed that his negotiating deputy, William Sullivan, would become the first American ambassador to North Vietnam. Sullivan would serve on a part-time basis, while concurrently working as U.S. ambassador to the Philippines, a post for which he had been nominated but not confirmed by the U.S. Senate.

By the middle of 1973, the pattern of North Vietnamese cease-fire violations in South Vietnam, Laos, and Cambodia became too obvious for the State Department to ignore. The idea of Sullivan serving as ambassador to Hanoi was dropped as quietly as it had risen. (The United States and North Vietnam would not have diplomatic relations for more than twenty years.)

Sullivan's confirmation for the Philippines got stuck in the Senate, mainly because Senator William Fulbright, chairman of the Foreign Relations Committee, still held a grudge against Sullivan for his slickly evasive testimony years before. Fulbright also held up the nomination of Sullivan's successor as Laos ambassador, G. McMurtrie Godley, to be assistant secretary of state for Far Eastern affairs.

The opinion-makers of the press chimed in with their disapproval of the two nominees. Most remarkably, Anthony Lewis of *The New York Times* wrote a column condemning Sullivan and Godley as war criminals. The two ambassadors, Lewis wrote, "played a decisive part in what must qualify as the most appalling episode of lawless cruelty in American history, the bombing of Laos." In the Sullivan and Godley years, from 1964 to 1973, the U.S. military dropped almost two million tons of bombs on Laos, which worked out to two thirds of a ton for every man, woman, and child. Few Americans had allowed the bombing of Laos to enter their consciousness, but it was even worse than the horrors next door in South Vietnam, Lewis wrote.

He continued, "The human results of being the most heavily bombed country in the history of the world were expectedly pitiful. They are described without rancor—almost unbearably so—in a small book that will go down as a classic. It is *Voices From the Plain of Jars,* edited by Fred Branfman, in which the villagers of Laos themselves describe what the bombers did to their civilization. No American should be able to read that book without weeping at his country's arrogance."

The columnist concluded that "Sullivan and Godley have the blood of more innocent human beings on their hands than just about anyone who has ever served as an American Foreign Service officer." That was a questionable assertion, because neither man had had the war entirely within his grasp. But a strange kind of justice had been meted out in the establishment press. Two career foreign service men had been condemned, and scruffy, rebellious Fred Branfman had been raised above them, and praised.

◆

In Laos, after the 1973 agreement was signed, the Americans were in the awkward position of trying to tell royalist Laotians that the U.S. government wasn't abandoning them. Rather, the Americans claimed, the U.S. was dedicated to the support of Prime Minister Souvanna Phouma and his quest for lasting peace through a coalition government.

That was a hard sell, even to people as passive and gullible as the Laotians. A lot of Americans found it hard to look the Laotians in the eye, or look at themselves in the mirror in the morning. Edgar Buell was one of them.

Buell knew that both the royalist army and Vang Pao's irregular force had been on the edge of collapse when the agreements were finally signed.

All that had saved the Meo was a new gadget from the U.S. Air Force, a portable radar beacon used to direct night bombing raids on enemy troop concentrations. It was a technological descendant of Commando Club, and it worked. In those last months, the new precision bombing raids had kept the North Vietnamese from attacking Long Tieng in force. But even with that, the tribal soldiers' most common injury had become bullet and shrapnel wounds to the back—wounds sustained while running away. There had been a surreal night in the mountains when a thousand tribal soldiers had panicked and fled en masse, suffering less from enemy attacks than from their own new footgear, which had given them trench foot.

To Buell it was embarrassing how close the Meo were to defeat, and how far the Americans had pushed them. He was glad that the fighting was over. But he was not optimistic for the future of the Meo and of the lowland royalists. He was saddened for the Laotians who were going to lose their jobs, who had grown to depend on the American-supported wartime economy. He had come to understand that the end of the war was also the end of a way of life.

For Buell, Laos at war had been better than anywhere else in the world at peace. The lowland Lao, though less clever than the Vietnamese, were friendlier to foreigners, and they lacked that underlying atavistic violence of the Cambodians. There was no terrorism in Vientiane. It was a safe, benign place. The standard of living was high and the cost of living low for those with American dollars. The Lao treated *farangs* graciously and politely and with deference. Laos had it all—hot and cold running servants, good food, cheap booze, and every vice obliged with a *wai* and a smile. Buell knew that he would miss the place when he had to go. The only question was when.

The cease-fire violations, daily at first, tapered off steadily. Without American airpower to back them up, the royalist side lost the last vestiges of their willingness to fight; but even the Pathet Lao troops had *jai yen,* or cool hearts, and little desire to fight their fellow countrymen. The Pathet Lao side didn't allow inspectors into "liberated" territory, which violated the cease-fire terms, but then Vang Pao didn't allow full access into his military region either.

To get around a cease-fire provision outlawing paramilitary forces, Vang Pao's irregulars were merged into the royalist army. Over the coming months, the combat pay given to the tribal irregulars stopped, and the payroll as a whole switched over to the royalist army, whose salaries were much lower. The U.S. military took over many of the supply and advisory functions of the CIA and USAID. On July 1, 1973, most of the CIA paramilitary advisers left Laos, and the fifteen thousand Thai SGUs began a process of withdrawal to the Thai side of the Mekong.

By August 1973, parts of the Long Tieng valley were overgrown with brush. The wartime spirit had left the place, and there was a miniature crime wave, as former soldiers with shrunken paychecks and nowhere to go began robbing fellow tribespeople at gunpoint and carrying out occasional reprisal killings.

Without a war to support, the American civilian contract airlines began cutting back on pilots and planes. The Vientiane airport grew noticeably quieter. Occasionally an Antonov biplane landed and took off again, a Soviet gift to the Pathet Lao leaders, who remained in their cave headquarters in Sam Neua. At night the occasional sounds of motor vehicles and the crackle of radio static were drowned by the croaking of frogs and chirping of crickets, as Laos's overwhelmingly rural character asserted itself.

By September 1973, the major topic at American parties in Vientiane was who was leaving when. Almost everybody seemed to be leaving within weeks. Bars and restaurants that had been crowded earlier in the year were almost empty.

After further protocols to the cease-fire agreement were signed, 1,500 Pathet Lao troops arrived in Vientiane in November 1973 to help oversee the "neutralization" of the capital. Nervously clutching their AK-47s, traveling in groups to avoid seduction by loose Vientiane ways, the Pathet Lao troops kept their discipline. It was hard for Buell to get used to the sight of enemy soldiers around him. "I guess this is what is meant by losing," he glumly wrote home.

Buell had become a social fossil, a holdover from an earlier time. His pilot friends and poker-playing buddies had either going or were going. His best friend, Doc Weldon, was going back to the States, bitterly disillusioned with the U.S. government.

For some time Buell had been looking into the possibilities of a disability pension for his heart trouble. Without waiting for final approval of his disability, he retired from the U.S. government at the end of March 1974. He stayed on in Vientiane, working at a school for blind children.

A few days after Buell retired, on April 3, 1974, the Pathet Lao's Prince Souphanouvong arrived in Vientiane for the first time in a decade. Buell did not join the crowd that met the prince, which was the largest in the city's memory. Young men jumped up and down to get a glimpse of Souphanouvong above the sea of heads and shoulders along the parade route. At a mass rally, introduced to thunderous applause by his half brother the prime minister, whose pride was visibly injured by the crowd's enthusiasm, Souphanouvong gave a rousing speech while flanked at the dais by eminent Buddhist monks. Then he took off in an unostentatious car without a motorcycle escort, pursued by hundreds of joyous celebrants. Prince Souphanouvong's return was so perfectly staged that few paused to wonder who had orchestrated it, or asked whether he was really the principal leader of the Pathet Lao.

Two days later the king of Laos formally invested the Provisional Government of National Union, as the coalition was called. Government cabinet posts were evenly divided between royalists and Pathet Lao. But the royalist elite didn't object with the Pathet Lao insisted on running their "liberated zones" all by themselves while sharing in the government of the royalist zones. "What is mine is mine," went a saying at the time, "and what is yours is half mine, too."

By prior agreement, all foreign troops were to leave within sixty days after the new government was formed. Some of the North Vietnamese units withdrew to North and South Vietnam to support the final offensive in the south while others changed into Pathet Lao uniforms to make detection nearly impossible. They governed the Ho Chi Minh Trail area of Laos as though it was theirs.

The American side obeyed the agreement more carefully. Project 404, which had provided the plainclothes air force men, was disbanded. Air America, which had been revealed to be a fully owned proprietary of the Central Intelligence Agency, withdrew its pilots and planes by the target date, June 3, 1974, and sold its big maintenance depot in Udorn. The CIA cut its paramilitary staff still further, and some of its case officers found themselves stateside and out on the street. The last of the war's founders, Pat Landry, transferred out of Udorn. By the time funding for Operation Momentum ended, on September 30, 1974, the Taj Mahal was nearly empty.

At the U.S. air bases in Thailand, a few warplanes remained in their covered revetments, shaded from the fierce tropical sun. Most of the military pilots and support staff had gone. Around each base the Thai tailor shops, restaurants, and go-go bars that had risen to service the Americans' needs were deserted.

"To put it very crudely," one of the last CIA men in Udorn said, on the changes in the local economy, "the price of pussy sure went down in a hurry."

# The Fall

$B$y the end of 1974, the Kingdom of Laos had sunk back into its habitual daydream. There was no fighting. The American embassy slowed the communists' creeping takeover of the government with judicious handouts of aid. Huge refugee settlements remained, and many wartime problems went unresolved, but the coalition government was functioning. Peace, by general consensus, was better than war.

The catch was that Laos was closely related by geography and history to the wars in South Vietnam and Cambodia, which were rapidly approaching their climax. In Cambodia, the Khmer Rouge communists had tightened their siege of Phnom Penh, sinking the river traffic, cutting off the roads, and shelling the last point of exit, the airport. In South Vietnam, the North Vietnamese had launched a full-scale blitzkrieg, using tanks and the tactics of conventional warfare rather than the guerilla ambushes of earlier years. Province after province of South Vietnam was falling, and the panic of the South Vietnamese generals spread throughout Southeast Asia. In Laos, as elsewhere, there was a distinct feeling in the air that the time of the Americans had ended.

In late March 1975, fighting flared at the crucial Route 7–Route 13 junction, connecting the main road from the Plain of Jars with the road between Vientiane and Luang Prabang. It was the same junction the neutralists and Pathet Lao had captured in 1960 and that Tony Poe had captured in 1964. This time the royalist generals in Vientiane assigned Vang Pao to defend it even though it was outside his military district. His men lost it to the Pathet Lao and then traded it back and forth a couple of times, until finally Vang Pao got fed up and sent T-28s to bomb and strafe the place after the Pathet Lao took it for good.

The fighting and bombing at the junction were minor compared to the all-out battles of a few years earlier. But Vang Pao still wanted to fight, and this put him at odds with the Laotian royalist high command. Vang Pao still had a *jai han,* a hot heart. The rest of the generals wanted to greet the Pathet Lao like long-lost brothers and embrace them.

For some time the Pathet Lao coalition cabinet members had been trying to convince Prime Minister Souvanna Phouma to get rid of Vang Pao. Their efforts got a boost when they convinced the king to visit the Pathet Lao headquarters in the caves of Sam Neua. The king's visit to the caves, like his visit to Long Tieng back in 1963, had a strong symbolic effect in Vientiane. It legitimized the Pathet Lao to the last few rightist lowlanders who until then had resisted accepting the new political reality.

In the neighboring countries events reached their conclusion. On April 17, 1975, Phnom Penh fell to the Khmer Rouge guerillas, and the war in Cambodia was over. "Year Zero" began, a radical restructuring of the country that started with the forced evacuation of all civilians from cities and towns into the countryside. The Westerners in Phnom Penh were herded into the French embassy and eventually taken by truck to Thailand, lucky to escape with their lives.

Less than two weeks after the fall of Cambodia, on April 29, 1975, a North Vietnamese tank smashed through the gates of the Presidential Palace in Saigon. The North Vietnamese flag was raised on the flagpole, and the two Vietnams were reunited. Hanoi began to impose its harsh, spartan character and its Marxist-Leninist ideology on corrupt, free-wheeling Saigon, renamed Ho Chi Minh City.

In Laos on May 5, 1975, convinced that further resistance was hopeless, Souvanna Phouma summoned Vang Pao to his Vientiane office. The prime minister said the time for fighting was over. An angry argument erupted between the two men, ending when Vang Pao resigned his army commission by ripping the two stars off the shoulders of his uniform and slamming them on the prime minister's desk.

Vang Pao then flew back to Long Tieng, where even without military rank he was the leader of his people. He had some spare sets of stars anyway and put them back on, knowing that he would need every bit of prestige and authority to make it through the days ahead.

An announcement was broadcast over the Vientiane government radio station: Vang Pao would be replaced as commander of Military Region II by Chao Monivong, a longtime friend and aide. This was good news, under the circumstances: The Meo rather liked Chao Monivong. But at almost the same time, roadwatch teams reported that a column of tanks was slowly rumbling up the road from the Mekong valley toward Long Tieng. The rank-and-file Meo were deathly afraid of tanks, and they became confused and frightened at the mixed signals they were getting from the government in Vientiane.

One of Vang Pao's advisers at the time was a young scholar named Yang Dao, who had come back from France with a Ph.D. degree, the first of his people to do so. It was Yang Dao who had told a *National Geographic* magazine journalist that the proper name for the tribe was Hmong, meaning "free people," rather than Meo, a corruption of a Chinese word for "barbarian." Hmong it became ever after, even though *farang*s who had worked with the tribe for years had used the term "Meo" without being contradicted by the Hmong themselves.

In front of Yang Dao and other senior aides, Vang Pao announced that he was going to send his T-28s to bomb Vientiane. He was thinking of attacking by land, too. He would go for the enemy's nerve center while the whole country was collapsing and his enemies closing in. It was the kind of long-shot gamble that he loved to take. To Yang Dao it seemed like lunacy. He asked Vang Pao what kind of army he had left. He reminded Vang Pao that his remaining units suffered from massive desertions by men who had not been paid in months and who had gone back to their farms to plant crops.

The short, dour intelligence chief, Hang Sao, added that if Vang Pao attacked Vientiane, Vientiane would strike back. Not just the Pathet Lao, but the royalists too. The royalists would attack Long Tieng with their own T-28s, and then what would Long Tieng use to defend itself? Those antiaircraft guns captured and put on the mountaintops years ago? Nobody had maintained the antiaircraft guns, Hang Sao pointed out. They were rusted and didn't even fire bullets anymore.

Vang Pao stubbornly said that he was still going to attack.

Yang Dao hurried to Vientiane to see the prime minister and pleaded with him to keep the Pathet Lao from attacking Long Tieng. Souvanna Phouma, listening thoughtfully, said he would telephone the top Pathet Lao man then in Vientiane, Phoumi Vongvichit.

The prime minister then reached for his rotary telephone, cradled the receiver against his ear, put his index finger in a hole, dialed, and frowned. No dial tone. He put the receiver in the cradle, lifted it up again, dialed again, and looked disconcerted. Still no dial tone.

The telephone wasn't working in the office of the prime minister.

Souvanna Phouma looked at the young scholar and shrugged. What could he do?

Yang Dao went over to the Pathet Lao headquarters and talked to Phoumi Vongvichit, who asked him sharply how long Vang Pao wanted to keep on fighting. Ten years? Twenty? The Pathet Lao were ready for whatever it took.

◆

"It is unreal the change that has taken place," Edgar Buell wrote to his children. "The U.S. is a sore word and a sore subject anywhere in S.E. Asia. There are very few safe places to go."

For his own safety, Buell moved from his house overlooking the Mekong to an apartment compound near the airport on the western edge of town. In the minds of the Pathet Lao and their sympathizers, who now made up the overwhelming majority in Vientiane, Buell symbolized the CIA and American imperialism, even though he had never actually worked for the CIA. He had not been the target of physical attacks yet, but he felt it could be only a matter of time. There had been demonstrations and strikes against organizations associated with the U.S. government. Students were trying to prove their revolutionary credentials, and because they were not subject to military discipline they were much more unpredictable and dangerous than the Pathet Lao soldiers themselves.

Buell wasn't quite sure how everything got turned inside out, how the most powerful country in the world had allowed itself to get beaten and was slinking out of Asia like a dog with its tail between its legs. He had always blamed the bureaucrats and the "educated fools" who never got out of their offices, but he knew there was more to it than that, and it frustrated him that he could not put together a coherent explanation.

He could not put it all together, so he concocted ugly racial explanations, that Kissinger sold Laos out because he was a Jew, that the white race would have to accept some communism in Asia because there weren't enough whites and niggers to fight all those Asians, and so on. His racial tirades didn't make sense and they were out of character for him because he had always treated people according to their abilities. But he was drinking too much and he was under stress and his mind was not clear.

Above all, he needed to have the hill people absolve him of blame. He traveled north to see his old friends. "I spent two nights at Long Tieng. V.P. very depressed. They can see the hand writing on the wall. They know it is only a matter of time till they will be living under the Reds. They are all bitter at the U.S.

"Even though it is a sad time," Buell added, "I enjoyed it and everyone was kind to me. I think I am respected for being able to face them. Many said, 'Pop, you needn't feel bad. You did all you could and what you thought was right.' " That was exactly what he wanted to hear.

Back in Vientiane, the weather was oppressively hot, up to 110 degrees by day and nearly 100 at night. Then a heavy rain fell and left the city refreshed. The rainy season was about to begin, the cycle start anew. Sitting by the pool in his apartment compound Buell wrote, "I have never saw the trees more beuitful. The red flame trees are in full bloom. So many flowers you can't see the bark. Looks like one bouquet. The trees which have the weeping yellow flowers are in full bloom, then all the bouginvilla colors mixed in. I have been thinking about the many things I will miss here. Surely the flowers are one."

On May 10, 1975, at the urging of friends and of the U.S. embassy, Edgar Buell flew out to Thailand on a Continental Air Services Pilatus Porter. His luggage consisted of three small battered, mismatched suitcases carrying all he owned. His eyes were watery, the pilot noticed, but Buell sat staring straight ahead and didn't say a word.

◆

Long Tieng was awash in rumors of assassination plots. For Vang Pao himself, the immediate danger was not so much from the Pathet Lao, although they were drawing near, and rifle fire was sometimes audible in the distance. Nor was it even from the column of Pathet Lao tanks, slowly rumbling and clanking northward toward Long Tieng.

The greatest danger was from the inside—from infiltrators, from people who had changed allegiances, and from those who were angry at him and the course of events generally. The Ly clan, whom he had displaced from power at the outset of the war, was believed to be the most dangerous. His own Vang clan provided private muscle, and he spent much of his time in the "Sky," or CIA offices, with Jerry Daniels, the case officer who had decided to stay to the bitter end.

Vang Pao could not make up his mind. At one point he told Daniels to go ahead and kill him; it would be better that way. An hour later he was talking about leaving Laos and going into exile. The next day he said he would fight to the last bullet. Various emissaries came up from Vientiane, trying to persuade him to leave, and then went away again. Eventually it fell to a midlevel officer from the Vientiane CIA station to give him the bad news. The U.S. would help any legitimate government of Laos economically but not militarily, he said. It was time for Vang Pao and his top aides to leave the kingdom.

The U.S. decision to evacuate Vang Pao was made in reaction to the fiascoes of the withdrawals from Saigon and Phnom Penh the month before. In both capitals there had been scenes of chaos and panic: helicopters taking off from the embassy rooftops, crowds of loyal Asian employees abandoned to the enemy. Hoping to prevent a replay in Laos was a small group of Americans who had known Vang Pao for many years and who had been promoted to powerful positions in the government: The director of the

Central Intelligence Agency was Bill Colby. The chief of the CIA's East Asia Division was Theodore Shackley. The commander of the U.S. military's assistance and advisory effort in Thailand was the Air Commandos' Heinie Aderholt, who had been called out of retirement and promoted to air force brigadier general.

Aderholt, working out of the Joint U.S. Military Advisory Group's headquarters in Bangkok, found a big, four-engine C-130 cargo plane the U.S. Air Force had rented out, or "bailed," for airdrops in Cambodia. After the fall of Phnom Penh, the C-130 had landed on the long runway built for B-52s at Utapao air base in Thailand, and it had not moved since. Finding a pilot was harder since most of them were gone from Southeast Asia. Ultimately he located an Air America C-130 pilot named Matt Hoff just as Hoff was about to board a commercial flight back to the States. Hoff agreed to fly from Thailand to Long Tieng and back at five thousand dollars a trip.

By May 8, 1975, Vang Pao had already flown his wives and younger children to Thailand. The crowds began to gather around the Long Tieng airstrip and the evacuation proper began on May 12. A couple of C-46s and some other planes made one shuttle trip each between Thailand and Long Tieng before getting caught in Thai and Laotian red tape about needing official permission to enter their airspace—no such permission had been needed during the war itself. The next day saw a few more flights and more red tape. A small Pilatus Porter utility plane, sent to bring another midlevel Agency emissary up to Long Tieng, returned with two cases of Olympia beer. Jerry Daniels was an Olympia beer drinker, and this was interpreted by the pilots as a sure sign that the end was near. An evacuation flight to the big refugee center nearby at Ban Xon was canceled when a Hmong telephone operator reported that about a hundred Pathet Lao had captured the base with little gunfire and were busily looting the USAID warehouse. In Vientiane, about a thousand Hmong had collected surreptitiously, trying to get information and pooling their money to get across the river to Thailand.

The Pathet Lao tanks rumbled through Ban Xon, and then stopped outside the Long Tieng valley.

On the roof of Vang Pao's house, soldiers from the Vang clan readied antitank weaponry. The crowd around the runway had grown to an estimated five to seven thousand, with perhaps another fifty thousand hiking in and out of the valley in small groups, talking worriedly and assessing their chances of getting seats on the planes. Everybody wanted out. Nobody had panicked yet, but a few majors and colonels drove onto the tarmac in their vehicles and threatened to shoot the pilots and the cargo kickers if their families were not allowed aboard. The Americans planning the evacuation agreed that if Vang Pao was seen leaving in an aircraft the crowd would go berserk. It would be necessary to sneak him out of Long Tieng to keep him from being killed by his own people.

May 14, 1975 dawned with a four-thousand-foot ceiling and ragged clouds drifting along the tops of the karst outcroppings and mountain ridges above the valley. Early in the morning, as the American pilots started landing, the surly crowd gathered again. Around the perimeter, abandoned suitcases, shoes, and other possessions lay scattered with the trash. In the Sky building where Vang Pao had gone for safety, he and Jerry Daniels were still arguing and revising the plan. Vang Pao was reluctant to go. Daniels's mission was to get him to agree to a plan and stick with it.

When a helicopter pilot named Jack Knotts and a Porter pilot named Dave Kouba entered the room, Daniels remarked that there were a couple of huckleberries out there, meaning potential assassins. He and the pilots discussed another problem of red tape: The Porter but not the helicopter was cleared to fly into Thailand. Together they concocted a plan to divert the crowd's attention, sneak Vang Pao out in the chopper, and then switch to the Porter for the flight across the Mekong. Kouba asked Vang Pao about nearby sites to make the transfer, and Vang Pao gloomily said there was no place, adding, "After today it will all be communist."

Knotts arranged for Vang Pao to have a signal panel, a piece of reflective Mylar about a foot high and five feet long. Then Knotts went back to his helicopter to wait. The big C-130 appeared in the sky over the southern ridge and landed. As it taxied by, the cockpit window opened and Matt Hoff waved. Without stopping, the plane rolled to the end of the runway, slowly turned around, and kept moving. The rear cargo ramp went down, the bottom of the ramp scraping the runway, the plane still moving forward, and a crowd ran up into the plane, elbowing and pushing each other, until Hoff raised the ramp and picked up speed and took off again.

After that a twin-engine C-46 landed, the pilot waving to Knotts and pulling around to stop by the control tower. By prearrangement, scores of specially favored tribespeople, most of them from the Vang clan, had already clambered onto two-and-a-half-ton trucks. These trucks backed up to the cargo doors of the C-46, but the mob of ordinary people from the runway got there ahead of them and swarmed inside, taking most of the places. Not long after the C-46 took off the C-130 came back again from Thailand.

Knotts had been waiting the whole time in his Bell 206 helicopter, a relatively small and delicate aircraft. He wondered whether the people on the runway would realize the chopper's fragility or whether they would try to hang onto his skids when he took off, the way people did during the evacuation from Saigon a few weeks before or the doomed South Vietnamese invasion of Laos a few years before that. If they hung onto his skids he was likely to crash. Finally lantern-jawed Jerry Daniels drove up in a white Ford Bronco and gave Knotts the word. Knotts took off in his chopper and flew along Skyline Ridge, then around the far side of the Long Tieng valley, out of sight of the crowd on the runway.

Among the people on the runway was a son and aide of Vang Pao, Vang Chu. After persuading a soldier who had been aiming his rifle at a pilot not to shoot, Vang Chu went back to Sky headquarters. His father asked him to fetch his briefcase from his two-story stone house. Vang Chu obligingly went off to his father's house. The ground floor was occupied by fifteen armed men he had never seen before, dressed in the uniforms of the royalist army. He was sure they were imposters. Without telling them what he was doing, he went upstairs to his father's room and got the briefcase. A large walk-in closet that was normally kept locked, known as the "money room," was unlocked and open; boxes and boxes of Lao kip lay inside, from a payroll shipment that had arrived not long before. Vang Chu left the money there. On his way out the strangers asked him whether his father was coming back. Vang Chu told them he was coming right back and that they should guard the place in the meantime.

Near Sky headquarters he saw his father and Jerry Daniels running downhill to Vang Pao's jeep. The general had taken off his stars again and was wearing a black floppy-brimmed hat to make it harder for ordinary Hmong or for assassins to recognize him. Vang Chu and a few others got in the jeep and drove up the valley to a little earthen dam in back of the king's house. They saw Knotts's Bell helicopter approaching and held up the Mylar reflecting panel. The helicopter landed on the lip of the dam. Vang Pao, his son, another clansman, and a bodyguard got in quickly, all but Vang Pao loaded down with rifles and grenades. The helicopter took off low, cleared the back ridge, flew across a river valley to a seldom-used chopper pad on the next ridge to the west, in the village of Phou Khang. They got out. When a small crowd of villagers gathered, Vang Pao exhorted them to hide their guns and wait for him to return to liberate the country. He promised them that he would be back.

Knotts flew the chopper back to Long Tieng, landing on the pathway leading to the king's house. Down below in the valley, tribespeople on the runway were still pushing and shoving to get on the evacuation planes. They hadn't noticed that their leader had deserted them. Six or eight uniformed tribal soldiers walked over a rise near the chopper just as Jerry Daniels drove up. Daniels calmly got out of his Bronco, opened the back end, and got his briefcase. The pilot, sitting inside the helicopter with the rotors turning, silently prayed for the case officer to hurry. The soldiers were looking at the helicopter and the Bronco and then back again. As though he had all the time in the world, Daniels looked up in space and saluted the cloudy sky, his own private sign-off to the Laos war. Then he got in the chopper.

Knotts picked up gently. Out of the corner of his eye, he saw the tribal soldiers shouldering their rifles and jacking rounds into the chambers. He maneuvered the chopper behind a rise out of their line of fire, and then flew around and over the ridge to rejoin Vang Pao and the others. They all got in the helicopter together and flew to Muong Cha, where Kouba's Pilatus Porter was ready to go, the propellors already turning. The transfer of the passengers took less than a minute, and then the Porter was airborne, heading south.

There was a case of beer in the Porter. Daniels opened beers and passed them around. Vang Pao refused to take one and asked Daniels sharply how he could just sit there and drink a beer when everything had been lost. Daniels shrugged it off. He seemed relieved; he had done what he had been asked to do, get Vang Pao out of Long Tieng in one piece. There was some casual conversation in the helicopter cabin; the other Hmong, too, were glad to make it out alive.

Soon they were in sight of the bright reflective ribbon of the Mekong River and the flat expanse of Thailand beyond.

◆

At Long Tieng, with the discovery that their leader had deserted them, an exodus began, by motor vehicle for a few, by foot for most. There were paths through the hills for those who were nervous about the tanks, and then the road toward the lowlands. The road crossed the Nam Lik River, a tributary of the Mekong, on a bridge. By the time they reached the bridge all the Hmong soldiers and officers had changed into civilian clothes.

When the first Pathet Lao entered Long Tieng a day or two later, they met no resistance. Intelligence operatives proceeded directly to Vang Pao's old headquarters, where Lao-language records dating back to the beginning of the war sat neatly in filing cabinets. These records listed the company commanders, the spies, and all kinds of other information the Pathet Lao and Vietnamese could use to hunt down and persecute Hmong who stayed under a communist regime. Other Pathet Lao soldiers peacefully disarmed those Hmong who remained in the valley and who had not made up their minds what to do, or who were waiting to see what things would be like under Chao Monivong. He arrived a few days later and found himself only nominally in command, and nearly a prisoner. Long Tieng was under firm Pathet Lao control.

Toward the end of May, the newly unified army of the Pathet Lao and royalists blocked the bridge over the tributary of the Mekong, at the village of Hin Heup. The flow of Hmong backed up until there were several thousand camped on the side of the river nearer the mountains. They ran out of food. Early one morning when the soldiers had left the bridge for guard houses nearby, several hundred unarmed tribesmen started walking across. When they refused orders to stop, the Pathet Lao and royalists opened fire. Four to eight were killed and several dozen wounded. The "massacre" at the bridge sent an electric shock through the tribal communities. The Hmong scattered through the mountains. Over the next few weeks thousands more made their way to the banks of the Mekong, where some were fired on by government soldiers. Before the end of the year others were robbed, raped, or killed by increasingly violent and unprincipled private river pilots.

"They were good soldiers," Prime Minister Souvanna Phouma remarked to a foreign diplomat, referring to the tribesmen. "It's a pity that peace will mean their extinction."

◆

The fall of Long Tieng and the start of the persecution of the Hmong were eclipsed by other events in Laos. The U.S. ambassador and his USAID chief left a few days after Vang Pao. Student strikes followed, and then the occupation of the USAID compound in Vientiane, house arrests of Americans, and gunpoint confrontations in other towns along the Mekong. Those were tense days, but no Americans lost their lives, and the embassy succeeded in paring its mission down to a skeleton staff rather than pulling out completely. This relative lack of drama made the events in Laos seem anticlimactic—a footnote to the larger catastrophes of the U.S. evacuations from Cambodia and South Vietnam.

In Thailand, the only remaining U.S. ally in the region, the 2,500 Hmong airlifted from Long Tieng camped at the empty Namphong air base, fifty miles south of Udorn. Vang Pao stayed in the base commander's quarters with his wives; and other tribespeople who had entered Thailand on their own sneaked through the fences, adding to the population.

At a mass meeting, many of the tribal elders angrily denounced Vang Pao to his face. About thirty thousand Hmong had lost their lives in the war, more than a tenth of the tribe's population in Laos. They declared that he had led them to their destruction and that they would never follow him again.

No other major leader emerged to take Vang Pao's place. Nobody else had his stature. To the tribal rank and file, who spoke no English and had had little personal contact with the Americans during the war, Vang Pao was not just a mortal like themselves but almost semidivine—a sort of super-shaman able to reach the spirits and manipulate them on the tribe's behalf. This was also true for the hundred thousand or so pro–Vang Pao

Hmong left behind in Laos. Even though Vang Pao had abandoned them, they wanted to go to Thailand, too, for their own safety from the communists, because it was their ingrained habit to follow leaders, and because Thailand had been a part of the original escape plan if the Sayaboury plan failed.

Ten to twenty thousand other Hmong had already crossed the Mekong by boat or raft and were living in squalid temporary camps along the border. The Thais didn't want them there and gave them no assistance. Adding to the Thais' aggravation, Vang Pao was acting like a big-shot military commander rather than a guest. When he didn't get permission from the Thai military to travel freely in the country, he appealed over their heads to the Thai prime minister.

The Thai generals told the U.S. embassy in Bangkok that Vang Pao had two choices: He could stay in Thailand in handcuffs or he could leave the country. For the sake of Thai-American relations, and Thai-Lao relations, the U.S. embassy reluctantly decided to deal with the problem of Vang Pao. Cables flew back and forth from Bangkok to Washington. The State Department bureaucrats could find no piece of paper in their files recording a decision to resettle Vang Pao in America. If it hadn't been on paper, they said, it hadn't been the policy.

The CIA stepped in to break the deadlock. Vang Pao had in mind a place to go to, the agency revealed: Missoula, Montana. The CIA said it would get Vang Pao into the country and help him buy a home. It would also bend the immigration laws on his behalf, which was useful—he was, after all, a known polygamist with a history on the periphery of the opium trade.

The American embassy then told the Thais that the United States agreed to take in Vang Pao, plus a few of his followers, and a few others who had worked for the CIA or USAID.

◆

On June 18, 1975, just before he was to fly to the United States, Vang Pao was taken to the CIA offices on the third floor of the U.S. embassy building on Wireless Road in Bangkok. After a formal farewell to the station chief, he encountered in the hallway the quiet man from Texas who had sought him out south of the Plain of Jars some fifteen years before.

There wasn't much to say. Both men were diminished by events and by the passage of time. The meekness and humility that had been part of Lair's camouflage had merged with his real personality. He was older, grayer, and more withdrawn. Vang Pao also seemed smaller than before, now that he was outside his own country. He seemed uninspired and generic—just another short, overweight Asian ex-warlord, like the right-wing leaders and generals from Cambodia and South Vietnam.

In the hallway of the embassy, Bill Lair wished Vang Pao good luck. But as Vang Pao walked off, Lair wished to himself that the tribesman had disobeyed all the orders and had led his people across the Mekong into Sayaboury Province in Laos. It wouldn't have been easy for them there, but a lot of them would have survived by dispersing into the mountain wilderness as they had always done. They belonged in the mountains as free people, rather than in refugee camps in Thailand, or in America.

Alternatively, thought Lair, it would have been good if Vang Pao had been killed in battle. Better for him to die in his prime in Laos and become a legend than to go into exile. Because Vang Pao had been a great man once, back when the operation was young.

# Land of the 847 Elephants

After Vang Pao left for the United States in June 1975, meetings were held in Udorn and at Nong Khai to discuss the continued influx of Hmong tribespeople into Thailand. The Hmong were represented by second-tier leaders who had worked with the Americans. The outfit was represented by Jerry Daniels, who did most of the talking, while Bill Lair, the assistant station chief for special operations, sat quietly at the table with his eyes downcast.

Lair went back to Bangkok and asked his boss what he should do. The station chief told him he wanted the Meo problem swept under the rug and to take care of the broom work himself. Lair mulled it over, then got in his diesel Mercedes and drove across town to see his wife's brother, Siddhi Savetsila.

Siddhi, an American-educated scion of an influential Bangkok family, was a rising star in Thai governmental circles. He sat on Thailand's National Security Council, which was more powerful than the organization of the same name in the United States. On the Hmong refugee matter, Siddhi moved so quietly behind the scenes that afterwards nobody could quite recall who had been responsible, the same style that Lair had always favored.

The Thai government established a camp for the Hmong south of the Mekong in the foothills of Loei Province, in a place that came to be called Ban Vinai. It was not supposed to be a resettlement area, because the Thais wanted the Hmong of Laos to move on. It was a "temporary" refugee camp, but with enough land so that each family would have a little plot to grow vegetables. As soon as it was set up, the CIA faded out of the picture, except for Jerry Daniels, who collected intelligence information while work-ing at a cover job to screen and process refugees. Veterans of Pop Buell's old outfit, USAID Refugee Relief, took over in the pots-and-pans depart-ment; and the United Nations ran the place with the Thai government and an alphabet soup of voluntary agencies.

Lair never went up to see Ban Vinai or any of the other refugee camps established for Laotians. He tried to blot the war out of his mind.

He didn't want to hear about the new regime, the Lao People's Demo-cratic Republic, when it replaced the old monarchy in December 1975. It was led by a man he had known about for decades, a secretive half-Lao, half-Vietnamese named Kaysone Phoumvihane, who ranked number one in the Lao People's Revolutionary Party, the secret communist organiza-tion behind the Pathet Lao front. Prince Souphanouvong, the public face of the Pathet Lao, had never ranked higher than seven.

In the months that followed, Lair did not want to hear about the "sem-inars" or re-education camps that people from the old regime had to at-tend. The camps for the higher-ranking royalists were far off in the wilderness, and many died of neglect, disease, or starvation. A few were executed, including the drug-dealing Gen. Ouane Rattikone. The king and queen of Laos and their son the crown prince eventually died of neglect or were killed, but Lair didn't really want to listen to the rumors about the royal family, or about the regime's campaign to exterminate the Hmong.

He avoided reminders of Laos whenever he had a choice. A number of Americans he had known from the war years had resettled in Bangkok, where the style of life was similar to Vientiane and the people were still friendly to *farang*s. The American expatriates frequented the bawdy estab-lishments of a street called Patpong, which was beginning to make the old days at the White Rose and Madame Lulu's seem tame by comparison. Pat-pong was a combination red-light district, meeting point, and watering hole for the expatriates. Pop Buell and Pat Landry were regulars, but not Lair.

He stayed away from the whole scene, the men who got rowdy and cursed the hippies and the Reds, and who pounded one another on the back and told themselves what great Americans they were. He preferred getting drunk in the quiet and privacy of his own home.

In the gloom that followed America's debacle in Indochina, Lair had one last professional success. His brother-in-law Siddhi, soon to become Thai-land's foreign minister, was invited to China as a member of a Thai delega-tion. In Beijing, the Thais visited the hospital room where Mao Zedong lay slowly dying. Mao bade them sit down on the bed and put his arm around them, the Great Helmsman and his little Asian brothers. Siddhi returned with a detailed, firsthand look at Mao's declining health and at the power struggle under way in the wings. He shared the intelligence because it would not harm the Thai government, because it might help the American government, and perhaps because he thought it might help his brother-in-law's career.

In Washington, Lair's cable on the Chinese succession was brought to the attention of President Gerald Ford, who had taken office after Richard Nixon resigned, and Secretary of State Henry Kissinger. It was a minor bombshell, one of those intelligence triumphs that are treasured ever afterwards. But there were no more to follow.

The CIA's dark years had begun. In the aftermath of its many failures in Indochina, the outfit had come under fire for its mediocre, uninspired performance around the world. What made it harder for Lair was that people he had worked with for years, like Bill Colby, were at the heart of the controversies. In the hearings to confirm Colby as director of Central Intelligence, the whole ugly business of the Phoenix operation had come up again, the unsupervised killings of South Vietnamese in the poorly run hunt for communist leadership.

Colby got his directorship, but Congress formed the Church committee, named after its chairman, Senator Frank Church, to look into the Agency's misdeeds. To the bewilderment of his old colleagues, Colby gave the committee "the family jewels," an internal study of the CIA's illegal deeds—fixing elections in the name of democracy; destabilizing and overthrowing foreign governments; and conducting undeclared, covert "Presidential" wars, such as Laos.

The assassination attempts of foreign leaders got most of the attention. The CIA had tried to get Castro but failed, and it had been indirectly responsible for a number of assassinations that had succeeded, from Diem in South Vietnam to Lumumba in the Congo. Either way, the outfit looked bad—blamed for the immorality of planning and encouraging assassinations, but too inept to pull them off.

When Jimmy Carter was elected president in 1976, he replaced Colby with Adm. Stansfield Turner, a moralist who knew little about the intelligence business. To Lair's way of thinking, Turner's management replaced the old vice of excess activism with the new vice of excessive caution. At least in the old days, Lair thought, people had believed in what they were doing, even if they made mistakes. Now they didn't do anything at all, even for the right reasons and with the right people.

The most glaring example was Cambodia. Renamed Democratic Kampuchea, and ruled by the secretive Pol Pot, it had turned into a murderous totalitarian state. Upwards of one million Cambodians died of illness, starvation, and execution. For years, around the world, the CIA had been meddling in the affairs of even innocuous governments. Now, against a truly evil regime, the CIA did nothing, not even to publicize Pol Pot's genocidal policies.

Another example of inaction was the issue of American prisoners of war left behind from the Vietnam War era, particularly in Laos. Some 566 airmen had been shot down over Laos during the war, along with some civilian pilots and Green Berets captured on the ground. Most of those who survived their plane crashes and who had been taken captive appeared to have been taken to North Vietnam, but the U.S. government had never discovered how many had survived their crashes or how many had been kept prisoner in Laos by local Pathet Lao commanders. After the 1973 agreement was signed, Hanoi had released only nine Americans taken prisoner in Laos. The Pathet Lao never released any of their own prisoners and never answered U.S. requests for information.

There was only one branch of government with a proven track record of collecting intelligence in Laos, and that was the CIA. But after Vietnam, Watergate, and the Church committee revelations, the White House didn't want the CIA operating in Laos again. A third-rate military bureaucracy, the Joint Casualty Resolution Center, was in charge of prisoner-of-war and missing-in action discrepancies. The JCRC field investigators were novices in the culture, languages, and history of Laos, and they were hamstrung by regulations, such as not being able to go to refugee camps in Thailand to talk with resistance fighters there.

In the absence of any well-organized U.S. governmental effort, a cottage industry of POW/MIA sightings and amateur expeditions into Laos sprang up along the Mekong River. On the Laos side the business was based on small-time scams and phony reports, and on the American side it was based on grieving relatives' desperate need for information. American private citizens, most of them ex-soldiers who had served in Vietnam, went on secret expeditions into Laos but never found any live prisoners. They brought back a few airplane parts and genuine human remains from crash sites in Laos, along with a greater number of ox bones and even chicken bones.

It got so Lair dreaded coming to work in the mornings. He queried Langley about returning to the States. Perhaps he could be useful at The Farm, in Virginia, teaching young men who were still wet behind the ears. After all, he had started the run the covert war that men like Colby and Shackley said was one of the best-run operations ever. Or maybe he could teach a course in counterterrorism, a subject on which he had a few ideas.

Headquarters told him there were no openings in the States.

Lair quietly made preparations to leave Thailand and retire. Even more quietly, he was summoned by the ultimate behind-the-scenes operator in the Kingdom of Thailand, the king himself. Lair was driven to one of the royal palaces in Bangkok and shown in for an audience.

King Bhumibol, a constitutional monarch who reigned but did not rule, had known Lair for twenty years and did not put him in the category of evildoers. To the king, the war in Laos had been a forward defense of Thailand, a war that had stopped the North Vietnamese from crossing to his side of the Mekong. He knew the sacrifices the Paru had made, and he had personally looked after the surviving Paru veterans. The audience was his way of telling Lair that his career had not been in vain and that he would always be welcomed and honored in the kingdom.

Feeling a little better, Lair left Thailand and retired from the outfit to start a new life.

◆

Edgar Buell's years in Laos made him a minor celebrity in Bangkok's expatriate community. It was good for his self-esteem to go out drinking with his old pilot buddies when they came through Bangkok on vacation from Saudi or the Indonesian oilfields, and to have old friends in high places in the U.S. embassy.

He lived modestly on his U.S. government pension in a midrise apartment off Sukhumvit Road. He was forever helping out Hmong, Lao, and Thais of Lao descent who came to him with problems of one sort or another. When he visited refugee camps he took an overnight bus, a hard way to travel but cheap.

He knew as well as anybody how the Hmong had suffered after the communist takeover. Some were hunted down and shot; others were put in prison camps. They were fired on by MiG jets and 130mm artillery. They fled into the deepest forests and were never in one place long enough to grow their own food. Starving, they traded their children to childless couples for handfuls of salt, or flour made from wild roots. Hundreds were shot trying to cross the Mekong into Thailand on bamboo rafts. Hundreds more drowned. There were stories, though Buell wasn't sure whether to believe them, that the North Vietnamese used Soviet-made chemical weapons against the Hmong. In a sense it didn't matter how the Hmong were dying because there were so many ways. From what he could figure, roughly ten thousand died under the communist regime, in addition to the thirty thousand Hmong killed during the war.

Buell figured that the U.S. government owed the Hmong. But he also knew that the Hmong were not the innocent victims, or "noble savages," that some idealistic Americans liked to believe. It was much more complicated than that. If Vang Pao hadn't sent messages from the United States telling his people to stay in Laos and wait, more of them would have escaped to Thailand when it was safe to do so. And if the tribal leadership hadn't collapsed, rival resistance factions wouldn't have firefights with one another on the Laotian side of the Mekong. The refugee camps in Thailand were the strangest places of all: part prison, part feeding and vacation

center for resistance fighters, part travel bureaus where Iron Age tribesmen could sign up to emigrate to the West. Buell didn't like the idea of
Laotians going to America and other Western countries. Resettling in Thailand, so similar to their own country, would have been more sensible; but
the Thais weren't accepting refugees.

The war and its aftermath left Buell traumatized but able to speak his
mind. When people asked him about the war, he said the U.S. lost because
the other side fought better. He said America sold out the Hmong.

Toward the end of 1980 he took a vacation trip to the Philippines. He
was staying in Manila at the house of a CIA friend and planning to visit Dr.
Charles Weldon, who had retired along the Luzon coast, when he had another heart attack, his fourth, and died.

There was a huge memorial ceremony for Buell at the Ban Vinai refugee
camp. Everybody in camp showed up. He was the only *farang* who had stuck
with them for the entire length of the war, and who had sided with the tribal
leaders against the U.S. embassy on issues such as going to Sayaboury. He
had entered their mythology—the little old white man who never carried a
gun and who only did good, building schools and hospitals, making the rice
fall from the sky. Since few of the refugees could read or write, they tape-
recorded the songs and speeches at the memorial ceremony and sent the
tapes as "letters" to their relatives who had resettled in America.

The funeral itself was in Edon, Ohio, the one-stoplight town where
Buell had always done his shopping, just across the Indiana line. It was a
snowy day when the pallbearers brought his casket into the Edon United
Methodist Church. At the service, the organist played the songs he had
loved to sing, "Springtime in the Rockies" and "Let Me Call You Sweetheart." Tribespeople who had resettled in Minnesota were there and so
were Americans who had known him in Laos years before. As the mourners filed out of the church, a car drove up and Vang Pao emerged, visibly
angry with his driver for missing the right exit from the Ohio turnpike.

The funeral-goers went from the church to the cemetery. They buried
him in the family plot, next to his wife on the grassy rise within sight of the
grain elevators and the railroad tracks. Then everyone went back to the
family farmhouse. Vang Pao was still in a bad mood, acting haughty, and
speaking only in French to the Americans. He left after half an hour, leaving Buell's children to wonder about this great Laotian leader they had
heard about all these years.

◆

For most of the 1980s, Vientiane was an empty city. The markets at either end of town were open, and so was the Soviet cultural center, with its
color photographs of the workers' paradise. But in the central business dis-

trict, storefront after storefront was closed, with metal grills drawn across the doors, or, if the stores had been converted into living spaces, with a child or two making the premises look more abandoned by contrast. The streets were deserted. Most of the educated and entrepreneurial people in Vientiane—to use Lenin's phrase—had voted with their feet, including Laotians who had initially been in favor of the new regime.

The exodus from Laos eventually included 340,000 people, or more than a tenth of the population, hilltribes as well as lowlanders. The refugee camps on the Thai side of the river offered safety, free food, and the possibility of resettlement abroad in countries like the United States, Canada, Australia, and France. Between the refugee camps in Thailand and the "seminar" camps in upcountry Laos, which held about ten thousand officials and military officers of the old regime, hardly anybody competent was left to run the government. The new leader, Kaysone, hardly ever appeared in public because of assassination scares. Forty thousand Vietnamese soldiers and advisers kept the regime from falling apart, but the top economic project, the building of roads through the Annamite Mountains to Vietnam, bogged down, and few of the other projects of national reconstruction were even started. On the walls of government ministries, maps of the United States, left over from the previous regime, hung side by side with portraits of Marx and Lenin.

In the depths of the communist era there were four Americans living in Laos in addition to the skeleton crew at the U.S. embassy. Two young married couples, sent by Quaker and Mennonite organizations, ran small aid projects. They found the lowland Lao unchanged, which is to say extremely nice and almost impossible to motivate. Knowing that the country had once been called the Land of the Million Elephants, the Mennonite man went to the appropriate government office of the Lao People's Democratic Republic and asked how many elephants there were now.

"Approximately 847," came the prompt, decisive answer from the government official.

Approximately? the American inquired, eyebrow raised.

"We took a census of the elephants in the entire country," the official explained proudly. "There were 347. But one province didn't sent in results, and we know there are five hundred there."

Laos under communism was Wonderland all over again. There were about two thousand Soviet advisers in the country, mired in the tracks of their predecessors. The Soviets taught in French at the medical school in Vientiane. They paid their hotel bills in U.S. dollars since the new regime wouldn't accept rubles. The Russians could be seen strolling around Vientiane with their shabbily dressed wives, wandering into the markets and affecting nonchalance while glancing over their shoulders as they

changed money at black-market rates. At the sight of them, or any Caucasians, the children of Vientiane pointed their fingers and shouted, "Soviet! Soviet!" but without malice. The children, like the adults, just didn't
care.

The Lao People's Democratic Republic was one of the ten poorest countries in the world. There was no modernization, and parts of the country
regressed. On the Plain of Jars, and in some towns in the southern panhandle the prewar communities never recovered. The people were gone,
the buildings obliterated. A generation after the fighting and bombing
stopped, these places were pockmarked with bomb craters and littered
with *bombi*s and other ordnance. Almost every week children playing and
farmers working their fields accidently detonated explosives, and amputees on crutches were a common sight.

The drug trade was another form of regression. As the central government in Vientiane began going broke—Hanoi and Moscow had less and
less money to give—it farmed out most of its duties to the provincial gov-
ernors. Officials and commanders in the boondocks didn't have any
money either and they operated like the regional warlords of old. They
found that the only way they could make any money was by growing or
transporting opium for export through Thailand or Vietnam or even
through Burma and China. Hmong resistance fighters grew opium, too.
Outside Vientiane, hardly any area of Laos was under regular, systematic
government control.

About 1985, the year Laos hit rock bottom, Kaysone decided on a
change of course. First he let the remaining political prisoners out of the
"seminar" camps upcountry and closed the camps one by one. Then the
Vietnamese soldiers started pulling out of Laos, without explanation. One
year pith-helmeted soldiers had crowded the markets upcountry and the
next year they were gone. The Museum of the Revolution in Vientiane shut
down for repairs. When it reopened, the North Vietnamese had almost disappeared from the exhibits. History had been rewritten: There was no
mention in the museum of the Ho Chi Minh Trail.

By the time the Berlin wall fell in 1989, most of the Soviet advisers had
gone, too. Moscow, like Hanoi, was broke. The sons of the old-line Pathet
Lao leaders began to make contact with the remnants of the old elite families in exile in France and America, to discuss joint ventures. A construction boom got under way, financed by wealthy Thais. In the dry season,
when the Mekong's water level fell, heavy machines drove out on the sandbars next to the city, loading sand into dump trucks for mixing with ce-
ment. Nightclubs opened again. Opposite the exit from the Vientiane
airport, an advertising billboard rose, proclaiming "PEPSI: THE NUMBER ONE
SOFT DRINK IN LAOS."

It took until the breakup of the Soviet Union in 1992 to understand the magnitude of the change. Communism had failed as an economic system and as an ideology; and the Pathet Lao who had won the war had lost the peace. They were gradually giving in to the free-market system because they had no choice. Most of the rest of Asia was prospering as never before in history, and Laos, which always lagged behind its neighboring countries in everything it did, decided to climb on the free-market wagon.

Slowly but surely, Laos was heading back to the fold. Though it retained the hammer and sickle on its national emblem, it began to resemble more and more the mildly repressive, cheerfully corrupt, right-wing regimes of its Southeast Asian neighbors. Even before Kaysone died in 1992, Laos had joined the Southeast Asian trade group, ASEAN, with observer status. It allowed the Australian government to build a bridge across the Mekong near Vientiane, ending Laos's isolation and connecting by road two of the fastest-growing economies in the world, Thailand and China.

The regime mended relations with the United States. When USAID came back in, its first project was providing artificial limbs to Laotians who had lost them to *bombi*s. The U.S. military sent archeological teams to crash sites from the war, sifting through the wreckage, resolving MIA cases, Laotians and Americans working amicably together. A few of the refugees came back, too, some of them willingly, most of them not, as Thailand gradually closed the refugee camps.

It was as though this small, obscure, sweetly retarded country had ridden on a Cold War roller-coaster ride, starting with the coup of 1960: fifteen years of American domination, followed by fifteen years of Vietnamese and Soviet domination, and then a few more years for Laos to calm down and find its own destiny again, which was merely to be its own sweet, goofy self. When it was all over, even the Americans who had been part of the war effort found they could return to Vientiane and wander the streets, smiled at by locals who either didn't have a clue or didn't hold a grudge over the destruction of their country.

# THIRTY THREE

# The American Aftermath

Long after he retired, G. McMurtrie Godley, the U.S. ambassador to Laos during the peak years of fighting, offered this epitaph.

"We *used* the Meo," Godley admitted. "The rationale then, which I believed in, was that they tied down three first-rate North Vietnamese divisions that otherwise would have been used against our men in South Vietnam.

"It was a dirty business," he added.

Godley was right, as far as he went. The war was a dirty business. Though Operation Momentum began with a different motive, to help defend Laos, America ended up sacrificing the tribals and the lowland Laotians for U.S. goals in Vietnam. These allies, or proxies, were abandoned once the war was over, and the results were a permanent stain on America's reputation.

For those few Americans who worked in the field in Laos and really cared about the country, however—a group of perhaps a hundred people—Godley's summary was a little off the mark. Quite apart from his use of the old term "Meo" for the new, correct term "Hmong," the ambassador's assessment did not fully cover what the old hands experienced, and what they believed.

The multitour veterans from the CIA and USAID, the Bill Lairs and the Edgar Buells, were not cynics. They did not deliberately attach themselves to a losing cause. They gave willingly of themselves, hoping to help the Laotians at the same time that they helped their own country. The paradox was that even though they helped run the Laos war for their government, the outcome was the opposite of what they intended. Somehow, and they didn't know how, events had slipped out of their grasp. In some mysterious way, as the war became institutionalized, the system they worked for betrayed them and turned the war inside out.

What hurt them the most was that the United States had used the tribals for nothing. The Hmong hadn't been able to save Laos, and nothing tried in Laos was able to salvage the American effort in South Vietnam. It had backfired; and it had been no wiser or effective than shooting at the moon.

◆

Vint Lawrence became an artist.

He was a regular contributor of pen-and-ink political caricatures to *The New Republic* magazine, in Washington, D.C. His drawings were witty, detailed, and erudite, and every few years he had a show of his recent work in an art gallery. For his own pleasure, he also painted rural scenes with pen-and-ink and watercolor. The colors filled in the spaces between the ink lines and sometimes dappled or skitted across the lines, a technique he handled skillfully. He and his wife, a reporter for National Public Radio, had a house in Washington, D.C., and another in Connecticut. They lived quietly, but they knew a great many accomplished and influential people in government and journalism and in the East Coast intelligentsia.

Lawrence believed the work he had done in Laos, until his departure in early 1966, was worthwhile. The mission was nation-building more than fighting, and things started going wrong, he said, when people forgot that the middle letter in SGU stood for guerilla.

"As long as the Hmong maintained at least the semblance of fighting as a guerilla unit, there was every reason to suspect that they could survive almost indefinitely," said Lawrence. "It was when they, at our urging, decided to fight as large conventional forces that they got in such terrible trouble. The Hmong have never stood and fought anywhere. They were not good that way."

He didn't put all the blame on the American government. "Vang Pao wanted to be more of a force than he was, and thought he was capable of doing more than he was in fact capable of doing. As long as I was there, and as long as some of the other people were there, we were able to keep Vang Pao under wraps, because of the very fear that if you attracted too much attention, you were going to get your nose badly bloody. And that was what happened.

"Summed up in terms of our involvement in foreign lands, it's a very cautious lesson. I argued at *The New Republic* about our involvement with the Contras. Not on the basis that it was or wasn't morally correct. I argued against involvement simply because we would leave them worse off than when we started. We're incapable of supporting for a long period of time a people like the Hmong without trying to co-opt them or to change them into little versions of ourselves. You should give yourself real pause before you start in down that road. Because the end result may well be, as it was with the Hmong, that your help pushes people into political positions from which they can't retreat, and then makes them a target, and destroys them."

He did not think about Laos often, but every once in a while reminders came to him unbidden. One February he went walking through the woods of northwestern Connecticut with his young daughter. She was then learning that there was a body of beliefs and practices called religion, and she was curious about it in an innocent, six-year-old way.

As they walked along, Lawrence remarked to his daughter that different people think of God in different ways. In Laos, for example, the people whom he had known felt that there were spirits, and God was in every rock and every tree.

She looked at him as they were walking along a valley. Above them sloped a forested hillside. She stopped and her eyes went big and saucer-like. "You mean, there's a spirit inside every single tree?" she asked him. He said yes. She was dumbstruck that, to a Hmong, there could be a spirit inside each tree. They were looking at what seemed like millions of trees.

Lawrence began to form a perception of what was going through her mind. And then he was dumbstruck, too.

◆

Vang Pao became an American citizen. After a few years of farming outside Missoula, Montana, he joined the great secondary migration of Hmong refugees to California, settling in Santa Ana, south of Los Angeles. He became naturalized in a ceremony with immigrants from all over the world.

He has told fellow tribesmen that he receives thirty-five thousand dollars a year as a pension from the U.S. government, and that he can get medical care from Veterans Administration hospitals for the rest of his life. No other Hmong gets such treatment from the U.S. government. He is said to share his home with Wives Number Four and Six, who get along well, both being from the same clan.

His life in exile has not been happy because of his loss of stature, and because he came to America too late in life to be able to adjust to a culture radically different from his own. The first organization he helped start, Lao Family Community, was supposed to help Laotian refugees of all ethnic groups acculturate. Gradually, it became so biased in favor of the Vang clan that most other Laotians abandoned it. The national leadership got in so much trouble for sloppy accounting that local chapters became autonomous—not that they have done much better. At least one local leader has been convicted of embezzlement, and some of the local chapters, according to Americans familiar with their pattern of operation, exist essentially as money-raising fronts for the Laotian resistance and as a means of lining their leaders' pockets. Other Lao Family Community chapters, however, play genuinely useful roles by promoting education, discouraging the Hmong tradition of taking brides by force, and acting as go-betweens for indigent Hmong families who refuse to accept government-provided Western health care.

The second organization Vang Pao helped start, the Neo Hom, his branch of the Hmong resistance, has not fared much better. The young, educated Hmong who proposed the organization to Vang Pao were dismayed, they said, when he took over the leadership from them and decided to run it himself. Rank-and-file members lost faith when they bought Neo Hom certificates entitling them to high-ranking positions in a postcommunist Laotian government, only to find that those same positions were sold to somebody else the following year.

Because of the resistance's failure to topple the Vientiane government, and because of the questionable money-raising schemes, Vang Pao's support has fallen off in the United States. Law enforcement agencies have investigated the selling of Neo Hom certificates for fraud, but they have not brought charges; and those who understand Hmong culture believe that it is fairer to judge Vang Pao from an Asian perspective. Vang Pao, they point out, lives relatively modestly. He has never been particularly interested in money. If money is taken inappropriately, they say, blame it on his supporters and henchmen, who would use any system they were part of for their personal gain. Furthermore, they say, Vang Pao has to satisfy his people. Many of the older refugees, who still use shamans and believe in the parallel spirit world, have vivid dreams of returning to their homeland. These dreams seem more real and desirable to them than their waking lives in run-down urban communities, collecting welfare and fighting cockroaches. If Vang Pao ever gave up the idea of the resistance, his sympathizers say, he would risk some old tribesman coming up and shooting him in anger.

Nevertheless, it is widely stated in resistance circles that half the money collected in America is stolen by Neo Hom members, and half of the money that makes it to Thailand is stolen by the Thais. In Laos itself, the resistance, which has two main factions and many splinter groups, has never amounted to much. From time to time the leaders have their pictures taken with their raggedy soldiers holding their few weapons in remote camps in the boondocks, and proclaim that the parts of Laotian territory under their control are independent of the Vientiane regime. The outside world pays no attention.

The Neo Hom resistance soldiers have another photograph that they treasure as a talisman of their faith and show to few outsiders. In this color snapshot, an older and fatter Vang Pao carries a rifle slung over his far shoulder. Wearing brand-new camouflage fatigues and Adidas running shoes, he is walking down a hill through a grove of trees, looking at the ground so as not to lose his footing. Behind him walk other men in identical brand-new fatigues. The picture could have been taken anywhere, but the resistance fighters insist that it was taken inside Laos, in Sayaboury Province; and other sources confirm that this is true.

The resistance has its natural stronghold in Sayaboury Province, just as Bill Lair knew it always would. But Vang Pao's brief and secret return to Laotian soil has had to stay unpublicized. It would anger his handlers in an intelligence branch of the Thai army if word got out; and it would cause trouble with the U.S. government, since private U.S. citizens are by law not allowed to wage wars on foreign soil.

In the long run, Vang Pao is hoping to outlive the last of the doctrinaire Pathet Lao leaders. He will return when the regime has further softened its position and when it is ready to reconcile with the greatest of its former enemies. Perhaps, he will be able to live once again in the two-story stone house in Long Tieng, a valley now totally overgrown with jungle vegetation. But if he does, he will always need bodyguards to protect him against the last of the die-hard communists, and against those members of his tribe who believe that he betrayed them.

◆

During the 1980s a tiny, nonprofit advocacy organization called the Christic Institute filed a lawsuit against twenty-nine defendants, including Theodore Shackley, Thomas Clines, Richard Secord, the leaders of the Nicaraguan Contras, and, for good measure, the two biggest kingpins in the Colombian cocaine trade. The brief accompanying the lawsuit outlined an elaborate conspiracy theory alleging that "The Secret Team," a right-wing cabal including Shackley, Secord, and Clines, had originally formed in Laos, where it trafficked in narcotics and used the profits to support the Meo fight against the communists, and then turned up again in Central America, running cocaine to support the Contras. It also alleged that Shackley et al. were behind a 1984 bombing whose target was a Contra leader but which killed five journalists instead.

Subsequently the Christics put out a comic book, or "graphic docu-drama," version of their charges. The comic book portrayed, in more accessible form, the most cherished myth of conspiracy theorists and of the crowd that loves to hate the CIA. The myth is that the CIA finances operations through profits from the drug trade and arms smuggling, and uses the money to assassinate foreign leaders and overthrow governments.

The conspiracy theorists overlook an obvious fact—that throughout the Cold War the CIA had an easy time getting all the money it wanted from Congress. The Christics' suit was thrown out of court before it came to trial, and the judge levied a 1.2-million-dollar fine on them for bringing what he called a frivolous action. The Christics appealed the judgment, and the case went all the way up to the Supreme Court, which declined to review it, letting the lower court's decision stand. Most serious students of the CIA, and most heavyweight investigative journalists, agree that the courts acted correctly.

The irony of the Christics' clear-cut legal defeat is that the myth lives on. There is enough justifiable resentment of the CIA, and just enough nuggets of truth in the conspiracy theory, that some people will always believe that it is completely true. The Meo did sell opium. Secord was involved with both the Meo and the resupply of the Contras. Secord, Shackley, and Clines were all socially acquainted with Edwin O. Wilson, a former CIA operative who helped Libya's Col. Muammar Qaddafi build a terrorist organization, and who gave Clines financial backing for a shipping venture. Clines was convicted on four charges of underreporting his income to the IRS and concealing foreign bank accounts, and eventually went to prison. Secord made a rather unconvincing appearance at the Senate Iran-Contra hearings, and later pleaded guilty to lying to Congress; he paid a small fine for buying a security system for Oliver North. And so on. People are not to be blamed for connecting the dots, even if the picture they get isn't true.

Secord, Shackley, and Clines retired from the government after what they believed were honorable careers. They grew tired of being on the defensive, angry at the press, angry at the government for everything that happened to them in the 1980s. But for them, the Laos of the 1960s belonged to a better time. They felt they had served their government well there, in a cause they believed in, working with people they admired.

Of the three of them, Major General Secord was the most outspoken. He came to an interview with his friend Clines, whose case was then under appeal. The two men talked about the Laos war and the conversation turned to the battle for Phou Pha Thi, and the mystery of why the top-secret installation fell so easily. It had been a central event of that earlier stage of their careers, and the details came back readily. The Commando Club radar had always been underutilized, they agreed; and they wished they could have pulled the installation off the mountain long before it fell.

The two men were asked to assess the successes and failures of the Laos war. Clines, a practical, nuts-and-bolts man, believed gunships were a great tactical success. After Phou Pha Thi, the gunships came in, and no more sites were lost at night. Secord, more of a conceptual thinker, talked about the failures.

Secord believed that there were two strategic blunders of fatal proportions during the Indochina war, the failure to achieve unity of command and the failure to interdict the Ho Chi Minh Trail in a way that made sense. "Not with the McNamara Line, not with 'magic,' not with air alone," he declared. "We all wanted to do it without facing, as we used to say, the Dreaded Enemy. We'd spend however much money it took as long as we didn't lose our soldiers. Christ, look how many soldiers we lost! For doing nothing. For achieving nothing." He said that battle-hardened American ground troops, supported by artillery and airpower, particularly gunships, could have shut the Trail down. There would have been American casualties, but there are always going to be causalities if you try something worthwhile, he said.

He added that the idea of bombing the North Vietnamese back to the Stone Age was not a bad idea, either. "We could have done it—bomb 'em back to the Stone Age—had it been our objective," he said. "But it was always my understanding that the war was very limited, and that it was to maintain the integrity of South Vietnam and then later Laos. And if that is your objective, the way to go militarily is the way I just mentioned," by cutting the Trail with U.S. troops and by forming a unified command.

"Or else we could have nuked them, too," Secord said as an afterthought. "There was no shortage of things we could have done. But I'm just trying to give you my view of reasonable strategies, given the objectives laid down by the president."

◆

When the Vietnam War ended in 1975, Fred Branfman moved to California. He worked for Tom Hayden, the antiwar radical who had entered state politics, while his wife, Thoa, looked after the Hayden–Jane Fonda children. After that, he was an adviser to California's Governor Jerry Brown. Then he worked for Senator Gary Hart's presidential campaign until Hart self-destructed with the revelations of his sexual affairs. Politically, Branfman was moving steadily from the far left toward the center; and it became easier for some of his old critics to see that perhaps he had been patriotic all along, even if his understanding of the national interest was different from theirs.

Divorced, Branfman went back to Washington, D.C., where he started a nonprofit organization called Rebuild America, whose agenda was restructuring the U.S. economy with fiber-optic information freeways, industry-led consortia, an industrial policy for government, and so on.

Branfman remained an idealist who was always a step ahead of reality, always wanting the nation to improve itself. Shortly before the Clinton administration came along and pushed for some of the same causes, Branfman
dismantled Rebuild America. By then he was spending most of his time on
a personal quest. He went on meditation retreats. He traveled to Hungary
to learn from a spiritual teacher there. He went to India, and from there
back to Laos and to the Plain of Jars. He visited a cave where American
bombs had killed a large number of Laotians twenty years before. He felt
that he had spent much of his life trying to answer philosophical questions
that the Laos bombing had raised. Why does man hurt his own race? What
does that say about mankind's place in the universe?

"History is usually told from the air," Branfman wrote from his travels.
"We reconstruct it from the top down—as we look into the minds of leaders and discover their originally decent motivations and the constraints and
pressure under which they operated. But I didn't learn history that way in
Laos. I learned it in the eyes of the Laotian peasants who didn't know where
America was, let alone why its leaders dropped bombs that blew their
grandmothers to bits, burned their children alive, or blew the heads off
their brides before their eyes. I learned it in the eyes of folks who were
driven underground like animals for years, saw everything they had destroyed, and could still be more decent, loving and gentle than any people
I have ever met.

"Never this century has there been so much bombing for so long in such
secrecy by such a great power against so weak a people," Branfman continued. "Nine years of bombing, two million tons of bombs, whole rural
societies wiped off the map, hundreds of thousands of peasants treated like
herds of animals in a Clockwork Orange fantasy of an aerial African hunting safari."

He believed that the American leaders who bombed Laos acted as human monsters. "That is, they committed monstrous acts, killing thousands
and thousands of innocent human beings, in violation of the rules of war.
I say this without bearing personal animosity to the gentlemen in question
in Laos. Indeed I see them today as rather interesting and often endearing
chaps in their non-bombing Laos roles." Branfman said he admires Robert
McNamara and MacGeorge Bundy, two of the original architects of the
Vietnam War, for their later work on nuclear nonproliferation. Likewise,
he appreciates Bill Sullivan in retirement for having pushed for normal-
ization of relations with Hanoi. "I would look forward to spending a night
on the town with Tony Poe, Secord, or any of the other boys.

"And I say this without questioning their motivation. Indeed, I am perfectly willing to admit that it was, at least in many cases, no better or worse
than my own. I have been persuaded that those on the ground who really

hated communism were at least as 'idealistic' as those of us who opposed the war. And I am even more than willing to entertain the notion that I, too, am capable of acting monstrously in the unlikely event that the U.S. Air Force was placed at my disposition.

"And I say this without the need any longer to make the Pathet Lao and North Vietnamese more 'right' than we. Events since the war have shown that the Vietnamese and Pathet Lao probably would have behaved just as badly had they been the more powerful parties. If the Pathet Lao and North Vietnamese were more heroic during the war, it was largely due to cir-cumstance—a successful guerilla war against foreigners required doing more to secure the willing allegiance of villagers. They didn't have the tech-nology to drop millions of tons of bombs as did we—if they had they might well have used it.

"Indeed, all these caveats are precisely the point. What is most signifi-cant about Laos is these monstrous acts were committed by decent, not evil, men."

◆

William Sullivan served for four years as U.S. ambassador to the Philip-pines when that country was still under the rule of Ferdinand and Imelda Marcos. He then became ambassador to Iran, just as the Ayatollah Kho-meini's revolution was beginning to gather steam.

In his final hectic months in Iran, after the Shah's departure but before he retired in protest from the U.S. Foreign Service (and before the takeover of the American embassy in November 1979), Sullivan met with batches of reporters on a "background" basis. A gang of veteran journalists came in, along with one very serious young man stringing for an American news-paper. At the end, the young man asked, "Mr. Ambassador, I want to ask you a question. When the histories are written, the question is going to be asked: 'Who Lost Iran?' Aren't you going to be a principal candidate?"

Sullivan asked whether he could give his answer off the record. The young reporter said sure.

"I've lost a hell of a lot better countries than this one," Sullivan said.

With his gift for deflecting serious inquiry, it was hard to discover how much Sullivan cared about Laos and how he summed up his role there. Years later, when he was asked about it, he waved the questions off. "I tend to forget things or dismiss things from my mind so that I'm not haunted by them," he said. "If I were haunted by all my past life I'd never be able to sleep quite as equably as I do. So I don't keep things in mind."

He added. "You know, if you're really a professional in this business, you don't get emotionally too much involved. You have to try to stand back and see things objectively. If something didn't work out, you can't afford just to wail and gnash about it. You have to try to work your way out of it somehow."

No single American had a greater effect on Laos than Sullivan. He helped negotiate the agreements in 1962 and 1973 that bracketed the most serious fighting, and he was ambassador with extraordinary powers—a virtual proconsul—from 1964 to 1969, the crucial years.

He was Mr. Wonderland. He kept Laos ostensibly "neutral," only it was a battleground. His greatest achievement was keeping regular U.S. ground troops out of Laos, but there were instances, like Phou Pha Thi and at least arguably the South Vietnamese invasion of the Ho Chi Minh Trail, where U.S. ground forces might have made all the difference between failure and success.

He tried to control the bombing of Laos, which became one of the most heavily bombed pieces of real estate in the world.

He helped form two coalition governments that fell apart. And in the end, the communists took over anyway.

The unresolved question about Sullivan was whether he was a brilliant diplomat who had been dealt a bad hand and worked hard to make the best of it or just another one of those American war barons who never quite saw to the center of the problem in Southeast Asia, and who jealously protected their turf at the expense of their nation's higher interests.

Pushed on Laos's fate, Sullivan restated his thesis about Laos being subordinate to Vietnam, and Vietnam being subordinate to America's larger interests in the Cold War. "The great irony of our involvement in Vietnam," he said, "is that we were better off having lost the war than we would have been if we had won it," because losing it enabled the Chinese to make their opening to the Americans. China's opening to the United States, Sullivan pointed out, pushed the nervous Soviets into building up their eastern military flank along with their western flank, and the cost of that buildup, coupled with the inherent weaknesses of the Soviet economic system, bankrupted the Soviets, which brought an end to the Cold War.

This explanation makes sense from the geopolitical perspective; but when Sullivan goes beyond that, and implies that he knew the U.S. would win the Cold War all along, or that the U.S. "won" the Laos war after a fifteen-year lag of "temporary" defeat, it raises the suspicion that he uses this line of thinking as retroactive spin control, to excuse his blunders and those of his generation in government when the changing course of history enabled him to do so.

He was asked how he felt personally about the Laos epic.

"Let's leave Laos aside for a moment," replied Sullivan, "because Laos was in my judgment a greater personal tragedy to nicer people than what happened in Vietnam. On Vietnam, I think it was inevitable in the post-war world and in this whole accumulation of American hubris that sooner or later we would get ourselves into some situation from which we couldn't extract ourselves successfully.

"Given that fact, and given that Vietnam taught us a pretty severe national lesson, my thought is that we were just damn lucky that it happened in someplace like Vietnam, where we could put our tail between our legs and lick our wounds and walk away, rather than have it happen in someplace like East Berlin, where it could have led to an explosion of the Third World War. It was useful for our nation to learn, and particularly for some of our military types to learn, the limits of our capabilities. A brutal lesson, perhaps, and one that tore the country up pretty badly, but not as badly as it might have been torn up had it been someplace of greater strategic significance."

And Laos?

"In the case of Laos, I place the primary responsibility for what happened on the ambitions of the Vietnamese. Their intentions were evil. Our intentions were good. The fact that we were not successful in accomplishing our goals doesn't mean the Vietnamese were successful, either. Their failure was greater than ours."

And the Laotians themselves?

"In Laos," Sullivan said at last, "the people were sort of gentle and pleasant and innocent, and one can't help but feel a great sense of concern about it. But if you're asking, do I have personal anguish about these things, probably no. Maybe again it may sound a little cynical to you, but professionally, if you're in the business I was in, you can't allow yourself to get anguished and concerned in these things. You have to try to stay as far removed from it as you can.

"We're supposed to have ice water in our veins, I guess."

◆

Tony Poe came walking down the dirt lane near his house in Udorn Thani holding a quart bottle of Singha beer by the neck. He wore dirty gray pants, a gaudy Hawaiian-style sports shirt with the tail out to hide his bulging belly, and new running shoes. He wasn't a runner. Several of his toes were dead; the nerves didn't work from the various pieces of shrapnel he was carrying around. He could not walk through an airport metal detector without setting off the alarm.

Tiredly, he waved hello and said he wasn't feeling good. His wife was out of town. He hadn't eaten for three days, which meant he'd been drinking instead. The day before he'd gone to his favorite red-light establishment and, lo and behold, three women working together did him justice, for which he was grateful, particularly since he'd forgotten to bring any money. He was headed back to pay the whores now, but he couldn't feel any sensation in his feet, so maybe it would be a good idea to sit down in the café around the corner, just for a little while.

He sat at the café, brushing flies away from the table, and ordered beer for lunch. His two front teeth were missing, pulled out to get false ones, which had not yet been made. The two middle fingers of his left hand were missing, too—"let's just call it a training accident," he said. He was overweight and mostly bald, and his liver was getting tested monthly. He was taking nitroglycerine for his heart trouble and he said he wouldn't last long. Yet apart from his fatigue he seemed gregarious and cheerful.

The following day, when he was feeling better, he showed up at the big hotel in Udorn Thani, the Charoen, and sat by a window in the coffee shop. On the other side of the window, a gibbon in a cage climbed a dead tree, swung on a rope, jumped down, and climbed the tree, over and over.

Much of what Poe said that day was not to be taken literally because he was drinking. He gabbled, he talked gibberish, he had moments of lucidity, and then he launched into digressions. When he declared, for example, that there should have been marines at the Kent State antiwar demonstrations instead of the National Guard, because the marines shot better, he did not really mean that he supported the killing of American antiwar demonstrators. He was merely pledging his allegiance, stating his patriotism in a kind of far-right barstool jargon.

Beneath the surface of his words, Poe was mourning the loss of America's preeminent place in the world of nations—the America he had helped build in World War II, and arguably had helped destroy in Laos and elsewhere. He veered off on another long tangent about wanting to impeach the Supreme Court justices who recently had ruled that burning the American flag was protected by the constitutional freedom of expression. "I don't wanna be a pseudo-fucking flag waver," Poe said. "Goddammit, it means a lot to us. Hey! If we destroy the *fabric,* you know, this cloth, which was made up, you know, of *fabric,* and you put it all together, it creates strength. What in the hell are we talking about? We're talking about the *flag.*"

He took another sip of beer. "These things have nothing to do with—ah . . . because you're a Jehovah's Witness or a Holy Roller or a fucking Jew. Or a fucking Catholic like me or some other goddamn asshole. That's a lot of bullshit. This goddamn thing is—*fabric*! That makes us strong. These fucking pricks today, aw, 'It's my civil rights to burn the fucking flag.' If they want to be civil rights, give 'em a free ticket to go to Russia. Or wherever they want to go. Get the fuck out of here. Fuck 'em. We don't need this kind of people. Oh, that really pisses me off."

Poe drained the bottle of beer and turned around to signal the waitress for another. Then he got up to go to the men's room. He had to go to the men's room every few minutes. Having been badly wounded in combat in northeast Laos, he had an intestinal system that didn't work too well, either.

When he came back, he was asked whether drinking had ever hurt his career.

"No," said Poe. "I never drank. I never drank until I was about, uh, twenty-eight or twenty-nine. And then I didn't drink a lot. I never *drank* until, what, until Laos. I think Laos was the first one, when I was with VP. I think that's the first time I really started drinking."

He went off on a diatribe about Vang Pao. How Vang Pao should have been a colonel at most, and never had the training to be a general. How Vang Pao didn't delegate authority. "He wanted to be the biggest man in the business. And that's why he fell on his ass."

On the other side of the windowpane, the gibbon climbed up the tree, swung on the rope, jumped down, climbed up the tree, in a never-ending, neurotic cycle.

"Should we have gone into Laos in the first place?"

"Knowing what we knew in '75, no, I wouldn't," said Poe sadly. "Leave it alone. Bypass it. Bypass it.

"We went in because a lot of the big families in Laos wanted us to protect their interests. They were assholes. If we didn't go in there, there wouldn't have been any problem. I don't think the enemy would even have disturbed the people in the villages. If we'd left the Meo alone, they would have made some sort of compromise with the opposition."

Poe then wiped his mouth and declared that the opposition wasn't ready to cooperate with the Meo. "The Vietnamese and the bottomland Lao always called them the crazy people," he said of the Hmong, "because they do everything exactly the opposite of what you want 'em to do. They do it opposite."

In losing Laos, was Thailand saved?

"That's what all the big strategists ask," he said. "By our being in Laos, by our 'volunteers,' by our support for the Meo, we prevented the enemy from coming to Thailand."

Tony Poe had just said that we should have bypassed Laos, but that by going in we had saved Thailand. That the hilltribes would have been able to make an accommodation with the communists, but the communists wouldn't have accepted it. It didn't make the usual kind of sense—it didn't reduce to a single, coherent line of thought—but then Laos hadn't been that kind of war, and it wasn't that kind of country.

So what did we learn?

"We didn't learn shit," said Poe. "Come on. *Come on.* We were always in the majority, with the Hmong and our other people over the Pathet Lao and the North Vietnamese. But half of our guys wouldn't fight. Half of 'em'd run away in the nighttime. In the daytime, we'd end up with half of the troops.

"You can just take a frame," continued Poe, "without a picture in it, and put it over Laos or over some other part of the world and it's the same. It fits every goddamn situation. We still don't accept it. We go through the same—the Sandinistas, the Contras. Hey, the fucking Afghanistanis, the mujahedeen, these fucking rebels are fighting each other. You can't work it that way.

"The real tragedy," said Poe, "is that on both sides we lost so many good people. And what're we fighting over? A lot of bullshit. A lot of bullshit. A lot of personal prestige involved. Nothing really great. What's the great thing? Huh? What's the objective?" said Poe. "What's the *objective*? A bunch of goddamn hill people who don't want to fight? Who don't want to do anything? What did we accomplish? Nothing."

Did he feel that way at the time, when he was getting shot at and arguing with Vang Pao and collecting enemy ears?

"No, no, no," he said. "When you reflect back on it, when you think about all those people that are gone, when you think about all the people that are dead today, I don't think that the end justifies the means."

Tony Poe walked out of the coffee shop, bellowing loudly, scattering waiters and waitresses before him, and staggered through the lobby to the hot outside air.

◆

When Bill Lair retired from the CIA he went back to Texas. He enrolled his two grown children in state colleges and moved onto a ranch that he had bought on the installment plan for 127 dollars an acre. He was fifty-three years old. He had no idea what he was going to do with the rest of his life.

For a while he raised quarter horses with his son, a business neither of them knew much about. The horse operation folded rather rapidly, leaving the Lair family in serious financial trouble. He had reached GS-16 in government service, a civilian grade equivalent to one-star general in the military. His pension gave him enough to live on, but not enough to get him out of debt. He sold off part of the ranch and decided to get a job. The trouble was that around Waco, Texas, there was not much demand for organizing tribal trailwatch teams or planning guerilla campaigns against North Vietnamese.

He knew one way to get rich quick, and that was to go back to Thailand and work in the private sector. He knew he could be enormously useful to foreigners wanting to do business there, because of his contacts and his knowledge of the culture. He had friends from the CIA and the military who had taken that route. When they left the government they went to work in the areas of their specialty—for defense contractors or multinational corporations or as registered agents and lobbyists for foreign governments. He could understand that. They had been underpaid in government service, in comparison to their responsibilities. They were bright, aggressive people who wanted to live well and send their children to the best schools and colleges.

He couldn't bring himself to do it. He'd had the respect of the Thais he worked with, because they all knew that he worked for something larger than himself, that he would never ask them for anything for his own sake. Without that respect, he never would have been able to get anything done.

He tried several lines of work around his hometown but nothing panned out. He grew restless. The initial pleasures of returning to the States had long worn off, and something was bothering him inside.

One day he saw an advertisement in the newspaper for independent truck drivers to haul recreational vehicles from the factory where they were built to RV dealers around the country. On impulse he bought a used white International Model 4080 with a bunk in the back of the driver's seat and a Cummins diesel under the hood. He started hauling RVs on an orange fifty-four-foot-long trailer.

He knew what his old friends would think about his driving a truck, and he didn't care. He didn't have to write any memos. He didn't have to report to committees, work for a boss he didn't like, or work at all when he didn't feel like it. He drove the rig three or four days a week, and made as much money as he needed.

He liked the view from his truck cab, high above the cars. It was a little like flying in cargo planes in Thailand and Laos, only now he was in the pilot's seat. In the open landscape of the high plains states, he could see the weather unfolding from horizon to horizon, the cumulous clouds rising and building into thunderheads in the vast western skies. In clear weather, when he drove up the front range of the Rockies, it was nothing to see the snowcapped mountains from fifty or eighty miles away.

He was alone on the road for days at a time, puffing on an occasional cigar, needing the solitude and liking it.

He retraced the whole history in his mind, beginning with his arrival in Thailand and organizing the Paru and then going across the Mekong. He played the events over and over again, searching for the dynamics, the hidden forces that had made things turn out the way they did. He thought about his first meetings with Vang Pao, and getting the go-ahead from Desmond FitzGerald. About Tony and Vint, and then Shackley taking over the war and everything turning sour after that.

It took him tens of thousands of miles on the road to get over his anger at Shackley.

Thinking back on Laos, Lair wished he could have limited it to a handful of Americans at the most. Younger guys who would have stayed in place and understood about keeping the Laotians and Thais in charge. They couldn't have won the war, not with the North Vietnamese being as determined as they were; but it would have been possible to manage the war better by keeping it small and better connected to Thailand from the start.

He blamed himself for not forcing Vang Pao to build a following in Sayaboury. If he'd only pushed Vang Pao harder, and convinced the Thais that it was in their own interest to give the Meo quasi-legal status in Thailand, when the war was over Vang Pao could have crossed the river into Sayaboury and on up into the mountains along the Thai border. The Meo would still be there, on one side of the border or the other, living in close to traditional fashion. Which wasn't exactly happily ever after, but it would have been better than living in refugee camps, or collecting food stamps, or being shot up by MiG jets.

Because—yes. The Meo had been abandoned and they were always going to be abandoned. From the start he had known that the U.S. was going to leave. But it would have been possible to leave them better off than they'd been in the beginning. Better armed and better schooled, with their tribal integrity intact. Left with some reasonable hope for the future.

It took Lair years of solitary truck-driving to figure it out to his satisfaction. How at the start he had a program that worked, on a small scale. How as Vietnam grew next door, the failure to stop the traffic on the Trail gave the air force and the military their foot in the door; and how the bureaucracy had overwhelmed Momentum until it grew beyond its natural size.

As time went on, with only his thoughts for company, Lair began to take a more forgiving view of his own role. For as much as he tried to blame himself, he knew he had tried his best, and he had gotten some results.

He had been a founder and leader of a thirty-thousand-man army. Not many men could say that. He'd worked with the finest men he'd ever known, the Thai Paru, and with generals and ambassadors and kings.

He'd had a full career, and not without victories. He could accept the defeats. *Jai yen.*

And maybe, thought Lair, as he drove his truck down the interstate, everything was supposed to turn out the way it did.

# Notes

## Chapter 1: The Coup

On Edgar Buell: letters, photographs, and other documents in the Buell family archives. To assemble a coherent narrative, it was necessary here and in other Buell sections of the book to splice excerpts from different letters, though this was done without altering the sense in which they were originally written.

On the Kong Le coup and the events before and after: The best of many written sources, in my opinion, is Bernard B. Fall, *Anatomy of a Crisis: The Laotian Crisis of 1960–1961* (Garden City, N.Y.: Doubleday, 1969). The specifics about Kong Le's use of transistor radios come from Fall's account; and I have supplemented this with information from interviews with former employees of the CIA.

## Chapter 2: The Quiet Texan

Phoumi's attack on Vientiane is covered in the standard books of the period, including Hugh Toye, *Laos: Buffer State or Battleground* (London: Oxford University Press, 1968); Bernard Fall, *Anatomy of a Crisis: The Laotian Crisis of 1960–1961* (Garden City, N.Y.: Doubleday, 1969); Arthur J. Dommen, *Conflict in Laos: The Politics of Neutralization* (New York: Praeger, 1971). Thomas Lobe, *United States National Security Policy and Aid to the Thailand Police,* vol. 14, bk. 2 of Monograph Series in World Affairs (Denver: University of Denver Graduate School of International Studies, 1977), gives useful background on the Paru's formation. Alfred W. McCoy, *The Politics of Heroin in Southeast Asia* (New York: Harper & Row, 1972), has fascinating—but incomplete—information on Thai politics and its relationship to the drug trade. The rest of this chapter is derived from my interviews with Bill Lair and four other retired CIA officers, and with Ron Sutphin. Wherever possible, information from one source has been cross-checked with information from other participants; and where this has not been possible, effort has gone into checking the reliability and the reputation of the sources.

## Chapter 3: The Meeting

Buell archives; interviews with Lair, Sutphin, and others.

Eisenhower administration's planning at the beginning of 1961: "U.S. Increases 'Readiness' to Meet Crisis Over Laos; SEATO Studying Invasion," *The New York Times,* January 3, 1961, p. 1.

Removal of the trees from the airport road: interview with Fred Walker, an Air America pilot, who talked with the contractor.

Vang Pao's life up to the time of his meeting with Lair is largely based on a lengthy tape-recorded interview Vang Pao gave to the Hmong scholar Yang Dao in later years. The interview forms two chapters of a French book Yang Dao wrote with Jean Lartéguy, *La Fabuleuse aventure du peuple de l'Opium* (Paris: Presses de la Cité, 1979). While the account is colored by Vang Pao's selective memory, it generally tallies with information from other Hmong and American sources.

The French intelligence agency and the opium trade: See Alfred W. McCoy, *The Politics of Heroin in Southeast Asia* (New York: Harper & Row, 1972). On Vang Pao's early involvement with the opium trade: Ron Sutphin, the pilot, personally saw Vang Pao in the late 1950s loading opium onto airplanes at airstrips in northeast Laos; and Hmong refugees interviewed in the United States have spoken knowledgeably of Vang Pao's role as an assistant to Touby LyFoung, who handled much of the opium trade volume.

## Chapter 4: Momentum Begins

Interviews with Lair, Anthony Poshepny ("Tony Poe"), Jack Shirley, Bill Young, and other retired CIA officers.

Eisenhower quote to Kennedy: Secretary of Defense Robert McNamara to John F. Kennedy, "Memorandum to the President, 24 January 1961," declassified copy in the Lyndon B. Johnson Library.

The ex-marine helicopter pilot who crashed with Lair and Pranet was Clarence Abedy, later chief helicopter pilot for Air America. Abedy lost his logbook in later years, which makes it difficult to pinpoint the date, but from all other available evidence this flight seems to have taken place sometime in the first week of January 1961.

On the U.S. Army Special Forces in Laos: Years later Arthur "Bull" Simons became famous in military circles as the leader of the Green Beret raid on the Son Tay POW camp in North Vietnam.

## Chapter 5: Shooting at the Moon

Buell archives; Lair interviews.

U.S. response to Laotian crisis: news accounts and other written sources, notably Arthur M. Schlesinger Jr., *A Thousand Days: John F. Kennedy in the White House* (Boston: Houghton Mifflin, 1965), pp. 323–42.

Operation Millpond, Heinie Aderholt's B-26 force in Takli: interviews with Ronald Sutphin; and Timothy Castle, *At War in the Shadow of Vietnam: U.S. Military Aid to the Royal Lao Government, 1955–1975* (New York: Columbia University Press, 1993). pp. 34–36.

Story of the lunar eclipse in Vientiane confirmed independently in Peter T. White, "Report on Laos," *National Geographic,* August 1961; and in interview with Wilbur Garrett, the photographer for that story. Animist myths about eclipses abound in technologically undeveloped cultures. For Ojibway and Peruvian examples, see the one-volume edition of James Frazer, *The Golden Bough: A Study in Magic and Religion* (New York: Macmillan, 1962), p. 78.

Kennedy news conference: *The New York Times,* March 24, 1961, and other sources.

## Chapter 6: Vang Pao's Mistake

Padong: interviews with Lair, Young, Shirley, Chance, Vang Pao, and Fred Walker; and contemporaneous newspaper stories. On the Special Forces men donning their uniforms after the Bay of Pigs: It was at this point that the Green Berets were told that they were part of Operation White Star, the army's name for the Special Forces operation that lasted from April 19, 1961 until October 6, 1962. On the CIA explosives expert and his nervous break-down: The story was told to me in nearly identical versions by Chance and three CIA men in separate interviews. On rescuing American prisoners: interview with Bill Chance; sup-plemented by Don A. Schanche, *Mister Pop* (New York: McKay, 1970); p. 94; and Shelby Stanton, *The Green Berets at War: U.S. Army Special Forces in Asia, 1956–1975* (Novato, Calif: Presidio, 1986), pp. 39–40.

On the U.S. strategy at Geneva: interview with William Sullivan, plus two declassified documents from the John F. Kennedy Library: Case # NLK-87-84, with the hand-letter identification "1,3(a)(4)c," apparently a CIA memo with its date and title blanked out; and NLK-77-657, "Sanitized Copy: Status Report of the Task Force of Southeast Asia, Covert Annex—Laos (11–24 July)," no date given but apparently 1961. The United States dis-continued weapons drops to the Meo on June 27, 1961, less than two weeks after the fall of Padong.

Sullivan and the Soviets: William H. Sullivan, *Obbligato: Notes on a Foreign Service Ca-reer* (New York: Norton, 1984), pp. 162–65.

## Chapter 7: The Withdrawal

Interviews with Lair, Young, Sutphin, Vint Lawrence, and others. Information on the com-munist attacks' generating Meo refugees: press reports, Edgar Buell's letters, and an un-classified International Cooperation Administration report from Vientiane by John Tobler, director of U.S. Operations Mission, Laos, August 22, 1961.

On the difficulty of finding good CIA men to work in the field: Lair still believed that it was better to have Thais in the field than Americans. His right-hand man was the Paru Dachar Adulyarat, a smart, homely looking, overachieving Moslem from the south of Thailand.

Prince Souphanouvong's communist beginnings: See Arthur J. Dommen, *Conflict in Laos: The Politics of Neutralization* (New York: Praeger, 1964), pp. 23–36; and Tran Van Dinh, "The Birth of the Pathet Lao Army," in *Laos: War and Revolution,* ed. Nina S. Adams and Alfred W. McCoy (New York: Harper Colophon, 1970). Souphanouvong's and Sou-vanna Phouma's exile in Thailand, and the later Khang Khay incident: interview with Sul-livan and from Sullivan's book, *Obbligato: Notes on a Foreign Service Career* (New York: Norton, 1984).

"After another flare-up in the Laos civil war": in May 1962 the Royal Lao Army suffered a major embarrassment at the town of Nam Tha, in northern Laos near the Chinese bor-der, where a lowland Lao garrison took to its heels and fled seventy-five miles to the Mekong River and then across to Thailand at the mere rumor of an attack by Chinese troops. See Charles A. Stevenson, *The End of Nowhere: American Policy Toward Laos Since 1954* (Boston: Beacon, 1972), pp. 167–75.

The Buell story in *The Saturday Evening Post* was published as "An American Hero," by Don A. Schanche, in two parts, June 2 and June 9, 1962. Incidentally, the *Post* piece puts Long Tieng's population at five thousand; my lower figures come from a sketch map with population figures Buell made about two weeks before Schanche's arrival. Buell was a ha-bitual exaggerator except when it came to matters like airdrop requirements, when he was careful to be precise.

## Chapter 8: Udorn and Long Tieng

Interviews with Lair, Landry, Lawrence, Poe, and other retired CIA officers. On Tony Poe's background: Anthony Alexander Poshepny was born in 1924. He seems to have told many people in the early years of his CIA career that he was a Hungarian refugee, but he told me that the Poshepny family had come to America in the late nineteenth century from Bohemia and settled in Milwaukee. Ralph W. McGehee's *Deadly Deceits: My 25 Years in the CIA* (New York: Sheridan Square Publications, 1983), pp. 7–16, discusses Poe's CIA training. McGehee and Poe were in the same class at The Farm; Poe, the most colorful member of that class, is identified under the pseudonym Jimmy Moe.

## Chapter 9: Hard Rice

Harriman and Colby: William Colby, *Honorable Men: My Life in the CIA* (New York: Simon & Schuster, 1978), pp. 192–94; and interview with Colby. Hilsman's Burma war stories and his hawkishness on Laos: Colby interview.

Aftermath of the Geneva accords. The State Department's policy was to support Kong Le; so the army attaché at the U.S. embassy in Laos dutifully flew up to the Plain of Jars to talk with the neutralist commander, who was not always receptive. (The army attaché wasn't even allowed to land at Long Tieng, which was under the control of the CIA.) Attachés of the other countries signatory to the Geneva accords were also trying to befriend Kong Le, and their offers of friendship grew into a tug-of-war, as the Westerners and the communists tried to seduce him with competing aid packages. Geneva accords or no, the three Laotian factions had never entirely stopped fighting and skirmishing, and the level of paranoia stayed high. In late 1962 the neutralists even shot down an American cargo plane bringing rice to their own troops on the Plain of Jars.

Sullivan section: interview with Sullivan and his book, *Obbligato: Notes on a Foreign Service Career* (New York: Norton, 1984), pp. 178–82. U.S. decision to get militarily involved in Vietnam: Many books have been written on this subject, my favorite being David Halberstam's *The Best and the Brightest* (New York: Random House, 1972). I believe that Sullivan's recollections make a minor but useful addition to this literature, first because the Omega war games have not yet been fully written up, and second because his sense of the Soviets and the Chinese putting a geopolitical squeeze on Southeast Asia fits in with American perceptions at the time. Dean Rusk's memoir, *As I Saw It,* as told to Richard Rusk, ed. Daniel S. Papp (New York: Norton, 1992), does not specifically confirm Sullivan's recollections, but neither does it contradict them; and partial and indirect corroboration comes from Deborah Shapley, *Promise and Power: The Life and Times of Robert McNamara* (Boston: Little, Brown, 1993), p. 318.

On National Security Council removal of Geneva restrictions for Laos: separate telephone conversations with William Leary and Ken Conboy, scholars of the Laos war.

## Chapter 10: The Bureaucracy

Interviews with Dr. Charles Weldon, his daughter Rebecca Weldon Sithivong, and (by telephone) his ex-wife, Dr. Patricia McCreedy; letters and reports written by Weldon and Buell, and supplementary interviews with CIA and USAID staffers. Weldon's "Report of Recent Activities in Regard to Cholera Outbreak in Sam Neua," August 10–11, 14–20, 1963, was particularly helpful. Corroboration of Buell's practice of "testing" his Americans comes from interviews with several people who worked for him, including Tom Ward and Paul White.

## Chapter 11: Nation Building

Interviews with Lawrence, Poe, and Lair.

## Chapter 12: The Wedding

Interviews with Lawrence, Poe, Lair, and former members of Vang Pao's staff who do not wish to be identified.

Colby's maneuvers in Congress: Ralph W. McGehee, *Deadly Deceits: My 25 Years in the CIA* (New York: Sheridan Square Publications, 1983), pp. 82–84.

Vang Pao's changing role in the opium trade: confidential interviews with retired CIA officers, and with former members of Vang Pao's staff. Touby LyFoung's share of opium exports had declined in 1958, when a number of growers and local chiefs consigned a large shipment to him for sale, expecting later payment. The plane Touby hired crashed on the forested slopes of Phu Bia, the large mountain south of the Plain of Jars, and wasn't found for ten years. Touby didn't have money to pay the growers, and he lost credibility with them. That, and the removal of a Corsican syndicate from the Plain of Jars in the early 1960s, threw the Hmong opium trade more or less open to anybody who wanted a piece of it. At that point the main outlets for Meo opium were Touby LyFoung's brother in Vientiane, a Meo chief in Pha Khao, and ethnic Chinese traveling on trails to villages throughout the Laotian northeast.

Vang Pao agreed to separate proposals from Vint Lawrence and Dr. Patricia McCreedy to have the U.S. buy the entire raw opium crop at a fair price from the growers. The crop would have cost about a quarter-million dollars. The plans would have channeled most of the Meo opium crop away from illicit export and given the U.S. the option of destroying the raw drug or refining it into pharmaceutical morphine for hospitals. (The U.S. later used a policy like this successfully in Turkey.) But in Laos the proposals never made it through the American bureaucracy, and the status quo was maintained—in other words, U.S. policy was deliberately ambiguous.

Poe's story of the twenty-six helicopters: The analysis of someone who knew Poe well was that whatever the incident was it passed fairly easily. "It probably occurred but became exaggerated in Tony's mind." Vang Pao giving injections: confirmed, in general, by Hang Sao, Vang Pao's intelligence chief, in interview; he also confirmed that Buell and Poe sometimes worked together to curb corruption. Poe's wedding: With a U.S. embassy marriage certificate, Poe married the same woman, Ly Sang, in about 1974, which made their marriage legal by U.S. government standards. The two were still together twenty years later.

## Chapter 13: The Trail

Interviews with Lair and other CIA veterans. Meo factions: An old rival of Touby LyFoung's, Faydang Lobliano, had allied himself with the Pathet Lao and North Vietnamese. Their split grew out of historical quarrels over opium marketing and out of an old feud between leaders of the Ly and Lor clans. There were also Meo villages in Sayaboury Province on the south side of the Mekong and across the border in Thailand that worked closely with communist Chinese and North Vietnamese agents, mainly out of resentment against the lowland Lao and lowland Thai. The CIA would have liked all the Laotian Meo behind Vang Pao, but total unity was never possible.

Roy Moffitt and the Pakse operation in far southern Laos: As a bona fide USAID employee, Moffitt had advised the U.S. Army Special Forces when they set up a paramilitary force among the Lao Theung of the Bolovens Plateau in 1961 and 1962. When the Special Forces left Laos in October 1962, Moffitt hired on with the CIA as a contract employee and did what he could to pick up the pieces of the Bolovens operation. He used hunting expeditions as an excuse to travel around the Bolovens and farther east. His main contact was a Bolovens plantation owner named John Cadoux, who knew the local tribes and their territory well. With help from the regional Lao military commander and Lair and Landry at Udorn, and advice from Vang Pao and even Bill Young, Moffitt and Cadoux ran a reconnaissance and self-defense operation among the Loven, Lave, Nha Heun, and other Bolovens tribes.

The Ho Chi Minh Trail: The Vietnamese communists had used southeast Laos for transportation since the end of World War II. In May 1959, the North Vietnamese created Doan [Group] 559, tasked to manage and improve the Trail as necessary. In 1961 and 1962, the U.S. Air Force ran reconnaissance flights over the area to try to figure out what the North Vietnamese were up to. President Kennedy also ordered the CIA to conduct secret commando raids from South Vietnam, but the CIA's montagnards didn't like traveling far from home and weren't up to the task. The Agency then used South Vietnamese special forces to watch the Tchepone airfield, where North Vietnamese planes landed every now and again. Many of these teams were caught and killed. Subsequently, even before the CIA turned over the montagnard operation to the Special Forces, Green Berets led mixed-nationality cross-border teams. CIA officers who do not wish to be named; Douglas Pike of the Indochina Archives at Berkeley, California; former Ambassadors Leonard Unger and William Sullivan; Mark Pratt, former political officer at the U.S. embassy in Vientiane; Professor William Leary, University of Georgia; Stanley Karnow, *Vietnam: A History* (New York: Viking, 1983), Jacob Van Staaveren, *USAF Plans and Policies in South Vietnam and Laos, 1964,* U.S. Air Force Historical Division Liaison Office, December 1965, fn. p. 73; Brig. Gen. Southchay Vongsavanh, *RLG Military Operations and Activities in the Laotian Panhandle* (Washington, D.C.: U.S. Army Center of Military History, 1978), p. 9; *The Pentagon Papers as published by The New York Times* (New York: Bantam, 1971), p. 233.

The deterioration in South Vietnam in early 1964 and Lyndon Johnson's secret plans for building up the war there: A number of excellent histories examine this period in detail. My major sources were Karnow, *Vietnam: A History,* pp. 322–66; and *The Pentagon Papers,* pp. 234–306.

Airpower: The T-28s were technically known as AT-28s, for "advanced trainer." First use of airpower Van Staaveren, *USAF Plans and Policies in South Vietnam and Laos, 1964,* pp. 72–73. The first American pilots were U.S. Air Force Commandos from Udorn; they were soon replaced by civilian Air America pilots, and phased out entirely a few years later when enough Lao were trained to do the job. Kenneth Conboy, *The War in Laos, 1960–1975* (London: Osprey, 1989), p. 46; and other sources. Vang Pao's first request for airpower: Lair cables, released years later under the Freedom of Information Act. CIA cable describing airpower at Padong: My Xerox copy, unfortunately, is undated and without a heading. I believe it was from late May or June 1964. Airpower's early effect on Laotian commanders' confidence: Col. Robert L. F. Tyrrell, U.S. Air Force Oral History Interview, May 12, 1975 (Washington, D.C.: Office of Air Force History, U.S. Air Force Headquarters), pp. 32–34, p. 71. The first American retaliatory air strikes: Arthur J. Dommen, *Conflict in Laos: The Politics of Neutralization* (New York: Praeger, 1971), p. 275; and Charles A. Stevenson, *The End of Nowhere: American Policy Toward Laos Since 1954* (Boston: Beacon, 1972), p. 202.

The big Laotian logistical connection between the two Vietnams: *The New York Times,* May 28, June 26, and September 20, 1964. Unger's meeting with Souvanna Phouma: interview with Leonard Unger, December 27, 1990, Washington, D.C.

## Chapter 14: The Seesaw War

Overview of the "seesaw" war: Basic knowledge derived from various interviews and from the standard histories of the period, such as Charles A. Stevenson's *The End of Nowhere: American Policy Toward Laos Since 1954* (Boston: Beacon, 1972). Operation Triangle, known as Operation Sam Sone ("Three Arrows") to the Lao: various government cables of July and August 1964, many of them written by William Bundy, and deposited at the Lyndon B. Johnson Library; and other sources. Poe's role in Operation Triangle: various interviews with Tony Poe, and a July 31, 1964 cable from U.S. Ambassador to Laos Leonard Unger to Washington, confirming that the Meo did take the junction on July 29. This was not part of the plan as reported in previous cables and memoranda to and from Washington. Tonkin Gulf incidents: The best source is Stanley Karnow's *Vietnam: A History* (New York: Viking, 1983), pp. 365–76.

Colonel Thong: Buell letter to his children, June 26, 1965; and interviews with Dr. Charles Weldon. Late 1964–early 1965 North Vietnamese troop levels in Laos: CIA Office of Current Intelligence Memorandum, "The Communist Buildup in Laos," January 16, 1965, declassified 1976. Poe being wounded in January 1965: interviews with Poe, Weldon, and two retired CIA operatives, cross-referenced with letters from Buell and his Lao assistant, Thongsar Boupha, from the Buell family archives.

### Chapter 15: The Ambassador

Interviews with Lawrence, Lair, Weldon, Vang Pao, and other sources.

On Ouane and the royal opium concession in the northwest: interviews with Dr. Charles Weldon.

Phoumi's business interests: Charles A. Stevenson, *The End of Nowhere: American Policy Toward Laos Since 1954* (Boston: Beacon, 1972), p. 218; and other sources.

The attempted coups: William H. Sullivan, *Obbligato: Notes on a Foreign Service Career* (New York: Norton, 1984), pp. 219–27; interviews with Sullivan, Dr. Weldon, the USAID American who inadvertently tipped off the embassy to Colonel Karpkeo's location, and others. The other colonel who went and stayed on the lam was a Colonel Khamsao.

The Laos bombing campaigns were formally begun on December 14, 1964. The Rolling Thunder campaign against North Vietnam was postponed several times and eventually started in March 1965. On early bombing mishaps in Laos: Col. Robert L.F. Tyrrell, U.S. Air Force Oral History Interview, May 12, 1975 (Washington, D.C.: Office of Air Force History, U.S. Air Force Headquarters), p. 114. (Tyrrell was Sullivan's air force attaché.) Sullivan interview. Telephone interview with a retired CIA case officer who does not wish to be identified.

### Chapter 16: Vietnam

Interviews with Lair, Rhyne, Sullivan, Blaufarb, and others. Ernest Brace affair and its aftermath: Brace himself gives a slightly different construction to the events of his capture in his book, *A Code to Keep: The True Story of America's Longest-Held Civilian Prisoner of War in Vietnam* (New York: St. Martin's, 1988), pp. 32–33.

### Chapter 17: High-Water Mark

Interviews with Lair, Lawrence, Poe, Weldon, Vang Pao, and confidential sources; Buell archives. Vang Pao's first jet air strike: interviews with Dr. Charles Weldon. Laotian commanders who had been able to beat the North Vietnamese: Besides Vang Pao and Colonel Thong, two other lowland Lao colonels who worked for Vang Pao had impressive records: a Colonel Chansom, who was Vang Pao's number two in the royalist Military Region II command; and a Col. Duongta Norasing, who worked closely with Thong. Laos hands often pointed out that leadership was the most important factor in combat—that a March 1965 Vietnamese attack on the Dong Hene military training center, for example, was also repulsed because the Lao soldiers there fought hard and just wouldn't quit.

Colonel Thong's wounding, death, and funeral: Journal entries of June 23–24, 1965 of Dr. Patricia McCreedy; Edgar Buell's letter home of June 26, 1965; and author's correspondence with William Leary and Douglas Blaufarb.

Poe's departure from Long Tieng: interviews with Poe, Lair, Lawrence, Weldon, Young, and various high-ranking Hmong.

On Congressman "Tiger" Teague and his son, the forward air guide: phone interview with the junior Teague (now a retired colonel living in Texas) on March 2, 1991. Letter from Capt. John O. Teague to Pop Buell, December 9, 1965; and Buell letter home, November 16, 1965.

## Chapter 18: From a Country Store to a Supermarket

Lawrence's departure: interviews with Lawrence and William Colby.

February 1966 battle for Nakhang: Capt. Melvin F. Porter, *The Defense of Lima Site 36,* report of Project CHECO (Contemporary Historical Evaluations of Combat Operation, based in Udorn), Pacific Air Force Headquarters Tactical Evaluation Center, May 25, 1966. Sullivan convincing Vang Pao to accept a steel pin in his shoulder: William Sullivan, *Obbligato: Notes on a Foreign Service Career* (New York: Norton, 1984), p. 216.

Comparison of B-52 bombing in the northern Laos theater with Ho Chi Minh Trail and South Vietnam: Col. Gene Gurney, *Vietnam: The War in the Air* (New York: Crown, 1985), p. 213; Agent Orange and Agent White: "Ranch Hand Herbicide Operations in SEA," Project CHECO report, July 13, 1971, pp. 1, 13. Use of Nung tribesmen east of Bolovens Plateau: Kenneth Conboy, *The War in Laos, 1960–1975* (London: Osprey, 1989), pp. 7. U.S. troop levels in South Vietnam: *The Pentagon Papers as published by The New York Times* (New York: Bantam, 1990), pp. 385, 460.

Lair's station chiefs: interviews with Lair, Blaufarb, and Shackley. Blaufarb and Weldon: interview with Weldon. Shackley's initial meeting with Lair and Landry: interviews with all three men, plus Tom Clines and Richard Secord (who came to Udorn a few months later and heard about Shackley's first meeting from staffers there). The phrase firmly attributed to Shackley, "from a country store to a supermarket," became part of the Agency folklore in the war in Laos. Shackley, in an interview, did not recall having used the phrase, but did not deny using it, either, saying that it was not the kind of phrase he was likely to use.

Shackley's background: See David Corn, *Blond Ghost: Ted Shackley and the CIA's Crusades* (New York: Simon & Schuster, 1994). Additional sources include interviews with William Sullivan, Tom Clines, Ted Shackley, and others; and Shackley's book, *The Third Option: An American View of Counterinsurgency Operations* (New York: Reader's Digest Press, 1981). The CIA and Cuba: For a good overview of Mongoose, see Thomas Powers, *The Man Who Kept the Secrets: Richard Helms and the CIA* (New York: Knopf, 1979), pp. 132–52. In my interview with him, Shackley was reluctant to talk about Cuba, as he had not cleared any of his own recollections on the subject with the CIA. On the issue of finding the Soviet missiles he told me, "I think it's clear that the basic information about the Soviet ICBMs came from the station in Miami [of which he was then chief]. And it's also clear that on the basis of that, people flew the U-2 missions. I think that is as straightforward and simple as one can make it during that period of time."

Shackley in Laos: interviews with William Sullivan and various other Americans from the State Department USAID and CIA; and from Buell archives. Shackley-Mendenhall arguments from Ernest Kuhn in a letter to author. Douglas Blaufarb writes, in *Organizing and Managing Unconventional War in Laos, 1962–1970* (A Report Prepared for Advanced Research Projects Agency by the Rand Corporation, Santa Monica, California, January 1972), pp. 39–41, 98–99, of the collapse of CIA-USAID cooperation in the Sedone valley security project north of Pakse; and though he doesn't name names, blames the collapse on both Mendenhall and Shackley. Weldon-Shackley meeting: interview with Weldon. On Weldon's memory of the meeting, Shackley responded, in his interview with me: "The specific incident that he [Weldon] has recounted, I have no memory of that whatsoever. But honestly, if he went off in a huff, and it was an important issue to him and if it did take place, it obviously didn't register with me. It had to be in the years '66 to '68. That's a long time ago."

On the changes Shackley brought to Pakse: interviews with five retired CIA personnel with direct knowledge of southern Laos. See also Brig. Gen. Southchay Vongsavanh, *RLG Military Operations and Activities in the Laotian Panhandle* (Washington, D.C.: U.S. Army Center of Military History, 1978), p. 38.

After reading this and the following chapters in manuscript form, Shackley objected to the book's central theme. He wrote: "Yes, the war in Laos was designed to meet the purposes of the kingdom of Laos and the United States. When the original balance in this partnership shifted because American policy makers expanded America's role in Vietnam, the tasks in Laos also changed. They became, as you say, . . . to tie down North Vietnamese divisions in north Laos and make Hanoi pay a price for using the Ho Chi Minh Trail. This is a reflection of what historians call national interest. In essence, the United States felt the protection of 500,000 American troops in Vietnam was more important than the preservation of the fig leaf of Lao neutrality. Your argument, therefore, should be with the policy formulators not the implementers of policy if you think such a change betrayed the Lao peoples. Couldn't it be that some Udorn observers were looking at a tree in the Indo-China war and not a forest?"

### Chapter 19: The Taj Mahal

Secord: Most information on Secord comes from face-to-face and telephone interviews with him, supplemented by interviews with Clines, Lair, and others who were then serving with him in the CIA. An additional source was the book Secord wrote, with Jay Wurts, *Honored and Betrayed: Irangate, Covert Affairs, and the Secret War in Laos* (New York: Wiley, 1992).

USAID's Ernest Kuhn contributed information on Operation Night Watch and on the Nakhang battle. Another Nakhang source was an air force report, *Second Defense of Lima Site 36*, by Capt. Melvin F. Porter of Project CHECO, Pacific Air Force Headquarters Tactical Evaluation Headquarters, May 25, 1966. Where Kuhn and the CHECO report disagree, I have gone with Kuhn's account, which is based on a closer understanding of the terrain and the people involved.

Lair on airpower and the Taj Mahal: interviews with Lair and others who served with him in the CIA.

### Chapter 20: Commando Club

Secord: same sources as in Chapter 19, plus Sullivan.

The "Hobby Shop" projects for detecting and harassing Ho Chi Minh Trail traffic were run overall under the cover name of the Defense Communication Planning Group (DCPG). Other nicknames and code names also became attached to this effort, including McNamara's Line, after the secretary of defense, Robert McNamara; and Igloo White, one of the principal code names for the electronic operation that eventually was run out of Nakhorn Phanom air base in Thailand.

Sullivan's problem with Secord: Both Fred Branfman (in a manuscript from the early 1970s called "Control of an Air War") and Seymour Hersh (in "How We Ran the Secret Air War in Laos;" *New York Times Magazine*, October 29, 1972, p. 97) relate stories similar to Sullivan's about a denied request for a bombing raid that went ahead anyway and was later discovered. Neither Branfman's nor Hersh's account, however, mentions Secord.

Planning for Phou Pha Thi radars: interviews with Lair, Secord, Col. Gerald Clayton (Ret.), and others; and a study prepared by the air force's Project CHECO in Udorn, *The Fall of Site 85*, by Capt. Edward Vallentiny, August 9, 1968, declassified in the late 1980s. Organization of 7/13th Air Force: Col. Gene Gurney, *Vietnam: The War in the Air* (New York: Crown, 1985), p. 212. TACANs and Skyspot: The air force had also installed TACANs outside Nakhorn Phanom air base in Thailand; at Long Tieng; at Muang Pha-lang near Savannakhet; and on the north edge of the Bolovens Plateau.

Lyndon Johnson's order to Sullivan: interview with Sullivan. Colonel Clayton's meeting with air attaché and Sullivan: telephone interview with Clayton.

Lair's disagreements with Shackley: In an interview Shackley disputed this view. He said, in part:

> To the best of my knowledge, there aren't any conflicts between Bill Lair and my-self. . . . I think I understand what you're saying. But that needs to be put into a slightly different perspective. . . . Bill Lair and Pat Landry . . . understood that air-power had to be harnessed as the North Vietnamese kept increasing the commit-ment they were going to make to the north of Laos, as far as putting in additional divisions and troops. And certainly we were all of the same line, that we needed to use the slow technology, in terms of the airpower, rather than what was being put forth by people like General Momyer from the 7/13th Air Force.
>
> I think, as you know, that the Meo, for instance, of the northern hilltribes, had no role in the south. So that war didn't really impact on it. Now, did it impact on the managers and theoreticians and others who were involved in the war? Yes. A lot of their area knowledge was drawn on, and their experiences in the war were brought to bear on developing and enhancing the techniques that were used in the south. I saw that really as a collegial effort, of melding various different techniques and ap-proaches to a problem. And sure there was tugging and pulling. But there's always tugging and pulling. . . . In the final analysis I didn't always accept their recommen-dations. I made my own. Followed my own judgments. I don't think that ever—that I know of, anyway—with Bill Lair and Pat Landry and others created any lasting fric-tions or irritations or dissatisfactions.

## Chapter 21: Branfman and Lawrence
Interviews with Branfman and Lawrence.

## Chapter 22: Ted Didn't Know Shit about Tactical Warfare
Interviews with Lair, Secord, Weldon, Kuhn, Clines, Shackley, Clayton, and others; for dates, sizes of military units, and embassy policy: Capt. Edward Vallentiny, *The Fall of Site 85*, Project CHECO report, August 9, 1968, declassified in the late 1980s. The CHECO study is useful, but also seriously flawed, as it was written hastily and without interviews of most of the principals. It reflects an institutional bias of the air force, and is at heart a bu-reaucratic exercise in rationalizing the air force failure at Pha Thi. The thesis that the North Vietnamese decision to send sizable forces into Laos was a reaction to the Pha Thi radar is derived in part from Douglas Blaufarb, in correspondence and in his book, *The Coun-terinsurgency Era: U.S. Doctrine and Performance, 1950 to the Present* (New York: Free Press, 1977).

Pilots' dislike of Commando Club: Clayton Interview. Statistics on use: CHECO Site 85 report, p. 2. Shooting down the biplanes: CHECO Site 85 report and Statement of Capt.

Theodore H. Moore of Air America, in Timothy Neil Castle, "At War in the Shadow of Vietnam: United States Military Aid for the Royal Lao Government, 1955–1975" (Ph.D. dissertation, University of Hawaii, 1991), p. 210.

Nam Bac and its fall: interviews with Lair, Shackley, Clines, Secord, and others; and various published sources. Accidental air strikes: August 1990 interview with two former Royal Lao Air Force T-28 pilots who flew missions in defense of Nam Bac. On Vang Pao's commitments and losses east of Nam Bac: Buell letter of February 11, 1968 to Joseph Mendenhall, the USAID director for Laos. On Sullivan's role at Nam Bac: interview with Sullivan. Douglas Blaufarb notes, in *Organizing and Managing Unconventional War in Laos, 1962–1970* (A Report Prepared for Advanced Research Projects Agency by the Rand Corporation, Santa Monica, California, January 1972), pp. 61–62, that Sullivan's approval was needed for "[s]izable movements for Lao military personnel requiring lift by U.S.-controlled aircraft" and "[o]ffensive operations by Laos forces requiring close air support or preliminary air attack or any special logistical support."

Shackley's role at Nam Bac: interview with Richard Secord and Tom Clines. In my later interview with Shackley, I mentioned the view at the CIA's Udorn base that he had a lot to do with the failure at Nam Bac. Shackley responded:

> Like a lot of these things, there is a kernel of truth in this. . . . Nam Bac was essentially a FAR [Force Armée Royale] operation. It was a royal Laotian conventional force operation. The instigator/primary proponent and planner of that operation was the military attaché. . . . He was the primary mover and planner for that particular operation. Now within the mission council we were all asked to contribute to that operation. And I did agree that we would make a contribution with the forces that we had. . . . But that was not our operation. We were providing essentially support— intelligence, guerilla harassment, and an agreement that within the total resource package of firepower and so forth that certain amounts of that would be allocated on a priority basis to Nam Bac.

Buell in the post–Nam Bac period: Excerpt from a confidential memo from Edgar M. Buell, area coordinator of Xieng Khouang, to Joseph A. Mendenhall, director of USAID/Laos, February 11, 1968; and excerpts from Edgar Buell's letters home of February 26 and March 7, 1968.

Pha Thi narrative resumed: CHECO Site 85 report, pp. 3, 6, 21–23, 32; interviews with Clayton; author's communications with Ernest Kuhn of USAID, who was stationed on a neighboring mountain the night Pha Thi fell. Howard Freeman declined to be interviewed for this book.

Blanton and Etchberger information: two telephone interviews with Clayton, their commanding officer, October 1991. Information largely but not completely corroborated by a source in the Defense Intelligence Agency.

## Chapter 23: Sayaboury Time

The fates of the American men and the technology from Phou Pha Thi are still unresolved. In 1994 a Defense Intelligence Agency team interviewed the leader of the North Vietnamese unit that captured the installation, who claimed that no Americans were taken prisoner; but a source close to the DIA team said that the story still had loose ends. Another DIA source told the author that Soviet or Soviet-bloc technicians were spotted on Pha Thi a few days after it fell.

Sullivan and the early Paris negotiations: William H. Sullivan, *Obbligato: Notes on a Foreign Service Career* (New York: Norton, 1984), pp. 227–33.

Buell section: letters, March 26 and April 5, 1968.

Lawrence section: interviews with Vint Lawrence, with quotes from "National Integration of North Laos," a paper he wrote at Princeton; and Robert Shaplen, "Letter from Laos," *The New Yorker,* May 4, 1968.

On the fall of Phou Pha Thi being the turning point of the Laos war: interviews with Lair, Secord, Weldon, Shackley, Blaufarb, and others.

Secord and the increase of U.S. tactical aircraft in northern Laos: A State Department cable dated March 31, 1968, informing ambassadors in Asia and the Pacific of the impending partial bombing halt, stated, in part: ". . . air power now used north of 20th can probably be used in Laos (where no policy changes planned) and in SVN." [South Vietnam] (*The Pentagon Papers as Published in The New York Times* [New York: Bantam, 1971], p. 623). Nevertheless, a short-lived bombing halt north of the 20th parallel ensued, and the CIA made strenuous efforts to have it overturned. Excess of air force planes: Douglas Blaufarb, *Organizing and Managing Unconventional War in Laos, 1962–1970* (A Report Prepared for Advanced Research Projects Agency by the Rand Corporation, Santa Monica, California, January 1972), p. 99. The decision to send more planes to Laos was not made for the sake of the men on the ground but rather so that the air force could justify its force structure in Southeast Asia. See Col. Robert L.F. Tyrrell, U.S. Air Force Oral History Interview, May 12, 1975 (Washington, D.C.: Office of Air Force History, U.S. Air Force Headquarters), p. 59; and other sources.

Organization of the Ravens: The primary catalyst behind the formation of the Raven program was the U.S. embassy's air attaché at the time, Col. Paul "Pappy" Pettigrew, who served during Tyrrell's absence.

Lair's departure: interviews with Lair and others in the CIA. Photos of the medal-awarding ceremony were taken by Thais present at the king's house in Long Tieng, 1968, and copy sets circulated among the Americans later.

## Chapter 24: The Opium Trade

Landry's takeover of Lair's job: interviews with various CIA veterans. Diminished importance of Landry's job: This was also due to internal CIA reshuffling. A new layer of subordinates—the chiefs of unit—made many of the decisions in the field. They reported to Landry, who reported to the Vientiane chief of station, whose job had expanded under Shackley's tenure to include supervision of paramilitary matters.

Further buildup of air war: With the total bombing halt over North Vietnam, the monthly total of U.S. flights over southern Laos jumped from 4,700 to 13,400, including 600 carpet-bombing sorties by B-52s: John Morrocco, *Rain of Fire: Air War, 1969–1973,* in the series The Vietnam Experience (Boston: Boston Publishing Co., 1985), p. 38.

Poe in the northwest: interviews with Poe; several retired CIA officers who do not wish to be identified; William Sullivan; USAID veterans including Dr. Charles Weldon, MacAlan Thompson, and Ernest Kuhn; Ron Rickenbach; and several Mien and Lahu tribesmen. Resupply of wiretapping teams in China: In Burma and even over the border in Laos the CIA coexisted with these opium traders because it had no practical choice—or so the old-timers said. The connection to the opium trade was not believed to be enough reason to stop the operation. The reconnaissance went on for years, until 1972, when Nixon visited China and his new hosts asked him to put a halt to it. For a fuller account, see Alfred W. McCoy's *The Politics of Heroin in Southeast Asia* (New York: Harper & Row, 1972), pp. 301–308.

Poe and the "reverse medevacs": interview with MacAlan Thompson and Ernest Kuhn, both of USAID. Young and Poe: Young believed, with some justification, that if the CIA really wanted good reports it should give him one of its Ivy League intelligence types, someone like Vint Lawrence, to do the writing for him. It was too much to expect a specialist like himself to be a generalist, good at everything he did. Young claimed that the reason he left the Agency in 1967 was that he was getting disillusioned with Shackley's changes and also because he was planning to get married. (Young did marry an American woman about that time.) Americans who knew both men said that neither was a reliable source of information but that Poe fired Young and that Poe's account of Young's shortcoming and misdeeds was basically true.

The opium trade: interviews with Poe, Weldon, Young, and others. General Ma's refusal to take part in the drug trade and the lead-up to the 1967 Opium War: The standard account is McCoy's *The Politics of Heroin in Southeast Asia,* pp. 293–328. Other sources were my own interviews and a memorandum of the 1967 Opium War shootout by Dr. Pat McCreedy of USAID, August 15, 1967. T-28s in the 1967 Opium War: interview with an ex–Royal Lao Air Force pilot who flew one of the T-28s.

Poe collecting information on the drug trade after the 1967 Opium War: This is a controversial point. Some of the CIA people supervising Poe denied that this was true, perhaps because they were trying to protect the Agency from the age-old charge that it was involved in any way in the opium trade. But Sullivan, in a 1990 interview, confirmed Poe's expanded assignment. Vang Pao's role in the opium and heroin trades: see notes for Chapter 25.

## Chapter 25: My Favor

Determining what Vang Pao did or didn't do in the drug trade is not easy. The trade was always secret or semisecret, even though poppy cultivation was legal in Laos (until theoretically outlawed in 1971). Both the Hmong and the Americans who knew most about it were reluctant to speak; and most Americans from the CIA, except for Poe, made a point of not learning too much because of an unstated policy of leaving the trade alone. The drug war wasn't the war the CIA was interested in fighting.

The truth is further obscured by hidden agendas. Generally, those who said that Vang Pao was a drug kingpin were trying to prove something much larger—that Vang Pao, because of his involvement, was a bad guy through and through; or that the CIA because of its role (whatever it was) is a bad institution. Those who insisted that Vang Pao was uninvolved were trying to protect the reputation of the CIA—just as unrealistically.

Long after the war, Tony Poe told an American TV journalist for the PBS *Frontline* series about Vang Pao's supposed connection with Ouane and heroin trafficking to South Vietnam. The journalist, a woman of the political left, deftly edited the review to buttress her thesis, the venerable myth that the CIA itself participated in drug trafficking. My own conclusion, after talking extensively with Poe and after interviewing other CIA veterans and some of Vang Pao's staffers, is that this was one of many occasions when Poe mixed up or embroidered stories after the fact and later came to believe in his own inventions. If I had reasonable evidence to back up the claim that Vang Pao was a drug kingpin or that the CIA actively abetted the drug trade I would not hesitate to say so.

The other extreme position taken by some CIA supporters—that Vang Pao's household and his organization knew nothing at all about opium—is also ludicrous. Opium was part of Hmong tribal culture. Two of Vang Pao's own wives smoked opium occasionally. One of his brothers was a heavy opium smoker and Long Tieng local opium trader of no particular importance. A major who worked for Hang Sao, Vang Pao's intelligence chief, was arrested on opium charges in Vientiane during the latter part of the war, and Vang Pao had him freed a few days later. The exact link between the major and Vang Pao was not clear then or now; but it is likely that Vang Pao benefited in some way from the hierarchical relationship, whether in the form of money or loyalty.

Vang Pao's wives: interviews with various Hmong refugees in the U.S., including one who lived in Vang Pao's household as a boy; and one of VP's top aides. Vang Pao's remark on his marital situation comes from an interview with Tom Clines. Vang Pao's tour in the U.S.: a CIA source who helped arrange the trip and was familiar with many of the details. Vang Pao and the fishing trip in Florida: interview with Richard Secord.

Operation Pigfat, the attempt to retake Phou Pha Thi: Much of my information comes from Ernest Kuhn of USAID, who spent a month in the field with Vang Pao and his CIA adviser on this operation. Casualty figures in Pigfat: letters home of Edgar Buell, January 16 and 29, 1969. The information about the partial evacuation of Sam Thong later in the chapter comes from the same Buell letters. Ten thousand refugees: Ernest Kuhn, "Refugee Policy of the USAID Mission to Laos" (first draft typescript), p. 13.

Buell section: undated handwritten memo from Edgar Buell, found among his letters home. Last few paragraphs taken from Buell letters of February through May 1969.

Vang Pao and the capture of the Plain of Jars: various sources, including interview with Vang Pao, Buell letters home, news accounts, Christopher Robbins's *The Ravens: The Men Who Flew in America's Secret War in Laos* (New York: Crown, 1987), and U.S. Air Force documents, particularly the U.S. Air Force Oral History Program Interview of Capt. Karl L. Polifka Jr. by Lt. Col. Robert G. Zimmerman, December 17, 1974, Washington, D.C., declassified 1982. Muong Soui losses: Col. Gene Gurney, *Vietnam: The War in the Air* (New York: Crown, 1985), p. 238. Vang Pao's grief at Ly Lue's funeral: interview with Vang Pao. Flying in the rain in canyons: see, for example, Polifka, pp. 44–46.

Will Green's role: interview with Clines, and other sources. Vang Pao, Clines, and the cave on the Plain of Jars: interview with Clines. The Polifka and Maj. Michael E. Cavanaugh interviews of the U.S. Air Force Oral History Program both describe similar supply caves in and around the Plain of Jars (Cavanaugh interview by Lt. Col. Robert G. Zimmerman, November 21, 1974, Randolph Air Force Base, Texas). Enemy matériel captured on the Plain of Jars: The written sources—Colby, Gurney, Blaufarb—all vary on the statistics of enemy materials seized on the Plain of Jars; I have given low, safe figures taken from them.

On Vang Pao wanting to be the big man of Laos: interviews with Lair, and with Americans and Laotians who knew him well and do not wish to be identified. Vang Pao and the torture of the North Vietnamese prisoners: Henry Kamm, "Laotian Generals Concede Prisoners Are Tortured," *The New York Times,* October 20, 1969. Pha Khao interrogation center, spies in Long Tieng, and heavy-handed recruitment: interview with a former high-ranking officer in Vang Pao's G-2, or intelligence apparatus, and other confidential sources.

September to October 1969 forcible evacuation of civilians from the Plain of Jars: numerous sources, including newspaper stories; Polifka, pp. 99–100; interview with Ernest Kuhn.

Branfman section: interviews with Branfman, supplemented by interview with T. D. Allman, and published sources.

## Chapter 26: No Commitment

All quotes in the Senate hearing section are taken from a transcript, published as "Part 2: United States Security Agreements and Commitments Abroad, Kingdom of Laos; United States Senate, Committee on Foreign Relations, Washington, D.C., April 3, 1970" (reprinted by Dalley Book Service, 90 Kimball Lane, Christiansburg, VA 24073). In some instances I have edited and abridged the quotes, though without altering their meaning. Symington's opening statement, pp. 365–66. Other passages, pp. 367, 377, 402–405.

Buell section: Buell letters, and author's visit to Buell family farm, now owned by his son, Howard Buell.

U.S. Air Force bombing on and around the Plain of Jars (Operation West Wind): U.S. Air Force Oral History Program, Interview of Capt. Karl. L. Polifka Jr. by Lt. Col. Robert G. Zimmerman, December 17, 1974, Washington, D.C., declassified 1982, pp. 82, 102, 118–19; and other sources. Bombs missing the shanty on the Plain of Jars: interview with Jerome Doolittle, who served as the press spokesman for the U.S. embassy in Vientiane.

Branfman and Perot: interview with Branfman; Christopher Robbins, *The Ravens: The Men Who Flew in America's Secret War in Laos* (New York: Crown, 1987), pp. 204–205, 277–78; U.S. Air Force Oral History Program, Interview of Maj. Michael E. Cavanaugh, by Lt. Col. Robert G. Zimmerman, November 21, 1974, Randolph Air Force Base, Texas, p. 68; *The New York Times,* December 28, 1969; July 1992 deposition of Ross Perot to the Senate Select Committee on POW/MIA Affairs; and other sources, including Edgar Buell's letters home.

Buell's illness and subsequent events in and around the Plain of Jars: Buell reports and letters home; published news stories; interviews with USAID employees, including Dr. Charles Weldon, Paul White, and Mac Thompson; and CIA employees who do not wish to be named. Dog-and-pony show at Sam Thong: interviews with Tom Clines, Fred Branfman, Tim Allman, and Jerome Doolittle.

Vang Pao's request for a Sayaboury evacuation: interviews with knowledgeable American and Hmong sources; and Henry Kamm, "Laotian Said to Ask Massive Evacuation," *The New York Times,* March 12, 1970.

Nixon's misstatements on American casualties in Laos: A few American servicemen had been killed on the ground, including the plainclothes air force men on Phou Pha Thi, and, as Sullivan had pointed out in closed-door testimony, about two hundred servicemen, most of whom were Green Berets stationed in South Vietnam, had been killed in Laos on the Ho Chi Minh Trail.

Vang Pao installing antiaircraft guns at Long Tieng: interview in the U.S. with a high-ranking aide to Vang Pao.

## Chapter 27: The Invasion

First Branfman section: interviews and other sources; news accounts.

Failure of the fallback plans for Sayaboury: interviews with Lair and other CIA veterans, Vang Pao, various Hmong refugees in the U.S. who do not wish to be identified. Thai participation in agreements with U.S.: In 1965 the U.S. made a secret agreement with Thailand in exchange for the use of Thai air bases. It committed the U.S. to defend Thailand from the communists if necessary. But the agreement said nothing about the Meo and crossing over the border from Sayaboury Province in Laos. Meo reconnaissance in Sayaboury: interview with an American who worked closely with Vang Pao. This source also pointed out that by 1970 the Thai government, which earlier would have welcomed Vang Pao's army into Thailand as a border defense force, had lost its enthusiasm. By then Thailand had its hands full with its own communist insurgency—in part, ethnic Meo tribespeople who lived on either side of the Sayaboury border, and who were being supplied and trained by the North Vietnamese and Chinese.

Vang Pao's address to his people and his plans for moving from Long Tieng: Henry Kamm, "War in Laos Imperils the Survival of the Meo," *The New York Times,* March 16,

1971; Pop Buell support for move, and rationale for staying within the second military reason: interview with one of Vang Pao's principal aides.

Thai casualties at Long Tieng in early 1971: *Air War in Northern Laos, 1 April–30 November 1971,* Project CHECO report, U.S. Air Force Headquarters, June 22, 1973, p. 47. On the Thais being "good on defense" and on Vang Pao throwing them into the bloodiest combat situations while favoring the Meo: This assessment was almost universal on the part of Americans familiar with Vang Pao.

Accidental air strike on Long Tieng: The U.S. government appeared to have tried to cover up the casualties. The official air force report (*Short Rounds,* Project CHECO, Pacific Air Force Headquarters, July 15, 1972, p. 4) states that the cluster bombs "probably contributed to one foreign national killed and seven wounded." However, it should be said that even the approximate number of casualties remains unknown. The AP and UPI wire services reported on the accidental bombing the following day, as did *The New York Times.* The fullest and best account appears in Christopher Robbins, *The Ravens: the Men Who Flew in America's Secret War in Laos* (New York: Crown, 1987), pp. 265–72, including reminiscences by the American forward air controller who ordered the air strike.

Lam Son 719, the South Vietnamese invasion of southern Laos: news accounts; Stanley Karnow, *Vietnam: A History* (New York: Viking, 1983), pp. 629–31; and other sources. Another useful account is John Morrocco, *Rain of Fire: Air War, 1969–1973,* in the series The Vietnam Experience (Boston: Boston Publishing Co., 1985), pp. 87–93. Firebase Sophia anecdote: interview with Robert Schwab 3rd, a young American who for a brief time worked as a freelance correspondent.

Second Branfman section: interviews with Branfman, and other sources, including G. McMurtrie Godley. Branfman's three-part series on the air war was published in at least four newspapers in the U.S., including the *St. Louis Post-Dispatch,* where it ran December 7, 8, and 9, 1970. Branfman being kicked out of Laos: Branfman interviews; and "For the Record," Branfman's communiqué to newsmen, prepared in Vientiane, February 13, 1971. Branfman at Yale: transcript labeled "Speech at Yale Teach-in," Branfman's papers. The teach-in was held February 22, 1971.

The Kennedy hearing: "U.S. Congress, Senate Committee on the Judiciary Subcommittee to Investigate Problems Connected with Refugees and Escapees. Hearings, Ninety-Second Congress, 1st Session" (Washington, D.C.: U.S. Government Printing Office, 1971). The relevant quotes are from pp. 32–37.

## Chapter 28: Cat and Mouse

Sullivan's discomfort in return to Washington, his phone being tapped by Nixon's aides, and being left out of the loop in Lam Son 719 planning: interview with Sullivan; Sullivan's, *Obbligato: Notes on a Foreign Service Career* (New York: Norton, 1984), pp. 236–38. Newspaper headline after Sullivan hearing with Branfman and Kennedy: *The New York Times,* April 23, 1971.

The Symington ceiling and the Laos money trail: confidential source. Costs of Laos war: Any attempt to assess costs of the Laos war should be treated skeptically. As Douglas Blaufarb points out, in *Organizing and Managing Unconventional War in Laos, 1962–1970* (A Report Prepared for Advanced Research Projects Agency by the Rand Corporation, Santa Monica, California, January 1972), p. 54: "The unconventional war in Laos has such a variety of inputs from different agencies with different practices that no common basis exists for an overall accounting. This is particularly true when one attempts to identify the costs of the air war." Ho Chi Minh Trail figures are the softest of all since the air assets used there were deployed in South Vietnam and used in Laos only as they could be spared.

Vang Pao's 1971–72 campaign: telephone interviews and correspondence with two CIA men who worked closely with Vang Pao during this period; *Air War in Northern Laos, 1 April–30 November 1971,* Project CHECO report, U.S. Air Force Headquarters, June 22, 1973; William M. Leary, "The CIA and the 'Secret' War in Laos: The Battle for Skyline Ridge, 1971–1972," unpublished paper; and various newspaper and U.S. Air Force reports. Another useful air force document is United States Oral History Program, Interview #663 of Maj. Jesse E. Scott by Lt. Col. V. H. Gallagher and Hugh N. Ahmann, April 6, 1973, Maxwell Air Force Base, Alabama. Vang Pao breaking down at Padong: newspaper reports, Scott Oral History interview, plus telephone interview with Jack Knotts, the Air America helicopter pilot, who was an eyewitness. Savannakhet troops: interview with two retired case officers in Long Tieng for the battle. The lowland Lao mutiny at Long Tieng: *The New York Times,* March 20, 1972.

Vang Pao and Nixon's trip to China: interview with Vang Pao. Vang Pao's visit to Missoula: Buell quotes from Edgar Buell letter to his family, June 20, 1972. Vang Pao's intentions and the changes in his behavior when he returned to Laos: The main source was a longtime CIA employee who worked undercover for another branch of the U.S. government and who knew Vang Pao well. Supplementary sources include CIA veterans, a former senior aide to Vang Pao, and other thoughtful and well-informed Hmong refugees resettled in the United States.

## Chapter 29: Peace Was at Hand

Sullivan section: interview with Sullivan; Sullivan, *Obbligato: Notes on a Foreign Service Career* (New York: Norton, 1984), pp. 240–42. Additional background on the Sino-Soviet split: Stanley Karnow, *Vietnam: A History* (New York: Viking, 1983), p. 637, and other accounts. "PEACE IS AT HAND" headline, with Kissinger and Sullivan photo beneath: *The New York Times,* October 27, 1972, p. 1.

Secord's role in the Christmas bombings: Richard Secord, with Jay Wurts, *Honored and Betrayed: Irangate, Covert Affairs, and the Secret War in Laos* (New York: Wiley, 1992), pp. 101–110, and interviews with Secord.

Negotiations between Laotians and Americans in early February 1973: My paraphrase of their positions and statements is based on a Henry Kamm *New York Times* story, February 3, 1973.

Tony Poe section: interviews with Poe and other CIA veterans. Chao La, the Mien (Yao) leader, told the author in a 1990 interview that the attack on Nam Yu occurred on the Yao New Year, when a lot of troops were away visiting their families.

Buell section: Buell letters home of the period, plus supplementary interviews with people who knew him then.

Kissinger in Vientiane and Hanoi: Henry Kissinger, *Years of Upheaval* (Boston: Little, Brown, 1982), pp. 9, 18–43. On North Vietnam's embassy in Laos noticing the softness in the American position and passing it on to the regime in Hanoi: Timothy Castle, *At War in the Shadow of Vietnam: U.S. Military Aid to the Royal Lao Government, 1955–1975* (New York: Columbia University Press, 1993), p. 260.

## Chapter 30: The Second Withdrawal

Lair section: interviews with Lair and others.

Branfman's return to Southeast Asia: interviews with Branfman, and supplementary information from Sydney Schanberg, and from Dean Boyd of Jack Anderson and Dale Van

Atta's office in Washington, D.C. Jack Anderson's columns on Nakhorn Phanom, based on reporting from Branfman in the field, appeared on June 24 and August 10, 1973.

Sullivan section: interviews with Sullivan, and Anthony Lewis column, "Another Senate Test," *The New York Times,* July 9, 1973, op-ed page. Sullivan said that Lewis later personally retracted the comment about blood on his hands.

Section on U.S. drawdown in Laos: Buell archives, news accounts, interviews with CIA and USAID personnel, and "December 1974 End of Tour Report of DEPCHIEF Maj. Gen. Richard G. Trefry." Trefry was the deputy chief of the joint U.S. military advisory group (DEPCHIEF JUSMAG) in Udorn, and concurrently the defense attaché at the U.S. embassy in Vientiane.

## Chapter 31: The Fall

Buell Section: Buell letters, March through May 1975.

Vang Pao's departure, and related events: interviews with Vang Pao, Yang Dao, Yang See, Hang Sao, and other Hmong; with Gayle Morrison; and with the pilots Les Strouse, Dave Kouba, and Jack Knotts. These pilots recorded a tape of their experiences soon after the evacuation, and this was helpful in reconstructing the details. Gayle Morrison was extraordinarily helpful in adding and correcting details.

Aftereffects of Vang Pao's departure: interviews with knowledgeable Hmong refugees who do not wish to be identified, plus Gayle Morrison and several USAID veterans. Souvanna Phouma quote: cited in Stanley Karnow, "Free No More: The Allies America Forgot," *Geo* (U.S. edition), January 1980, p. 26, and other sources. The original remark seems to have been made, in French, to the French ambassador in Vientiane.

Vang Pao's semidivine status to the Hmong rank and file: Henry Kamm, "End of Laos War Has Brought No Peace to Thousands in Meo Clans," *The New York Times,* July 13, 1975. My interviews with Hmong refugees made clear that Kamm was right. Vang Pao's departure: interview with Lair.

## Chapter 32: Land of the 847 Elephants

Lair section: interviews with Lair, Yang See, and other sources; supplementary information on POW/MIA issue from author's travels and personal experiences in Thailand and Laos; Gayle Morrison.

Buell's later years: author's acquaintance with Buell in Bangkok; interviews with people who knew him, including Dr. Charles Weldon; Buell archives; author's visit to Buell's farm and conversation with his two grown children, Howard Buell and Harriet Buell Gettys.

Lao People's Democratic Republic: author's travels in Laos in 1981 and 1991. The 847 elephants anecdote: related to author by Fred Schwartzendruber of the Mennonite Central Committee, Vientiane, spring 1981.

## Chapter 33: The American Aftermath

Ex-Ambassador to Laos G. McMurtrie Godley's statement: interview with Godley, Hamilton, Massachusetts, November 1993.

Lawrence section: interviews with Lawrence.

Vang Pao section: interviews with Vang Pao and about forty Hmong refugees in the U.S. and Thailand. Supplementary information from Americans who work with Hmong refugee organizations, particularly in Minneapolis-St. Paul and Fresno. See also Ruth E. Hammond, "Sad Suspicions of a Refugee Ripoff," *The Washington Post,* April 16, 1989.

Shackley, Secord, and Clines: interviews with Shackley, and with Maj. Gen. Richard Secord (Ret.) and Thomas Clines. Clines conviction: Richard Secord, with Jay Wurts, *Honored and Betrayed: Irangate, Covert Affairs, and the Secret War in Laos* (New York: Wiley, 1992), p. 348.

Branfman's thoughts on the war: abridged excerpts from a letter from Fred Branfman to the author, October 31, 1991, Budapest, Hungary.

William Sullivan section: interview with Sullivan. Sullivan and "Who lost Iran?" anecdote first related to author by T. D. Allman and later by Sullivan himself.

Tony Poe section: interviews with Poe.

Lair section: interviews with Lair.

# Acknowledgments

Researching a book on a secret war is a challenge, particularly when the author was not an eyewitness, and most of the records are classified and unavailable.

I was a student during the Laos war, graduating from college just after Vang Pao left Southeast Asia for his life in exile. My first trip to the region was in 1980, when Indochinese refugees were in the news, especially the Vietnamese "boat people" and Cambodians fleeing the Khmer Rouge holocaust. On a freelance magazine assignment, I traveled to northeast Thailand to the town of Nong Khai, near the Mekong River, and there beheld to my surprise a refugee camp for Laotians the size of a city—acres and acres of dusty thatched shacks, tens of thousands of people. My vague awareness that Laos had been part of the Vietnam War, and that the CIA had run the Laos theater, did not reduce my astonishment. What are these people *doing* here? I wondered. What was the American role in their war? This book, published fifteen years later, is my attempt to answer those questions.

During the two years I lived in Thailand, 1980–82, a friend named Susan Walker helped me get started with the research. The daughter of an Air America chief pilot for Laos, Fred Walker, she arranged for my passes into the refugee camps and generally made it easy for me to meet veterans of the Laos war, including Pop Buell, Jerry Daniels, and Dr. Charles Weldon. I traveled to Laos as a journalist but was denied permission to travel outside the Vientiane area. My researches, which started with such promise, gradually met with more and more obstacles and frustrations, including the deaths of both Buell and Daniels. I returned to the United States, interviewed Vang Pao, and then put the project on hold.

Two books and seven years later, Alice Mayhew of Simon & Schuster publishers encouraged me to try a Laos book again, and this time the pieces fell into place. The polarization of the Vietnam War era and its aftermath had eroded over time; and now the old hands were able to reflect on their experiences with greater equanimity. In fact, to my surprise, a number of retired CIA officers were not only willing but almost eager to talk about Laos with someone who could ask them the right questions. The people I talked with belonged to interconnecting networks, and once in a network it was possible to travel along it from one person to the next, tactfully and patiently, in many cases waiting for the right telephone calls to be made between old friends, as they discussed whether it was okay to talk with me or not.

Most of the information in my book comes from these interviews, about 150 in number. I talked with retired CIA officers, USAID and State Department veterans, U.S. Air Force pilots and scholars, civilian pilots, Laotian refugees—anyone who would talk with me whose experiences were germane. Since there was then no overall reliable book on the Laos war to create a framework of knowledge, knowing what to ask these people and making sense of their answers was not easy, at first. Fortunately, my friend and former teacher, Thomas Powers, author of *The Man Who Kept the Secrets: Richard Helms and the CIA,* probably the best book ever written on the CIA, advised me to assemble a chronology. Ken Conboy, who was researching the military aspects of the war in Laos, further suggested using *The New York Times Index* of Laos stories as a backbone for the chronology, and this I did, using a database program to enter names, dates, and events from all the sources available. This chronology led me in some wrong directions for a while—I know of no other subject where logical deductions based on partial evidence prove wrong so often—but it gave me a structure to work with, a thesis to test, correct, and revise as time went on.

Another basic challenge was trying to get the geography of Laos straight, since former pilots and spooks routinely referred to airstrip numbers and village names that appeared on no map. A valuable key to the site names was the 1974 edition of the Air America Air Facility Data Pamphlet (reprint available from Dalley Books Service, 90 Kimball Lane, Christiansburg VA 24073, along with many other publications on Southeast Asia not available elsewhere). For maps, the 1:500,000 scale Tactical Pilotage Charts from the Defense Department proved a workable if less than ideal substitute for the maps used by the Americans during the Laos war (to get them, write: DMA/CSC, Attention, PMSR, Washington, DC 20315).

Among the few partial histories of the Laos war that I found I could rely on in my researches, pride of place goes to Douglas Blaufarb's *Organizing and Managing Unconventional War in Laos, 1962–1970,* which was written as a study for the Rand Corporation and later declassified. Most of the documents on the Laos war are still classified, and the Freedom of Information Act proved to be little help in getting materials released from either the CIA or the State Department. The U.S. Air Force was my best source of archival information, both in its Project CHECO reports and its oral history series (particularly the interviews conducted by a Lt. Col. Robert Zimmerman). For the Vietnam War, which to a large extent provides the enveloping context of the Laos war, the literature is, of course, excellent; my favorite sources were those two classics, David Halberstam's *The Best and the Brightest* and Stanley Karnow's *Vietnam: A History.* For background reading and for insights into the situations that develop when Westerners involve themselves in Asian or Third World affairs, books like Barbara Tuchman's *Stillwell and the American Experience in China, 1911–45* were deeply if indirectly rewarding (compare Stillwell and Chiang Kai-shek with Bill Lair and Vang Pao).

Several scholars of the Laos war provided encouragement, suggestions, and information: Professor William Leary of the University of Georgia; Maj. Timothy Castle (Ret.) of the Air Force Academy and other institutions; and Kenneth Conboy, formerly of the Heritage Foundation. Gayle Morrison, who is associated with the Hmong community of Santa Ana, California, and who is compiling an oral history of Hmong experiences from 1975 onwards, was extremely helpful on the subject of the fall of Long Tieng and the start of the communist dark days in Laos; Gayle's rigorous researches have been self-supporting, and if ever there was a worthy recipient of a foundation grant she's the one. Douglas Blaufarb, a recognized scholar and expert on counterinsurgency as well as a former CIA station chief in Laos, was also among those who read the manuscript and kindly offered corrections and suggestions.

The CIA veterans who talked with me have my thanks. All but two or three approached were willing to talk, but few wished to see their names in print. Former Director William Colby was my first interview; and I am grateful to Bill Lair, Vint Lawrence, Tony Poe, Tom Clines, Ted Shackley, and all the others, the great majority of whom wish to stay anonymous. None of these men attempted to control what I wrote in my book, and it stands to reason that they do not necessarily agree with what I wrote, either: Their views are their own.

Another impressive group of people were the USAID veterans. Above all, I am grateful to Dr. Charles Weldon, a gracious host, and Ernest Kuhn, a wonderful archivist who wrote me a couple of twenty-page letters in answer to my questions; Ernie deserves his own book about Laos someday. Thanks to Bob Dakan, Blaine Jensen, Dr. Patricia McCreedy, Edwin Mc-Keithen, MacAlan Thompson, Tom Ward, Paul White, and Jack Williamson. For their hospitality and for access to Edgar "Pop" Buell's papers I am grateful to his two children, Howard Buell and Harriet Buell Gettys.

A note on the Hmong: As I hope is clear from the text, I used the old outsiders' name for the tribe, the Meo, because it was in use among *farangs* at the time. Nothing derogatory is meant, nor would it appear that the tribe itself considered it particularly derogatory at the time, since no tribal member, including Vang Pao, ever told Lair, Lawrence, or Buell then that "Meo" was inappropriate.

In interviewing Laotian refugees in Thailand and in the U.S., I found that many were reluctant to have their names used, for fear of retribution. The ranking Hmong interviewed included Vang Pao, Hang Sao, Yang Dao, and Yang See. A special tip of the hat to Cher Pao Moua, the commander of Bouam Long, the base that never fell to the communists, whom I interviewed back in 1980, and who is a leader of the resistance in Laos today; and to Col. DouangTa Norasing, Colonel Thong's right-hand man and an accomplished guerilla leader in his own right. When I saw DouangTa he was working the night shift at a factory in California, assembling circuit boards. It's painful to see the lowered status of Laotian refugees who were prominent leaders in their own society.

Among others willing to be acknowledged, thanks to Gen. Harry "Heinie" Aderholt, Tim Allman, Bob Anderson, Jim Anderson, David Andreanoff, Kaori Aochi, Soradetj Bannavong, Mrs. Norma Blanton, Tom Blanton, Dean Boyd, Fred Branfman, Kevin Buckley, Mike Carroll, Jim Chamberlain, Lt. Col. Billy Chance, Eli and Arlene Chavez, Col. Gerald H. Clayton, Sandy Cochran, John Crowley, George Dalley, Alan Dawson, Inkian Devongsa, Jerry Doolittle, Maew Pareena Duangdara, Mike Eiland, John Everingham, Adam Foster, Peter Vincent Foster, Andrea Fowler, Wilbur Garrett, G. McMurtrie Godley, Fred A. Gologi, Denis Grey, Erika Hagen, Ruth Hammond, Neil Hansen, Lor Ngia Her, Burton Hersh, Seymour Hersh, Doug Hulcher, Houmpheng Insixiengmay, Robert Karniol, Tia Kha, Jim Kitchens, William Klausner, Jerome Klingaman, Jack Knotts, Dave Kouba, Toua Kue, Kwa Chong-Teck, Chang Lee, Chong Moua Lee, Eric Lincoln, Ethel McConaghy, Ralph McGeehee, Charles McLaughlin, Yong Kay Moua, Col. Rod Paschall, Nick Pavlesky, Nick Peck, Douglas Pike, Mark Pratt, Don Ranard, William Rees, Ron Rickenbach, Dave Roseneau, Jon Sawyer, Al Schinkel, Robert Schwab 3rd, Maj. Gen. Richard Secord, Vang Seng, Jack Shirley, Vang Shur, Becky and June Sithiwong, William Smalley, Harvey Sommers, Gen. Singkapo Srikhotchoumnamaly,

Jinny St. Goar, William Sullivan, Ronald Sutphin, John Teague, Ly Teng, Leonard Unger, Bea Vang, Claude Vincent, Bea Vue, Jeremy Wagstaff, Fred Walker, Liz Walker, Carol Leviton Wetterhahn, Dan Weiss, Carl Wykoff, Neng Sao Xieng, Jer Xiong, Vu Yang, and Steve Young.

I am grateful to a congressionally funded organization, the United States Institute of Peace, for a grant that helped defray my travel and research expenses. The opinions, findings, and conclusions in this book are mine and do not necessarily reflect the views of the United States Institute of Peace.

Special thanks go to my brother, Sturgis Warner Jr., who read the manuscript at several stages and gave me sound advice. My agent, Joy Harris, and my editor, Alice Mayhew, stuck with me during the rough part of this project, when the manuscript was too long, and when there were serious disagreements on the direction the revisions should take.

Above all, thanks to my wife and children for enduring my long research travels and my many weekends at the office.

# Index